Mitra Phukan is a writer, translator, columnist and trained classical vocalist who lives in Guwahati, Assam. Her published works include four children's books, a biography, two novels—*The Collector's Wife* and *A Monsoon of Music*—and a collection comprising fifty of her newspaper columns, titled *Guwahati Gaze*. In addition, her short stories have appeared in various journals. Her works have been translated into several languages. As a translator herself, she has brought the works of some of the best-known contemporary Assamese fiction writers into English. Her widely read column, 'All Things Considered', appears fortnightly in *The Assam Tribune*. She is an active member of Aradhana, an organization that takes music to the underprivileged sections of society, and a founder member of the North East Writers' Forum.

a full night's thievery

~ STORIES ~

MITRA PHUKAN

SPEAKING
TIGER

SPEAKING TIGER PUBLISHING PVT. LTD
4381/4 Ansari Road, Daryaganj,
New Delhi–110002, India

First published in paperback by Speaking Tiger 2016

ISBN: 978-93-86050-60-1
eISBN: 978-93-86050-62-5

10 9 8 7 6 5 4 3 2 1

Typeset in Arno Pro by SÜRYA, New Delhi
Printed at Sanat Printers, Kundli.

For Dulal and Bubi Borkotoky
Bhindeo and Baideo…
With gratitude,
For always being there for me.

Contents

The Choice

You may well look amazed, sir. Yes, yes, I can read the look in your eyes like a book. Haven't I seen this look, hundreds, thousands of times throughout my life? Whenever I take up this instrument to play, or indeed, whenever people see me carrying it about with me, as though it is my first-born babe, as I go from concert to concert, venue to venue—yes, I have seen this look in a million pairs of eyes. The same look of wonder and amazement.

I can guess your thoughts, sir, at this very moment, as I sit in your beautiful air-conditioned drawing room, sipping tea from your expensive china, nibbling on nuts from sparkling crystal… I'm a little worried about the air-conditioning—will it harm her? I mean, my instrument. Most likely not—but one never knows, she can be so temperamental at times. If I could request you, sir, to switch it off, and turn on the fans instead—thank you. Yes, that will be fine. She's not used to air-conditioning, though the concert halls where we play these days are mostly air-conditioned. But my house, my music room, where she sits and sleeps, is not… Thank you.

Where was I? Yes, of course. You're wondering, aren't you, how it is that you, who pride yourself on being such a connoisseur of music, haven't actually heard this instrument being played?

And you're amazed, aren't you, at its beauty, the sheer majestic grandeur of its looks? Just look at her—how beautiful she is! Most people don't know that she was created by Rudra himself, for his wife, Parvati. An instrument designed by God the Destroyer, for the creation of music, for his divine consort. They call her the Rudra Veena, but she is Parvati's instrument all the same. Rudra fashioned it after Parvati, didn't you know that? He watched her while she was asleep, and the veena took shape echoing what he saw. Look at these two resonators, two perfect globes covered with such intricate carvings. They are her heavy, blue-veined breasts, of course. And the stem of the instrument, wrought just so—that's her delicate arm as it lies across her breasts while she sleeps. And these frets, what else are they but the bangles on Parvati's arm, yielding divine music when one plays on them?

See how she responds to my touch, sir. She comes alive with music, like a woman ... no, I mustn't talk in this way.

You are curious now, aren't you?

Yes, I know you've heard of me. Anybody with any interest in our music will have heard of me. After all, I am one of the very few Rudra Veena players around in this country today. And possibly the best one. No sir, I don't believe in false modesty. It's a fact that my fees are more than most organizations can afford. Only the really big sabha and concert organizers can come up with the money for my payments. It's a different matter that you haven't actually seen or heard me perform. I am mostly abroad these days, sir, performing at the festivals and concerts there. Like so many of my fellow musicians, I spend summers there, and only a bit of winter here, in our country, doing the music circuit of our metro cities. It's not just the money that attracts me, though I must say that today I am richer than I had ever dreamed would be possible. It's the ... well, let's just say that I like the seriousness with which the students come to me in Europe, or America, or Japan, to learn this Rudra Veena from me.

They haven't heard of the Curse, you see. And even if they have, they are too ... well, perhaps, they are too far away from the darkness of their distant pasts, to pay much attention to it. Whereas we, here in this country—we are too close still to the elemental forces; we cannot afford to ignore these myths, these legends, which are so often not fictitious at all, but true in every aspect. They talk of the Curse as though it's a curiosity, something that is totally removed from the everyday, ordinary reality of their lives ... whereas here, the dark shadow of the Curse looms over everything connected with this instrument, this veena of Rudra ...

You mean you haven't heard of the Curse? Well, that's amazing. Yes, that's really amazing. Practically the first thing that people ask me about is the Curse. I mean people from this country, of course, not foreigners. They want to know—was I aware of the Curse when I took up this instrument? Why did I take the risk of turning to the Rudra Veena for my profession, when I could just as easily have taken up the sitar, or sarod, or flute, or why not, the violin? These instruments make beautiful music, too, (though nothing like the music of my Rudra Veena, everybody says so ...) they are popular, here as well as abroad, they travel better than my instrument ... yes, and besides, they don't have the Curse hanging over their heads as my instrument does ... Well, it's my turn to be amazed now. Truly amazed. How come you haven't heard of the Curse on those who play this instrument? Everybody in the music world knows it. But ah, I was forgetting. You are not a musician, are you? Indeed, you talk so knowledgeably; you are so sensitive to the sentiments of us musicians that for a moment I had forgotten that you are not one. Of course you are a connoisseur, but not part of the music world itself. But we need people like you, people with huge business empires who can patronize the arts like you do. In the old days, it was the kings who patronized musicians. Today, I say, thank God for people like you, cultured and refined businessmen who promote the arts… that is, of course, why I have come to you today. I, along with my instrument, the Rudra Veena. And the Curse that hangs over us.

The Rudra Veena and the Curse, they go hand in hand. It is as though Rudra, jealous of those who would caress and stroke this instrument that was Parvati's echo, thought up this jinx to keep them away. He wanted to touch, to play, to bring alive with music this instrument *himself*. What better way than to hurl a Curse to keep merely human aspirants away?

Yes, I'm coming to that. The Curse. I don't know how it started, of course, but it seems that it has been around since… well, how can I say how long? All I can say is, that anybody who plays the Rudra Veena is doomed to die without a child to carry on his name. Not a male child, mind. He is doomed to be childless—no sons, no daughters, nothing. Tell me, sir, can anything be worse? For us, the people who live here on this subcontinent that we call home, to die without a child to take us to the burial ground, or to light the funeral pyre so that we can proceed on our journey to the next world, our next birth—can anything be worse? To die with no one to carry on the family name, to perish without leaving our blood behind in the veins of our sons and daughters, to have no grandchildren in the evening of one's life to play with, to tell stories to, to sing to, to teach our music to… can anything be worse?

I can see that you are startled. Yes, this is a terrible thing, a terrible thing indeed. And of course it's one of the reasons, perhaps the main reason, why my beautiful Rudra Veena is falling into disuse. Who will dare come to learn from me, knowing that he or she is bound to die without any progeny? It's different for foreigners; in any case they don't feel as deeply about things like continuity of the family and so on, in the way we do. But Indians... no sir, I don't have any Indian students on the Rudra Veena. Foreigners, yes, several, but no Indians. Nobody has come forward to learn from me, though many approach me to learn the sitar. I play that instrument, too, you know—but not on the concert circuit. Not yet. Well, perhaps we shall soon have to go to Europe and America to learn the Rudra Veena!

Ah, yes, of course you want to know about my ancestors, my gurus. I learnt from my Mamu, my mother's brother, the famed Ustad Ali Hussain. He died several decades ago—a bachelor. He never married, never had any children. Of course I was his child in all senses but the biological—the real inheritor of the mantle of his musical heritage. He, in turn, learnt from his Chacha, his father's brother, who had four wives and several mistresses—he was a very handsome man, and fond of women, but no, he never had any children. This Veena was his child, his daughter, he always used to say... he gave it to my Mamu, who, at his deathbed, gave it to me... Yes, this very instrument that you see before you now. Who knows how old it is? It is priceless, my Rudra Veena.

I can see the wary look in your eyes. No sir, don't worry, I am not flogging my instrument, holding her up to a prospective buyer like a slave girl in a marketplace, enumerating her best qualities. No sir, my Veena is too much a part of me, of my life, for me to hold her up for auction. That is why I have come to you, and not to others ... But let me continue ... am I taking up too much of your time? You did tell me that you had kept the whole evening free for me ... thank you. It is important for me, a poor artiste like me, that you hear my story. I don't mean poor in material goods, but poor nevertheless. Why I have had to come to you with my beautiful, my cherished Rudra Veena.

Thank you, I am quite comfortable. No, tea is fine, I am a teetotaller, a strict and devout Muslim, though you know how it is with us musicians, the lore connected with the music we play draws us inexorably to the myths of this ancient land. But I fast during the holy month, I say my Namaz at the prescribed times ... yet when I play my Veena, I feel the presence of Parvati near me ... I don't know, it confuses me, but I have come to accept the fact that there is something greater than all organized religions, and I mean *all*, sir—a Power that cannot be pinned down through ritual or rite, through ceremony or sacrament—a Power whose shadowy form can be discerned only through Art ... and Music. Especially through Music. That is why, when I play on my Veena, I worship.

Forgive me for straying from the topic, sir. I have hardly slept at all this last week, hardly closed my eyes as I kept vigil ... And the turmoil in my heart is something that nobody can understand.

As I was saying, this instrument is priceless. Not just because it is old, or beautiful, or because it is so rare, though these all contribute to its value. The music it makes, the fact that it has been played by so many of the best Veena players the world has ever known—which, I can say quite without any false humility, includes me—all this gives my Veena a value that cannot be quantified.

In any case, the Rudra Veena is now almost a museum exhibit. The best museums around the world place them behind glass, where they are seen ... but not heard, never heard, no, by gawking crowds. Or there are the private collections, housing instruments such as Stradivarius violins, and maybe even a Rudra Veena. (Yes sir, I may be a Rudra Veena player, but I do know the value of a Stradivarius. Priceless, like my Veena). They are kept in climatically-controlled walk-in vaults, for the pleasure of their billionaire owners. Yes, of course I do know that your private collection is one of the best in the world. I also know that you take the best care of your collection, not just looking at them, but even handling them, strumming them, getting musicians in to actually play them once in a while ... that is why I have come to you, sir, and not gone to others, though I could have taken my instrument anywhere in the world, anywhere at all ...

But like Stradivarius violins, Rudra Veenas are becoming rare because there are hardly any makers around. Indeed, why should anybody make Rudra Veenas? For whom? There are practically no new players around. The students that I have live in places such as Berlin, Tokyo, Manchester, Toronto ... A veena maker cannot live by making four or even eight instruments in a lifetime ... In any case, where is the fine, seasoned Burma teak, where is the ivory for the bridge work, where can one get the materials needed to craft an instrument of this kind?

Long ago, when I was just this high, and my voice was still that of a child's, my Mamu had taken me to the workshop of a veena maker. Who knows, that may have been the last Rudra Veena to have been made! The craftsman was, I remember, regarded as being the best at that time. He had invited my Mamu to the ceremonies that were always conducted when work on a Rudra Veena began. An auspicious date was chosen, and at the favourable hour, work on the carefully selected piece of seasoned teak would begin. There was, I remember, prayer and ritual, all conducted in the ancient Hindu tradition. We two, my Mamu and I, were outsiders, Muslims, but we were very welcome nevertheless, because the maker of the instrument and my Mamu belonged to the same religion, the creed of Music. Amid the lighting of fragrant incense and aromatic joss-sticks, the first ceremonial cut on the wood was made by a sanctified tool. It was a moving moment, I remember, and I treasure the memory of it till today. It is not something I am likely to see again in my lifetime... I remember that the craftsman took a whole year to finish that instrument, which was being made, not for my Mamu, but for a ...yes sir, you are right, it was for a private collection, a Maharaja's museum if I remember right.

Am I boring you, sir? I hope not...thank you for your patience. You are kind, very kind...yes, they were right when they told me to come to you, for you understand the mind and heart of musicians. As for me, I never tire of listening to tales about my instrument, my Veena.

Yes, I knew we would come to that. You are still thinking about the Curse, I see. Yes, it is a riveting myth, isn't it? For me, now, at this moment, it is of course much more than a myth, though there was a time not so long ago when I had thought that it was just that: a myth and nothing more. Till the other day, I was like those foreign students who hear about this Curse and forget about it, or at most remember it only as a strange and interesting tale, which has nothing to do with them. Not now, though, not any more. Oh no, I believe, I truly believe in it, though my religion forbids me to do so. But I am past rationalizing about these things.

Yes, of course you want to know whether I, one of the few remaining Rudra Veena players alive today, have a child. I am coming to that, sir; that is indeed the point of my story...

When I began to show an interest in this Veena of Rudra, my relatives, even my own Mamu and Guru, were uneasy. I was a kind of child prodigy, you know, I could recognize at least six raags and identify them by their basic notes when I was not even five years old. But musical genius was something that was taken for granted in our family of musicians. There have been eminent instrumentalists right from the time my forefathers came from Peshawar, and even further West, from Afghanistan, and ultimately, from Persia. There have been wonderful vocalists, too—indeed, Chhote Wajid Ali of the Agra Gharana is my own uncle. Nobody would have minded if I had become a pakhawaj player, for instance, or a sitarist, or a sarod player. Indeed, it was expected that I join the family firm with some kind of instrument in my hands. But the Rudra Veena?

The threat of the Curse was in everybody's minds when I began to go across to my Mamu's house to hear him play, watch him perform... Even he tried to dissuade me, you know. My father was a pakhawaj player, my first cousin an excellent Dhrupad singer—he tried, yes, everybody knows, he tried to get me to take up other instruments, even singing. And my mother—she actually forbade me to go to her own brother's house, she was that afraid of the Curse. But I would run away, and hide behind the screen in my Mamu's music room, and listen to him play. And when my Mamu went out of the room, I would creep out and try to reproduce those magical sounds on the instrument—this very instrument—myself.

The things they told me, just to get me to give it up! Of course nobody mentioned the Curse directly, but they thought up a lot of disincentives. The instrument was frightfully difficult to play, they argued ... but I countered each and every argument of theirs logically, painstakingly. Yes, the Rudra Veena is difficult to play. But so is, say, the shehnai, and nobody put obstacles in the path of my cousin when he began to take up that instrument in earnest. The breathing exercises that his Guru gave him were excruciatingly difficult. He would have to take a bowl of soapsuds, and blow on it for an hour at a time, making sure that the bubbles he produced were all exactly the same size. But my family never tried to dissuade him from learning it just because of the difficulty... so why were they putting all these hurdles in my way?

Eventually, of course, they all gave up. My Mamu, my father, my uncles—all their cajoling, their threats, their scoldings stopped short in the face of my perseverance, my dedication. And of course, the beauty, the sheer magical beauty of my music. (No, I told you before, didn't I, that I am not falsely humble). My mother was the last—but even she stopped the day I brought home Suraiyya.

By then, of course, I was already a well-established player. Radio and TV programmes, concert assignments, foreign tours—I had them all under my belt. My earnings were much more than I had ever imagined would be possible. And then, to be paid for doing something that I loved so much, that was as much a part of me as breathing... I felt fortunate, indeed. And the day Suraiyya entered my home as a bride, I felt ... well, what can I say? Any man who has in his life the woman he loves will know what I feel.

Suraiyya knew about the Curse, of course. Her family, too, is one of musicians. As daughters, they were not taught the secrets of the art, for daughters move away and take the knowledge to enrich the homes that they marry into—homes that house competitors! But Suraiyya, in spite of being born to a traditional family, is educated. She is a graduate, a rare thing for a daughter in our community of musicians in those days. Yes, a graduate, and a Science graduate at that. Of course she didn't believe in the Curse.

But now... today... she is the one who begged me, weeping, to bring the Veena to you. My Rudra Veena, which has been my companion for so many decades... Forgive me, sir, I am old now, and easily moved to emotion. No, no, I am fine, don't worry. Well, as fine as can be expected from an old man in my condition...

Yes, of course, I'll continue. I can't let you have my Veena without telling you why I have to part with her; why it is that I am snapping all ties with Shiva's beautiful instrument, an echo of Parvati herself.

Majid, our son, was born within a year of our marriage. Nobody had much time to fret about whether the Curse was going to swing into action. He was a healthy, happy, chubby, chuckling boy. He grew up to be a mischievous little lad, totally disinterested in music. Well, that was fine with me. Times are changing, there are so many options open to young people today... I never forced him into music; indeed, I was happy that he was going into a world where he would get a steady job, a nine-to-five occupation, a normal life.

But we never had any more children. I don't know why... but Majid is everything that I or Suraiyya could have wanted in a child. Tall and handsome like his Pathan ancestors, with blue eyes and straight brown hair... ah, he is nothing like me, who am hunched now, not so much with age as with the postural problems of playing this instrument all through my life.

We sent Majid to the best schools in town. English medium, of course, though Suraiyya has taken care to teach him the traditions, the values that we have always lived by. He passed his school exams with excellent marks, went to one of the best colleges in the country. He is a CA now, you know, a Chartered Accountant. With his own flourishing practice, a pretty wife... Yes, Majid has been a wonderful son. He has respected my wishes in all that I have ever asked of him. Except...

He was always fond of speed. Even as a child, whenever he was taken for a ride on a car, he would tell the person at the wheel to drive faster, more fast... Professionally, he is cautious, judicious, but when he is driving anything on two wheels or four, he throws caution to the winds... I have told him many times, not just me, Suraiyya, too, has said it many times, to drive with a little bit of care.

He is fighting for his life now. Battling to survive, on life support systems, with a serious head injury that has the doctors at his bedside round the clock. And his wife, his pretty, sweet Rukhsana, who was carrying their first child... she was beside him in the car when it crashed into the truck that was coming from the other side. She's unconscious, too, and she doesn't know that she's lost this child.

No, I'm all right, really. Yes, a glass of water, perhaps. Yes, thank you.

So you see, don't you, why I have to give away my instrument? We may live in times during which man has walked on the moon, when technology shows us that much of what our ancestors have believed in, in the past has been nothing more than superstition. But things happen, when you are forced to believe, when a cold hand from some distant past reaches across and touches you on the shoulder, reminding you that in spite of all the changes that you see all around, some things can never be ignored. It catches up with you, just when you think you have beaten it. And then you realize that it was just biding its time, waiting, choosing the one moment when its blow would be most devastating…

We have been keeping vigil around the clock. Rukhsana will wake up to find her baby gone, and Majid—ah sir, I don't know about Majid at all! All I can hear now are voices whispering in my ear, filling the spaces of my mind with their derision, telling me that one can never run away from what is written.

Yes, I have made my choice. Indeed, it was hardly any choice at all, was it? There were times in the past when I could have gone another way, but I didn't. I could have chosen another instrument as a child: I didn't. I could have chosen not to get married: I didn't. We could have chosen, Suraiyya and I, not to have a child: we didn't. Ah yes, I can imagine how the voices must have waited, biding their time, watching me as I made my choices then. And now, at this moment, when I have no choice, absolutely none, they have done this to me. To die without a child is bad enough. But the very worst thing that can happen to a person is to have a child, watch him grow to manhood, and then lose him…

Even if Suraiyya hadn't urged me to bring this Rudra Veena of my musical ancestors to you, I would have stopped playing. Yes, the day my son went into the hospital, and the doctors told me of the seriousness of his injury, I knew that the time had come to pay my dues.

They are waiting for me at the hospital. They will look with questioning eyes at me as they keep their vigil around the hospital beds. And I will nod. And then ... my boy will stir, and open his eyes, and I will tell him, it's all right, my son, it's all right. I have removed it, I have finally removed the curse that was over your head since the day you were born ...

So you see now why I cannot accept any money for her. I made that clear over the telephone, did I not? Ah, I could see you were curious: why should an artiste give away his priceless instrument to a collector for free? No, all I want is a good home for her. And that, I am sure, you will give her —perhaps a better home than I, or my gurus, ever have. And I know you are a modern man, and don't believe in curses and other such dark forces, but let me tell you this, nevertheless: the Curse falls only on those who play the Rudra Veena. And you are a collector, not an artiste ...

Let me touch her one last time, my Rudra Veena. She knows that I am giving her away. She knows the reason, too, I am sure. But I doubt if she can understand. Music is a harsh taskmaster, one that doesn't acknowledge the ties of friendship or family. She will not understand why I have chosen my son's life over her.

The Reckoning

THE LETTER, AWAITED WITH SUCH ANXIETY, REACHED THEM at last. Okon found the plain white envelope just inside the front door, lying innocently on the polished wooden floor as though it was an everyday missive, an invitation to a flower-show, perhaps, or a letter from a friend in the city.

The night-chowkidars were questioned. They knew nothing of how it had got there, though they swore that they had been patrolling throughout the night. The policemen who had been appointed to keep a picket outside the gates were as surprised as anybody. How could someone have entered the Manager's compound in the Betbagaan Tea Estate and slipped a letter under the doorway in the dead of the night? That, too, such an important letter!

Actually, of course, it was quite easy. The bungalow was situated in a vast compound. Many stretches along its perimeter were unfenced. Tea bushes and kitchen garden merged into each other at the back, undivided by pale, hedge or fence. And even the white-painted picket fences in the front sweep of the deep-green lawn were decorative rather than functional. Anybody could have got in, slipped in the note when the chowkidars were on the other side of the enormous garden, and then run fleet-footedly away.

The address on the envelope said, 'Mr Ranjit Choudhury, Manager, Betbagaan Tea Estate.' But Ranjit was away at the moment, having left at dawn, as usual, for his supervisory rounds of the garden. Yet it was so obvious that this was *the* letter. Should it be given to the policemen outside? Should she, Shrabana, open it? What about such things as fingerprints, evidence and so on? What should she *do*?

Okon stood before Shrabana, proffering the letter respectfully to her on a polished silver tray. Shrabana put up a hand to her forehead. This scene—this feeling of deja vu—it had all happened before. This tension-filled wait for an expected missive, its arrival one morning, and the liveried bearer holding it out respectfully… she shook her head. With trembling fingers, she took the letter.

Rahul. Where was he now? What were they doing to him? Was he aware that this letter had been written to his father?

'What's the matter, Baideo? You're looking very unwell.' Jona's voice broke into her thoughts. Wordlessly, Shrabana turned to her, and held out the unopened envelope. Jona's eyes widened. 'It's come, then?' She reached out a hand to steady Shrabana, and led her to a chair. 'I'll call Ronojoy…'

Shrabana watched Jona rush off to call her husband in. She was glad that they were here, at this time. Perhaps it was human nature that people should turn to each other in times of crisis. Children to parents, brothers to sisters, wives to husbands. And vice versa. She, who wasn't even on talking terms with her husband any more, hadn't been for months now, she felt the lack of these binding chains in her life most acutely now. This would be the time for a husband and wife to draw sustenance from each other. Whereas Ranjit and she…

The huge black weight that had lain on her chest for the last seven days seemed to grow larger and heavier as it turned over and settled back in its pit again.

Ronojoy strode into the room, followed closely by Jona. Their faces were tense, their bodies taut with fear and anxious anticipation.

Shrabana looked down at her hands and watched their trembling turn slowly into clenched fists. She knew exactly what would happen now, the sequence that was to follow. Deja vu. The past unspooled into the present, as Ronojoy questioned the now-nervous Okon about how and in which spot he had found the letter.

In that light, in that stance, Ronojoy looked just like Ranjit, his brother. The same tableau had been enacted just there, in that very spot. Six months, no, almost a year ago now.

Ranjit's hands hadn't trembled when he had read the first letter brought to him on a polished silver salver a year ago. But Shrabana, watching from this same chair, had noticed the habitual crease-line on his forehead furrow deeper as he had read it.

'What is it?' she had asked, wearing the right mixture of concern and innocence on her face. They had still been on talking terms then. Talking, but only of essential domestic matters, not communicating. And of course, not sharing a bed, or even a room.

He hadn't looked at her then, or replied. Thrusting the letter, envelope and all, into the breast pocket of his bush shirt, he had turned abruptly and walked out of the room. Minutes later, she had heard him start the Jeep. There had been the angry sound of furious wheels on gravel. And he had gone.

Looking at Ronojoy now, she shook her head slightly. Past images coalesced again with the present reality.

'Open it,' said Shrabana softly. 'I want to know…' She couldn't find the strength to continue further. Jona came towards her and held her close. But Shrabana refused to yield to the comfort of hysteria. Not now. Not until it was over, one way or the other.

'Shouldn't we wait for Ranjit...?' asked Ronojoy in an undecided voice. 'I have already sent the bearer to fetch him.'

'Open it,' said Shrabana again, not pleading. 'Rahul is my son, after all.'

The hands—Ronojoy's now, Ranjit's a year ago—carefully tore open the envelope. Ronojoy took out a single sheet of paper. He read it through quickly, then handed it wordlessly to Shrabana. Unclenching her fists, she took it from her brother-in-law.

The letterhead on the single white sheet was an incongruous, frivolous pink. But the message on it was as grim as she had expected. In a surprisingly beautiful copperplate hand, it informed the Manager, Betbagaan Tea Estate, that his son was safe. To ensure his further safety, as well as his return to his parents, his father would have to part with a certain sum of money, the amount to be negotiated, at a date and place that would be intimated later. If he valued his son's life, on no account was the respected Manager Saab to do anything rash. The letter ended with a salute to the Cause for which they, Rahul's kidnappers, were working.

Safe. Shrabana latched on to the word, written in black ink on the white notepaper, as though it was a lifeboat that would take her and Rahul away from the shipwreck of their lives. A small, insistent throbbing at the back of her head tried to tell her that what she perceived to be a lifeboat was after all only a straw. But she refused to let the pulse become an articulated thought. She did not want any voice, even her own inner voice, to give form and shape to her terror, to unlock the gates that would let the darkness come roaring in. She knew, of course she did, that a kidnapper's word was not to be believed, even if the kidnappers used pink letterheads and had highly-educated handwriting. But if life was to go on, if the Universe was not to come to a standstill, she *had* to believe that Rahul was safe.

A roaring, apocalyptic hurricane of unrest had been whipping the sky above all who lived in this unfortunate land for decades. 'Insurgency', 'terrorism', 'a breakdown in the law-and-order situation': these words had swirled around her for a long time now. But till a couple of years ago, safe in her cocoon of ordered domestic felicity, they'd never had the power to pierce the armour that had protected her from the chaos outside. She had within her a small candle-flame of conviction that these things happened only to other people, never to her. But all the while, playing out their lives in remote, far-flung tea-gardens where 'security' was just a high-sounding word for a lathi-wielding chowkidar or two, they had been completely at the mercy of whoever wished to target them for extortion, whether a terrorist group, or merely an anti-social outfit donning the guise of insurgents.

Shrabana slumped back in her chair, not even trying to stop the shaking in her hands, in her entire body, now. The thought came to her fevered mind that, through contact with the kidnapper's note, she had touched Rahul himself. Her fingers had touched the note, which had been written by the kidnapper, who had probably touched Rahul several times during these last seven days. It was a link. Tenuous, but a link nevertheless. Had the kidnappers' hands steadied her son as he had been marched through the snake- and leech-infested forests? Rahul feared snakes, though, like any other sixteen-year-old, he always tried to cover it up with bravado. But his eyes, and the look of suppressed horror in them when he saw a snake slithering across their garden, gave him away every time.

Rahul's eyes had had the same look in them when they had taken him away. The twelve people who had encircled Rahul on the veranda each had a gun. One of which was smoking. Lassie, their Labrador, had barked too loudly. Casually, one of the twelve had pumped three bullets into Lassie's leaping body.

Shrabana had been inside. She had come rushing out at the sound. Two guns were immediately lifted towards her. This wouldn't have stopped her from trying to tear Rahul away from the men. But the other ten guns had been aimed at Rahul's head.

'We're taking him.' The man had been brusque.

'Where? Why? Chowkidar!' Her voice had gone out of control. A scream had come bubbling out of her throat.

'Don't make a noise. It won't help you.'

'Please—what do you want? Take anything—please—leave him.' She couldn't bear to see that frightened-of-snakes look in Rahul's eyes. 'Take me—yes—I'll go instead of him.'

One of the men had laughed. 'You? The Manager won't pay even a paisa of ransom for you!' Even these men knew. She had felt no shame. Not then, not now. She was bottling up her emotions, she would take them out later. If there was to be a later. All her energies had been concentrated at keeping the darkness at bay.

Another man, whose eyes seemed to burn above his beard with the flame of idealism rather than greed, had spoken up. His voice had been soft. 'Don't worry. He will come to no harm.' All had had beards, all were young, all had had guns.

The cold of that January morning had seeped into her bones as they had marched him away. 'Let me give him some warm clothes, at least. He'll feel cold at night ...' she had whispered, despairingly. Rahul had been wearing just his jeans and a thin T-shirt with the name of a rock band printed on it. And, of all things, his Kohlapuri sandals. The twelve hadn't bothered to pause, or reply. But Rahul had turned around once. With the guns still on him, he had said, (the look still in his eyes, but his voice steady) 'Don't worry, Ma. I'll be back soon.'

Tall, with a tennis-player's build, but with a soft, open, vulnerable face still. Her Rahul, her son. Flesh of her flesh. Heartbeat to heartbeat for nine luminous months. And they had marched him away, guns to his head. 'Don't worry.' How often had Rahul said these words to her in the past couple of years? Trying to be a man, because his childhood had been taken away from him.

Rahul's words, the expression on his face when he had found out about Ranjit, were seared onto her mind. Perhaps she could have forgiven Ranjit if her own feelings, her own future had been the only ones involved. But Rahul's bewildered vulnerability had made her turn against Ranjit in a cold, unforgiving fury.

The Annual Winter Ball and Tea Meet had been held at the Gymkhana Club, fifty kilometres away from the Betbagaan Tea Estate. Ranjit had told her about his involvement with Noyona by then. They were already sleeping separately. But they had still, at that time, been keeping up the facade of appearing together for social functions at the nearby clubs, and for dinners and lunches at friends' houses. The chains and bonds of fifteen years of matrimony were being snapped apart, but slowly, link by painful link.

Rahul, of course, had gone along. Increasingly, he was being used as a shield by both of them. Without his constant chatter and schoolboy humour, the fifty-kilometer-long journey through lonely roads that cut across monotonous carpets of manicured tea-bushes would have been unbearable. For by then, Ranjit and she had reached an impasse: there had been nothing left to say. Recriminations, tears, on her side; defences, accusations and stubbornness on Ranjit's: all had been played out. There was only silence between them then. As now. Rahul had been home from his boarding school in the hills, and the desolate spaces between Ranjit and herself had been cushioned by his presence in the huge bungalow.

The next day, however, Rahul had been subdued. He sat opposite Shrabana in the sunny dining room with its French windows leading to the flower-filled garden. 'What's the matter?' she remembered teasing him. 'Didn't any of the girls pay you any attention last night?'

Rahul had always been frank and open with both his parents. But that morning, he had refused to even look at her. 'No—it's not that... ' he had mumbled.

This uncharacteristic reticence had caused a small ant-bite of worry to surface in her consciousness. She had asked gently, 'What is it, Rahul, sweetheart? What's bothering you?' She had half-expected him to flinch away from her in the pride of his newly-dawning manhood. But he hadn't done so. Instead, he had looked up at her. His eyes had been filled with sudden anguish. His upper lip, soft with a golden down of which he was inordinately proud, trembled slightly.

The iron weight on her chest shifted its weight and settled down even more heavily now, when she remembered the vulnerability of his young face that morning.

'Deuta's having—he's involved with another woman, isn't he?' The words had come out like weighted cannon balls in that sunny room with flowers outside and framed pictures on the walls.

She had thought that she could—that they, Ranjit and she, could—keep the whole thing a secret from their son. But chance words overheard, looks interpreted accurately by an intelligent, sensitive mind, and the whole sordid episode had been laid bare before Rahul. Besides, she could well imagine that nobody in the closed confines of their tea circles would miss an opportunity to gossip and make barbed comments about Ranjit's adulterous relationship. What did they care if the barbs homed in on a fourteen-year-old's mind, instead?

The anger that had festered within her had burst its skin and come roiling out at that moment. The humiliation of being cast off for a younger woman, the pain and insecurity that had followed Ranjit's unemotional announcement that he wanted a divorce, the sleepless, tortured nights spent imagining Ranjit together with Noyona, all coalesced into fury that a defenceless boy had had to find out, in the worst possible way, about his father's infidelity. Even the pain that she felt when she imagined Ranjit's familiar body in the embrace of another woman, even that sense of deep betrayal had paled against the glittering rage that she had felt at that moment, when faced with Rahul's uncertain, bewildered look.

Till that moment, she had only thought of the situation that she was in with despair. In some of her less controlled moments, with her pillow damp with fevered tears, her imagination had tossed up impossible schemes for revenge. Taking a lover, or better still, inducing Noyona to take up with another man, if possible a man who was richer, younger and taller than Ranjit... But these were only night-time schemes. In the bright light of morning, she knew that there was nothing that she could do to get Ranjit back.

Of course she had refused to give him an easy divorce, taking perverse pleasure in the knowledge that this would alienate him from her even more. But why should she make it easy for him? She had given up a promising career, a job with a multi-national company in Mumbai and followed him here, to this remote, terrorist-infested place. He would provide for her, he had said, after he had asked for a divorce. But how could he compensate for those lost years, those stilled ambitions, those silenced desires? She had channelled all her energies into this marriage, sublimated all her career ambitions into keeping a picture-perfect house and garden. Her home, her garden, her parties were the talk of the tea circles. People openly attributed Ranjit's rapid rise up the managerial rungs to his wife's wonderful way with all kinds of people. She was the woman behind his success.

And he had dared to tell her that he would provide for her.

Boyhood had fallen away from Rahul that morning, as she had looked helplessly on, unable to speak, numb with a double-edged dagger in her heart. Like greedy hands stripping away a warm garment from another person on a cold morning, his father's actions had stripped innocence and security away from Rahul. Her son's sudden maturity had sent waves of pain bludgeoning deep within her, the effects of which were quite different from those of his father's perfidy. Ranjit's actions had hurt her, yes, but that hurt had come wrapped in layers of humiliation and anger. The pain she felt when she saw her son's suddenly-quiet ways was a raw, aching hurt, which seemed to emanate from some primeval, maternal part of her psyche.

Shrabana sat with her eyes closed as Ronojoy, his voice sharp with urgency, made the necessary telephone calls. She did not attempt to follow the process of calling in the law-enforcers. It would take its course. All that mattered was that Rahul was not with her any more.

Ronojoy's urgent voice summoned the uniformed men who had been waiting for just such a letter to be delivered. Once again, her mind strayed to that earlier letter in Ranjit's hand, then twitched away, like a leech coming into contact with a grain of salt. Shrabana couldn't bear to think of the parallels any more. Was it just a parallel, a mere coincidence, that these things were happening in the same house, repeating themselves within such a short time? Or was this—the word, lurking in a membrane of denial, finally burst its thin, containing skin and popped into her consciousness, fully formed—was all this her Nemesis? Punishment by a sportive Being who had a weakness for the neat ironical retort, inflicted unerringly, where it hurt the most?

She pushed away the thought, and concentrated, instead, on Jona's palm on her head. It was a cool bandage across the iron band that had clamped down heavily on her brow at the moment when they had taken Rahul away... Rahul's hand on her brow had not felt the same. His were a teenage boy's hands, a tennis player's palms, rough and callused. Yet his touch had been more soothing than Jona's soft, well-intentioned palms.

That morning, Shrabana had not been able to answer Rahul's question. The anguish in her heart had been for her son, whose childhood innocence had vanished overnight. She had clasped him to herself and, stroking his hair, had rocked him gently over their mingled tears.

With his own chatter stilled, Rahul had become aware of the echoing silences in the house. Ranjit talked to her only to say the most perfunctory things such as 'Shrivastava from Head Office is dropping in tomorrow. He will probably stay the night.' And Shrabana, too, had stuck to the most essential of communications. Sometimes, especially if they'd had a series of company guests that month, she had to ask Ranjit for extra housekeeping money. She had always budgeted efficiently, and the occasions when she'd had to ask for extra money in the past had been rare. But now, knowing that Ranjit was probably spending large sums on Noyona, money that should rightfully have come to their own family—money that should have been set aside for Rahul's future— Shrabana began to take a secret delight in asking for more whenever the opportunity rose. She began to squirrel some of it away every month, and also to spend on things that had never interested her in the past—fancy face-creams that promised to keep even incipient wrinkles at bay, or bestow the user with a glowing skin overnight.

With his suddenly-mature, observant eyes, Rahul had noticed the lack of any proper conversation between his parents. He would reassure her, 'Don't worry, Ma,' when he caught her gazing desolately after Ranjit as he left in his car in the evenings, without telling either of them where he was heading.

Sometimes, when he was unaware that his mother was watching, Rahul would let his guard down. The cocky veneer would drop from his eyes, and a look of hurt and puzzled bewilderment would appear. Her son, who had always been a fun-loving, outdoorsy extrovert, now began to avoid his friends in the neighbouring gardens when he was on holiday. Every change, however small and in itself insignificant, that she had seen in Rahul, had added to the rage seething within her. How dare Ranjit forget, not just that he had a wife, but also that he was the father of a boy who was at an impressionable age? Couldn't he see what his behaviour was doing to his son? Or was he so besotted with that woman that he was blind to all else? An image of Noyona, small, slim, with a waterfall of hair to her waist, rose in her mind. What did Ranjit see in her, this woman who was twenty-nine to Ranjit's forty-eight, a nurse in the hospital of the Betbagaan Tea Estate? How could this woman make him forget that his son was at the age when he needed to hero-worship his father?

After Rahul's vacations had ended and he had gone back to school, the questions had continued to plague her. Sitting in that vast, echoing bungalow, with its carefully maintained perfection making a mockery of her marriage, alone except for the throngs of domestic help around her, the expressions on Rahul's face had continued to torment her. And for all she knew, Ranjit was away at that very moment with Noyona, seeking fulfilment in some secluded, tree-shaded patch of mossy coolness.

If only she could punish him. Her thoughts would always come back to this focus.

The idea had come to her suddenly, full-blown, one night. She had woken up from sleep, with the entire plan fully detailed in her mind. Of course. Since she couldn't actually do anything, she would learn from what the terrorists around them were doing so successfully all the time. She would terrorize him, make him so fearful that he would become a limp puppet. Fear would make him hers, put him in her power. Fear would castrate, would emasculate him. Unlike the insurgents teeming around them, she would not do it for money, or to score a political point, or for a convoluted love of country. She would terrorize him to get even. He, who had taken away Rahul's secure childhood forever, would pay for it by losing his own peace of mind.

It had all been quite easy, once she had made up her mind. The long hours when she was alone were now spent in composing threatening letters, instead of brooding. She had visited the families of enough victims of terrorist kidnappings to know exactly how to go about it. True, she did not have the official notepaper of any of the main terrorist groups that were active in the area, but it did not matter. In the chaos that prevailed in these anarchic times, there were many small opportunistic outfits that made the most of the general lawlessness to get themselves some easy money. She would copy them.

Shrabana spent long afternoons carefully cutting out alphabets and words from old issues of The Assam Tribune. *If ever some intelligent policeman got hold of the notes that she planned to send, the lettering would not point in her direction, since this was a paper seen in all homes, offices and business establishments around them.*

In any case, it was highly unlikely that any particularly zealous policeman would be assigned to the case. In the face of the frequent terrorist attacks, the bomb-blasts, the gun-snatchings and the train derailments that convulsed the land, the police forces were a demoralized, confused lot.

Remembered fragments from newspaper reports, the habits of successful crooks in detective novels, came back to her. She was careful to burn the papers that she cut up; careful also to paste the letters and words on plain foolscap paper, easily available even in the local village shops. The envelope that she used, too, was flimsy and innocuous-looking. She wondered for a long time how she should go about writing the address on it. Typing it out on Ranjit's typewriter was of course out of the question. She knew, once again from detective stories, that it was quite easy to trace the typed paper back to the typewriter on which it had originated. So easy, in fact, that even the local police could do it once they made up their minds to do so. She couldn't use the computer, because terrorists did not have access to computers. In the end, she had printed Ranjit's name and address in cramped capital letters, using black ink. She herself normally used only royal blue. It was amazing how different the writing looked from her usual bold, flowing hand.

Posting the letter posed a problem. Normally, the daak-wala collected all letters from the Manager Sahib's bungalow and took them to the office, from where they were again taken to the local post-office. Obviously she couldn't send her note that way. Nor was it feasible to go down to the village post-office and post it there. The postmark would point to the place where it had been dropped off. And if the police ever questioned the postal workers there, they would surely remember that the Memsahib of the Betbagaan Tea Estate had taken to posting her letters herself recently. In the end the solution had been quite simple, as easy as lying. After the houseboys had gone to bed, and she had locked the many doors that opened out to the deep verandas encircling the house, she had merely slipped the note under the main door. Half in, half out, with the address facing downwards. Okon, whose job it was to open the doors and windows every morning, would find it there, and hand it to Ranjit.

Shrabana listened to Ronojoy on the telephone now, but the images that flickered under her closed eyelids were of Ranjit.

Ranjit opening the letters as they were handed to him, one by one, at random intervals. Even though they were not communicating at all by then, it was quite apparent to Shrabana that the first few letters had disturbed him greatly. The police had been contacted, the servants had been questioned, a few token security men had been deputed to guard the bungalow. Token, because it was laughably apparent that they were painfully inadequate against any terrorists who might wish to attack them.

As expected, nothing had come of the enquiries. Nothing ever did. The letters had continued to arrive.

And each time Ranjit opened one, Shrabana had rejoiced. She would position herself in a nearby spot, unobtrusively, when she knew that it was time for Okon to deliver the letter. She savoured the way Ranjit's face appeared to shrink, the way worry lines appeared on his forehead, the way his expression tautened, every time he saw the letters. By the time he received the second one, he had come to recognize the handwriting, as she had intended he should. His hands hadn't trembled when he had received the first letter; but from the second time onwards, they had begun to shake uncontrollably as soon as he saw the handwriting. She had relished the way his hands shuddered as he opened the envelope, gloated over the way his face slackened with fear as he read the message. She had read along with him, silently, with burning eyes. In the scales of justice in her mind, each letter was a small blow of revenge for the way his behaviour had changed Rahul for ever.

The messages had all carried the same refrain, using different phrases. The Manager of the Betbagaan Tea Estate should leave as soon as possible. Otherwise, there would be drastic (though unspecified) consequences. It hadn't been difficult to vary the phrases. She had sent out eight letters so far, over a period of a year. And each one had arrowed into the vulnerable place in Ranjit's mind.

With her eyes still closed, she heard the door open, and Ranjit's unmistakable footsteps walk heavily across the wooden floor of the veranda outside. Now. She would have to tell them now. Tell them that Rahul's kidnappers were not the same people who had sent those eight letters. Tell them, tell Ranjit especially, that those threats had been hollow. That it was no use wasting time trying to find links between those letters and this one, or those letters and Rahul's kidnapping, as the police were trying to do. It would lead them nowhere, it was a waste of time.

Why weren't they *doing* anything, she thought with a sudden, despairing spurt of fresh anguish. She wanted to run out of the house in eight different directions at once, barefoot, with her hair streaming behind her, screaming out to the winds for her son. But of course it wasn't possible. The impulse subsided as soon as it came. They might shoot him if they were pursued. There was nothing left to do but wait. Count the nano-seconds as they crawled endlessly by, and remember Rahul's afraid-of-snakes look as he had been led away.

And wonder, always wonder, whether this heart-stopping thing had happened because of her. Because she, by indulging her craving for revenge, had invited disaster with her letters.

Tempted Fate. Given ideas to the gods, who were now laughing mockingly at her. Was this what was meant by retribution? Was this Nemesis? Yes, it was.

Ranjit was in the room now. She opened her eyes and looked dully around her. Gently, but with steady hands, she pushed away Jona's palms from her forehead, and took a deep breath.

It was time to talk. This was it. The time to pay for her actions of the past year.

Ekalavya

Being the Culture Correspondent for *The Eastern Guardian* suits me fine. The work, if indeed it can be called that, is extremely light, while the returns are excellent. I don't of course mean the economic returns, which are meagre at the best of times, and non-existent when the paper lurches into one of its frequent crises. No, the dividends are more intangible, as I have found out over the years of being involved with this paper published from Parbatpuri, our medium-sized, but rapidly expanding city.

Just last month, for example, we had a vocalist of the Agra Gharana here for a concert. As usual, in addition to reviewing his performance, I was asked to do an interview with him. Quite an opportunity. Over the years, I've found that readers are more interested in the personal slant than in the strictly professional aspect. I mean, who is *really* interested in reading about the nuances of a particular raag, or the presentation of a particular bhav? I've always, therefore, sprinkled my interviews with questions about the artiste's personal life, about the rumours and gossip that inevitably surround such stars. And the cheekier the questions, the better. I don't know about other celebrities, but the musicians, dancers, painters and theatre-people that I've interviewed over the years have always been almost painfully polite to me.

I see them lording it over their chamchas, their students and their hangers-on, making outrageous demands of the organizers of the function for which they've come, asking for out-of-season grapes and exorbitantly-priced dry fruits. But the minute they hear I'm from a newspaper, they're like putty in my hands. They may stutter when I ask them about the wife they abandoned when successes began to come their way, or blush when I innocently inquire if there's any truth in the story that they've moved in with so-and-so. But never once, so far, has any one of them shown any anger. Indeed, the vocalist of the Agra Gharana sent me an effusive thank-you note after he received a copy of my interview, along with many entreaties to visit him when I was next in Delhi. This, even though I wrote more about the two nubile young students hovering adoringly around him all the time I was there, than on his approach to the Raag Lalit he had performed at that morning's concert.

Power, that's what this job is about, and that's what I like about it. You'd be surprised what a publicity fiend even the most committed artiste can be. He may be steeped in decades of sadhana, but even a dilettante journo like me gets a warm welcome from him. And of course the organizers of cultural events in our city send me special invitations to attend their functions. I make it a point to enter the hall a good half-hour or so late, so that the audience gets a chance to whisper among themselves, 'That's Shibani Barua. You know—the musicologist.' Of course the performer's concentration is disturbed. But, I reason, what's his riyaaz worth if it can't stand up to a small distraction like a late entry? The organizers run around getting me the best seat and soft drinks while I stand rock-like, uncaring that I'm blocking the view.

Over the years, I've written so many reviews that now I can spout the jargon while I'm only half-awake. For local and still-struggling artistes, I use a patronizing tone: I hint at mistakes, without of course actually committing myself to specifics. 'The raag structure could have been built up more carefully' is one of my favourite phrases. On the other hand, I am safely laudatory about the performance when a Big Name visits our Rang Manch. I talk of the 'plaintive wail of the Komal Dhaivat' and the 'home-coming to an all-encompassing Shadaj' in effusive tones. Of course it's all drivel, but nobody can see through this verbal haze, least of all the musicians themselves. It's this nebulous, ambiguous language, coupled with my questions about the artistes' personal lives, that has done wonders for my reputation here in Parbatpuri. I hardly ever practice my own music now, though there was a time when I would diligently do my palta-riyaaz for a couple of hours every day. But I've stopped. Why should I sweat when there's an easier way to get into the limelight?

Yes, I've become cynical about the respect that I get here. The organizers pander to my whims because they need the publicity that my reviews bring them. A favourable review means more sponsors for their next programme. The paper needs me because there's nobody else who would work the culture line for the pittance they pay. Up-and-coming artistes buzz around me because they, too, need a good review if other programmes are to come their way.

At one time, I had dreamt of being spoken of as a musician, a vocalist. Maybe not a top-notch one, even then, but enough to call in audiences to my performances. I had wanted to move people with my songs, just as I was—still am—moved when I hear a fine piece of music. But not everybody can make it as a performer. Gradually, I had lowered my ambitions, till one day I stopped doing my riyaaz completely.

And in any case, this alternative career of mine, if it can be called that, is better than nothing. Certainly it gives me power. And, I reason, being a Culture Correspondent is better than moaning about neglect. Or taking a lover. Instead of being the bored, vegetative, childless, rich wife of a busy paediatrician—or indeed, a failed musician—I can revel in being introduced as 'Ms Barua, the writer.'

I've learnt to like my life, I've learnt to like what I'm doing. Only... sometimes, something... the raw emotions of an earnest youth who is out to touch the stars with his music, or something in the eyes, the expression on a veena-player's face, as he delves deep into Darbari... sometimes these get past the carefully built wall that I've erected around me. And then...

Just now, for instance. I have received a review copy of a CD. The local music stores send these over to the paper, and the paper in turn sends them across to me.

Visually, the cover of the CD is a beauty. It is beautifully packaged, with the picture of the performer, Pandit Deenbandhu Misra floating hazily behind a superimposed riverscape that is as serene as the look in the musician's eyes. The cover itself is an attention-grabber. The company has named the CD 'Pandit Deenbandhu Misra: A Riverain Muse.'

The title intrigues me. I play the CD immediately. The clear, digitally mastered cadences are flawless. The smooth, silky resonance of the maestro's sitar flows like a wide river, so deep that there is no trace of turbulence on the blue surface, even though it is racing swiftly towards the sea. The music pours through the house, it washes in little ripples around the nooks and crannies of my mind as I listen, entranced. The waves lap softly, but insistently, at the casements of my innermost being till I am shaken out of my usual cynicism.

Effortlessly, the sitarist has succeeded in evoking the mood of a great river as it flows swiftly, yet calmly, towards the sea. The music is so smooth that the listener forgets that he is hearing a stringed instrument, one from which each note has to be plucked out physically, with one's fingers. The infinity of the sea is just beyond the curve; there is joy in his music, pure and unadulterated, joy at the prospect of journey's end at the next bend in the river. Yet there is sadness, too, a deep resonant sadness that wells up from some subterranean place. It is the sadness that comes from the knowledge that the familiar world of hills and valleys, of forests and lakes, will soon be but a memory. The sadness that comes from the consciousness that the realm of people, children and little animals who had come long ago to drink of its waters when the great river had been but a clear, bubbling brook on an icy mountainside, will soon be lost to it. And at the end, there is peace, as quiet and final as the sound of the last raindrop falling from the leaf of a tall tree to the mossy ground below, in a shady forest after the fury of a monsoon storm has passed. Little ripples grow in ever-widening circles of silence till the mind is filled with the deep, hushed voice of the ocean.

The music on the CD is like nothing that has been tried by Panditji before. It is not, strictly speaking, a raag-based piece at all, though wisps and echoes of many raags wander in and out of the main narrative. It is not raag music, but river music. The main aria has poured out of a land where an immense river is the dominant feature of the landscape. Indeed, the basic melody, the substratum on which the entire shimmering aural structure is so carefully built, is none other than a tune that I am myself familiar with. It is neither a Bhatiali, nor a Baul, those melodies that have always been associated with river music; not a Bihu or even a Biya Naam, but an evocative mingling of all these various euphonious odes.

My mind goes back to the time, several months ago, when Pandit Deenbandhu Misra had visited our city.

~

Who hasn't heard of Pandit Deenbandhu Misra? Over the decades, he has built an awesome reputation for himself. Even those who know nothing about classical music are familiar with the story of his life. He was born into a prosperous family over six decades ago. His father owned a paratha shop in a Lucknow bylane which was famed for both the variety and excellence of its wares. It was a hereditary pursuit: it was said that the Nawabs at the height of Awadh's glory came to this narrow gali disguised as commoners to sample the various types of unleavened bread on offer at the shop. Even when Deenbandhu was a child, people came from distant corners of the state to taste his father's kulchas stuffed with spiced potatoes, and his legendary mooli parathas. The delicately spiced mixed-vegetable pickle served as an accompaniment was made from a secret recipe that had been handed down through five generations from father to son. It was assumed that Deenbandhu, as the only male offspring, would shoulder the burden of pleasing the shop's many customers, modernizing and mechanizing it, perhaps, as he led it to the next century.

But Deenbandhu was not inclined towards culinary pursuits. His interests lay, not in pleasing the palates of others, but in satisfying them aurally. On the pretext of going to the temple to offer evening prayers, or to visit friends, or to take part in a football game, he would sneak off to a local master to learn the sitar, instead. He did not even keep the instrument in his own house, for fear of his father's anger, but in a friend's bedroom where he would practice whenever he could. When his father the paratha-tycoon found out, Deenbandhu was thrashed soundly. But it had no effect on him at all.

He followed the sound of the sitar. He was mesmerized by it. Leaving his family and friends behind, he went to a distant village situated in the middle of a deep forest to learn the intricacies of this instrument from a recluse, a mystic who believed that the way to reach the godhead was through music. He was the only student there. It was a rigorous life, but the notes of the sitar filled all his waking hours, and echoed in his mind when he slept.

Much later, Deenbandhu came back to civilization. His years of struggle, his fight to be accepted into the closed world of those musicians who had been born to the pursuit of music through their gharanas, his taking to playing in film orchestras in order to make ends meet—all this is part of popular lore today. Now, of course, he is a colossus in the music world, a man who jets in and out of the country as a cultural ambassador, spreading the message of peace and brotherhood among nations with his music.

Sangeet Circle, the group that had managed to get Pandit Deenbandhu to agree to perform in our city, was quite euphoric about the coup. It was to be Pandit Deenbandhu's first performance here. So rarely was he in the country of his birth nowadays, that even the huge music conferences that took place in the metropolises had to book him at least a year ahead. Sangeet Circle had managed to get him to condescend to come to our city for a performance, only after they had agreed to all the conditions imposed by his Personal Assistant. This included a 25 percent advance on his fee of five lakh rupees. The remaining

75 percent would have to be paid to Deenbandhu's P.A. just before the maestro stepped onto the stage. If the organizers failed to comply, or if the Panditji's P.A. did not, for whatever reason, give the maestro the green signal, not a single note would he play till the conditions were met.

Besides the five-lakh-rupee fee, the organizers would also have to foot the bill to fly the six-member troupe from Mumbai to our city that lies sprawled on a curve of the Brahmaputra, way up in the North-East of the country. The other people in the group included a star tabaliya whose fee of one lakh rupees was to be paid separately. Besides, there were three students accompanying their guru. Two of them would play the taanpuras during the performance, for apparently the maestro did not trust small-city taanpura players. The third would provide support on his sitar during the performance. In addition, of course, the P.A. would also have to accompany Panditji. Indeed, he was as indispensable as the tabaliya. For he would be responsible for the actual collection of the fee. The maestro himself never sullied his spirituality by handling cash, at least in his own country, though the handling of dollars was, of course, a different matter.

Apart from the transport, the troupe's accommodation was to be five-star deluxe. Nervously and shamefacedly, Sangeet Circle had confessed that the most luxurious hotel in our city had barely three stars. After consultations with his boss who was then in Paris, the P.A. had told them, in an 'aren't you lucky' tone, that Panditji had agreed to three-star accommodation provided each member of his troupe was given an individual suite.

Our city, which is still a small town in many respects, was all agog as news of these details filtered in. Luckily the date on which the performance was scheduled was more than a year in the future. The organizers had enough time to run around raising funds and sponsorships, bringing out a lavish souvenir, and generally looking after the innumerable details that organizing an event of this type entails.

For Pandit Deenbandhu Misra is, unequivocally a star. Indeed, he is a supernova at its peak of brightness, the Amitabh Bachchan of classical musicians. He has left far behind him the days when he lived with his Guru in a hut in the forest. Once he had made his first crore, Panditji had tried to bring his Guru, by then a frail and irascible man, to live in Mumbai in a spacious flat to be purchased by him. However, the Guru had declined, even though he was now living alone in his forest hut—he had never married—saying that the pollution of Mumbai and the sea air would aggravate his rheumatism, as a result of which he would be unable to maintain the speed of his stroke-play.

As the day of Pandit Deenbandhu's arrival approached, it seemed that our city could talk and think of nothing else. Notices appeared in *The Eastern Guardian*, as well as its rival papers, both English and local-language, about the imminent arrival of the maestro. Red-and-white banners were strung across lampposts at strategic points around town, tom-toming the upcoming concert as the 'Event of the Decade'. It was decided that none of the nine public auditoriums in the city were big enough for the teeming crowds that were expected to attend the performance. Indeed, music lovers as well as pretenders to culture were anticipated not just from our city, but from the entire state. The city's indoor stadium, a huge, cavernous hall, was therefore readied for the event. A carefully built and tastefully decorated dais was placed at one end of the hall. Several smaller rooms adjacent to the hall were thoroughly cleaned and readied as greenrooms. White-sheeted, thick cotton mattresses were arranged on the floors, with several large bolsters scattered around, giving the greenrooms the look of conference rooms at political party headquarters. The microphone system, as well as technicians to operate it, were brought in from out-of-state at great expense, since only the very best sound system was deemed fit for Deenbandhu Misra's concert.

Even as the members of the Sangeet Circle were busy organizing the event and collecting money from donors to fill their coffers, the citizens of Parbatpuri went about their daily business with a sense of heightened awareness about the momentous cultural event about to come to a climax. People boned up on stories about Deenbandhu Misra, who began to figure quite prominently in the city's adda sessions. Youths, suddenly aware of the importance of the event, began to sport kurta pyjamas with ornate embroidery, as well as Kohlapuri chappals on their feet, and went around earnestly discussing 'our great heritage' even as they spoke of the approaching event with familiarity, as though they were in the inner circle of the cultural organization. They referred to the sitarist as 'Deenbandhuji' with just the right mixture of familiarity and respect, to show that they were well acquainted with the star himself, as well as with the nuances of his art.

Rishabh, a young man I have known for several years now, is very different from these poseurs. Unlike them, Rishabh actually plays an instrument. Indeed, he, too, is a sitar player. Though he has had some tutoring from two or three teachers, he is mostly self-taught. He listens to and absorbs the performances of the great masters on radio, TV, CDs and YouTube. His playing is sweet, melodious and true. He is slim and delicately-boned, with long fingers that caress the frets of his instrument when he plays, as though he were stroking the petals of a pure, unsullied lotus.

I like Rishabh because there is nothing pretentious or hypocritical about him. Unlike those whose appreciation of music consists of shouting 'wah wah' in all the wrong places, Rishabh knows about classical music. An appreciative nod and a quiet 'kya baat' from him is high praise. He is always present at the musical events that take place in Parbatpuri. Over the years, we have become friends. With him, I drop the jargon that I use for *The Eastern Guardian*. He supports himself by tutoring, and by giving performances on the radio, TV and on stage. And, unlike most middle-level performers, he is quite objective about his own standard of playing.

~

I met Rishabh on the pavement outside the Radio Station about a week before Pandit Deenbandhu's scheduled performance. He carried his sitar under his arm, and looked out of place amidst the hustle and bustle of the city at that hour.

'Coming to the function?' I asked him after we had exchanged greetings. There was no need to elaborate which function I meant. There was only one event on the minds of our city's musicians now.

'Of course, Baideo,' he replied. 'They've priced the tickets very high, but I bought one towards the front of the auditorium. Not in the very front row but good enough to watch Panditji's finger techniques. I can't really afford it, but ... how can I learn if I sit at the back?'

I felt a twinge of guilt. I could well afford the tickets, thanks to my husband's flourishing paediatric practice. However, I would be attending the show without having to buy one. As usual, I would see and hear Deenbandhu Misra's performance from one of the best seats in the hall, one which had the word 'Press' on a placard attached behind it.

'How's your riyaaz?' I asked, to change the subject. I knew that Rishabh practiced for at least four hours daily. Even though the mundane activities of having to earn his living kept him busy throughout the day, he always began and ended his waking hours with his riyaaz.

'You know I never miss it,' he answered. 'And now that Panditji's coming here, I've stepped it up.'

'Really?' I was confused. I didn't see the connection between Deenbandhu Misra's arrival and Rishabh's increased efforts. He, after all, was not billed to support the maestro in his performance, or anything like that.

'Yes, I don't want to sound amateurish when he listens to me,' replied Rishabh.

I must have looked surprised, for he continued, 'Sorry, I thought I'd told you. When I first heard that Panditji,' he breathed the honorific reverently, 'is to come here, I sent a message to him. Several messages, in fact. First I wrote. Then I sent emails. Then, after I got no response to even my third one, I sent a message through Pradipda. You know, the person who is liaising between the Sangeet Circle and Panditji.'

'What message?'

'I have requested him to take me on as his student.' Rishabh looked diffident as he said it, but earnest.

'So did you get any reply?' I was rather sceptical, for I know the casual attitudes of some star performers.

'Yes. Yes, I did! About a month ago, Panditji sent word that he would listen to my playing while he was here. A kind of audition, you know. If I'm good he'll take me on...'

'I'm sure you're good enough,' I broke in. It was not just politeness that made me say it. I had heard him playing, and knew that he has the musical sense required to make it to the top. He also has that quality which is even more essential for an aspiring student of classical music: determination, doggedness, the ability to keep one's nose to the grindstone of a gruelling regimen of practice, practice and yet more practice. I know now, after all these years, that lots of people have talent, and musical sense. Yes, lots. What is required to make it to the top is this determination, this passion that sustains all the hours of rigorous practice, and the ability to slog it out. And I know now, too, that this is what was missing in me. The lack of this passion and discipline is what made me ultimately give up on my attempts to become a musician professionally. This is why I respect people like Rishabh even more.

'I hope so,' said Rishabh now, but he looked worried. 'I've decided,' he said, 'to play Raag Todi for him, since I am to meet him in the morning. I know that it is one of Panditji's favourite raags. I've also prepared one of my own compositions—a light dhun based on a folk song, Baideo.'

'But what about, you know, finances?' I couldn't help asking. I knew that learning music from as renowned a guru as Deenbandhu Misra wouldn't come cheap. Besides having to live in an expensive metropolis, Rishabh would have to pay for his tuitions, his fare there and so on. And I knew he wasn't rich; far from it.

'I've been keeping aside a little money every month for a while now,' he replied. 'I'll live cheaply if I do get there, to Mumbai I mean. And perhaps in a little while I'll be able to earn a bit through performances. After all, I'm an approved radio artiste—something should come up. The main thing is that Guruji should accept me as his student, if I'm good enough, that is...'

I noticed the 'Guruji', though the student had yet to meet the teacher. He sounded like an Arjun who saw only the eye of the bird his arrow was aimed at. For Rishabh, the only thing that mattered was being accepted by the person he had come to think of as his guru. Details such as how he would survive while he took his lessons were trifles.

'You know I've been listening to Panditji's CDs for several years now. I mean, seriously listening. I've learnt quite a few things from them ... but everybody knows learning from CDs and TV and radio has its limitations. Now if only he accepts me as his student ...'

'I'm sure he will,' I repeated, with sincerity. 'Once he hears you playing, he can't refuse.'

I left him to trudge up to the Radio Station, where he had a recording, while I walked to my waiting car.

The day after Deenbandhu Misra's arrival in our city, all the Parbatpuri dailies carried four-column photos of the arrival of the maestro and his entourage. He was shown with a thick garland of marigolds around his neck, and an enigmatic expression on his unsmiling face. Behind him in the pictures were several other members of his troupe. Two or three papers included a view of the President of the Sangeet Circle in their frames. He looked nervous and bewildered, yet gratified.

In view of the erratic plane schedules to our city, the organizers had played it safe and brought in the troupe a day ahead of the actual programme. But it was well known that the maestro never met anybody outside his own entourage for twenty-four hours before a programme. To do so would disturb his concentration. Not only would he be unavailable to the press, he would meet and interact with only the President and Secretary of the Sangeet Circle till then. He would leave by the afternoon flight on Sunday. All this, though known, did not prevent eager fans from crowding around the front of his hotel. Several of the more enterprising ones tried to get to the maestro's room, but they were unceremoniously hauled back by the vigilant doormen who had been specially hired to guard the guru from such unwelcome attentions.

Rishabh, however, was not among this crowd. He remained at home, busy with his riyaaz.

The Eastern Guardian had reserved an hour with Pandit Deenbandhu on Sunday morning for my interview. Besides, of course, I was to go as their Cultural Correspondent to the concert. For once, I arrived well ahead of time at the venue. I was ushered in obsequiously to the seats reserved for the press by the members of the Circle. They had sent a card for Nitin, my husband, also, but of course, he hadn't been able to fit Deenbandhu Misra into his own busy schedule.

I settled myself into the deeply-cushioned chair, and looked around. The combined efforts of all the members of the Sangeet Circle had converted the normally functional-looking indoor stadium into a beautiful venue for a classical music performance. Stalks of fresh tuberoses, interspersed with rosebuds, were attached to the walls. Large vases filled with gladioli and tuberoses were placed at the corners of the white sheet-covered dais.

Though there were still about fifteen minutes for the programme to start, the hall was already crammed to capacity. I recognized several people sitting in the rows behind me. There was Srijata, a buxom ghazal-singer who favoured low-cut blouses and an affected manner when she performed in local concerts. There were quite a few high-level bureaucrats who had been especially invited to lend gravity to the gathering, even though their knowledge of classical music was likely to be scanty. Parbatpuri's rich businessmen were there in strength. And, squeezed between a corpulent, sweaty lady on one side and a morose-looking man who was already looking bored on the other, was Rishabh.

I knew that the seats in that row were a thousand rupees each. Normally Rishabh would no doubt have bought a twenty-five-rupee ticket for one of the back rows, where the real cognoscenti in classical music concerts are to be found. I knew he could ill afford those thousand rupees. He saw me looking back at him, and managed a small smile. In his simple kurta-pyjama, with a cloth bag balanced on his knees, Rishabh looked lost and out of place amidst those safari-suits, twinkling jewels and swishing silks.

I caught the eye of one of the ushers and beckoned. 'Could you please call that young man there,' I waved my hand towards Rishabh, 'to sit here?' I showed him the invitation meant for my absent husband. 'His card is with me.'

Rishabh was happy to be sitting in the press row. His new seat offered him an unobstructed view of the stage. Murmuring his thanks, he took out a tablet from his jhola, and tested the recording app. Like all musicians, he had invested in the best gadget he could afford when it came to recording music.

For once, the show began punctually. The President of the Sangeet Circle gave a rather nervous speech. The gathering gave him a polite hearing. He was followed by Ram Kumar, the tabaliya who was to accompany Pandit Deenbandhu. Since it was unthinkable that the maestro would begin the evening's function with his recital, and since our city had no local artiste deemed good enough to give a performance just before Deenbandhu's programme, Ram Kumar had been prevailed upon to begin the evening with a brief recital. I had been following Ram Kumar's career for some years, and he had now become one of my favourite tabaliyas. For a while, he had vanished. Rumour had it that he'd suffered some kind of trauma a few years ago. But whatever that ordeal, the truth was that he had returned with an added depth, a kind of humility and spirituality to his music. As I listened to him then, I realized that suffering had actually enriched his art. Even though the instrument he played was a percussion one, he made his tablas sing. The audience loved his recital, and he took bow after bow, the gold buttons on his kurta flashing in the light.

After a fifteen-minute interval, it was announced that Pandit Deenbandhu, the internationally renowned sitarist, would now come on stage. His bio-data was read out in three languages. People listened breathlessly as the announcer went through the list. The maestro's childhood, the names of his gurus, his awesome achievements, the several schools he had set up around the world, the list of honours that had come his way from all corners of the globe, Panditji's successful forays in fusion music—the catalogue was as impressive as it was long.

And then Pandit Deenbandhu Misra made his appearance.

Of course, all of us in that hall had seen the sitarist's photographs many a time, but as he strode on stage and settled himself among his troupe, we felt the sheer magnetism of his personality for the first time, even from our seats in the audience. With a deep 'Namaste' to the wildly applauding hall, he ensconced himself between the tabaliya, the taanpura players and the supporting sitarist. He listened intently to the tuning of the instruments, made a few last-minute adjustments to his own sitar, checked the settings of the microphones, then spoke briefly of his pleasure in being with us and about the raag to follow. He closed his eyes, touched his earlobes, and meditated for a few seconds. Picking up his sitar, he began to play.

Glancing sideways at Rishabh, I was struck by the rapt look on his face. I had seen this kind of expression only in holy places before. He was oblivious to his surroundings: his eyes, glistening with emotion, were fixed on the seated figure of Deenbandhu. He was face-to-face at last with the Dronacharya whose teachings he had followed for years, without his guru being even aware of the existence of his worshipful pupil.

Puriya Kalyan was the first raag. Panditji centred the whole structure around a meditative pancham and a serene shadaj, punctuated by a grieving Komal Rishabh. With small glides to begin with, then in ever-widening arcs and swoops, he brought in the ambience of evening prayers in front of a powerful yet benevolent deity. His quicksilver stroke-play was structured to give the impression of an aarti offered by a beautiful, white-robed devotee with golden censers, from which fragrant clouds of smoke rose up in a rhapsody of devotion.

By the time he ended his first composition, the audience had been lifted to another realm of the spirit. The sponsors sitting in front of me looked bewildered but happy. Glancing behind me, I saw that even the bureaucrats and businessmen were glowing with appreciation. As for Rishabh, he seemed to come out of a trance as the sound of the final note died out. He sighed and blinked as his eyes focussed on reality again. He quickly checked the tablet on his lap. The sound was clear. He smiled slightly with satisfaction.

Next, Pandit Deenbandhu took up a Megh. As he moved in to the heavy curves around the main notes, I studied his appearance. He had a full, swarthy face as pendulous as the lowering monsoon clouds that he was now describing. Though of a medium height, under his embroidered ivory-coloured kurta, he was as muscular as a footballer. Deep lines were etched from his nostrils to the corners of his lips. But his eyes glistened like the diamonds on his kurta front, and were as sensitive and as limpid as a wild fawn's. What struck me most about him were his fingers. Most instrumentalists have long and sensitive-looking fingers, be they sitarists, flautists, or tabla-players. Pandit Deenbandhu's fingers, however, were short and doughy, like the digits of a paratha-maker who spends his working hours kneading mountains of flour every day.

Panditji's recital lasted for well over two hours. In all that time, there was not a murmur from the audience except for the frequent 'Wah!' and the occasional burst of appreciative applause after a vivacious round of rhythmic feinting with Ram Kumar.

Afterwards, crowds of people clustered around the troupe in the greenroom. Some wanted autographs, others wanted to tell Pandit Deenbandhu how much they had enjoyed his programme, while others simply wanted to touch his feet. I did not join them. I knew that Pandit Deenbandhu would be tired. And though every artiste laps up praise, especially after a recital, I did not wish to jostle and elbow my way in through the throngs to give him mine.

Rishabh gathered up his tablet, and placed it reverently in his jhola. He stood up to leave. 'I'm glad you saw me,' he said simply, by way of thanks. 'It wouldn't have been nearly as pleasant if I'd had to sit back there.'

'Aren't you going in to pay your respects?' Neophytes, in my experience, always clustered around their gurus like moths around a candle-flame.

'Not today,' he answered unexpectedly. 'I have an appointment with him at nine tomorrow morning. In his hotel room.'

'Mine is for ten,' I told him. 'I'll probably meet you then. Your Todi must be shaping up well.'

'I've been practicing. But I'm more proud of the dhun that I've composed. It's based on one of our own folk-melodies, you know, a Biya-Naam, a marriage song. I've given it a raag base. I hope Guruji likes it. I'm sure he's never heard anything like it before.'

I noticed the 'Guruji,' again. His eyes glistened with hope. I realized that the next day would be truly a momentous one for him. If he were accepted as Pandit Deenbandhu's disciple, his future would unspool at a much quicker pace. Through his guru's influence, he would be able to perform at all the prestigious festivals and conferences, if not on his own, then surely as an accompanying sitarist. Trips abroad with his guru would become routine. Fans would clamour around him, too, for a bit of Deenbandhu's starshine would surely rub off on him. Of course, if he was not careful, his musical individuality would be swamped, and he would become a Deenbandhu clone. But perhaps for him that was preferable to toiling in oblivion in a small, obscure city like ours. And anyway, I reflected as I watched Rishabh's slight figure moving out of the hall through the crowds, perhaps his own unique style, his individual temperament, would manage to survive the weight of his guru's superstardom.

Next morning, I collected the photographer from the offices of the paper, and went to the hotel where Pandit Deenbandhu Misra and his troupe were staying. There were crowds of people everywhere. I knew many of them by sight. Most were music-buffs, but there were also signature hunters who knew nothing of music but were well aware of the value of Deenbandhu's autographs. There were also several other press people around. The security guards who stood around looked somewhat bewildered.

The harassed receptionist put me in touch with Vishnu Vyas, the maestro's Personal Assistant. I explained to him that I was from the press, and had an appointment. The P.A.'s haughty tones at the other end of the line thawed perceptibly at the mention of the press. 'Please come up, please,' he said with an accent that was an intriguing mixture of small-town Gujarati and a nasal American drawl. 'We are expecting you. From ten to eleven is for you only. You have camera? Oh, a photographer? Good, good, bring him up also, please. Please come to 305.'

The entire third floor of the hotel had been booked for Pandit Deenbandhu and his entourage. Once there, it was easy enough to find the maestro's suite. Several pairs of shoes and chappals were ranged neatly outside the corner suite. I knocked gently on the door. It was opened almost immediately by a short, wiry-looking man with an earnest expression and thick glasses on his pigmented face. Vyas. After ascertaining our identities, he led us inside.

Several people were lounging around in the sitting area. I recognized some of them. Members of the Sangeet Circle, a musician, and four pretty young girls, probably college-going autograph hunters. Vyas led us straight into the inner room. 'Please come in,' he said quite politely to us. 'Panditji is expecting you.'

The inner room was large, and had a comfortable-looking double bed at its centre. The usual hotel furniture of overstuffed chairs and tiny writing and dressing tables made up the rest of the appointments. A TV stood silently in the corner. A medium-sized suitcase, covered with colourful labels from various international airports, stood at the foot of the bed. Several mythology-based pictures decorated the walls. They formed a series showing the early training and martial education of the Pandavas. One print showed Arjun aiming his bow in concentration at a bird on a branch. Another depicted Bheem wrestling mightily with his brothers. Yet another showed a tribal boy slashing off his thumb in front of a venerable old man, even as the Pandavas watched from behind. But the most eye-catching feature of the room was the large picture-window that almost covered the entire far wall. Through it, one could see the vast expanse of the Brahmaputra, red now and turbid with the monsoon floods, flowing deceptively calmly. Behind the width of the river, in the distance, were the hazy blue hills of Bhutan.

Deenbandhu Misra was sitting on a chair beside this window. He did not glance in our direction as we entered. It was Vyas who whispered and gestured us towards two chairs, indicating that Panditji would soon be free to talk to us.

The room was drenched in music.

On a blue rug at Deenbandhu's feet sat Rishabh. He, too, was unaware of our entrance. His eyes were closed. In his hands was his sitar. They, his hands, seemed to have a life independent of him as they stroked and strummed, plucked and caressed the gleaming instrument, making it come alive as it sang out in joy.

I had last heard Rishabh at a small baithak a year or so ago. He had improved tremendously since then. He was now performing at a level that placed him much higher than a mere 'local artiste'. I could see that his sadhana in the last year must have been intensive.

Apparently, the guru's interview with Rishibh was coming to an end. The Todi that he had said he would play first was evidently over. Rishabh was now pouring out his very being through his self-composed dhun. The main melody of this air was based on a wedding song. The tune was heavy with tears, yet there was an expectancy, a sense of happiness, too. Rishabh had woven many raags into the main melody. These glinted and glistened like the lapping wavelets of the mighty river that flowed behind him. The meends that he played were the heavy curves of the river; the taans that rippled through his fingertips were the birds that quested eagerly on its banks, sometimes taking wind in a flash of vivid colour. Indeed, Rishabh had blended raag and folk melody so seamlessly that it was impossible to say where the folk idiom ended and the classical mode began. And through it all came the voice of the river which was always a living presence in the music of this region, the river as it fell headlong from a crystal lake near the top of an icy mountain, down through purple-rock gorges, then through green, verdant plains, till, aware at last of a new life before it, the river glided on to mingle with the waters of the sea. And then there was just the peace of a calm sunset, and the joy of the boundless deep.

With his eyes fixed on a spot above Rishabh's head, Pandit Deenbandhu was listening expressionlessly to the music that poured out. Not a single nod, not a single laudatory exclamation came from him. He was not even tapping his foot or moving a finger in time to the beat. Only his jaws moved occasionally as he chewed the paan to which he was addicted.

As the last note died away, Rishabh opened his eyes. He laid down his sitar gently, and looked up diffidently at the maestro at whose feet he was sitting.

'Wah', said Pandit Deenbandhu Misra finally. He did not, however, sound effusive or even enthusiastic. I caught Rishabh's eye and smiled encouragingly. He smiled back.

'This is your own composition?' asked Deenbandhu.

'Yes'. Rishabh sounded breathless. He explained, briefly, about the particular folk genre on which it was based.

'Play the main melody for me again,' commanded the maestro. 'Without any ornamentation.' He looked at his secretary, and said, 'Just get the iPad on record mode, will you?'

Vyas bustled around. He took out the gadget from a brief-case, and twiddled around with it a bit. Deferentially, he handed it over to Deenbandhu.

Apparently, Deenbandhu had been briefed on who I was, for he turned to me and asked in excellent English, 'I hope you don't mind waiting a bit—?'

I assured him that I didn't. He switched on the iPad, and Rishabh began to play again. The maestro listened intently, occasionally interjecting commands such as, 'Repeat that,' or 'Play the antara now.' But even then, no laudatory comment escaped him, though the music was exquisite.

I studied the man surreptitiously. He had a heavy, swarthy, faintly pockmarked face and muscular neck. A thick growth of hair covered his arms and also the back of his stubby fingers. His eyebrows, however, were delicately curved and surprisingly well shaped.

In ten minutes, Deenbandhu Misra had captured the essence of the dhun on his iPad.

Rishabh put down his sitar and looked up at Pandit Deenbandhu Misra. There was an unbearably eager expression on his face. But the maestro looked impassive as he carefully put away the iPad in its case and handed it back to the hovering Vyas.

'Good,' he said at last. I noticed that he did not look directly at Rishabh. He shifted the wad of paan to his other cheek, and said, 'Some of your phrases are good, and your grasp of the raag structure is clear.'

This sounded to me as though he was damning with faint praise. But Rishabh looked gratified. 'Does that mean—' He stopped, swallowed and began again. 'Shall I make arrangements—I mean, will you accept me as your pupil then?'

Pandit Deenbandhu did not reply immediately. He continued to gaze over Rishabh's head. At last, he said, 'Leave your address with my secretary. I am going out of the country soon. Amsterdam day after tomorrow, then San Francisco, after that Tokyo, I think. Vyas will let you know when I return to Mumbai. He'll tell you when to come.'

I looked at Rishabh. He had an expression of reined-in ecstasy on his face. Catching my eye, he smiled as he covered his sitar with its cloth case. Then, with a deep pranaam to the man who had agreed to become his guru, he went out of the room. Vyas followed him out.

~

Pandit Deenbandhu Misra was a cooperative interviewee. Polite and courteous, he made all the correct statements in a soft, soothing voice. 'The Parbatpuri audience was impressively knowledgeable,' he said expressionlessly. And 'I hope to come to your beautiful city again, quite soon.' He was less cooperative about the personal aspects of his life, even though I tried hard to ferret these out of him. He deftly changed the subject whenever I tried to talk about his live-in arrangement with an American girl, his student, who was less than half his age. He also talked at length about his schools abroad, though he became reticent when I asked him why he hadn't set up a school in his home country yet.

But all in all, it was a successful interview. Pulak, the photographer, clicked away through it all, and I was confident that he had caught Panditji's personality on film.

As I put away my own recording gadget, the smartphone I used for interviews, I said casually, 'I'm so happy that you're taking on Rishabh as your student. It means a lot to him, you know. We're very proud of him in Parbatpuri ...'

Deenbandhu raised a delicate eyebrow. 'Rishabh? Who ... ?'

'The boy who was here before me—the one who played the dhun ...' I was surprised.

'Ah, yes—he has a good understanding,' said the maestro. He looked at Vyas, who had returned while the interview was in progress, and asked him to send in some tea for us. I declined the offer, and got up to leave.

'A paan, then?' said Pandit Deenbandhu as he courteously opened his little silver box. It had several tiny compartments, which contained two or three elaborately folded paans covered with thin sheets of silver, as well as a variety of fragrant spices. I picked up a clove from the tiniest compartment. Then, with a final 'Namaste', Pulak and I walked out.

That was many months ago.

My interview with Pandit Deenbandhu Misra appeared in *The Eastern Guardian*, along with my review of his performance at Parbatpuri. I sent a copy to his address in Mumbai, along with the links to the online edition. After a few weeks, I received a neatly-typed letter from Vyas, thanking me on Panditji's behalf. Panditji was in Singapore at the moment. He himself, however, had forwarded the links to him.

Months passed. Occasionally, I met Rishabh at various concerts around our city. He always came up and greeted me courteously whenever he saw me. I invariably asked him when he would be leaving for Mumbai. His answer would always be the same: 'I'm waiting to hear from Guruji.'

And now, as I sit listening to the review copy of the CD, those images of the past race through my mind. I look carefully at the inside cover. '*This composition is Pandit Deenbandhu Misra's original creation.*' The small print is unambiguous, uncompromising.

I close my eyes. Clearly, I see Rishabh's intent face in front of the vast river that flows swiftly past behind him. The unique timbre of his sitar sounds clearly in my mind, superimposing itself on Pandit Deenbandhu's more recently heard composition.

Unbidden, a picture that I had seen in the maestro's hotel room comes to my mind. The picture of a young boy, a marksman with a bow and arrow, slashing off his right thumb, and placing it reverently as guru-dakshina at the feet of the man who had not even been aware that he was the boy's teacher.

A Full Night's Thievery

The late forties of the last century. The air was clean and the streets uncrowded. True, there were very few cars in the town, people preferring mostly to walk it to nearby places. At a pinch, they would cycle to work, or perhaps take a ricksha. Even so, there was an air of spaciousness about this little town of Rupohi in Western Assam that was not seen in too many places in the state, even at that time. The British, who had moved out only recently, had left the town with a legacy of parks that fronted the broad and beautiful river; enormous fields where football could be, and was, played with gusto and skill, and large, spacious bungalows that gave the elite quarter of town an air of gracious charm.

It was still a town where people had appellations based on their professions. Himadri Dutta, the doctor whose jolly exterior hid a fierce determination to keep Yama away from the town, was known, inevitably, as Himadri Daktor. Or sometimes, if the person referring to the middle-aged medic was much younger, he was called 'Daktor Babu.' Lawyers Prasanna and Tridib were known as Prasanna Ukil and Tridib Ukil. Teachers in the school were known as This Mastor or, if a woman, That Mastorni. The policeman was naturally Daroga Babu. The merchant selling groceries in the largest store in town was known as Ajoy Dukani. This was because the town was not yet crowded enough to have more than a few people of each profession.

Of course, it wasn't as though the town consisted of upright and learned people only. Like any other self-respecting town, it had a thief as well. For having a local thief was a marker of the affluence of the town itself. Those neighbouring villages and little townlets that did not have a known thief were looked upon with pity by the people of Rupohi. Poor things! They were not deemed to be prosperous enough to support a thief, somebody who could proudly sport his own designation of Sur. Of course, there were cattle lifters and grain pilferers in these other towns, but they did not really count, for theirs were deemed to be petty larcenies.

Modon, the official thief of Rupohi, therefore, held a position, if not of honour, exactly, at least of recognition in the town. Modon Sur. That was the name he was known by, and he never objected to being hailed by this handle in Rupohi's marketplace. 'Oi Modon Sur, do you know anything about the disappearance of the chair from my veranda last week?' somebody would shout across from the fishmonger's shop. Modon would put on an injured air and say, 'Chair? Wooden chair? What would I do with a chair, Dada, I have only a hovel, where will I keep it?' And his demeanour would be so humble, so convincingly honest, that it would not even register with the victim—if Modon Sur had not taken the chair, how did he know it was a wooden one?

It wasn't really true, though, that Modon Sur lived in a hovel. His residence was a hut on the outskirts of town, beside his paddy field. For Modon Sur, in spite of his designation, was only a part-time thief. Rupohi was not actually large or prosperous enough to support a full-time one. And he could hardly expect the townspeople to support him financially, in a more direct way, through donations and handouts, just because they were honoured by his presence there. In any case, he had a wife and two young children to support, and thievery in a place like theirs was still a chancy business.

Modon Sur hadn't been born or brought up in Rupohi. He had only settled down there because paddy land was available. In the village where he had been born, he had been quite a successful cattle thief. Still, he hadn't started practicing his original trade in Rupohi till his crop had failed in the third year of his residence there. He had wanted to become respectable, and in any case all these night shifts had been taking a toll on his health. He had heard the big educated people, sitting on their verandas in their bungalows, talk of this many a time while he lurked in the bushes nearby, waiting for an opportunity to enter the house and go about his work. Night shifts for nurses and such people were ruining their health. Well, he too was a night-shift person, though like many in his profession, he had a day job too. These days, he only practised his craft in order to keep his skills honed. He didn't want his thievery skills to turn rusty. After all, who knew when they would be required?

Even now, so many years after settling down in this friendly town, he only stole things that he was almost sure that the stealee, the person he was stealing from, could replace without too much trouble. Things such as a pira, a wooden stool left outside the kitchen, or perhaps a few brass utensils that had been left out to dry in the sun and forgotten by the careless new cook's assistant. And of course the alnas, wooden clothes horses, on which were placed the gamosas, saris, mekhela sadors, dhutis, panjabis, and other articles of clothing owned by a family, which tempted him with irresistible invitations to be purloined, whenever he saw them.

Modon Sur was thin of build and dark of colouring, as befitted one whose work required him to blend into the night.

He also had a philosophy, a doctrine, about the justifiability of his alternate profession. A thief like him, he believed, was highly beneficial to society. His work made people careful. Without the disciplining effects of his thievery, housewives grew lax and left their clothes outside on the line at night, even though it was well known that doing so brought evil spirits into the house. It gave Modon Sur a feeling of pride that women feared him more than they did evil spirits. He had heard matriarchs telling new and foolish daughters-in-law, 'Bring in the clothes, Bowari, it's almost dark, can't you see? While you sit and idle away your time with gossip, Modon Sur will come and take away all the clothes ...'

He was in the thoughts of menfolk, too, he knew, as shadows lengthened and lamps were lit and the evening prayers were chanted in the domestic shrines. Bicycles left leaning against a wall of the front veranda would be brought into the inside courtyard of the house and chained securely to the guava tree near the well. Shoes left lying carelessly here and there would be brought into the inner verandas, near the bedrooms. Even though he only came out on moonless and sometimes rainy nights to purloin from houses, his shadow lay on the homes of the town every evening.

Every true professional has an area of expertise in which his mastery remains unchallenged. In Rupohi itself, for instance, Jiten Mastor's knowledge of the history of the area was immense. Himadri Daktor's ability to chase out all kinds of aches and pains afflicting the legs and feet of men was acknowledged to be second to none. Similarly, Modon Sur, too, had an area of expertise. His skill in lifting clothes from alnas was widely respected. If the clotheshorse was near a window, it was practically an invitation to Modon Sur to take everything piled on it. But even if the alna was at the opposite end of the room, several yards away from the window itself, it was the work of a moment for Modon Sur to poke in the special iron contraption he had himself invented, and pull out the muga mekhela sadors, the paat panjabis, the eri shawls, and decamp. Sometimes, bags and jholas would be left hanging there, too. These would be a bonus for him. Clothing fetched a decent price, but if the jhola contained a purse with five or ten rupees and maybe a few annas, he felt that he had earned his keep for a whole month.

Another thing he was careful about was not to have any of the stolen goods in his home or shed. He took the purloined stuff straight to his contacts in the town from which he had emigrated, who would be waiting just outside the town's boundaries to receive the goods. It was this kind of clever planning that earned Modon Sur the admiration of even those who were the targets of his thievery.

The strange thing was not that Modon Sur was never caught. After all, many thieves roamed the land whose skills were of such a high order that they always eluded capture. The really amazing thing, the one that anointed Modon Sur as a master, was the fact that he always seemed to have a watertight alibi. He could never be nabbed and put behind bars for the disappearance of the butcher's bicycle because, why, that very night, at in fact at the very hour when the bicycle was likely to have disappeared, he was seen at a Naam Kirtan congregation at the other end of town, singing soulfully before the image of Krishna and keeping time with the cymbals in his hands.

How did he always have this kind of an alibi? It was a secret that he took with him to the grave (metaphorically speaking of course... he was cremated, with full honours when he died thirty years after the events that will presently be described here), a highly respected, even prosperous farmer who came to be addressed with respect. By then, the appellation Sur had dropped away from his identity.

But we are getting ahead of the story.

In the largest official bungalow of Rupohi lived the town's Magistrate, who was in charge of the administration of the town. Not a Collector, because Rupohi was not the headquarters of any district. Still, the simple townspeople held the Magistrate in great awe, because, even though he was a brown-skinned person just like themselves, the people who had lived in that house earlier had all been Sahibs and Memsahibs. They had gone back to their island across the seven seas after Independence. Some of the awe which the villagers had vested them with had rubbed off on the house, and on those who lived in it for a long time.

The current incumbent of the rambling red-brick bungalow was Animesh Choudhury, who had been posted there just a few months before the events of this story. Tall of build and imposing of demeanour, he brought dignity and a great reputation for fairness and efficiency to his post. But more stirring than even this was the fact that he brought to the town his large family, consisting of his wife and six daughters. The daughters ranged in age from nine to nineteen. Even though the eldest two were married, they were often at their parental home, for their husbands were on transferable jobs and they liked to come and stay with their parents while the husbands settled into their new postings and arranged for quarters.

The girls caused quite a stir in the little town. Though there was a good girls' school in Rupohi, they were tutored at home by a series of teachers who came in from the school. However, the girls were in the habit of taking the air on the river bank every evening. Though their large lawns fronted the river, the view was impeded by walls and hedges. All six girls therefore went right out of their gate, to the concrete promenade that bordered the river, without fail every evening. Often, they sat for a while in one of the parks adjoining the river bank, talking and laughing.

The girls were, of course, beauties. How could they not be good-looking when they came from such an aristocratic lineage? Tall, not thin, but not fat either, and with skins that glowed like the setting sun in October, they would stand out, singly, in any crowd of people. In a group, they were simply devastating. When they went to watch the Durga Puja celebrations that year, their beauty, whispered the awestruck townspeople, rivalled the Devi's herself.

And their clothes! It was said they went to Calcutta especially to shop for the latest fashions. Instead of the simple muga and paat and cotton mekhela sadors that the townspeople wore, they put on beautiful silk and muslin saris brought from Calcutta. Their blouses were bordered with fine lace, and their hair was always uptwisted into the latest fashion in chignons. As for their jewellery... ah! Of course the Magistrate Sahib was a rich man, but even so! It was said that his wife herself came from a family that was so prosperous that they had gifted her a huge black trunk full of the purest gold jewellery when she had got married. And probably the girls had added to that storehouse, for their necks, wrists and earlobes twinkled and gleamed and glistened in the light of the setting sun on the river bank as they took in the fresh air.

In short, they were loaded with jewellery. And costly apparel. Enough to get any self-respecting thief's hands itching.

Of course, Modon Sur was only a petty thief. Still, it wasn't as though he hadn't, in his time, pinched a gold chain here or a finger ring there. All that gold was really inviting. And it wasn't as though they would miss the stuff. There was that huge black trunk stowed away somewhere, from which more jewellery could be loaded onto their persons, after they had finished mourning the stuff that had been stolen.

Besides, (and here one falters in telling the story) the fact is that Modon Sur rather enjoyed some of the perks of his profession. One was the feeling of power that pinching even as small an object as a cushion from a cane chair gave him. The other was, frankly, more shocking, especially in those prudish days. In fact Modon Sur himself never actually admitted it even to himself, but…the fact was, he enjoyed the sight of all those women in the houses he had come to burgle, lying supine on beds, their clothes all awry, delicious bits of their bodies exposed, and even more delicious bits hinted at… In fact, many a time Modon would come away without having actually burgled anything, but quite happy nevertheless at the sight of the sleeping girls and women of Rupohi. Of course, in no way was this any kind of disloyalty to his wife, to whom he was quite devoted. But he felt it was quite all right to ogle the prostrate bodies laid out so invitingly in the houses he visited at night. It was like staring, open-mouthed, at the women he saw in the bioscope that came to town occasionally. They, like the women he burgled, were from a different world. He would never have dreamed of touching them, except in the line of duty, as it were.

Still, here was a double bonanza! And added to it was the extra thrill of actually going into the lion's den and decamping with the loot. Delicious! The Magistrate's house had two durwans, of course, who were supposed to guard the gates, and the house, taking it in turns. But that in itself posed no problem for Modon Sur. Many of the big houses had durwans, but in his experience, they were creatures of habit, and as prone to sleep-wake cycles as the rest of humanity. It was just a question of studying their schedules for a few nights and planning accordingly.

Of course, stealing jewellery was a totally different challenge from lifting bicycles. Modon Sur realized that he would need to hone his skills in this department further. This actually suited him fine. It was only February now, and quite chilly. The fog from the river crept into the town at night, laying its damp fingers on everything. It sidled into homes as well, making people sneeze and develop the sniffles. Everybody in Rupohi kept their windows closed at night in these months. It was only after Bihu, in mid-April, when the sun took on strength again, that people began to sleep with their windows open. Luckily for Modon Sur, electricity had not yet come to Rupohi. When it did, he was sure that people would sleep with their windows shut even in summer, as instead of punkha-walas this thing called 'current' would twirl the fans on the ceilings, making rooms as cool as January, even in August.

So the weather gave Modon Sur several months to plan a heist that was shaping up to be probably the biggest of his career. Big, in terms of risk, glory and spoils. If he could sell off the gold at a decent price, he thought he might retire from his night-shift career. Though, perhaps he would keep a couple of pieces of jewellery for Senehi, his wife. He would not be able to give them to her immediately, of course. He would bury them in the earthen floor under their bed, and take them out only after the Magistrate had been transferred to another town, which would no doubt happen in a few years.

In the meantime, there were two areas of research that he had to conduct. One: did the punkha-wala pull the rope to swing the cloth punkha on the ceiling even at night? Modon Sur was almost hundred percent sure that he was sent off when the women went into their rooms to sleep. After all, no woman liked the idea that the punkha-wala could at any time climb up and peep into the room of sleeping girls and women. Most women were prepared to sacrifice this comfort for privacy. This bit of information was easily obtained. Modon Sur sent out a few feelers to those professional punkha-walas who tugged at the cloth fans above the offices of Rupohi. Within a week, without drawing any attention to himself, he was in possession of the information that the punkha-walas at the Big House were all sent away at seven in the evening. In fact, none of the bedrooms had any provision for punkhas at all. And also, all the help—armies of them—but excluding the durwans, lived in a large complex connected to the main house through a pathway. They, too, retired there for the night after cleaning up after dinner. This happened by nine-thirty, ten at the latest. For Rupohi was a town that went to bed early in those days.

Secondly, and more important: did the women take off their jewellery at night? True, there were thieves who pulled chains from women's necks, but Modon Sur was not one of them. Purloining, not bodily robbery, was his job description. Well, he would take along his contraption, he thought. If he found that the jewellery was not accessible, he would make away with the clothes on the alna. That too would satisfy him, if not monetarily, then at least from the point of view of professional pride.

These researches took Modon Sur some time, at which point the weather grew warmer, and people began to sleep with their windows open again. And so it happened that now, the more prosperous villages and the little towns around Rupohi began to report a spate of jewellery thefts. Nothing much, to begin with. A small gold chain left carelessly on a table near the window. Perhaps a ring, kept under a pillow while its owner went to the outdoor toilet at night.

Modon Sur's greatest asset was his total calmness. He had nerves of steel, which ensured that his brain worked alertly and coolly, even as he was lifting a chain from right beside a sleeping girl. Besides, his fingers were deft, and his steps light. In all cases, without exception, it was only much later, when he was safely back in Rupohi, making sure he was seen in the shops or in the fields by potential witnesses, that the theft was discovered in the village or town an hour's journey away by bullock cart, when its owner went in to make her bed.

Gradually, over the summer, as Modon Sur's confidence levels grew, so did his boldness. He began to purloin jewellery in ever more risky situations. In the heat, most girls and women kept aside their jewellery while they slept, in order to be more comfortable. After all, even the purest gold chafed terribly against skin made even more tender in the horrendous humidity of Assam in summer. On the other hand, it was considered inauspicious for the house if its daughters and daughters-in-law went about with necks, earlobes, wrists and fingers bare of gold. To get around this, therefore, they usually took off their jewellery last thing at night, and pushed it under their pillows for safe-keeping. In any case, it was considered a sign of industriousness and good breeding to make one's own bed in the morning, even if the household had many helpers. There was therefore little risk of some maid purloining the gold in the morning if the mistress forgot to wear it after her morning bath.

Modon Sur was of course as well aware of this custom as anybody else. Gradually, it became ridiculously easy for him to lift jewellery from tables near the bed. He felt the need for further challenges. Cautiously at first, therefore, and then with ever greater degrees of confidence, he began to lift the pillows from beneath the heads of the sleeping beauties themselves. After a few such missions, he was able to judge to the last inch where the jewels were likely to be kept, at which precise angle and point they would be located. Usually, for some reason, they would be located almost directly under the flowers embroidered in red, green and blue at the corner, following the fashion of those times. It became the work of a moment, eventually, for Modon Sur to locate the jewels under the pillow. And in any case, the beds were always pushed against open windows in those summer days, in order to catch every cooling breeze from the river.

Once or twice, if the chain around the sleeping girl's neck was a thin one, and if the girl herself was alone in the room and, in addition, was a slender specimen of womanhood, Modon Sur even went so far as to snatch the chain from around the said neck. This was a new thing for him. He knew it was much more risky to snatch a chain from a neck than it was to pick it up from tables and from under pillows. Still, such was his confidence in his prowess that he attempted that feat with aplomb. By the time the girl in question realized what was happening and called out for help, he was already quite far away from the scene of the crime. Even so, he had decided not to attempt this again, even if things seemed easy. It was just too risky.

It was only after he had put away the jewellery in the jhola that he always carried slung crossways across his chest, that he allowed himself to indulge in the perks of office. If the girls and women were pretty and lissom, he let his eyes linger over the curves of their bodies, before finally making off. Modon Sur's eyes took in the offerings of female beauty spread out before him much as an art lover would a painting by Raja Ravi Varma.

In the meantime, he also familiarized himself with the lay of the land in the Magistrate's compound. This he did by sauntering past the gates every evening, his demeanour casual-seeming but his eyes taking in every detail of the house that was visible to him. He also located a fine, mature mango tree near the back wall. The long, leafy and sturdy branches of this tree spread out over the wall itself, and hung low over the adjoining lane. Fortunately, this particular lane was deserted, not just during the night, but also during most of the day. Modon Sur spent many an evening fruitfully employed in the mango tree, gazing at the grounds and the house before him. And the bonus was that he could take home some choice mangoes for Senehi and the children every night.

In a few weeks, Modon Sur knew almost as well as the occupants of the house themselves which rooms were occupied by the girls, and which by the Magistrate and his wife. He had of course no intention of disturbing that personage himself during his night's work. That would be tempting Fate. He also familiarized himself with the habits of the two guards. The day guard was not really of any interest to him. However, he was not surprised to find that the night guard would give a couple of turns around the compound, and then doze off in the guardhouse. He would wake up every now and again with a start, and start banging his stick against a wall or post, shouting something unintelligible all the while. After which, he would go back to sleep. Modon Sur had surmised right at the beginning that the guards would not pose any problem to him. And now he was proved right. Thank goodness though, the Magistrate was not a dog-lover. There were no dogs to wheedle over and feed sleeping draughts to in this particular house. With guard dogs, things became more difficult and time consuming. Not impossible, no, but difficult.

~

The decision that he was ready to 'work' the Magistrate's house came to Modon Sur quite suddenly, one night. He was on his way back from a heist at the neighbouring town. It had been a good night's work, one of his best so far. His jhola was chinkling satisfyingly at his side, full of gold ornaments and silver anklets. Besides, he had come across a plateful of pithas too while going through the rooms. It had been standing temptingly beside the kitchen window. Munching on them as he cycled back to Rupohi, Modon Sur was filled with satisfaction.

It was a beautiful night... not moonlit of course, for that would have not been suitable for his work. As a person whose toils made him think in ways that were different from most other people, Modon Sur's notions of natural beauty too were coloured by his line of work. While others extolled the virtues of a purnima night, lit up by the silvery beams of the full moon, Modon was happiest under a dark, amavasya sky, moonless and shadowy. Indeed, others would not find it easy to find their way home in this darkness, on a night as black as coal. But Modon was not a successful thief for nothing. Whistling softly to himself, he rode his cycle back quite confidently through the narrow mud lanes of the area. He could see in the dark, and relished the aromas of the night flowers all around him, as well as the soft breeze against his skin.

That was when the idea came to him. He was having a run of good luck. Like all thieves, Modon Sur too was highly superstitious. He believed that when luck, Fate, Bhagya, whatever you called her... when she smiled on you, she did so for a certain period of time. And when she looked somewhere else, or began to frown at you, then the bad luck, too, came for a fixed amount of time. Certainly, this was a time when Bhagya Devi, Lady Luck, was smiling on him. Why not take advantage of this, and strike at the Big House this very night? The conditions were just right, and he himself was as ready as he would ever be. His footfalls had never fallen softer, his fingers had never been nimbler. In a flash, he made up his mind. Yes, Tonight would be The Night.

The lane at the side of the house was empty, as usual, and quite dark. Soundlessly, Modon leaned his bicycle against the spreading branches of the mango tree and prepared to climb it. The jhola, with its burden of gold, thumped against his side and made a chinkling sound at every step he took. Besides, the buttons on the jhola left gaps through which the smaller items could slide out. He realized that it was not really practical to carry it around with him as he proceeded with his final heist. Impossible to leave the jhola on the bicycle. After all who knew better than him, how the minds of thieves worked? Even a person who was deemed honest would bend his morals if he found this bag with its precious burden lying unattended in that dark lane. Modon decided to take it into the compound with him, and leave it leaning against a tree. He could pick it up on his way out.

Carefully, making sure that nothing fell out of the jhola while he climbed the tree, he went across the wall, and then climbed down the other side. He had made this trip several times before, and was, by now, very much at home here.

First, he took the jhola off from his shoulder, and leaned it against the tree. Then, taking off his sandals, he tied them together and slung them around his neck. This was part of his preparations. All the while, he kept looking around the compound, which now lay under the blanket of darkness. If his eyes hadn't been used to it, Modon would not have been able to make out a thing.

He began to move quietly towards the girls' bedroom. Glancing back once, he saw that his jhola, with its precious contents, had fallen to its side. He came back again, and picking it up, stood undecided about what to do. What if a stray animal came up and scattered its contents…yes, he had it. Taking the jhola, he went to a nearby golonchi bush. The plant was now in full flower, its creamy blooms soft stars in the darkness. Carefully, he fastened the jhola to one of its branches. There. It was safe from the inquisitiveness of animals now.

In a couple of minutes, Modon was at the window which he had rightly surmised to be of the girls' room. Large and high-ceilinged, he could see, by the light of the hurricane lantern that burned dimly in a corner, that it was a kind of dormitory. Each of the five beds was placed against a window. Four of them had one occupant each, while one had two girls sleeping. The youngest two, he surmised, dismissing them. They were unlikely to have much gold on them. The women were certainly sound asleep. He could hear the even breathing of the six ladies. It was a strange sound. He had never, truth to tell, seen so many females all stretched out, somnolent, in one room. Resisting the urge to stare, he looked around.

The windows had the usual iron rods placed horizontally to deter people like him. No problem there. His practiced eye judged that he could easily put in his arm.

But where was it? The loot, where could it be?

And then, suddenly, he saw the pile. A hillock of gold that gleamed even in that darkness, heaped up carelessly on the table next to one of the girls. She was probably one of the older ones. Silently, Modon moved to the window beside her bed. Yes, he would be able to reach the table, he thought, quite easily. No doubt she, this older daughter of the Magistrate, had thought that by placing her sleeping form between the table full of gold and the window, she was protecting the pile. Well, in the morning, she would find out how futile it had been.

Modon rolled up the sleeves of his dark shirt, and flexed his fingers. All right then. This was it… He put in his hand, and slowly, moved it towards the table. Quietly, with practiced ease, he grasped the pile. Almost all of it came up in his grasp. Carefully, swiftly, he started to take out his hand. And then…

~

Reba, the Magistrate's eldest daughter, was spending some time with her parents and sisters. Soon, it would be time for her to return to her husband, who was even then shifting from one town to another. In the meantime, it was wonderful to be able to giggle and laugh with her sisters and parents, without a care in the world, as though she had no responsibilities…

That evening as usual, all the sisters took off their jewellery and put it on the table beside Didi's bed. It was quite safe there. And of course it was too hot to sleep with it on. All those chains, rings, bangles… and those earrings! How they made the skin itch!

The girls, as was their habit, talked and giggled into the night. It was well past eleven when they dozed off, one by one, their murmurs dwindling to occasional whispers, and finally dying out altogether. Reba was the last to drift off to sleep.

She awoke a couple of hours later, fully alert. She wasn't sure what had woken her up, but she knew there was something. Without stirring, she listened. She heard her sisters' even breathing. Everything seemed all right there. But something had woken her…

She remained quiet, but opened her eyes a crack. Not fully, but enough to see her surroundings. The light from the lamp in the corner showed… ohmyGod… Krisno, Krisno! Ohohoh!

Reba stifled the instinct to scream, and watched, fascinated, as the dark and hairy arm slowly came in through the window. Like a rabbit hypnotized by a cobra's hooded stare, she watched it lift up a fistful of jewellery, and then start to take it out carefully.

OhmyGod. She should do something. She should… ohmyGod what if no sound came out from her throat, like in nightmares…? What if he throttled her or something…?

The hand was almost out of the window now.

It was the sight of her thick gold mangalsutra dangling from the hairy hand that brought her to her senses. Her mangalsutra, given to her by Probir during their wedding just two years ago. And this thief, this robber, was actually taking off with it, that too, right under her very nose! Literally. And what would Probir and his mother say if they knew she was sleeping with it off her body? She was supposed to wear it night and day. Indignation coursed through her being, displacing the fear at last.

~

Modon's concentration levels while at work on his 'night duties' were always high. His brain seemed to work in top gear, and all his senses, his antennae, quivered alertly. He focused, at this moment, on drawing out the fistful of jewellery through the gap in the iron rods of the window without disturbing the sleeping owners. Yet he was aware also of all the other things that were happening in the room. The sleeping forms, the even breathing of the six girls, the shadows thrown by the lantern… he was conscious of them all. What he did not realize, though, was that the woman on the other side of the wall was now awake. To say he was startled when she decided to take matters into her own hands would be a gross understatement. He had in fact never been more astounded, frightened and shocked, all at the same time, in his life.

Reba's scream, 'Sur! Sur!' came out shrill and strong. But it was not that which stunned Modon so much. It was the fact that she simultaneously grabbed his arm. And right after that initial scream, she bit down hard on it.

Pain coursed through Modon Sur's arm, radiating upward in agonizing waves. Of course his fist automatically unclenched itself. The jewels fell in a shower on Reba's body, but she continued to clamp down with her teeth on his arm.

There was turmoil everywhere. The other five sleeping forms had of course woken up at the first scream. Through the pain, Modon's bewildered mind registered that after the first surprise, they, too, were now screaming at the top of their lungs.

'Sur! Sur!'

'Kon aasey! Who's there?'

'Deuta! Ma! Come quick! Something bad is happening… eeeee!'

'Eeeee! Durwan! Where are you? Eeee, bring your lathis…'

'Help us! Help! There's somebody inside the room!'

'He's murdering Reba Didi!'

Of course this was not remotely correct, but possibly they could not see him as he stood outside in the dark. Through the fog of pain and shock, Modon's mind registered this fact as a ray of hope. All was not lost, not yet.

The noise in the room was horrendous. Five women, screaming at the tops of their lungs, unnerved Modon Sur completely. The sixth still had her teeth around his forearm, but even she was uttering high-pitched unintelligible sounds.

Modon's instincts, honed finely over a lifetime of thievery, took over. With a supreme effort, ignoring the pain, he shook his hand free from the woman's mouth. He could feel blood dripping down from it, but he blocked his mind to it. Quickly, like the shadow of a fleeing bat, he ran back to the mango tree. Without looking this way or that, he was up and then over, in a moment. His cycle was as he had left it. Mounting it in a trice, he turned around and pedalled off into the dark.

Behind him, there was pandemonium. The Magistrate and his wife were told the whole story when they came rushing in. At first, there was consternation when the lamp was turned up and Reba's bloody mouth was seen. However, it soon became apparent that the gore was not hers. The screams had subsided, but the girls were still sobbing hysterically.

The room filled up quickly with the help, who rushed pell-mell into the house. The sight of the blood on Reba's face was enough to send two of the maids into a dead faint, while a third fell on the floor with a thud, screaming and thrashing her feet around. The staff became so engrossed in this little side drama that they gave it their full and fascinated attention.

'Such a huge man, Ma!' moaned Rina, the third girl. 'A monster, I tell you! Black as coal, with eyes that were full of blood. He was wearing nothing on top… such muscles, Ma, one flick of his wrist to Reba Didi's neck, and she would have been like a chicken. Dead in a minute.'

(Here, let us fast-forward twenty years. Rina has now become an acclaimed writer of fiction. Possibly this childhood trauma has had something to do with it.)

The durwan, disturbed by all this noise, woke up at last, and began to shout, 'Jaagte raho! Jaagte raho!' automatically, groping for his stick and topi.

(Here it must also be mentioned that though the durwan was in great danger of losing his job, the intercession of his weeping wife, who fell at the angry Magistrate's feet the next morning and refused to let go till he relented, saved the man his salary. The durwan retired many years later on a full pension. Till the end of his days, he recounted this incident proudly. It is a trifling matter that in the recounting of the tale, it was he who caught the famous dacoit and rescued the six damsels from all kinds of horrors. Perhaps if he had been literate, the durwan, too, would have been a noted fiction writer.)

Of course there was no question of sleep. Reba had a full and complete bath, while the others took turns to count the jewellery. It was all there, thank God. By the time they had all stopped chattering and counting, dawn was breaking.

'But how did the man come in?' wondered the Magistrate. Followed by his fluttering brood, he walked out, in full majesty even though he was wearing his pyjamas, following the trail of footprints that led to the mango tree. 'Ah!' he said, not without admiration. 'So that's how the thief entered the house! Mali!' he called the gardener. 'Make sure that no branches cross over the wall any more. Lop them all off!'

Turning on his heel, he was walking off when something in the golonchi shrub caught his attention. A jhola! A dark, buttoned bag, hanging from a branch. Curiously, he walked up to it, and unhooked it. The chinkling sound that it made could be heard even above the excited chattering of the women who had followed him out.

The Magistrate opened the buttons, and peered inside the jhola. Fistful after fistful, he took out the gold jewels. Balas, bautis, chains, jhumkas, even a slim waistchain emerged. The women watched, stunned into silence.

'Obviously, the thief came here after robbing some other homes,' he said, in his most impressive tones. In the silence of the dawn, not even a bird chirped. Finally, Rina, always known for her boldness, stepped forward.

'But Deuta ... now that it's here with us, we should keep it, na? It's ours now, na? That's the law, I'm sure ...'

The Magistrate turned and looked at this child of his loins. With a voice like thunder and eyes that sparked lightning, he roared, 'No, it is not the law! Teaching me the law! This will go with me to the office, where it will be held securely till the real owners are found. Real owners, do you hear! From wherever it has been stolen. Now we have to find out who the thief is ... should be easy. After all, he has Reba's bite marks on his arm.'

But Modon Sur was not caught, then or ever. For he had taken the precaution of having a bad fall before entering his own home that night. The bite marks on his arm were now unrecognizable, camouflaged as they were by the injuries he had incurred. Not just his arms and legs, even his face was bruised and bleeding when the Arm of the Law came in next morning to question him.

And only Modon Sur, out of all those people who figure in this tale, never talked about this incident to anybody else. Ever.

The Journey

SWIFTLY, LIKE A SNAKE SLIDING SINUOUSLY ACROSS A GREAT, dusty plain in search of prey, the train rushes on its tracks towards its destination. Outside, the hot August sunshine beats mercilessly down on the fields and small villages that dot the landscape. The sky is relentlessly clear, with not a single cloud in sight. It seems as though the land is muffled in a thick quilt of heat, transparent, but stiflingly hot. There are hardly any people in the fields. The few who have ventured out look exhausted as they plod slowly about their chores, dripping perspiration freely. Everything in that landscape moves slowly. The heat seems to have snapped something inside them, causing their movements to become laboured, lethargic. Cows and dogs seek the shade of the occasional trees that dot the fields, and sit there, panting. Even in the villages that flash past the train's windows, there is very little movement. Sitting inside the air-conditioned train compartment, it is difficult, almost impossible, to imagine the conditions outside. Through the darkly tinted windows, the scene outside looks as cool as it is, in reality, inside. The body does not realize the discomfort outside those frail tinted windows. But the mind, watching the landscape, the villages and the people outside, cannot fail to deduce and understand that there is a mind-destroying, soul-breaking heat wave in progress.

The difference in temperature between the summer afternoon outside and the air-conditioned coach is, in absolute terms, not too great. But in terms of comfort, this difference of just ten or twelve degrees is vast. No perspiration beads the brows of the people who sit inside. Indeed, a couple of elderly women have light shawls around their shoulders, while a toddler plays in the aisle wearing a warm jacket. An elderly man reclines on his berth with a muffler around his neck. The movements of the people inside, too, are slow. But it is the slowness born of comfort, even luxury, a delicious languor that comes from a successful escape from the horrific heat and humidity of the landscape outside. It is a lethargy made all the more precious by the fact that in a few hours, most of the people inside the compartment will have to re-enter that outside world once more.

It is the post-lunch hour. The white plastic trays, emptied of food now, are set out neatly in the aisles, awaiting the attendants who will whisk them away discreetly. People are settling down to their siestas, pulling sheets and blankets over themselves and succumbing, blissfully, to the soporific rocking of the train as it hurtles through the dusty landscape. The post-lunch siesta is always longer on AC coaches than the pre-lunch or pre-dinner ones. Indeed, unless the train halts at an important station, the post-lunch siesta can last well into teatime.

Gradually, the conversation in the cubicles, desultory even earlier, quietens down. The hum of the air-conditioners seems louder in the silence, a quietude that is only broken by the occasional murmured conversation in one cubicle, or a child's laughter in another. The thick curtains at the entrance to each cubicle, now laced up by the occupants, add to the cosy ambience inside.

Forty-five minutes after lunch, the train slows down. There is a stirring in the berths as the rhythm of the wheels changes. Heads are poked out of the cocoons of the railway-issue, navy blue blankets. Questions are asked. What station? It is a brief, ten-minute halt. Nobody gets out of the coach to brave the ferocity of the heat outside. No passenger is scheduled to get off here, either. Yawning, people peer through the windows at the station. They observe those outside, dripping perspiration, and settle even more complacently into their seats.

Several vendors enter the coach. A blast of hot air enters along with them, causing the people sitting nearest to the doors to glare at the new entrants. Unperturbed, the vendors begin to chant their wares. One hawks newspapers and magazines. Another walks up and down, saying 'coffee, coffee, Nescafe,' in a low but penetrating voice. He pronounces it 'café, café, Nescoffee'. The sound of the words is irresistible to the sleepy passengers. Soon, he is doing roaring business.

Another vendor, with rather poor timing, tries to hawk small clay pots of curd and ice-cream, but custom is slow. The lunch of an hour ago sits heavy in the stomachs of most passengers. A small boy, dressed in rags that reveal his malnourished body, begins to sweep the aisle and the cubicle floors. The passengers welcome this service, and pay a few coins to the urchin after he finishes, but they keep a hawk eye on the child's movements. It is well known that these vendors and children are quite likely to go out with a passenger's shawl or sandals stuffed under their shirts.

A family enters the compartment. Three adults and two children. They are preceded by two red-shirted coolies who balance the family's luggage on their heads. They move slowly down the aisle, looking for the numbers of their berths. Thirty-one, thirty-two, thirty-three—yes, here they are. They move into the cubicle. The sole occupant of the cubicle, a middle-aged man who has had the whole section to himself all this while, good-naturedly removes his luggage and reading material from the other three berths. He had assumed, happily, that this booth would be his alone for the length of the journey. But he is not annoyed, though he does look askance at the two children as they enter. He hopes that they will not make too much of a noise, and will allow him to continue his siesta, undisturbed.

The family carries a large amount of luggage. Suitcases are pushed under the berths, and chained and locked securely. Large carrybags and a huge tiffin carrier are stowed wherever space is available. A large water bottle is slung from a hook. Handbags are placed in corners, packets are put on the upper bunk.

The door opens again, and another vendor comes in. He is a young man, tall, with a smiling, open face. His face is shiny with perspiration, coating it with a sheen that makes his coffee-coloured skin gleam like satin. He wears a brown cotton sleeveless vest that is much cleaner than most other vendors' and a green checked lungi. Well-muscled arms carry bunches of green coconuts at two ends of a short pole slung across his shoulders. A huge dao, curved like a pirate's scimitar, hands innocently from the sash at his waist.

The passengers are not hot, but the dry air inside the coach has made them thirsty. The green-coconut vendor is soon busy. His dao flashes up and down as he neatly slices off the tops of the coconuts. He takes out a plastic straw from the bag slung from his shoulder, and inserts it into the hole that he has made in the coconut before handing it to his customer. The water is sweet, he assures them with a smile, the coconut is tender, just right for a hot day like this, cool and refreshing. Judging by the brisk sales that he makes, his claims are not tall. His customers hand him back the empty husks after they finish gulping down the sweet water thirstily. He collects them into a neat pile, and places them near the door, where they sit like a pile of moss-covered, discarded skulls. He will throw them out later.

With smooth, jerk-free movements, the train pulls out of the station and quickly picks up speed. Soon, the long train is once more out on the open plain. The other vendors have left through the door, probably to go to other compartments. The coconut-water vendor remains inside the AC coach. The passengers, refreshed with sleep, cooled air and tender coconut water, are in a mood to chat. It has been a long journey, across half the subcontinent. They have already talked with their co-passengers. Names have been exchanged, details of family, job, purpose of this journey—everything has been discussed. The coconut vendor, young, smiling and good-natured, is just the person to chat with now.

The new passengers have spread themselves out on the lower bunk. They have yet to settle down properly. The man sitting opposite them introduces himself. He is Sharma, from a city more than a thousand kilometres away in the North. He smiles in a friendly fashion at the two small children. The younger one, a toddler dressed, somewhat incongruously for this journey, in a Little Lord Fauntleroy suit, complete with red bow tie, smiles back and waves at him. His sister, seven or eight years old, stares at him, and looks away.

The man with them, the father of the two children, acknowledges the greeting briefly, and goes back to trying to arrange some more space for his family on the bunks. Sharma, shrugging, goes back to his *India Today*. Once, more, he hopes that the children will not make too much noise. He likes children, sure, who doesn't? But only up to a point.

The two women tuck their legs under their saris, and lean back. They are mother and daughter. The same features, the same colouring, are replicated faithfully. The only difference between them is their build, and the few lines and wrinkles on the face of the older one. The young girl also has the same features as the two women. But in her, something seems to have gone wrong. It is as though an artist's hand slipped while he was drawing her face. Every feature seems more exaggerated. The eyes are more bulbous, the teeth protrude. Indeed, the child cannot close her mouth properly over her teeth at all.

The women, like the toddler and the child, are overdressed for a journey like this. Heavy silk saris rustle as they move on the plastic-covered berth. Thick chains, bracelets, rings and earrings, mostly faux gold, gleam and glisten with their every movement. Black-beaded mangalsutras are prominent around their necks. Only their sandals are shabby, not quite in keeping with the splendour of their finery. Besides, their feet, now peeping out from under the borders of their saris as they sit cross-legged on the berth, are chapped.

It is apparent, even at a casual glance, that the younger woman is with child. Not heavily so, but the round bulge beneath her green silk sari is unmistakable. She sits in the way all pregnant women do, with her body thrown back to balance the weight of her belly. She carries the toddler in her lap, seeming not to care that his feet and hands occasionally kick her stomach. In spite of the cooled air that rushes out from the overhead ducts, the woman is still sweating. Perhaps it is because of her pregnancy, perhaps the heavy silk clothes that she is wearing. Or perhaps it is something else, some tension that she carries with her, a burden that cannot be left behind at the station, like the heat. The beads of perspiration continue to pop out on her forehead and upper lip, long after she has settled down.

The other child, the girl, sits with her grandmother. In spite of her age, she, too, has jewellery around her neck and arms. Hoops twinkle at her ears. All faux gold. It is obvious that something is the matter with the child. She lies with her head on her grandmother's lap, and her legs sprawled towards the walls of the coach. Her arms move constantly, and her hands clench and unclench by themselves all the time. But there is delight on her face. She laughs and chuckles to herself, drawing back her lips to expose strong teeth, as she feels the vibrations of the speeding train beneath her. Her grandmother talks to her at times, speaking as one would to any child. For the most part, her mother ignores her, except to sometimes roughly push back the child's wandering hands. Sometimes, after the girl laughs particularly loudly, or kicks too hard at the opposite wall, the mother glances covertly at Sharma as he sits opposite them, to gauge his reaction. There is shame in her glance, and guilt. The magazine in his hands hides Sharma's face.

But she is quite maternal in her care for the younger child.

The man, stout and dark, goes out of the cubicle. He has bought an ordinary second-class sleeper ticket for himself. The price difference between the two coaches—AC and non-AC—is after all quite large. He cuddles his son before going, and strokes his daughter's head.

The coconut vendor is still doing brisk business. His stock of tender coconuts has diminished considerably. His muscled arm moves up, the dao in his hand flashes in the light from the overhead lamp. With a swift movement, it comes down, and neatly slices off the top of the green coconut. Knowing that the next station is more than a couple of hours away, he stays to chat in each cubicle. He has the coach to himself, and a captive market.

He hands a coconut to a plump girl sitting on an upper bunk, who sips noisily on the straw. In turn, he hands a nut to each member of her family—father, mother and brother. Each is as corpulent as she is. The water splashes inside the nuts as the train rocks and sways into a curve in the tracks. They make a strange contrast, the customers with their rolls and pockets of fat drooping from their jawlines, their cheeks and their bodies, and the fit, muscular vendor, who has no superfluous weight on his body at all.

The family is in a mood to talk. Where has he come from? Where does he get the coconuts? He answers them cheerfully. His home has been left behind at the last station. He has bought these from the town's wholesalers. Hopefully, he will be able to finish them off by the time they arrive at the next station. He will get down there and catch another train going in the opposite direction. He should be home before it is too late, returning to his mother and sister who wait for him. Yes, he has a permit to vend in these trains ... but palms have to be greased, all the same ...

The older man wants to know whether business is better in the non-air-conditioned sleeper coaches or in the AC ones. The vendor laughs. It is hotter there, he says, and the need for the coconut water is definitely greater. Besides, there are more people, hence more potential customers in the other coaches, he says, but they prefer to share a nut between two or even three of them. They watch their paisas, and haggle endlessly before buying. Whereas in the AC coaches, even though the air is cooler and the people fewer, it is easier to sell one's wares.

Flattered, the family buys more tender coconuts.

In the other cubicle, the young girl, possibly feeling the effects of the enclosed space, becomes restless. She starts to wail, and thrashes her hands and feet about on the berth. The grandmother tries to soothe her with words and calming gestures, but it does not seem to work. She brings down the canteen of water, and offers the child a drink. The girl does not even glance at it. Helpless, the older woman puts it down on the floor as she tries to calm the child.

The mother keeps her gaze firmly away from the girl, and offers no help. But the beads of perspiration on her brow grow closer together, till they form little rivulets that trickle down the sides of her face. Runnels of moisture flow down the sides of her cheeks. Once or twice, without turning her head to look at her daughter, she pushes down, hard, on the child's arms. The girl screams louder, but the mother keeps looking ahead impassively. The boy in her arms hangs over her lap, playing quietly by himself.

The grandmother shushes the girl, and croons a lullaby, softly. But the girl will not be soothed. Once more, the mother leans over and pushes down with all her force on the child's body. She does not look at the child as she does so. The child screams even louder. The grandmother, without a break in her lullaby, reaches out and gently pats the mother.

Sharma gets up from his bunk and moves outside. After a few minutes, he returns. He has found an empty berth a few cubicles down the row. He gathers his things together, and moves away. He hopes nobody will come to claim it at the next station. If necessary, he will bribe the ticket collector to let him remain there.

The grandmother smiles sadly at him as he moves away. The mother stares straight ahead, refusing to meet his eyes or reply to his friendly farewell.

The family spreads itself out on the bunk vacated by Sharma. The grandmother carries the girl there, and lays her down to sleep. The girl is quiet for a few minutes, but begins to wail again. The mother takes down a bag from the upper bunk, and opens a packet of biscuits. She munches on one, and feeds the toddler also. She ignores the other two on the opposite bunk.

Outside, a train passes in the opposite direction, a blur of silent speed.

The coconut vendor has moved to the next cubicle. Two young students, on their way back to college after the holidays, sit on one bunk, earbuds from their smartphones attached firmly to their ears. A man and woman, both middle-aged but still youthful looking, sit on the opposite seat. The man is tall, and something about his demeanour suggests a military or perhaps a police background. His wife sits with her feet tucked in under her, gazing out of the window. All four are very casually dressed in jeans and T-shirts. Indeed, except for the new arrivals from the last station, everybody in this coach is extremely casually dressed, the men in shorts, jeans or summer pants, the women in old salwar kameezes or pants.

All four welcome the appearance of the coconut vendor, though it takes some time for him to attract the attention of the students. There is no question of refusing to buy one—eating and drinking are time-honoured time-pass activities on trains.

It is a pleasure to watch the vendor as he prepares the nuts for his customers. Choosing one from his dwindling stock, he hefts it lightly in his left hand, twirling it slightly till the angle is perfect. He takes his dao in his right hand, and brings it up, over his head. Even though he is squatting on the floor, the curved blade gleams and glistens from a height that is almost level with the upper bunk. Then, with a swiftness that is quite amazing, his right arm swoops down, and the dao slices off the top of the coconut in one stroke. The amount of husk thus sliced off the top has been calculated to a nicety, in spite of the seeming casualness of the act. An inch less, and the hole which allows the plastic straw in would not have been made. An inch more, and some of the water would have fallen out. In spite of the rocking of the train, in spite of the random lurches that throw people walking in the aisles off balance every now and again, never once does the vendor need to slash a coconut twice. Nor does he spill even a drop of the sweet water. The man with the military bearing marvels at the precision of the act, a precision that takes into account and accommodates the rolling movement of the train as well as the different sizes of each coconut thus decapitated.

Soon, they are engaged in conversation with him as they sip thirstily from the large green nuts. The vendor slings his dao carefully from the sash around his waist before he settles down on his haunches, waiting for his customers to finish, so that he can take the husks back to the entrance where he has piled the empties. There is no hurry. He answers their questions, regaling them with stories of how tender coconut water wins over such products as Coke and Pepsi on trains. For while these things can be, and often are, spurious and hence harmful, the products that he sells are natural and pure. No scope for adulteration here, he says with a laugh. That's why his products, humble though they are, always beat the products of the multinational companies.

The wife of the military man is curious. How does he, a vendor of coconut water on trains, know such words as 'multinational' and 'spurious'? She asks him as much, tactfully. He laughs and tells her that he attends early-morning classes in a local college in the town where the train stopped some time ago. The students sipping the sweet water are delighted to hear this. Soon, all three young men are exchanging stories about the subjects that they are studying, about the foibles of various teachers, about their fears about the coming examinations. The two young students, in their late teens or early twenties, take out a packet of savoury munchies and pass it around. It tastes delicious with tender coconut water, they assure the military man and his wife. They insist that the vendor, too, partake of a fistful of the fried snacks.

The train approaches a station. It slows down, but does not stop. The station is small, but clean and beautifully maintained. A large, leafy tree shades two empty benches, and the red earth of the platform has been recently swept. A neatly trimmed hedge borders the platform on the side of the town. The buildings are freshly whitewashed. A blue-and-white tiled ledge supports a basin. Over the basin is a sign saying 'Drinking Water' in three languages. At the end of the platform, the train gathers speed again, leaving behind the stationmaster dressed in spotless white, waving his green flag at the departing locomotive.

In the other cubicle, the little girl is wailing loudly. Nothing her grandmother can do soothes the child. The toddler has fallen asleep on the bunk beside his mother. Even his sister's loud cries do not rouse him. The grandmother looks harassed, but the mother continues to chew on food that she has taken out of a bag, looking calmly at the landscape outside as it rushes past her window.

The girl thrashes her legs against her grandmother, screaming something repeatedly. The older woman looks helpless. Though there is nobody else in the cubicle, she smoothes down the girl's dress, which has scrunched up around her waist, revealing bony thighs and a small undergarment. The girl herself is oblivious to the suggestiveness of her posture. Finally, the older woman lifts the girl, and sets her on her feet on the floor.

The train, powered by electricity, is moving at close to full speed now. The carriages sway heavily, this way and that, as they rush forward. There is no wind coming in from the glass picture windows to gauge the speed of the train, but the deep swaying is a sure indication that it is moving very fast.

The girl, set down on the floor by her grandmother, loses her balance. She falls heavily to the floor, and cries even louder. Her knobby knees and thin, almost rickety legs are splayed apart as she sits on the dirty floor, wailing loudly. Her grandmother tries to lift her up again, but the girl, with a strength surprising for such a thin child, resists her fiercely. Her mother continues to look out of the window. But she lets down a foot and stealthily pokes the child, hard, in the small of her back with her toes. The grandmother does not notice. She is busy with the child. There is no sign of the father.

In the other cubicles, people look at each other, faintly worried. The child's cries are loud enough to fill the entire compartment by now. One of the elderly ladies with a shawl around her shoulders walks down the aisle, and lifts the thick material that curtains off the cubicle. She wants to help. But there seems to be a language difficulty. The women in the cubicle are from the South, the lady with the shawl from the East. Besides, on seeing her, the child on the floor begins to thrash her feet on the ground, drumming her heels and flailing her arms. Her mouth is stretched wide, like a rubber band, over her large, protuberant teeth. It looks as though if her mouth is stretched further, it is quite likely to snap in two. She knocks over the container of water, and the floor is suddenly awash The grandmother tries valiantly to hush the child. The toddler sleeps undisturbed through the commotion. The mother still looks impassively out of the window, but perspiration flows freely down her face now.

The lady with the shawl notices that the mother's hands clench and unclench on her protuberant belly, opening and shutting synchronously with the thrashing arms of the child on the floor. The elderly lady retreats to her own cubicle, shaking her head worriedly. She holds on to the berths on the way as she passes, for the train is rocking deeply as it rushes forward. The swaying threatens to knock her off her feet. Why are they travelling with this disabled girl? Where are they taking her? It is obvious, from the way that they are all overdressed, that they are not used to travelling by AC coach. Perhaps they had thought that the child would be easier to travel with if the air was cool and comfortable. Instead, she is probably feeling acutely claustrophobic.

The coconut vendor appears at the entrance to the cubicle. He has just a few coconuts left now. If sales continue at this brisk pace, he will have no wares left to offer those sitting at the far end of the bogey. He takes in the scene before him. Deciding that this is not a good time to vend his wares to these people here, he turns away. But the grandmother, desperate to distract the child, calls him back. She wants a coconut. Perhaps the child will like the cool, sweet, faintly nutty flavours of the refreshing drink and will quieten down at last.

The vendor loosens his sash, and takes out the dao. He selects a nut from the bunch beside him. All the largest ones have gone by now. The quantity of water varies depending on the size of the nut, and the amount of flesh it contains. Besides, some nuts have water that is sweeter than others, while some have a faintly salty tang.

The girl on the floor continues to wail. But now she is sitting up, looking towards the vendor. The green nut in his hand, like the ball that she is sometimes allowed to play with in the garden of the home they have left behind, attracts her. She raises her arms, and tries to get it from the vendor. Her grandmother pushes her gently back.

This action seems to infuriate the girl even further. Her wails increase in volume. The grandmother looks helpless. The toddler stirs on his bunk, and begins to get up. He, too, begins to wail. The mother looks at the girl before her. There is a strange, intense look in her eyes. Her hands and jaws are clenched tightly.

The vendor is intent on his job. It is obviously impossible to try to chat casually with this particular set of customers. The noise level here is deafening now.

In the other cubicles, even the passengers who have been sleeping determinedly so far, wake up. They look at each other, at their watches, and frown. They had not bargained for a compartment as noisy as an unreserved Second Class one when they had paid the high fare for their berths in this coach. The lady with the shawl shakes her head, and wonders sadly what kind of handicap the child is cursed with.

The vendor takes the coconut, and hefts it lightly in his hand, finding the perfect balance in that wildly rocking train, getting the nut to lie at just the right angle in his palm, so that its top can be sliced off in one neat stroke.

The girl clutches the edge of the bunk, and stands up. She sways on her feet unsteadily. The floor is slippery with water. But her eyes are fixed on the nut. Her wails, though still loud, have subsided somewhat. The toddler, too, is quiet now. The girl reaches out her hands and moves towards the vendor.

Once more, her grandmother pushes her back, gently. She tries to distract the child, telling her that she is going to get her some tasty, refreshing cool water.

The vendor takes up the dao lying beside him. The silver blade in his hand begins its ascent. At the apogee of the arc, it pauses an instant, gleaming in the half-lit cubicle like Kali's scimitar in a dark temple.

The child, frustrated in her attempt to get the green ball, screams. Her shrieks ricochet off the walls of the small cabin, and bounce around, escaping through the curtains to assail the other passengers. She rocks to and fro, forward and backward, to the rhythm of the speeding train.

Something seems to happen to the mother. A low wail comes bubbling out of her mouth. It is almost the first time that she has uttered a sound since she came into the coach. Her eyes glitter with a sudden surge of emotion. Swiftly, she pushes out her leg from under her sari. Her chapped foot, so much at variance with her gorgeous clothes and jewellery, shoots out and kicks the child sharply in the small of her back.

The vendor's arm begins its downward stroke.

The child lurches towards the vendor, her body out of control in the rolling train, her balance totally out of sync. The slippery floor does not help. Her head is pushed forward, at just the angle that the heads of sacrificial animals are placed when they are taken before a goddess to be slaughtered.

A dull thud. And suddenly, there is silence.

Jogeshwari

THE ROOM IS FILLED WITH MOURNERS NOW.

News of a death spreads as fast as the flood waters of the Brahmaputra in spate. We all know that, of course. Still, the way the news of this particular death has spread is amazing. It's as though everybody—neighbours, relatives, friends—was just waiting for this moment. Which of course, if you think about it, they were.

For days, the doctors have been saying that it could be any time now. The boys were called from their boarding school, and they have been sitting around the sickbed most of the time. They took turns to stroke his forehead, his wasted limbs. These were automatic gestures of affection, a desperate negation and a pushing back of the inevitable. The gentle strokes of their fingers, unaccustomed to this tenderness, were also perhaps a way of memorizing the feel of his skin, his limbs, his head and hair. Sometimes their palms would pause over a bone, a wasted muscle, till the tactile sensations had settled into the memory centres of their minds. These memories, they knew, would have to last them a lifetime.

And through all this the man on the bed remained oblivious. Almost gone, but not yet. His breathing had been laboured, his chest had heaved, his head had sometimes turned from side to side, in obvious though voiceless distress.

And now, this morning, he is no more.

I have been preparing mentally, as well as in more practical ways, for this moment for so many days now that it all comes automatically to me. I bite my lips and blink my eyes, but remain, as people will say later, stoic. They will whisper to each other, 'Poor girl, she had to endure so much. She did her duty all right. And she never complained. She bore it all, whatever he did. All those women, those models and that line of starlets. But at least she had a husband. And now she has none. No man to take care of her, or her boys. Oh of course she has enough money to see her through. But then a husband is needed, after all she is still quite young and pretty!'

The doctors come, giving their declarations and certificates of death. Wrists and the side of the neck are felt with solemnity. Their faces are serious, as they go through the obligatory motions. Eyelids rolled back, the beam of light shone into pupils that do not dilate any more. That will never dilate any more. Oh yes, he's gone all right.

The boys stand at the side, I beside them. They are exhausted after the all-night vigil at the bedside. And it's not that they are that old, after all. College-going boys, teenagers still. Children, really. We look on as the formalities take place. Time of death. Place. Cause of death.

Cause. Of course there's no doubt about it. It's cancer. He's been battling it for months now; he was in hospital all this while. It was only because there was no hope, and he expressed a wish to return home, that he was sent here. It was understood that I, as devoted wife, would nurse him to the best extent possible. Oh I would have help, trained nurses who were with me around the clock, hired from an agency. But it was I who was in charge. It was I, through all these weeks, who watched as he wasted away till he became, every day, thinner than I had thought humanly possible. I fed him, gave him those little sips of water, sponged him, dressed him, cleaned him, did everything. They saw it all, those who came to enquire about his health, but stayed on, like the voyeurs they were, to exclaim, 'Oh, how thin he's become!' and, more grudgingly, 'She's looking after him well though, his wife. In spite of everything…'

Yes. In spite of everything. All those pictures in the papers of him with some beauty or the other, some starlet wanting to be cast in one of his movies. Both of them hanging on to each other as though he did not have a legally wedded wife waiting for him at home. Or some of those models with the endless legs and pouty lips who towered over him in their six-inch heels, but who looked quite joyous as they matched their smiles to his.

It was impossible to ignore what he was doing, even though, the next morning, he would always tell me that they had a late shooting schedule. He did not want to disturb me, he said, and had taken his stuff to one of the other bedrooms quite some time ago. I could have told him at that time that I would not have been disturbed. I never could get to sleep until I heard the car coming into the driveway and being put into the garage. As the key turned in the lock, and he walked into the house, I would finally be able to turn on my side, and close my eyes against the darkness that was wrapping itself around me from all directions, and filling my mind, my very being, through the hours.

He looks so very different now, as the doctors move away and the relatives come in. The rituals of death take over. This must be done, that, too, must be performed, before he can be taken to the cremation ground. The room is cleared of people except me and the boys, and the people who will wash and clean him. Sandalwood paste is smeared on his forehead. He is wrapped in purest white clothes, dhuti and sador. Flowers, marigold and tuberoses are strewn across his chest, his face is framed in garlands. This appears to give more substance to his corporeal self than he actually has now.

Once, he was tall. Well built. Burly, even. Before he went to seed, much before the disease wasted away his body, he was handsome. And then his habits, his debaucheries began to show on his face. The puffiness of his face and his eyes increased in tandem with the increasing obesity of his body. His face still had the same features, the same eyes, the same mouth. But he became, to me at least, repulsive looking. And then, after Jogeshwari arrived, the disease struck him, wasting it all away, till now he lies there, dead, a shrivelled shrunken travesty of the man he once was.

He has two sons. Lucky man. Two sons that I have given him. For that, at least, he was always grateful. He was a good father, and I want them, the boys to remember that. Whatever he was to me, no matter what he did to me, to my dignity, no matter how badly he humiliated me, I have kept quiet through it all because I did not want the boys' image of their father to be tarnished. They are good boys, and in their faraway boarding school they have no access to the papers and journals that show him in his true light. Till the moment of his death, they think of him with fondness, and love. I want it like that. For their sakes, not his. They will be the ones who will light the funeral pyre; the eldest will feed the dead mouth with the flame that he holds in his hands after he has circumambulated the bier of sandalwood logs on which his father's dead body rests.

I look at the people as they lift the body from the bed, and start to place it on the sheet laid out on the floor. I am watchful, even though to others I look grief-stricken. No, they haven't taken the pillow. Neither have they removed the mattress. Sometimes the body is carried on the mattress that the dead man used during his lifetime. Not today, though.

~

I realize that I must continue to keep a vigil, a watch, even now. It is done easily enough. I stagger a little bit, put my hand to my head. Solicitous hands lead me to the chair beside the bed. 'Here, rest a bit here. It's all been too much for you, we know. You looked after him so well... and now you need to rest, of course.' A glass of water is brought to me. Somebody else brings me another glass, fresh lime squeezed into the water, and sweetened with palm candy. It is the traditional drink in mourning houses like the one that this has now become. I look around, murmuring, 'Jogeshwari. Where is she? She has my medicine.'

Jogeshwari is allowed into the room again. I need her now, here with me, at this critical time. Critical in a way that the others are unaware of. Only she and I know why we must be vigilant... She comes in, silent in spite of her height and corresponding bulk. The duskiness of her skin, the seriousness of her demeanour speak of things which the other people in this room cannot even guess at. But those worlds, those universes are hinted at in the night-dark depths of her eyes. Shapes, formless and ever-shifting, seem to move in those depths, shapes which neither I nor anybody else in this room has ever seen in the world outside her eyes. And yet they exist, there. And elsewhere, too.

She comes and stands by me. Her glance is reassuring. I try not to look at the pillow on which he has lain all this while. The dent of his head as lay there for so many days, weeks, almost unmoving, is a definite, concave shape. My glance keeps going back to it. I stare at it, hard, even while I try not to appear to be doing so too obviously. Are there other shapes there? Perhaps if one is looking for them ...

I look up and see Jogeshwari's dark eyes on me. She shakes her head, almost imperceptibly. *Don't stare. It's all right. Nobody else will be able to make out anything.* I can hear the thoughts in her head, though her lips don't move. She brings me a pill. I take it unquestioningly, and gulp it down with the lemony sweetened water. She takes the glass from me, and places it on the shelf behind. She stands beside me, impassive, as always. It is reassuring to have her with me now. At least till I can figure out what to do about the pillow, the mattress.

What is the form in these situations, I wonder. I look around at the dark bulk of her beside me, as she stands in stark contrast to the sea of white in the room now. I try to focus my thoughts as I stare at her, so that she gets it. Sometimes she did, as both of us sat by his bedside, keeping vigil through the long and suffering nights. The hired nurses did not guess the thoughts we shared, the spells and incantations that she recited in her head, targeted at the man on the bed, but heard by me. Spells that brought me hope, incantations that made me see, at last, some light at the end of this coal-dark tunnel.

In spite of the crowd of people around me, I hear her in my head. *I'll take care of it, don't worry,* she says, her voice low in the space behind my eyes. Though she is only speaking to me, it is laced with the menace which is habitual to her, the menace which keeps people away from her, afraid.

So many times, my friends, his relatives, had asked me, 'Why do you keep her? With you, in the same house? She looks scary. Like one of those medieval devotees of Kali Ma, a female one ...

She looks a bit masculine, too, don't you think? That straight torso, in spite of those thrusting breasts. She's large hipped, too, but not in a womanly way... something about her is manly. As though this is a man, dressed for a woman's part in a jatra performance. That square jaw. Be careful. Have you had her verified by the police? You have. Ok, but still... She probably looks even more masculine next to you. You're so feminine, delicate...just the opposite of you, in fact. As though she is your contrast or something. You know, the opposite of you...'

~

Jogeshwari had come into my life just like that, one day, two years ago. He was in the papers almost every day at that time, starlets staring adoringly at him, pretty girls hanging from his arms. The gossip columns were full of him. I used to read them all, whatever I could get my hands on, as I lay in my king-sized bed, alone, at nights, waiting for the sound of his car. The despair I felt showed in the darkness around my eyes, the downturn of my lips.

She had come, just like that, one morning after a particularly despairing night. He had not returned till the sun had been up. He had looked surprised to see me in the drawing room, reading the papers, as he had gone into his room. 'Very good party, you should have come,' he had said vaguely, his mind full of other women as he had opened his bedroom door and stepped inside, not in the least discomfited. He must have forgotten about my existence the minute he had closed the door behind him.

Ten minutes later, the doorbell had rung. She had stood there, a dark bulk against the sunshine of the winter garden. The marigolds behind her seemed to dim their golden light as she said, 'I believe I am needed here.'

I had stared at her, feeling the despair of my mind drain away. It was as though the huge darkness of my mind had coalesced, and come out to create this dusky woman before me. The despair, the humiliation—everything was vapourizing away from my mind. It had been given a form, and that form stood before me now, seeking admission to my home. All the agony seemed to melt away, just like that. Instead, my mind filled with an unfamiliar feeling. I hadn't been able to place it then, but I knew later that it was solace. And confidence.

Not peace, no, not at that time. But now, as I look at him under his blanket of flowers, I can feel peace stealing into my mind at last.

'Sure, come in,' I had said. Her voice had had no menace for me, but the other staff had looked askance. I hadn't made any enquiries. Not from the police. Not from friends, not even from her. Once, later, I had asked her how she had known about me, and about how that thought had come to be planted in my head. And how she had known that I had needed her knowledge, her expertise. She had just looked at me, unsmiling. *Some things are better not known*, she had suggested, in my mind. And I had left it at that.

~

I look around. The room is now filling up with people again, people who are being allowed in to pay their last respects. They stream in, flowers and garlands in their hands, which they place on his body till the wasted, dead flesh looks substantial again under that floral mound. Even the face, all bone and skin, looks filled out as it lies surrounded by garlands. Is there peace on that face? Now that he is free of all that pain at last, does he lie in peace? I can't make out. But I think not.

The priests are busy with their work. There is much to be done before he is taken to the cremation ground. Mantras are being chanted. The boys, freshly bathed and dressed in pristine white dhutis, stand at their dead father's side. Their upper bodies are bare, covered only by thin white cotton sadors. I am thankful, again, that I have been able to shield them and keep their innocence intact. It was something their father cared nothing about. And now he will be sent to the other world by these two sons of his.

Two legitimate sons. Oh of course I have heard the whispers, the innuendoes, about this other child, the daughter whose unmarried mother never speaks the name of the man who sired her in public. But here, as we bow before Death, it is only my sons who will be able to perform the rites. Only they have the moral right. Just as only I, the widow, have the moral right to remain here beside his body. Of course I expect her, the mother of his love-child, to come in at any moment now, along with the girl. I will greet her normally, just as I am greeting these other visitors, these other women, some of whose names have been linked with his in the past, too.

It is this other thing that is making me more and more uneasy now. I find that my gaze keeps going to the pillow, the mattress. I have to wrench my sight away, make a conscious effort. I hear Jogeshwari's voice in my mind: *Don't stare. It will attract attention.*

If only the room could be emptied for just a few minutes. Only Jogeshwari and I ... the task would take only five minutes. But people are filling up this room and it is becoming almost suffocating.

An idea. I look towards Shyamol, his secretary, who is overseeing all the arrangements. He is the one who is busy on his cellphone, calling up people, near and dear ones, the press too I suppose, the priests, the cremation ground. I gesture to him to come near. He is solicitous as he bends his ear towards me even though he will probably have to look for another job now.

'Yes Baideo?' he asks, courteous as ever. Sympathetic. He too has no idea.

'It's becoming very crowded in this room, isn't it, Shyamol?' I whisper. My voice is faint, just as people expect it to be, even though actually I should be laughing with delight and relief and clapping my hands with glee.

I continue craftily as he nods, 'Why not take him...' I glance delicately at the body, and allow anguish to seep into my eyes. '...why not take him to the living room. There will be more space for the people there. And the priests, they will have some things to do, too...'

'Right away, Baideo...would have done it earlier, but I thought that maybe you wanted him in this room for as long as possible...'

People gather around, and lift up the pallet with his body. It must weigh hardly anything. The mandatory paati, the large mat of split bamboo on which pauper and king must both make the final journey, is lifted carefully and taken out. The boys look at me, asking me wordlessly if I will be going with them to the other room.

'In a while,' I answer. 'You go on...Shyamol, just see that they are ok, please. I need some time alone. A few minutes.'

Shyamol nods, understanding. Of course. A recent widow like me will need to compose herself. Never mind if she had been treated like dirt by the man who lies under the flowers now. It is inconceivable that a widow should do anything but grieve at this point. And indeed, ever after.

Jogeshwari moves forward and closes the door after the boys. It's only her and me in the room now. The sudden stillness seems strange, even though I can hear the murmurings through the door as more and more people come into the house.

Together, in movements that might seem rehearsed in their synchronicity, we move towards the bed. We are light and shadow, shadow and light, reverse images, binaries. Day and night, sunlight and darkness. Good and evil. Timidity and boldness. But in this we are united. We know that this work ahead of us has to be done, urgently. Before anybody else gets an inkling of it.

Swiftly, but carefully, I take the pillow out from its case. Jogeshwari already has the small scissors in her hand. While I hold the down pillow, she makes the neat incision at its side, and carefully puts her fingers in. I watch, fascinated, as she withdraws the three objects. The root of that particular plant, dug up on a moonless amavasya night from the edges of the cremation ground. The withered claw of the hen that had been sacrificed before the huge image of Kali on another moonless night. And lastly, the hair from the head of a person after he had been placed on the pyre, just before the flames had consumed his body.

Jogeshwari had procured them all those months ago, when it had become clear to her that I was determined to go ahead. She had gone out on three successive amavasya nights and returned at dawn with each of these objects. There had been a strange look in her eyes at those times. Stranger even than the way she normally looked, and that indeed was saying something. Something demented about them. And she blocked out her thoughts from me, so that I could not see how she got those objects. Not that I really wanted to, of course. Then or now. It's enough that the job was done, the task completed.

Even so, every now and again, as I have watched him dying, and suffering, these past months, some images have come into my mind. *The wind howling on a rainswept, deserted cremation ground, while a demented woman digs away, digs away, at the roots of that tree. The implement in her hand seems frail, but she gets the work done. Her face is horrifying, the bloodshot eyes glisten with manic emotion. Her mouth is twisted back into a contorted grin, baring large yellow teeth.*

Another image. *The same woman creeping into somebody's hen run, and catching hold of a black chicken, holding the mouth firmly shut so that it cannot squawk in any way.* My own head seems to burst as I watch her twist the hen's head off in one expert motion before a huge black image, festooned with a garland of skulls. *The blood comes squirting out of the severed neck. Throwing back her head, the long black hair flowing in matted profusion down her back, the woman lifts the still squirming body of the hen, and aims the flow of blood from the neck into her now open month. She drinks each drop greedily, careful not to spill even a single one, as though to do so would cause a thousand Raktabeej demons to rise from each.* I stare, mesmerized at the image. *Finally, slowly, she brings down the now-still body. Taking out some kind of dagger from the folds of her red sari, she cuts off the feet, with the toes now curled up in the rigor of death.*

But I never did get images of how she managed the last feat. Once or twice, while keeping vigil by his bed, I would get that strange sensation in my head again. Not a pain, but yet a pain, not a pounding, exactly, but yet a pulsation, a throb, that gradually filled up my skull. That was the way the other images had come to me. Indeed, whenever Jogeshwari's thoughts come to me, they are always accompanied by this throbbing. Sometimes, if I get visuals along with her voice, there are flashes of light in my skull, too. The area behind my eyes especially seems to become a seething cauldron of light.

But even though all these things have happened, even though the blinding headache that leaves me feeling faint for hours afterwards has visited me repeatedly, that final image does not come to me. Oh, I have felt her straining to put that thought, that image in my head too, but somehow, it has not. Maybe my mind has baulked at receiving it.

We have sat together side-by-side, she a dark looming shape in the dimness of the sickroom, as he fretted and muttered unintelligibly through his wasted mouth. Sometimes one of the night nurses would come in to check on her patient, and probably on me, too. At those times, Jogeshwari would vanish. Just disappear. I still don't know how she did it. She seemed to have an uncanny ability to know just when somebody else would be about to enter the sickroom, and she would just melt away. And then, when one by one they all went away, she would come back again, her voice a ringing in my mind and her presence a dark shape beside me.

~

I remember how it was when all three objects were finally collected, one by one.

Time for the next step now, her voice had whispered in my mind one night, as I had lain, once more twisting and turning on my bed and waiting for the sound of a returning car through the darkness. I had sensed, rather than seen her presence in the dimness.

I had got up then, and unquestioningly followed her through the darkened rooms. The help had gone to their rooms at the end of the garden. I was always alone in this bungalow at night these days, with the boys away at school and he in the beds of other women.

She had done it all that night. I had watched, with growing fascination, as she had carefully taken apart the seams of his pillow. Jogeshwari seemed to grow darker, and even more substantial as she began to chant verses from texts that were unknown to me. They were not the mantras that I heard chanted by priests and holy men before sanctified images. Her voice grew guttural and strange as she undid the knot at the end of her anchal and took out the three objects. Placing them inside the pillow, she stroked them into place, while her incantations continued ceaselessly. The walls echoed her voice, till my thoughts themselves began to spin. Her rasping utterances, full of consonants and rough sounds, whirled around the room. And the walls bounced them back, till it seemed as though the room had become a tomb that held its secrets, as shadows and half-heard screams ricocheted around its domed, doomed vault

It was amazing, really, how quickly and efficiently the spells and incantations had begun their work. When he returned at dawn, he went straight to his bed. He came out for lunch, and though we ate in silence, I noticed him looking particularly debauched. He kept touching his forehead, as though he felt something there. I did not ask if anything was the matter. I did not need to.

After that, things progressed very fast. Illnesses, fainting spells, blackouts. Doctors, and then the diagnosis. He had just a few months left to live, I was told, with sympathy. And everybody, all the specialists in the many hospitals that we visited, expressed surprise that the tumour could have reached such an advanced stage without any previous symptoms. I had tried, through it all, to look as blank as possible. Finally, when it became apparent that he would not be cured, we returned back home from the round of doctors abroad, and the best hospitals in the country. He knew he was dying, of course, and knew, too, that despite all those pretty women and starlets he had been with, it was me, his wife, who had complete authority over the way his last remaining weeks on earth would be spent.

That, for me, was enough. The terror, the dread in his eyes when he looked at me was enough to balance all those sleepless nights, spent waiting for his return. And yet there was nothing he could do about it. I had complete authority over him. And though I tried to feel some compassion for the man in my care, through all those nights and days of vigil, I felt only a triumph that nobody, not even the nurses, could guess at.

Once, he had asked me, gesturing, 'Who is she? Don't let her come into my room.'

Without turning around to where he was looking, with terror, behind me, I had replied, softly as usual. 'Jogeshwari. That's her. You never knew her all these years that you were with me, did you? Well, now you've met her at last.'

I had allowed myself a smile then.

A strange sound, something between a sob and a wail had come from his mouth. But I had just turned away.

~

But here we are, together, in this empty room now. The sandalwood-scented incense sticks that were burning here till a few minutes ago make the smell of death almost too much to bear. It is overpowering, that smell. And the three objects in Jogeshwari's dark hand now intensify that stench further.

I look at her face now, dark with a film of sweat on it, even though the air-conditioner is working busily. I don't even need to articulate my thought into words. She responds, putting the thought in my mind. *They will have to be burned. Outside, in the garden, at night. Burned carefully, so that not even a single shred, a single tiny bit remains. Fire will have to consume them, and purify the house with the smoke that will come from these. Smoke that will take away all the spells and the sickness, and bring order and normalcy to the house again. I will put them safely in this corner of the cupboard where nobody will see it now. It's not safe to take them anywhere else, any other part of the house.*

I watch, fascinated, as she tears up a bit from the anchal of her red sari, and wraps up the three objects in that piece. She opens a cupboard door, and shoves in the bundle into its far recesses, under a pile of his shirts. Nobody is likely to see it there now, till she—we—can take it out at night to burn.

Jogeshwari turns to me. The madness is in her eyes again, the madness that I saw after those three amavasya nights when she brought the objects back with her. I shrink back, but cannot go much further, because the walls are behind me. *Your job is done now,* I try to tell her, but cannot. Instead, images flood my mind. *A body on a funeral pyre; a demented woman in a red sari going up to it, snatching at the skull beneath the top layer of flaming sandalwood that covers the body, just before it bursts from the heat of the burning pyre.* I squeeze my eyes shut, clench my fists, trying to put the image away from me. There is light behind my eyes, my head is throbbing terribly. The image just grows stronger.

I open my eyes and look at her again. She is very close to me, her dark bulk a heavy silhouette against the white wall. Yet there is something insubstantial about her bulk now. Terror overcomes me at last, as I realize what is happening. I can feel it. Her mind, being, her consciousness is entering me. I can see terrible images, a whole eternity of them, streaming into my mind. Screams, groans, darkness, manic laughter. A horrifying stench of rotting flesh. They are coming into me now, and there's nothing I can do to push them back.

I hold on to a bit of furniture for support as I feel the heaviness of her within me. I look down at my hands, my body. They are still the same. But my breasts are chafing against my bra, heavier already. And some knowledge planted in my mind knows that with time, they will become large, rough. I will soon begin to look like a man dressed for a woman's part in a jatra. There is no escape. I realize my eyes are staring. I catch a glimpse of myself in a mirror. I look the same as I did, yet not the same at all. My eyes are bloodshot, my hair has come loose and is spread out in mad abandon all around my head.

There is a knock on the door. I am wanted outside. I look around, but Jogeshwari is of course nowhere else in the room. I start to go out of the door with her.

She. We. Us, together.

The Tabla Player

LIKE A HALF-REMEMBERED MELODY FROM THE PAST, THE uncorked bottle of attar gently spread its perfume. Its fragrance brightened the shabby room with a happier light than the one that came feebly from the naked bulb hanging on a wire.

Ram Kumar added one last dash of the scent to his muslin handkerchief before carefully folding its perfumed softness into the pocket of his kurta. Corking the vial, he put it back on the narrow, newspaper-lined shelf under the small wall-hung mirror. He could see his face reflected a little dimly in it. Still, it was the only mirror in the house. He took a last look at his reflection, adjusted the wave of hair on his forehead once more, and turned to leave the room.

Just outside the door stood Bhanu Devi. Gazing at the floor in front of her, she asked, 'Will you be going out as usual this evening?' Her words were a timid whisper, her glance fixed waveringly on the patchy cement in front of her.

Her husband adjusted the fold of the sleeve on his kurta to a level on his arm that was consistent with the demands of both a round of energetic tabla-playing on the one hand, and fashion on the other. Busy with the task, he barely looked at Bhanu Devi's smooth head, with its wings of deep, glossy black that swept back from a heavily vermilion-sprinkled parting. The folds of the anchal that covered the rest of her head highlighted the black and red.

Ram Kumar replied distractedly, 'Yes, I have to. There is to be a baithak in Bansi Babu's house. Ustaad Rafique Hussain himself has come all the way from Benaras to be present this evening at Bansiji's baithak. Such a big event, a soiree of the grandest kind. Ustaad Saheb has asked that I accompany him on the tabla. How can I decline such an honour?' Ram Kumar's tone was casual. He spoke slowly, almost as though he was talking to a child, as he spelled out his evening's programme for his wife.

Bhanu Devi balanced the weight of her swollen belly against the door jamb. Her eyes, lustrous with some secret thought, glanced beyond the front door of the cramped sitting-cum-music room. The road outside wound its way in lazy loops past the little three-roomed house. She looked back again, at the small front room. It was crowded with round-bellied tablas, which occupied most of the space on a large divan. The rest of the furniture consisted of a small stained table, three fragile-looking old chairs, and a large colourful framed picture of Saraswati, the goddess of music and learning, on the wall. In that dingy, dreary room, the tablas with their sparkling silver bodies and vividly printed cloth covers seemed to be alive with the rhythms and music that they contained. Even Saraswati looked drab in comparison.

'Will you be late?' she murmured.

It was the first time, in the year since they had been married, that Bhanu Devi had asked such a question of her husband. Ram Kumar was surprised. He looked down at her covered head, stroking his moustache thoughtfully, and said, in the same slow, patient tone of voice, 'Maybe, maybe not. It depends on whether the other artistes ask for me. I have heard that Bansi Babu is celebrating his son's engagement in style. The baithak this evening is part of the festivities. There are to be many musicians tonight. If they ask for me to accompany them, how can I refuse? This is the way I earn my living, after all.'

Something about her stance, about the way she doodled slowly, diffidently, with her foot on the ground in front of her, caught his attention at last. 'Why do you ask?' he questioned. 'Is something the matter?'

'No, it's nothing.' The words came automatically. Recollecting herself, she added, her voice unsure and soft, 'That is—I'm not feeling very well. Maaji says it's time. The baby—' her voice took on a tinge of pride. 'The baby is due to arrive. Soon. Any time now, your mother says. Perhaps if you could return early... to take me to the hospital if needed...' her voice trailed off again.

A shadow of concern crossed Ram Kumar's face. He almost reached out a hand to stroke the swelling that seemed a much heavier weight than his wife's once-slender body could possibly carry. But he could hear his mother moving around in the kitchen beyond the wall. Instead, he raised his hand to finger the brass buttons that gleamed on his kurta. While dressing, he had hoped that after this evening's concert, if all went well, he would be able to increase his fees... perhaps he would some day be able to afford gold buttons.

But now his thoughts were focussed completely on Bhanu Devi and their unborn child. He felt, once more, that wave of tenderness towards her that he had experienced ever since he had first seen her a year ago. She had been a young flower-bedecked bride, sitting, shy but trusting, on the blossom-strewn bed, waiting for her just-married husband to come to her.

Ram Kumar was not an articulate man. Often, his thoughts did not take the shape of words at all. He had never analyzed in his mind this tenderness, this overflowing of a nameless emotion that engulfed him without warning sometimes when he saw his wife. It was his fingers that spoke as they flew over the tablas. All the thoughts and feelings that he was capable of, inchoate, yet definite, were expressed, not through words, but through the soaring rhythms of his singing tablas.

'Let's see,' he said now, turning his attention to the matter at hand. 'Why don't we arrange it like this. Bansi Babu's house is not too far from here. Lalloo knows the place. If you feel unwell, send a message through Lalloo. I'll be back immediately. I'll take you to the hospital, don't worry. But if I stay back at home, and the need to go to the clinic doesn't come up till late at night, I will have lost my fees unnecessarily.' He almost added, 'We shall soon need the money.' But the protectiveness that he felt for his wife stopped him from saying the words. Instead, he asked 'I thought the doctor said there's still some time?'

'Yes, but ...' Bhanu Devi looked up at her husband at last. There was a look of complete trust on her heartbreakingly innocent face. She smiled at him, and added, 'Who knows when babies decide to come into the world?'

Ram Kumar smiled back warmly. With one hand, he hefted the canvas bag containing his finest pair of tablas. Already, his mind had gone back to the world of beats, of matras, of the complex combinations of rhythmic cycles that whirled around his head during most of his waking hours. Eight beats into two, sixteen beats into half, a complex flourish, a tehai of forty-eight beats so that the sam, the dominant beat, would land on the first note of the bandish with the accuracy of an arrow loosed from Arjun's bow... He gave an affectionate, though already absent-minded pat on his wife's head, and moved out of the house.

Tonight's baithak was truly special. Bansi Babu, the richest man in town, was known throughout the state as a patron of the arts. It was important for any ambitious musician of the district to perform at his gatherings, which were often stepping stones to the music conferences of the big cities. And since this particular evening's sitting was a celebratory one, there were bound to be connoisseurs who would come in from all corners of the district, even from the capital city, to congratulate Bansi Babu on the betrothal of his son to the daughter of a well-known lawyer. The music, as usual, would be excellent, the food superlative.

Bansi Babu's house was ablaze with lights. Laughter and scraps of conversation wafted out of the open windows as Ram Kumar alighted from the ricksha. The sight of Bansi Babu's house always aroused a curious feeling in Ram Kumar. As he looked now at the sun-like radiance of the huge, multi-colonnaded house in its setting of lush green lawns, Ram Kumar was conscious of a feeling that was less than a thought, but more than a desire.

'Arrey, here you are ... we've been waiting for you!' Bansi Babu was always cordial to the musicians he took upon himself to promote. Now, as he approached Ram Kumar, looking plump and sleek as a pet pigeon, he exuded affability. 'We were wondering if that fantastic review in *The Tribune* that you got last week had caused the delay. You know the saying: the greater the ustaad, the later he arrives.'

Protesting happily, Ram Kumar was led to the dais at the end of the huge music room. Chandeliers sparkled across the moulded ceiling. The glow was reflected back from the diamonds adorning the necks and wrists and fingers of the women in the room, the gold and silver in their saris competing in brightness with the radiance from the lights. The men, in spotless churidars or dhotis, the colour of the creamy jasmine on the lawns outside, were lounging on the velvet-covered bolsters scattered across the carpeted floors.

Shraddha Rani was the first artiste of the evening. She was at the same stage of her career as Ram Kumar himself was. He watched as she approached the dais, his fingers already playing exploratory tehais, almost without his being aware of the sounds rippling forth from his fingers. Shraddha Rani paused to speak and smile to several men on the way. Even when one of them touched her arm, her lipsticked smile never faltered. Near her, moving as officiously as an important drone bee, hovered the corpulent Raadhey Shyam, the agent who arranged Shraddha Rani's appearances and haggled over her fees.

She came up to Ram Kumar. 'So, here we are once more!' she greeted him, tossing back her glistening hair with a coquettish gesture. It was, Ram Kumar knew, meaningless. This coquetry that had become habitual with her was just part of the package. In reality, she was as deeply committed to her music as he himself was. And if provocative glances and pliant smiles attracted a larger audience, he saw no reason why she should not use them.

Shraddha Rani began with Raag Behag. The haunting notes of this evening melody found an echo in Ram Kumar's emotive tabla accompaniment. The thumri that followed, its romantic lyrics suggesting forgotten loves, called out longingly to a beloved.

Chhodo chhodo Shyam moray baiyyan…
Shyam, leave, let go my arms…

Ram Kumar, looking at the faces of the people around him, knew that she had succeeded in touching the innermost feelings of most of them. As rhythm and melody arched to a climax, he matched her, beat for beat, note for throbbing note.

At the end of the recital, Ram Kumar looked up. Wiping the perspiration from his forehead, he gradually became aware of his surroundings again. The applause sank sweetly in his mind. He was aware that a lot of it was appreciation of his playing, too. He sipped the chilled water placed in front of him, and munched on the dry fruits brought by attentive servants, his mind still on the rhythms that had come pouring out of his fingers.

At the periphery of his consciousness, Ram Kumar became aware of some note of discord. A small boy, standing near the entrance of the hall, was trying to catch his attention. Ram Kumar beckoned him to come closer. 'Yes, Lalloo, what is it?'

The little servant boy from his own house looked nervously around. In his shabby shorts and somewhat soiled shirt, he looked out of place in these opulent surroundings. 'Bhanu Bhabi sent me to fetch you. She is not feeling well, she says.'

Ram Kumar was reminded of the existence of another world. 'Yes, of course. You go along. I'll soon be there. Is Maaji with her?'

'Yes,' replied the little servant boy. 'She says it's time to take Bhanu Bhabi to the hospital. '

'I'm coming,' repeated Ram Kumar. 'Tell her not to worry.'

Ram Kumar packed his tablas into their canvas bag and got up from the dais. Om Prakash, that old tabla player from across the district, was present tonight. He would be more than happy to accompany the other artistes. Perhaps, if all went well with Bhanu, he could return in time for Rafique Hussain's recital. But a voice hailed him. 'Arrey, Ram Kumarji, what are you doing? You can't get down so soon, you know! Who will accompany the others?' Bansi Babu, unaware of Ram Kumar's domestic pressures, thought that he was being unduly modest in leaving the dais so soon.

Before Ram Kumar could think of anything to say, (unthinkable to mention Bhanu Devi's labour pains in this ambience!) Pandit Amar Singh was on the dais, taking out his sitar and tuning its strings.

Well, it was just a couple of hours more, thought Ram Kumar. He sat down again, and, taking out his instruments once more, he adjusted the tuning straps on his heavy, big-bellied tabla. In the meantime, his mother and the neighbours would surely take Bhanu to the hospital.

The majestic strains of Raag Darbari filled the minds of the listeners. The grandeur and the glory of Badshah Akbar's royal darbar shimmered in front of them as Pandit Amar Singh's delicate, almost girlish fingers plucked at the strings of his sitar. A caress of the frets, and a waterfall of golden notes ushered the magnificence of the Mughals themselves into the midst of Bansi Babu's reception hall. The virile, muscular Amar Singh, with his delicate, feminine fingers, and Ram Kumar on his tablas, together culled sounds and rhythms from the ether and, nodding in joyous understanding together, recreated palaces of majesty.

It was three in the morning by the time Amar Singh's recital was over. Exhausted, Ram Kumar leaned over his instruments, trying to get back his breath.

Once again, a young boy was looking at him with urgency in his eyes. He came up to Ram Kumar and said, 'Bhabiji is in great pain. She is asking for you.'

Once more, Ram Kumar felt a jolt that was almost like a blow as his consciousness moved to another plane of reality. 'Of course, Lalloo, you go ahead. I'm just coming,' he said. 'And call a taxi. I'll take her to the hospital as soon as I arrive home.'

But Ustaad Rafique Hussain of Benaras, the most important artiste of the evening, knowing nothing of Bhanu Devi, hailed Ram Kumar as he approached the dais.

'Ram Kumarji, what, are you getting up already? Are you going to leave me to the mercies of some raw tabla player? Come, you must accompany me as well. I had specially asked Bansi to get you for my recital: didn't he tell you?'

The taanpuras were already tuned. The sarangi player who was to accompany the ustaad was already introducing the opening notes of the raag. The ageing, white-haired Rafique Hussain, taking Ram Kumar's consent for granted, had seated himself in the centre of the dais, and, with eyes closed, was already beginning to finger his surmandal.

How could Ram Kumar leave?

It was Raag Lalit this time. A serene, peaceful melody, ushering in the dawn as it glimmered against the open windows of the reception room. As the darkness lightened, Rafique Hussain's mellifluous voice effortlessly conjured up images of a new life, new hopes and fresh beginnings untarnished by the murk of life. After the weariness and toil of the past, the future dawned, newborn, brushed with promise, bright with dew-sprinkled dreams.

It was almost six in the morning before Ram Kumar was able to get away. Tiredness slowed his steps as, paying off the ricksha, he walked up the path to his house.

The last shreds of the raags and bols in his mind scurried away like clouds before a hot summer wind, as the wails of women rose up from the house before him. Lalloo, crying out aloud, came out to meet him.

'She waited so long for you,' he sobbed. 'She kept saying you had promised to take her to the hospital yourself. She wouldn't go with anybody else ...'

Ram Kumar's mother, hearing his footsteps outside, came out of the inner room. Her eyes, swollen with weeping in her lined and weary face, rested without accusation on her son's face. 'The baby was stillborn,' she said. 'Bhanu died minutes after the birth. She wouldn't go to the hospital with any of us, even when she knew the end was near…'

Homecoming

WHEN SOMNATH BABU WOKE UP THAT THURSDAY MORNING, it was with no sense of expectation or anticipation. He more or less knew, even as he hobbled painfully out of bed, what the routine of the day would bring. Ever since Nandini, his wife, had died more than two years ago, day-to-day life moved within its narrow, predictable grooves. There were hardly any surprises left, nor was there much left in life to look forward to.

Somnath Babu had reconciled himself some time ago to the fact that now, in his old age, life had lost much of its colour. As long as he was able to get through the day without his arthritic knees hurting too much; without the fingers of his hands getting locked into an unopenable fist; without his heart having painful episodes; as long as he was able to take a little bit of a walk in the neighbourhood park, he was happy. Well, not happy, no, that was too vivid, too bright, intense a word. But if he could get through his day without pain, without any major mishaps or disasters, he was not unhappy.

Though that, reflected Somnath Babu, was perhaps too much to ask for. He shuffled stiffly across the front room to retrieve the paper from the porch. Mishaps occurred with unfailing regularity around him. His fingers, gnarled and stiff now, often lost their grip on things, fragile things that fell with a crash and broke into a hundred irreparable pieces.

Not that he hadn't had arthritis or a heart problem when Nandini had been alive. But he had been able to do so much more then, even with his knotty hands. He had not yet closed down his shop while Nandini had been alive. Every morning, while Somnath Babu read the *Ananda Bazar Patrika* and enjoyed the perfect luchis that were placed before him for breakfast, Nandini would busy herself with preparing the concoction. He had never found out exactly what it was that she put into the potions that she simmered gently each morning over the kitchen stove, what oils and unguents she added, but the effect would be quite magical. She would bring the small ceramic bowl of the brew she had prepared and place it, sputtering and steaming, on a stand on top of the Formica tabletop. She would take his palms between her own, and rub the unguent on the curled up fingers till, one by one, they opened beneath her gentle touch like a rose budding into flower. She would do the same to his knees, all the while chattering away about the events of the previous day, till it was time for Somnath Babu to have his bath. He would leave the table with a much jauntier step than when he had come for his morning repast.

Now, of course, there was nobody to minister to his needs. He could, perhaps, do it himself, if he set his mind to it. After all, his days were long, and empty, and it wasn't as if he had lots of work to fill his time. But he had no idea what Nandini had put into the oil, or where she had got the oil itself. In any case, he had long ago been convinced that it had been her touch, rather than her potions, that had kept the rheumatism from getting this bad while she had been alive. She had kept it away from him, like a zealous bodyguard defending her charge with a flaming sword.

She had left him so suddenly. True, she was plump, and inclined to shortness of breath, but she was never unwell, never sick in bed. And she had always been so active, so full of life. Yet it had been Nandini who had gone first. A short gasp of pain, a hand clutching her chest, and her eyes had glazed over as she had slumped to the floor. Dead.

Within a few months, Somnath Babu had had to close down the shop. Over the past couple of years, he had, in any case, been spending less time in his shop in the lane behind his house, with the paint on its once-green signboard saying in peeling letters, 'Ghosh and Brother: Instrument Maker' in both Bangla and English. It had been habit, and the burden of responsibility towards his father and uncles and grandfather, right back to his great-grandfather, the original 'Brother' of the signboard, that had kept him going. That, and the need to stick to some kind of routine, which Nandini had seemed to require at least as much as he did.

Customers had long since dwindled to a trickle, even before Nandini's death. Where were the people who would play, much less buy, the instruments that had once been crafted in his shop? 'Ghosh and Brother' had once been part of the throbbing heart of the music scene of Calcutta. When Nawab Wajid Ali Shah, bowing to British might, had finally reached Calcutta after leaving Awadh, many of his entourage of musicians had followed him. They had brought with them their treasure-trove of instruments, their sarangis, their dilrubas, their veenas, their pakhawaj and tablas. Their presence in the city had added to the rich cultural life of the place. By the time Somnath Babu's ancestor had opened his shop, the demand for musical instruments, and for people who would create or craft, and actually repair those instruments, had been high indeed.

Those had been glory days, certainly. Even after the influence of Awadh had waned, there had been the zamindars who had vied with each other to patronize the arts. But then had come the country's Independence, and with it, the decline had set in. No longer did people want to listen to the old instruments, the old music. Surbahar, sursingar—the very names had rolled off one's tongue musically. Now, of course, very few people even knew what they had looked like, or were acquainted with the magic and amazing beauty of the sounds that they produced.

Instrument makers, mused Somnath Babu after he finished reading about India's latest cricket debacle in the West Indies, lived in a world full of shadows. They were anonymous, yet indispensable. Their work brought them no public accolades; no auditoriums full of connoisseurs put their hands together in rousing appreciation of their work. A sixer lofted into the air by a cricketer, for instance, would be frozen by numerous cameras, made immortal for future generations to laud. The entire stadium would rise to its feet in appreciation of the perfect arc that fell into the stands. Whereas the musical instruments played in concert halls across the country were seen merely as mediums for the music that was produced through them. Yet each instrument that the maker created was as much a work of art as the music that the maestro played on it.

Sighing, Somnath Babu folded his paper with difficulty, and kept it on the table. There was nobody he could even discuss his thoughts with these days. He had lived his life through his profession, leaving the socializing to Nandini. And now that she had gone, he could hardly begin, at his age, to chat up the neighbours and visit them. Even if he had the inclination to do so, which of course he did not.

It was cold today. The late-December nip in the early morning air was becoming sharper each year. Somnath looked at the clock on the wall, with its large numerals. He would have to kill more than an hour of time before Shanti put in her appearance. She lived halfway across the city, and though she tried, poor dear, to hurry to work in order to give him his breakfast earlier, it was not always possible. When Nandini had been alive, it hadn't mattered. Food had appeared on the table at the appointed time, the house had been a home. And of course Nandini had spoilt Somnath. He had only learnt how to make himself a cup of tea after she had died. But his culinary skills had not progressed beyond that.

Below the clock, on a shelf that was often dusty nowadays, was a row of photographs, coloured as well as the old black-and-white ones. Nandini's was the newest on the shelf, and it showed its recent origin in the rawness of its colour and the shininess of its aluminium frame. He had not put the mandatory garland of flowers around it. That would make her, for him, irrevocably dead. Of course she was no longer in this world, that was true. Indeed, he would have to be out of his mind to deny it. But putting a garland there was an act he could never bring himself to perform. It was as though by doing so, he would be putting her away in some camphor-scented box, away from the bustle of life, her home and what had been her domain. There were several other pictures as well, each showing Somnath Babu with some very well-known musician, who held in his hands one of the creations of 'Ghosh and Brother', either a sarod, a sitar or, in one instance, a Rudra Veena.

Beside Nandini's picture was one of Shobha. Proximity to her dead mother, at least on the dusty shelf in Somnath Babu's house, made her seem, somehow, dead as well. It was just the one picture of Shobha as a young girl, with huge Bangla eyes that looked out seriously from under her heavy head of black hair. This had been taken when Shobha had just about entered college. And then, of course, she had done what she had ... There were no more pictures of her after that. No pictures of Anup, her husband, with the remembered heavily-mustachioed face. No picture of the wedding. No picture, even, of Babloo, Shobha's baby son—now possibly a school-going child—whom neither Somnath Babu nor Nandini had ever seen.

Shanti had told Nandini several times while she had been alive that Babloo looked like him, Somnath Babu, and not like his father. Thank God for that. It was bad enough having a man who looked like a goon for a son-in-law, without having a grandchild with the same looks. True, Anup not only looked, but was a goon—the neighbourhood goonda, who had terrorized the para with his gang. God only knew what Shobha, artistic and quiet always, had seen in him. Glamour, of course. He was rich, too, but Somnath Babu did not believe that money had had anything to do with Shobha's decision to run away from home to marry Anup, rather than face their—no, not wrath, wrath was something that gentle Somnath Babu and Nandini were quite incapable of expressing—but dismay, and sadness. True, they had forbidden Shobha to marry that good-for-nothing Anup, but that had been only out of concern for her. The para people whispered about Anup's lawless and violent ways, of his propensity to get into fights and fisticuffs at the slightest provocation. They had not even come afterwards to seek their blessings, as eloping couples usually did in the course of time, hoping that by doing so, they would mollify the parents somehow. Even after Babloo had been born, there had been no sign of them.

The news that he was a grandfather had been brought to Somnath Babu by Nandini one evening after her return from a visit to some neighbour. He had wanted to weep then, and fold Shobha in his arms, but how could he do that? It was not possible to present himself at that goonda's door, in his white dhoti and with his furled umbrella in his hand, and announce, 'I am your father-in-law, how about letting me in, I want to see my daughter and grandson…' And of course, Shobha had not come herself. Not when her son had had his first rice ceremony, not even when her mother had died, though living as she did, not too far away, it was impossible that she would not know about it. No doubt Anup would not permit his wife and child to go to a house where he himself was not welcome… Besides, in spite of her quietness, Shobha had always been stubborn and full of pride.

Puzzled and perturbed by the turn of events, Somnath Babu and Nandini had not known what to do. Conflicting bits of advice had been doled out to them by well-meaning neighbours. Do this, don't do this. In the end, matters had drifted along for such a long time that they became accepted, petrified into actuality. Perhaps if Nandini had been alive, something would have come of it—but now…

Somnath Babu, alone with the *Ananda Bazar Patrika,* found his mind drifting frequently to Shobha these days. He had not let his grief show when Nandini had been alive, for her sake. Just as Nandini had remained, after the first stunned days, cheerful always, at least before him. But Shobha… He had always looked forward to the day when he would give her away, in front of the sacred fire, to a suitable boy, chosen perhaps by Nandini and himself. They said one of the most blessed acts that a man could perform was that of giving away a daughter in marriage. It brought a man, a householder, the greatest merit.

There was a knock at the door. Ah, Shanti. His stomach already rumbling with hunger, Somnath Babu let her in. Tall and bony, Shanti had been 'doing' for them ever since Shobha was a baby. These days, she did not need the money that cooking and cleaning for Somnath Babu fetched her. Her family, consisting of five sons and two daughters had prospered. All the boys were working at regular jobs and looked after their widowed mother well. And though, gradually, Shanti had left off working in all the other houses that had been part of her regular routine, she had not been able to stop coming every morning to Somnath Babu's place. Especially now that Nandini Didi was no longer around to look after her husband. She had spoiled him, she had, waiting on him hand and foot as she always did. He was hopeless in the kitchen; couldn't cook to save his life. And if she, Shanti, stopped coming, he wouldn't even be able to find himself an alternative cook-cum-housekeeper, though he had lived in this neighbourhood, near that shop of his forefathers, all his life.

Shanti began preparations for breakfast as soon as she entered the kitchen. The man was of course famished, though he was too gentle to say so. She began to knead and pound the dough for his chapattis energetically. As usual, when she saw the helplessness of Somnath Babu's expression, her thoughts went acerbically to Shobha.

Shanti had glimpsed Shobha just last evening, with the child, what was his name ... Babloo at her anchal. Indeed, Shanti bumped into Shobha quite often, which was quite natural, considering that the girl lived in the same neighbourhood as Somnath Babu, after all. She had seen Shobha grow up in front of her eyes. Indeed, she had given the child her babyhood oil massages every day, and had watched her start and finish school, and enter college. Such a well-behaved, modest girl. Of course she had known, long before these people, her parents, that she was going around with that highly unsuitable boy. She had spoken to Shobha about it, drawing her away to a corner of the kitchen. But had the girl listened?

Finally, when the whole para was agog with speculation and scandal, it had been Shanti herself who had decided to take matters to her own hands. Wiping them on the anchal of her sari one day, she had said to Nandini, 'Shobha comes home late from college these days, doesn't she?'

'Yes,' Nandini had agreed, placidly. 'She is taking part in that drama that they are staging there, she told me.'

It had taken an effort of will for Shanti to stop herself from snorting. But she had said, calmly enough, 'Drama. Sure, there is a drama taking place. A natok. But not in the college, no, everybody knows that.'

Surprised, Nandini had looked up from the paper she had been reading. 'What do you mean?'

'What I mean is this. I mean, I look on you as my older sister, my Didi ...' Shanti had fumbled in an uncharacteristic manner before the limpid simplicity of her employer's eyes. 'Well, please don't mind, but Shobha, whom I love and care for very much, as indeed I should, for haven't I seen her growing up in front of my eyes ...' Nandini had waited patiently for the kernel of Shanti's speech. Finally it had come: '... so even though I didn't believe what they were all saying at first, these last few days I have seen her myself, with that fellow, that goonda, Anup. Practically arm-in-arm. Can you imagine our Shobha doing such a thing unless that man cast a spell on her? Yes, a spell, one of those tantra-mantras that can easily be purchased from a shaman. Otherwise our Shobha is not like that, not like that at all. What I'm saying is, talk to her, tell her you are fixing a good match from a bhadrolok family for her, there is still time, true, people are talking, but they will stop when Shobha ends this, after all she has grown up here, and everybody loves her…'

And, she knew, Nandini had tried to talk to Shobha. So, indeed, had her father. But who knew what had got into Shobha's head? Instead of listening to her parents, she had shamed them by running off with that fellow. And then, rubbing salt and green chillies in the gaping wound it left in the old people's lives, she had even settled down here, in the same neighbourhood. After all, her husband was the parar goonda, the neighbourhood muscleman, and he had to live near his place of work, she supposed. Though people said he was much more than a parar goonda these days, he had progressed from petty criminality to much bigger things, and had his finger in all sorts of unlawful activities. Even drugs, she had heard.

Shanti glanced at Somnath Babu as she set his breakfast before him. It would break his heart if he knew. She would have to talk to him, of course, but how? Poor man, poor man… But she said in her usual brisk voice, 'There, now, eat. I'll be in the other room, cleaning up, if you need me.'

~

Somnath Babu looked at the dish of pressed rice cooked with vegetables as well as the curry and chapattis that Shanti had set before him. It was an effort even to unloose the knots in his hands in order to start eating.

Of course, even when he had been going regularly to Ghosh and Brother, his hands had often felt like this. But Nandini's unguents had kept the worst of the pain and stiffness at bay. And there had been his instruments, of course. The tanpuras, the sarods, the sitars, the Saraswati Veenas that he manufactured with so much care and love: they seemed, in return, to give him something that kept the pain and stiffness away while he worked at them…

Nandini had sometimes expressed regret that they had only a daughter. No son to look after them in their old age… And if God had decided to bless them with only girls, why not give them more, at least three or four of them, instead of just one, so that at least a couple of them would be likely to be around at any point of time. But Shobha had remained an only child. Somnath Babu, however, had never felt the need for more children. It was enough that they had one, God had been kind enough to them. And didn't he have those instruments at the shop, whom he could mould and shape just like his own children?

Trying to push the food, clumsily, into his mouth, his mind went to the remembered feel of the wood under his hands as he had shaped the instruments. The best, of course, had been the Rudra Veena. Starting work on one had always been a major event in the life of the shop. Just as an auspicious day was chosen for the first rice ceremony of a child, so, too, a day deemed propitious was chosen to start work on the instrument. Amid the fragrance of incense sticks, with the sound of the conch shell resounding on all sides, Somnath Babu would pick up a previously-sanctified chisel, and make the first auspicious cut. The person for whom the instrument was being created would be present at the time. Often, they were Muslims, in one instance, even a Christian, but they had all been united in their religion, that of Music. He remembered how the famed beenkar, Ustad Ali Hussain would come to look at his instrument take shape, slowly, over the months. Once, he had brought along his little nephew, who later also became a renowned Rudra Veena player, though he'd heard that he had now given it up completely. Indeed, he, Somnath Babu, had created instruments for generations of maestros.

Yes, they were his children, his daughters, in more ways than even Nandini had ever known. They would have remained imprisoned within their respective blocks of wood, unborn, if he had not set them free and given them life. The Rudra Veenas would take almost a year to make. True, they were few and far between, for how many actually played that difficult instrument? But daughters were rare too, daughters were a gift. Somnath Babu would make the whole instrument all by himself, not delegating any of the work to his employees. He would spend long hours in the shop, bent over the wood that would slowly take shape under his hands; through the long nights after the shop had closed, he would sit alone with the veena, working lovingly on the instrument. First, create the shape... But even before that, when the instrument was a mere idea, just conceived in his mind, he would give her a name. Tarangini, Ragini, Sruti, Antara, Gandhari, Shivranjani, Bhairavi—they were all his creations, the daughters of his skill and love.

He would put the resonators, the huge seasoned gourds, on the main body. The crocodile or snake or bird-shaped decorations at either end would be carved separately by him, and then put gently into their designated sockets. The frets, the ivory or bone decorations, the painstaking carvings into the seasoned wood, the final varnishing—yes, he was indeed, in those midnight hours, a loving father, moulding the daughters of his heart with his own hands. And when the first copper and steel wires were stretched taut over the frets, and the first auspicious note was plucked, and the veena resonated in its own individual, bell-like voice—yes, he was as ecstatic as any father with his child's first words, as rapturous, in fact, as he had been when Shobha had first lisped, 'Baba!'

But his work with his veenas wouldn't end there. There would be tonal adjustments to be made, strings to be matched, seasoning to be done. In the meantime, the musician for whom the veena was being made would come and strum a few notes on her, getting the feel of the instrument. Somnath Babu would already have the body measurements of the musician, for each veena would have to be tailor-made for the person playing it. And when, finally, the time would come when the Rudra Veena player—always a man, for which woman had the stamina to play such a complex and heavy instrument?—would take away the instrument, Somnath Babu would stand at the door, tears streaming down his eyes, like a bereft father on the day his son-in-law took his daughter away.

Of course the musicians would come to him, like sons-in-law, bringing their instruments for repair and adjustments. In fact, they still did even now, for although Ghosh and Brother did not exist anymore, he, Somnath Babu, was one of the few people alive today who could repair a Rudra Veena, in spite of his arthritic hands. And when they did, he would feel that his home was full, once more. Like daughters who came from their marital home to their father's house; like Ma Durga herself who came to her father's house to rest for a few days away from Shiva; his veenas, too, would come, wounded, perhaps, with scratches on their resonators caused by too much travelling through the concert halls of the world, or a gouge on their stems, which would alter the very tone of their voices. They would need to be coddled, and made much of, just like married daughters always were when they came to their father's house. And when finally, the musician came to take the instrument away, Somnath Babu would once more feel a father's grief as he watched the man pack his Tarangini or Bhairavi or Shivaranjani into its modern fibreglass case and take her away once more. 'Don't tire her out with too much work, look after her, her voice needs constant care, she doesn't like the air-conditioned halls to which you take her all the time ... !' he would want to say.

But of course he never did.

~

There was something that Shanti needed to tell Somnath Babu today. Even as she bustled busily about her duties, she wondered how she would frame it. If Nandini Didi had been alive now, it would have been different—no problem at all—in fact things wouldn't have come to this at all. A pretty pass, indeed. Shanti pursed up her lips and attacked the clothes that she was washing with a great deal of force, as though they, poor Somnath Babu's blameless clothes, were that asura Anup himself, in person.

Shanti heard all the neighbourhood gossip, but discounted a large part of what she heard, even as she relished repeating most of it to others. But what she had been hearing, of late, about Shobha, was not something that could be enjoyed and ignored. Slapping Somnath Babu's dhoti against the floor with great violence, she thought angrily about what she had seen. Now, of course, there was no way in which she could ignore the gossip—she had seen with her own eyes the proof...

She was setting Somnath Babu's lunch in front of him when the words came blurting out from her mouth. 'I saw Shobha yesterday, as I was leaving, you know.' She didn't look at him as she said it. 'In fact I sometimes do...'

Somnath Babu looked up, surprised. When Shanti spoke to him, it was usually about mundane domestic matters. She was looking at the table with a strange, set expression on her face, as though she had seen something unpleasant there, a cockroach perhaps. His heart began to thump, and the familiar constriction began to clamp down on his chest. Luckily, she didn't seem to require him to give her a reply...

'She didn't know I had seen her. She was walking down the road, on the other side, with her child, Babloo, near her. What I want to say is... I mean, I have heard this many times from others, but...'

Somnath Babu waited silently.

'That no good Anup, he's been using his fists on her.' There, it was out. 'People say he beats her up every time he comes home drunk, which is often, as you can imagine. But I didn't believe them... Till today. I saw her, you know. Her face was swollen, her eyes were blackened.' Shanti permitted herself to glance fearfully at her employer, but what she saw in his face made her look quickly away again. 'I mean, I have lived in a slum all my life, I know what a battered woman, a woman beaten by a man, looks like.' Her voice uncertain now, Shanti continued. 'What I am saying is this. Shobha won't come to you, especially not now, when she needs help. She was always a proud one. But there's nothing to prevent you from going, is there? Talk to her, ask her to come here, stay with you for a while, with Babloo, it will be good for her, and for you...'

Without waiting for a reply, she went back into the kitchen. From behind the shelter of its door, she added, 'If you like, I can go to her house today, or tomorrow, and tell her you want to go over... Prepare her a bit, like...'

Somnath Babu said nothing. Mechanically, he pulled the dishes towards him, and began to eat. His heart was pounding now, and he could feel himself perspiring. His mind seemed to have gone fuzzy, too, in a way it sometimes did these days... What was she saying, Shobha...?

He was washing his hands after having finished his lunch when there was a knock at the door. Shanti opened it to let in a tall, well-built middle-aged man.

'Namaste Somnath Babu, I hope this is not an inconvenient time, but my veena urgently needs your attention.'

It was Akhtar Hussain, the famed beenkar.

'No, not at all.' Force of habit made the words come out courteously, though his heart seemed ready to burst. 'Come in, I'll see what I can do…'

'No, I think I'll leave the veena here, in your music room, if I may. Some people are waiting for me. In fact, I'm already late. I'll come back later, in a day or two, perhaps…'

Shanti closed the door behind him as he left, after depositing the fibreglass case in the adjoining room.

An hour or so later, Shanti went in again to the music room, to tell Somnath Babu that she had finished her work and would be leaving soon.

The sound of someone speaking came to her. Had that musician returned, then? Perhaps she should give him a cup of tea before leaving. She went closer to the door.

Somnath Babu was all alone in the room. In front of him was a veena, probably the one that the afternoon's visitor had brought.

Unaware that Shanti was watching, Somnath Babu continued speaking. Indeed, he would probably not have noticed her even if she had been standing in the room as he crooned to the veena before him. In his voice was all the anguish of a helpless father. His hands, gnarled and knotted, moved over the varnished wood of the stem of the veena as though he was stroking away its pain with unseen unguents.

'My poor child, my Gandhari, what has he done to you? Your eyes, your arms … Ah, that must hurt. But don't worry, you've come home now. Home to Baba, don't worry, I'll take care of you, these bruises around your eyes, just let me put the medicine on them, you'll see, they'll heal in no time at all. There won't even be any marks after I finish. I won't let that man take you away again, Gandhari, you will stay here with me just as long as you want to, with Babloo, he can go to school from here, it's no problem … You can stay with me just as you used to, before …' His voice broke.

Shanti backed out of the door, a stunned look in her eyes.

The Gift

SUNDAY. FLAT ON HIS BED, ADITYA SQUINTED UP AT THE LIGHT coming in through the curtained window. It was quite sunny outside. He could tell by the golden glow that came in through the green material that it was going to be a fine day. Just right, in this late winter-time, for a last picnic on a sandbar, or maybe a long drive through the outskirts of town to one of the forest bungalows outside. It was the beginning of spring, really. The greyish mist that had blanketed mornings for the past so many weeks had now retreated. The fog and morning haze would appear again in autumn, bringing with them the fragrant, creamy white, orange-stemmed sewali blossoms.

It was a day to be up and about, a day to bound out of bed and make preparations for fun events. Upstairs, he heard footsteps moving around. Probably Rishi and Priyanka were getting ready for just such an event. They were not, otherwise, given to rising much before nine on a Sunday, no matter how wonderful the weather outside. A half-smile formed in his mind, not quite reaching his mouth, as he lay in bed listening to the footsteps of the young people upstairs. Usually, it was he, Aditya, who was the early riser now. He would wait in his bed, closing his eyes but resigned to sleep eluding him, till he could make out the dawn breaking through the curtains. It was only then that he allowed himself to leave his bed, and give up all pretence of sleep.

Today was different though. In spite of the sunshine outside, he pulled the blanket up closer to his chin and closed his eyes determinedly again. There was really no need to get up just now. It wasn't as though he was going to a picnic or an early morning boat ride or even a temple.

The faint fragrance of Ishita's perfume came to him. Strange how these blankets and quilts held the scent even now. It came to him at unexpected moments from these materials that had once touched her body. The thick quilt that he had set aside just a couple of weeks ago, when it had started to get warmer, had been strong with the fragrance in December. It had spread through the entire room when he had taken it out from its summer storage in the box under the bed.

He pulled up the blanket further, up to and then over his eyes, trying to shut out the brightness that was nudging him out of his bed. He breathed in deeply, surrounding himself with the fragrance. Maybe, he thought, since it was a Sunday and such a nice day outside, he would allow himself the luxury of opening her cupboard. Her clothes held her scent, that mixture of the perfume she usually wore and the scent of her body, a fragrance that was as unique as a fingerprint. He would inhale it again, just for a couple of minutes, and then close the steel doors firmly, blocking even the keyhole so that the lingering fragrance would not vanish, like the morning mist on a warm spring day.

His breath inside the blanket was warm. The scent, though, was already becoming fainter. That was the thing about fragrances, he realized. They came and went at their own whim, almost. Maybe the olfactory apparatus became used to the smell, or maybe it could just take in that much and no more. In any case, he could no longer smell her perfume inside the cave of the blanket. Like so much else, that whiff from the past too had been impermanent.

His mind went to the recurring leitmotif of his thoughts these days. Everything on this earth was temporary. The intensity of that realization, an intensity that had hit him when he was sitting among the fading flowers of last year's spring, still had the power, even today, to make him pause in whatever he was doing to think about it. Everything. The little anonymous flower that bloomed, blue and fresh in the grass, had a life of a few hours. And those hills beyond his bungalow, they had a span of some thousands of years. Millions, probably. But hours or millennia, it was all the same. It was just a case of different life spans. In the end, everybody, everything had to go.

Strange that he had not realized this before Ishita left them. And now, at this point more than a year later, he found it even stranger that he had not realized this from the moment he had been born, from the time he had begun to understand about life. Oh, he had read about it all right. Poets penned verses about the transience of life, singers sang about the passing of love, of life, novelists kept writing of loss. But it had all been a kind of theoretical thing, something that people talked about. He had recognized the truth of all that was written, of all that the various sages and holy men had spoken about, but in a kind of distant way, something that did not affect his life, and the way he thought and felt at all.

And then, one day, it had hit him. It had been a month or so after the cremation, a few weeks after he had returned with the other mourners, with Rishi in a dhuti and white panjabi, bearing the urn that contained Ishita's ashes. By then, the stream of people coming in to offer their condolences, their heartfelt sympathies, had dwindled to a trickle. He was sitting in his usual place on the porch, looking at the garden, trying not to remember, and yet wanting to remember the way Ishita had always punctuated her morning half-hour with him with little dashes to the garden to prop up a drooping stem here, or to tweak a dead leaf there. The sharpness of the pain just seemed to be getting worse. He had looked at the garden, seeing not the green of the grass and leaves and the brightness of the flowers, but a slim figure, moving swiftly, happily, as she set about putting the garden to order.

The little patch before him was showing signs of neglect, even though Hari the gardener came in twice a week as he had always done. But in that moment of epiphany, he had seen that the soul of it was gone. There were dead leaves on the branches, flowers were drooping. True, Hari would twist them off when he came, but he was due only the day after tomorrow. The flowerbeds bordering the little lawn were bare, the brown earth turned up by Hari's spade. Ishita would have had saplings planted in them. He didn't remember seeing a bare bed like this in the garden ever before. By the time one row of flowers drooped and became too old for flowers and fragrance, another row was already ready behind or in front of it. Young, vibrant, full of colour and perfume. It used to be a continuous process. But now with Ishita gone, the continuity was missing as well.

That was when it had struck him, suddenly. Everything around him was impermanent. The flowers were here momentarily, just as Ishita had been, just as he himself was. Time was arrowing ahead, and it was just a matter of a few years, a few decades, before he too left this place.

He had felt comforted by the fact. He still did. Now, as he pushed aside the blanket and got up from the bed, the same thought that came to him every morning appeared in his mind again. Another day, another night was over. A new day was before him. Soon, this too would be in the past. He would be one day closer to his own death at the end of this span of a few hours. Once more, the thought comforted him.

The day outside was indeed beautiful. Sometime in the past fifteen months, he had resumed his old habit of sipping morning coffee while reading the newspaper. In the beginning, with Ishita gone, he had thought he would never be able to do it again. They had always sat down there, exchanging interesting tidbits of news from their respective papers, with Ishita occasionally darting to the garden if something caught her eye. This was how they had eased themselves into their days then, before they left for their different jobs. He had thought he would never be able to do it again. For weeks, he had gulped down his coffee in the dining room, reading the papers there. But now here he was again, continuing the habit. Alone.

He gathered the papers that the newspaper boy had flung into the driveway, and sat down on the cane chair. He had got used to the emptiness of the other chair now. Strange, how people got used to everything. Anything that reminded him of Ishita's absence had brought on the agony then. And now... he was used to it.

Such a mundane phrase. And yet, so comforting. There was comfort indeed in the ordinariness of the way life moved on, in predictable patterns. As he well knew, it was the ordinary, the mundane that held up the drowning person, providing a gentle buoyancy, unobtrusive because it was habitual. No grand climax, only the routine of the everyday.

That sense of loss would probably be part of his life for ever now, he knew. But sometimes, hours passed before thoughts of Ishita came to his mind, though she was always there, behind his conscious thoughts. Sometimes days, even a week, passed during which he would not need to rub away the moisture in his eyes.

~

Footsteps. Rishi and Priyanka, dressed in their nightclothes still.

'Up so early?' he asked, affectionately. 'And no late night yesterday either, I notice!' This bantering about their love for late Saturday nights and even later Sunday mornings-after was part of his easy relationship with them.

Both young people smiled. Rishi pulled up the other chair for Priyanka to sit on. 'I'll get the tea,' he said.

Aditya looked at his young daughter-in-law. She had come into the house, her head ablaze with sendur just a few months before Ishita's illness had been diagnosed. What happy months they had been. Now, in this bright spring sunshine, she seemed to be a whiff of fresh air. He was suddenly grateful, again, for the fact that Ishita had been there to welcome this gentle, quiet girl into their lives. Priyanka had shown unsuspected reserves of compassion and strength through all the months of illness and suffering that had followed. He was always quietly thankful for her presence in their family, though he was not dependent on his son and daughter-in-law to run his own household downstairs. It was their presence that comforted.

Priyanka was looking at the patch of garden before them. He followed her gaze. A little bird was hopping busily on the grass, pushing its beak into the earth in an exploratory manner. But the earth had not yet yielded any worms to it. 'The early bird does not seem to be getting the worm,' he observed.

She laughed. It was a cascade of silvery notes, a simple laugh on a cheerful and sunny spring morning. A young person's laugh. The morning brightened up a little more. 'Earlier birds got them,' she said. 'Early worms got caught!'

He smiled. They did not usually get to meet up like this, on Sunday or indeed any morning. It was ... nice. On weekdays they all left for their workplaces by nine. No time then for them to dawdle like this. The younger ones were not like he and Ishita had been, easing themselves into their routine in cane chairs overlooking a garden. They would get up at eight, rush through their baths, fling on their clothes, not have any breakfast, and then move off in different directions to their jobs.

He looked beyond the bird at the garden. It could hardly be called that now, he thought, trying to ignore the pang that came with the reflection. Hari still did his quota of work on those two days of the week. But there was no life in the garden. The grass looked brown in patches. It could hardly be called a lawn any more. The edges, near the flower beds were bare, with the naked earth showing through. A garden had a life of its own. It was like a child, needing constant nurturing, round-the-clock care and unconditional love.

Hari tried, but he had not been able to get through the fog that had engulfed his employer. Looking guiltily at the barren flower beds now, Aditya remembered the many times Hari had told him that seedlings needed to bought, fertilizers and pesticides had to be sprinkled. Aditya had always said, 'Later, tell me that later ...' For fifteen months. And now Hari had stopped asking. He came in, cleaned and cleared, but there were no new flowers to greet the season now. The gerbera plants looked droopy and sick. And the pots that every year at this time had been a blaze of colour, were now empty. Aditya closed his eyes, recollecting, in a sudden bright flash, the golden marigolds, colourful white-bordered frilly-petalled petunias, white chrysanthemums, bright blue larkspur, pink and yellow phlox, crimson salvias that had spilled out in such joyous profusion from all the planters and window boxes and tubs around the garden. Almost all of them were empty now.

He opened his eyes, taking in, for the first time, the barrenness of the front of the house. Strange, he was only noticing it now.

Priyanka was saying something. 'Hear that, Deuta? The kuli bird!' It was indeed the first cuckoo of the season, calling out from a neighbour's tree. Soon the brain-fever bird, the keteki, would begin to cry out also.

He looked at this girl by his side. She was leaning forward, trying to see the kuli bird from whose throat the calls were coming. 'You won't be able to see it, you know,' he told her. 'They are very good at hiding in the foliage.'

She was from a different part of the country. Even after these four years of marriage, she still found excitement in all the new things around her. The kuli, herald of spring, always excited her with its clear, sweet, plaintive voice. Ishita, too, had loved the bird's voice. When its song had kept them awake on warm summer nights, Ishita had felt a sense of calmness, even during those terrible days when the disease was eating into her vital organs. It would bring her some relief from the agony in a way that even the pain-killing injections couldn't.

Aditya remembered how Priyanka had come to their house. Rishi had been working in a different city then. But her name had figured increasingly in his conversations with them over the phone. He had always had many friends, but one day Ishita had observed, 'Have you noticed? This girl, Priyanka. She seems to be with Rishi all the time.'

He remembered looking at her, surprised. She had read his thoughts, and said, 'No, I'm not being all possessive about Rishi—you know I wouldn't be. Maybe I should have put it another way. Rishi seems to be with Priyanka all the time. To the exclusion, it seems to me sometimes, of his other friends, girls and boys.'

'You think there's something going on there?' he had asked. Ishita had always been more perceptive than him when it came to divining things about other peoples' relationships.

'Time will tell, won't it?' she had said. But there had been a smile on her lips, as though she knew more than what her words implied.

In a few weeks, Rishi had called, saying that he was coming home for ten days. No, it wasn't his annual leave, he had just felt like taking a bit of a break, and he had managed to swing it. And yes, he had said, almost as an afterthought, he would be bringing a friend. Priyanka.

Bringing home a girl with him during the holidays was nothing unusual. They had welcomed all his friends, boys as well as girls, over the years. Mostly, they were friendly and, like Rishi himself, effervescent and talkative. Unlike Priyanka. She was a quiet person, they had discovered with some surprise. The tranquility of her demeanour was reflected in her quiet manner and calm eyes. She had spent quite as much time with them, Rishi's parents, as she had with Rishi during that visit.

He had Skyped them after his return to Bangalore. 'Did you ... do you like her? Priyanka?' he had asked.

They had made the enthusiastic comments expected of them. Indeed, what was there not to like about her? She had, they thought, hidden depths and a fine character.

'Hm.' There had been an uncharacteristic pause in the conversation then. The picture of their son on the computer screen had been as clear as though he was in the room with them, every little nuance in his expression, his voice, magnified by technology.

Aditya and Ishita had leaned into each other, touching, waiting for the next words. Words that they knew would change all their lives.

But what came had been totally unexpected. 'She ... Priyanka I mean ... she can't have children, you know,' he had said, his voice careful. 'She was—she doesn't have a uterus. She was born without one.'

It was Ishita who had spoken first. 'Ah. I won't say "poor girl" or anything like that, but she does have my good wishes. My best wishes. Her life ahead of her is likely to be difficult because of that.' But of course they had both known what was coming next. They had reached out to touch each other, waiting for their son's next words.

'I ... am going to marry her,' he had said then, in a rush to get the sentence out.

'That's wonderful ... it's a wonderful choice ...' they had both spoken the words immediately, spontaneously. Indeed, the fact that they would never have grandchildren had never, in any manner, come in the way of their affection for this girl.

'Thank you Ma, Deuta ... I knew it would be all right with you,' Rishi had said, quietly. 'Priyanka insisted that I should tell you this ...'

Just then, Rishi came in with the tea. 'It's becoming warm, isn't it?' he asked. Inconsequential words, but that was what companionship was about. Not the words or what they signified, but the fact that they were sitting here, together, looking at the changing weather, and thinking, all three of them, of the fourth person, whose absence Aditya felt in every aching breath. He was still lost in his memories of that call. They had never spoken about it again. In fact, he hardly thought of it. Indeed, he wondered why suddenly that memory had come back to him now... He shook his head to clear it away. It was almost as though he was being disloyal, in some way, to this girl sitting beside him by remembering that conversation.

But Rishi had that same expression that he remembered from the Skype call. Perhaps that was why he had been reminded of it. Aditya watched as his son set down his cup. He could not read the expression in his eyes. 'There's something we...' Rishi's glance took in his wife '... need to tell you,' he said.

It was something important of course. Otherwise why this build-up? Thoughts and worst-case scenarios raced through Aditya's mind. Were they being transferred? Would they leave this city, and go back to Bangalore, leaving him here, alone? Well that would be all right, why the clearing of the throat and the strange looks? He could look after himself, he had made that perfectly clear to them. He would visit them, they could come here for their holidays...

'It's like this...' began Rishi.

But he had to stop. The click of the gate leading out to the road made them swivel their heads.

A woman stood hesitating at the gate. Middle-aged, probably the same age as Aditya himself. She was a stranger. He was quite sure he had never seen her before. He would have remembered the distinctive head of white hair above her bright eyes and aquiline nose. He looked questioningly at Rishi, then at Priyanka. They shook their heads.

The woman saw them, and walked up to the veranda. Aditya stood up and waited for her to come. A large cloth bag bulged down from her right shoulder. He noticed that she supported the bag with her right hand as she strode down the garden path towards them, so that it would not swing against her hips.

She looked straight at Aditya, then at Rishi. Confidently, with no hesitation, she smiled. It was an open smile, a friendly one. There was something about her bearing, her demeanour that invited automatic respect.

'Ah…come in, please…' said Aditya. He still had no idea who she could be.

The woman made no attempt to introduce herself. Instead, she unslung the cloth bag from her shoulder and placed it on the topmost step of the veranda. There was a deliberateness to her movements. What was she going to take out? The papers and news channels were always full of bombs that were planted around town, lethal things that killed and maimed. But in those seconds that she stooped over the bag, Aditya felt no fear. He waited to see what she would take out.

A flower pot. A clay pot, with a plant, about a foot tall. Its green stem and darker leaves were topped by a single flower. A rose, yellow, like the sunshine outside.

The woman held up the pot carefully in both her hands. Looking straight at Aditya, she said, 'This is for your wife.'

In automatic response, he held out his hands to receive it. Only when he heard Rishi's quick intake of breath beside him did realization come to him. His hands fell to his sides. He felt their heaviness. In his head, thoughts whirled. Feelings, bottled down firmly for months, popped open a cork and flooded his mind in a confusion of foam and fume.

But the woman was still holding out the flowerpot to him. 'My wife… she's… I mean, she passed away.' He heard himself stammering.

The woman answered, her voice steady, 'I know…'

The three of them looked at her, speechless. Her voice was quiet, but had authority. She was still holding out the flowerpot to Aditya, though she was looking also at Rishi and Priyanka now, including them in her gift.

Aditya held out his hands again and took the pot. The flower glowed in his hands. It seemed to have a life of its own. The goldenness of it was concentrated sunshine, which the flower had taken into itself, and then scattered, carelessly, all around.

A rose. Of course Ishita had loved roses. The bed at the end of the garden, raised a few inches above the rest of the plot still had some of her shrubs. A few were flowering now, brave in spite of the neglect. But the blooms were small, nothing like what Ishita had coaxed out of them. Even the colours seemed washed out. As though they were already dead, as though they were anticipating the time when their very existence would seep out of them. And yet it wasn't as though they had aphids feeding on them or anything like that. Hari saw to it that they were not diseased. And yet they were almost dead. Lifeless.

'Fifteen months ago, wasn't it?' asked the woman. They nodded, all three of them on the veranda, still speechless.

'Four seasons,' said the woman. She picked up the empty bag, and slung it on her shoulder again.

Priyanka found her voice first. 'Please ... come in ... you must have a cup of tea.'

'Did you know her? My mother?' Rishi too seemed able to speak. Only Aditya remained as he was, holding the pot with the bright flower in steady hands. He felt he would never be able to tear his gaze away from the woman. Or indeed, find his voice ever again.

The woman continued, as though she had not heard either of them. 'Four seasons. It takes that much time. At least.'

Unexpectedly, she smiled, her teeth white and strong against her darkish face. She turned to Priyanka and said, 'No, that's fine.' Her voice, Aditya noticed, was kind. Compassionate, even. Not a voice full of pity though, no, not that at all.

Ignoring Rishi's question, she turned to Aditya. 'I hope you will do the garden again. It's time. Spring, summer, the rains, winter. Four seasons, they've gone. And now it's spring again. Basant. You've noticed that, haven't you?'

Slowly, Aditya nodded.

'A garden needs tending. Nurturing. It's like life. Like a child.' She looked at them, smiling, not noticing, perhaps, their confusion and wonderment. Or perhaps prepared for it, but unwilling, nevertheless to say anything else.

And with that, with no further words, she turned around and walked down the driveway towards the gate.

They watched her, unable to move their feet to run towards her and block her exit and make her tell them who she was, how she knew so much about them. And about Ishita. Their voices were frozen, as in a dream, the kind of dream where it was impossible to get a sound out of the throat, a word or a laugh, even though the dreamer tried and tried.

The woman walked purposefully on, away from them, never turning back to look at them. Only once did she glance up at the Krishnosura tree as she neared it. It was on the brink of blossoming now, the bright red flowers that would unfurl from the tight buds showing through in a promise of colour. She reached out a hand and patted the curving trunk of the many-branched tree, heavy with foliage. Without breaking her stride, she walked through the small revolving gate at the side of the main gate. And then she was gone.

On the veranda, they found their voices at last.

'Did you ...'

'Do you ...'

'Ever seen ...'

They all shook their heads.

Aditya looked at the pot. 'I should get this planted…'

Rishi reached out a hand and took it from him. Priyanka cupped her hands around the flower, caressing it. Her fingers seemed to be speaking to the bright bloom.

'It's… it's a sign,' said Rishi, slowly. There was a faraway look in his eyes. Aditya saw that they were glistening.

They put down the pot carefully, in a place on the veranda that was sheltered from the wind and the noon sun, but was bright just now with the morning light. 'We'll water it… not too much, I seem to remember Ma saying. You have to be careful about the amount of water a rose plant needs. Not too much, not too little…' Rishi's voice was still soft.

'Yes. I'll get Hari on his mobile. He's not due for a couple of days yet, but maybe he can come in today or tomorrow. That rose patch needs to be cleaned, probably hoed and weeded before this can be planted there. Manured also. I'll have to buy some… maybe I'll take him with me to the nursery tomorrow on the way to work. He can pick out what he needs and I'll have them sent here…'

Aditya paused. He realized that for the first time in his life, he was talking about getting things done in the garden. And for the first time in more than fifteen months, he was planning something.

They sat down again, and looked at the rose in its corner. The brightness of it was at one with the brightness of the sunshine around them.

'Breakfast?' asked Aditya finally. 'I was going to make my famous omelette, the Dak Bungalow one.'

'Totally flat, with lots of chillies,' explained Rishi to Priyanka, smiling. 'Of course, why not, Deuta. We'll help you with it. But just a moment before we go in… I was about to tell you something when the lady came in…'

Aditya remembered. Yes, perhaps Rishi would now tell his father about the transfer. He wanted to break in, tell them it didn't matter; they shouldn't worry; he would be quite all right here, and if he wasn't, he would go and stay with them; he knew he would be welcome in their home. He had a few more years to retire; he was still able-bodied; he could manage.

But Rishi was already continuing. 'We've been visiting some doctors, Deuta, Priya and I.'

He waited, bracing himself against the storm that rushed into his mind. Doctors. Disease. Not again, oh no, please God ... not again ... pleaseplease ... take my life, please, not that again, not for these children ... pleaseGodplease ...

'About getting a child. Ever since we knew about this procedure, Priyanka felt that we should go ahead ... in fact she's the one who feels that we should give it a try ...'

'Procedure? What procedure?' Relief, then puzzlement, replaced worry. But his son was speaking again.

'Surrogacy. It's all done quite efficiently these days. The doctors have identified a person who will carry our baby to full term.'

Aditya stared at them.

'The baby will be ours, Deuta, Rishi's and mine,' said Priyanka in her usual soft voice. 'That ... really means a lot to me. I never thought I could have a baby, and now I can.'

'We had thought of adopting, but for Priya, to have one's very own child, like this, our own ... with our genes, her parents', yours, Ma's ... This is a miracle, Deuta. A miracle.'

'And this morning we got the news that the fertilized ovum is safe in the surrogate's womb. God willing ... in another nine months ...' Priyanka's voice broke. She shook her head, unable to continue. Bending down, she touched her father-in-law's feet.

As Aditya stooped to lift Priyanka up, he got that familiar scent again. A mixture of Ishita's fragrance and the aroma of her body, the same scent that he had got a whiff of that morning. It seemed to be all around them now. The veranda, the garden, the house, their minds ... everything was full of it.

The Rings

The office peon brought in the afternoon mail. Harish Babu stretched his arms and yawned. This was the time when his energy levels flagged and his concentration wandered. He wondered if he should ask for another coffee to be brought in, then decided against it. Acidity, heartburn, gastric problems—at sixty, Harish Babu was fighting what seemed to be a losing battle with them. Going easy on the caffeine had been on the cards for a while.

He reached out for the bundle. Several letters, two pamphlets and a rather luridly coloured magazine vied for Harish Babu's attention. His somewhat bored expression brightened perceptibly as his eyes fell on the cover of the magazine. He had been dictating an important letter, but now Harish Babu sent his secretary away. 'Hold back all calls and visitors,' he told her. 'On no account am I to be disturbed.'

Pushing aside the letters and pamphlets as well as the papers he had been working on, he took up the magazine eagerly, and, tearing off its wrapper, began to read it. No matter how busy he was, Harish Babu always set aside all his other work when this fortnightly journal on astrology arrived, giving it his undivided attention. Of all the magazines of this kind that flooded the market, Harish Babu counted this as the best. Not only were their calculations of the movements of celestial bodies perfectly accurate, their forecasts and prognoses, too, were exact. Of course he did subscribe to several other such journals, too, but *Astrological Fortnightly* was his favourite.

What did the stars foretell for him that fortnight?

For the next thirty minutes, all that could be heard in the room was the quiet hum of the air-conditioner, and the rustle of the magazine's pages. Occasionally, a frown would crease Harish Babu's placid, moon-like face. Often, his large frame seemed to tremble with distress. Finally, he looked up, and closed the magazine. A sigh escaped him.

No longer did Harish Babu look like the successful businessman that he was, a pillar of the local Chamber of Commerce and various industrial associations, a shrewd, highly respected gentleman whose opinions were analyzed endlessly on the business pages of the national journals, the strength of whose forecasts had the power to send the Sensex and other financial indices either shooting up or plummeting down by several points. Indeed, he looked, just then, like a man in deep despair. As, indeed, he was.

With his head in his hands, Harish Babu thought over what he had read. 'My stars!' he muttered sadly to himself. 'Shani is as grumpy as ever—no sign of him moving away or smiling on me from another house. Brihaspati is behaving very naughtily as well, casting a malefic eye at Venus. Rahu is sulking all alone by himself as usual, and Chandra is at loggerheads with the Sun once more.' He shook his head again, and, casting caution to the winds, rang for a cup of coffee to calm his nerves. 'My horoscope is a battleground for all the planets, it seems. They have been at war with each other ever since I can remember. It's a wonder I'm still standing on my feet.'

He took two antacid tablets from a little box in his pocket, and swallowed them along with the coffee. 'Send in Som,' he spoke into the intercom. 'I'll be going out for a while, so hold back everything for some time, okay?'

He was already beginning preparations for departure when Som, the second-in-command in Harish Babu's organisation appeared. 'I'll be away for a couple of hours,' he said, adjusting the folds of the heron-white dhoti that fell smoothly down to his ankles. The sleeves of his creamy kurta were immaculately pleated. As he flicked off an imaginary spot of dust from one of his sleeves, the light caught the jewels that sat, row upon row, on his fingers, in all the colours of the rainbow.

Som looked perturbed. 'What about the meeting tomorrow?' he asked. 'You still have to okay the final papers on it. After all, the meeting is extremely crucial—you should have a look at the papers personally before going to it.'

'I told you, I'll be back in a couple of hours.' It wasn't like Harish Babu to snap so testily at his executives. 'I'll have a look at them after I return.'

'Ratna Bhandar,' Harish Babu directed his chauffeur tersely as he settled his bulky frame in his spacious new car. Normally, Harish Babu luxuriated in the seat, using his commuting time to catch up on the latest Jagjit Singh ghazal or Anup Jalota bhajan. Today, however, he made the journey to his destination in tense, worried silence.

The proprietor of Ratna Bhandar, a portly man who tended to waddle, hurried up to Harish Babu as soon as the doorman admitted him into the cool, luxurious interior of the shop. Rubbing his plump hands together, he escorted Harish Babu himself to the most comfortable seat in the shop, uttering little exclamations of delight and distress at the same time.

'Arrey, Harishji!' he exclaimed, 'It is my fortune, my extreme good fortune, that my humble shop has been graced by the dust from your feet today. But really, why did you bother to come? It's so hot and dusty outside... I would have sent one of my boys to you, along with whatever you needed...'

A little flurry of excited assistants left off whatever they were doing, and hovered around Harish Babu, leaving several hapless customers unattended. One whisked off invisible flecks of dust from the counter in front of Harish Babu, another brought a small footstool for his feet, yet another placed a pad of thick black cloth on the counter before him. They urged him to have either something cold to soothe his parched throat, or a hot cup of ginger tea to revive him, or perhaps an espresso coffee from that new shop across the street? And he simply couldn't leave without tasting some of the excellent burfis that he liked so much from the halwai's shop around the corner. 'No, no,' murmured Harish Babu, sinking into the chair, 'nothing for me, thank you ... not today... I don't feel like eating anything...'

'And how are the planets behaving, then?' asked the proprietor, offering Harish Babu a fresh green paan wrapped in complicated folds that were held in place by a clove and covered with silver foil. He nodded to the scurrying assistants, who melted away discreetly.

'Not well, not well at all ...' confided Harish Babu, spreading out his hands in a despairing gesture.

With the movement, the bright lights of Ratna Bhandar were suddenly reflected in the many precious stones that adorned Harish Babu's fingers. Red, blue, green, yellow—all the colours of the rainbow seemed to have been caught on the fingers of his two hands.

'Just now,' continued Harish Babu, letting his bright hands fall helplessly to his side, 'just now I've learned that Brihaspati is actively working for the downfall of my business. And the other planets are conspiring to help him. This very business that I've worked so hard to build, brick by brick, rupee by rupee…you know how it's been, haven't you?'

The proprietor nodded, too occupied with chewing his own fragrant paan to say anything. His face, however, had a concerned look.

'Malefic effects of one planet can be cancelled if the positions of other planets are satisfactory,' continued Harish Babu dolefully. 'But me, I'm getting no benefit from a single one of them! As for Shani, that rascal is occupied in keeping my family life unhappy. It's all becoming too much for me,' he ended dolefully.

The jeweller shifted the wad of paan to his cheek, and spoke soothingly. 'Now, don't worry. Just leave it in our hands. Things are never that bad. We can block the evil designs of even the most powerful planet, you know that. After all, haven't we been doing that for the last so many decades that you have condescended to grace our shop? Remember the time when the astrologer said that you would have an accident for sure, and break at least your leg or arm, if not your head, unless you wore a cat's eye of many carats on your left index finger? Well, the inauspicious time came and went, but with my jewel on your finger, did even a scratch fall on you?'

His words made Harish Babu's face brighten a little.

'There's a gemmological cure for every astrological disease, a jewelled solution for every planetary problem,' continued the shop-owner. 'What are we here for? I'll have our resident astrologer go through your chart once more. An adjustment of a few carats here or perhaps there, may be all that's necessary. And while you're sitting here, perhaps you would care to look at a new consignment of rubies that's come just this very morning… Rubies suit your horoscope, a few more carats can only help, never harm…'

Hours later, Harish Babu left the shop. He had been fitted with two more jewels as a new line of defence against the mighty planetary forces that seemed bent on destroying his life and career. It was most unusual for any jeweller to deliver anything so quickly. But Harish Babu was special. Two gold rings ordered by other customers were stripped of their jewels, and new ones, suggested by the astrologer, were put in their place. The proprietor himself slipped them onto Harish Babu's already laden fingers, while the astrologer and two assistants hovered helpfully nearby.

'Thank you,' said Harish Babu as he stepped into his waiting car. 'Send the bill to my house, as usual, then. I feel much easier in my mind now.'

'Yes, yes, what are we here for if not to ease your mind?' said the jeweller soothingly. He had left the air-conditioned confines of his shop and come outside to the dirty street, even risked soiling the zari-bordered edge of his pearly silk dhoti, in order to see off his most valued customer personally.

'No, you don't understand,' said Harish Babu earnestly. Normally he hardly spoke of his business to others, preferring to keep his cards close to his chest. Today, however, relief had made him garrulous. 'I have a big meeting, a very important meeting, you know, tomorrow. It's about a tie-up between my own firm and a national giant. A kind of collaboration, in fact, not a buyout at all.'

The jeweller looked suitably impressed though, truth to tell, he hadn't a clue what Harish Babu was talking about. All he knew about the work life of his client was that he was a person who had built up his business from scratch. An engineer by training and education, he ran, thought the jeweller, some high-level engineering firm, which, he had heard, produced very sophisticated equipment. What that equipment was, the jeweller hadn't a clue. But it must be something quite in demand, for Harish Babu never demurred over paying for any of the many jewels that he bought from him on a very regular basis.

~

Harish Babu returned to his office, where Som was waiting for him, an anxious look on his face. 'Come now, Som, don't look so worried,' said Harish Babu. His tone, his very step was different from what they had been when he had left the office a few hours ago. His irritability had disappeared. He was not just genial now, he positively exuded confidence. 'We've worked hard for this, you and I, for the past so many months now. All the spadework is done. A few final details tomorrow, then ... aah!' Putting an avuncular arm around Som's shoulder, he led him gently into his chamber. 'Call the others of the team, we'll go through the papers one last time ...'

It was quite late by the time Harish Babu returned home. But he didn't feel tired at all. Indeed, his new rings seemed to have given him an extra edge of confidence. He was sure things would work out for him tomorrow.

He had sent word home that nobody was to wait up for him. He had already had a simple dinner at the office. Quietly, without disturbing his sleeping wife, he slipped into bed. He decided not to tell her of his latest visit to the jeweller's that afternoon. Though Rina supported him in everything that he did, and had stood by him uncomplainingly during all those difficult years when he had struggled to set up his factory, in this one area of astrology they had had many differences of opinion. Many times, she had said that it hardly suited him, an engineer who had modern views on everything, to believe all that stuff about, firstly, the bad influences of planets, and then, secondly, those same bad influences being deflected by the wearing of jewels. He wondered, as he got ready for sleep, what being an engineer had to do with believing or not believing in astrology... He felt the heavy weight of the new stones on his fingers, and was comforted. He held up his fingers before his eyes. In the semi-darkness of the shadowy room, they gleamed and glistened in all the colours that one could think of.

Harish Babu fell asleep with their colours dancing in his mind's eye.

Indeed, next morning, Harish Babu looked cheerful and confident as he stepped out of his house for the meeting. The new stones certainly seemed to have given him that extra something that he needed so desperately.

His meeting that day was with Rathin, the fourth-generation part-owner of a giant heavy-engineering manufacturing concern. Harish Babu hoped that his firm would be able to bag a lucrative contract for supplying some vital components to the larger concern. If the bid succeeded, it would mean that his worries about marketing his products would be over, for the big manufacturer would need whatever Harish Babu's firm could produce. In fact, Harish Babu would probably need to plan for a lot of expansion, in order to be able to keep pace with the big manufacturer's growth. The spadework was done, and all that remained was the final nod.

And now, thanks to his new rings, it seemed that things were moving along satisfactorily. Rathin appeared to be quite amicable about the deal. 'Of course,' he was saying, 'all this is subject to my father's approval, but I think we can safely shake hands on the deal.'

Harish Babu sighed with satisfaction. Lovingly, he caressed the rings on his fingers.

The movement attracted Rathin's attention. He had been too busy with the facts and figures presented in the papers before him to notice anything else so far. He now checked his words in mid-flow, and gazed wonderingly at the older man's hands.

Why, they were like a shelf in a jeweller's shop! Gems of all colours winked and sparkled at Rathin. He could barely see the older man's fingers, they were that heavily encrusted with gems. Trying not to seem as though he was staring, he looked at them. Emeralds, rubies, topazes, garnets, diamonds, sapphires, corals, pearls—yes, they were all there. Not just one of each kind, but several, in various shades of the same colour. Never before had Rathin seen such a dazzling collection on one person.

He covered up the long pause with a feigned bout of coughing. Waving his hand at Harish Babu to signify his apologies for the interruption, he took a long sip of water from the glass before him. 'Of course,' he resumed smoothly, 'you must understand, Harish Babu, that there are many other considerations besides our own wishes and ideas in this matter. We shall let you know of any further development.' Standing up, he ushered the older man courteously out of his office.

~

It was Rathin's habit to discuss the day's happenings at work with his father in the evenings. He used the older man as a kind of sounding board, and valued his decades of experience in running this firm that had been set up by his, Rathin's, great-grandfather. Through the generations, the firm had grown by leaps and bounds, till it was now one of the leaders in several fields of manufacturing and commerce.

Rathin was the only child of his parents, and had been regarded as the heir apparent to the office of CEO from a very young age. Like his father before him, he had been groomed to take over the mantle of leadership. In keeping with the changing needs of modern times, he had been educated at one of the best schools in the country, then a prestigious engineering college, after which he had been sent to an Ivy League college in the US for his MBA degree. He had done brilliantly in all his examinations. Gradually, over a period of several years, his father had passed on the reins of management to Rathin. And under him, the business was poised, now, to become a multinational. Yet, in spite of his degrees and training, Rathin found, many a time, when he was floundering in a confused maze, looking for a solution to a tricky problem, that his father's words provided him with just the right clue to the correct solution.

That evening, however, while talking to his father over dinner, Rathin sounded emphatic. It was obvious that he had already made up his mind. 'We shouldn't have anything to do with Harish Babu, Father,' he said.

The older man was surprised. 'Why?' he asked, but he was careful to keep his tone mild. 'He has a reputation for dependability, honesty, and for manufacturing quality products. Besides, he's a very experienced hand in this field. He's built up his business over a lifetime, I hear. In fact, I've heard you extolling the virtues of his product many times. I thought you favoured him.' He looked at his son, and asked, 'You were scheduled to have the crucial meeting with him today. What went wrong, then?'

Rathin hesitated. 'Dependability and experience are not everything,' he said slowly. He looked up from his plate and said, 'Father, you should see the number of precious stones he wears on his fingers!'

If the old man was surprised at this apparent change of subject, he did not show it. In any case, he knew that among his son's many hobbies, the study of astrology ranked quite high. He had long ago ceased to be surprised at Rathin's passion for astrology, even though he himself was indifferent to it. Still, he had wondered, many a time, how a young person who had been educated in the Western way, and, indeed, in the West itself, had become so well versed in the intricacies of this subject.

'So?' he asked patiently.

'It seems every planet worth its name is against Harish Babu!' blurted out Rathin. 'He wears a large ruby on his left hand. This can only mean that his financial state is not nearly as solid as it's made out to be. I suspect his health is bad, though I was taken in at the beginning of our meeting with his glowing appearance. How do I know it? Because he wears two corals on his fingers to propitiate Mars. He sports a large emerald, too. He's most likely to be hypertensive, which is why he's trying to keep Mercury happy.

'That's not all. His marriage is not what it seems. He's got pearls and sapphires of many carats to keep the Moon and Saturn out of harm's way. I may not be an expert in these matters, but, as you know, I do have some knowledge about the effects of planets on mortal beings. And as far as I can make out, he's involved in some litigation. I saw a large cat's eye bound in silver on his middle finger. And that's only the beginning. His fingers are so thick with precious stones that it's a wonder he's not been mugged on the streets and relieved of them yet... The stones must cost a fortune!'

Pausing to chew on a mouthful of daal-rice, he continued, 'I wish I had met him earlier on, while the negotiations were at the preliminary stage. I wouldn't have allowed the discussions to continue to this level at all. Though our teams have been meeting regularly, he and I met only today, as you know. Still, it can't be helped—we can't have anything to do with Harish Babu. Father, that man's a walking disaster! At any moment he may get a stroke, or get clapped into prison. He may even get divorced from his wife. At his age! Think of the scandal! Our company shouldn't get involved with him. Not only will he sink, poor man, but all those adverse planets would drag us down as well, if we associate ourselves with him in any way. How can we defeat the combined forces and malefic effects of the Sun, Moon, and all the planets together?'

His father looked at Rathin, being careful to keep his expression as neutral as possible. Over the past few years, he had made it his policy to allow his son freedom in most business matters. Believing as he did, that experience was the best teacher, he allowed Rathin to make his own mistakes, so that he could learn from them. To be fair to his son, however, he had made very few business blunders so far. As for this matter of astrology—he himself didn't believe in any of it. But he was the old guard, in the process of passing on the baton of leadership to his son ...

The older man took a bunch of grapes from the table before him. He snipped off a luscious drop, the colour of perfect Chinese jade. Popping it into his mouth, he said thoughtfully, 'You're probably right.'

A few days later, Harish Babu got the news that the deal had fallen through.

He was philosophical. 'With so many planets stacked against me, what else can one expect? I'll go this very evening to the jeweller's shop again. Somebody recommended a garnet to me the other day…'

Spring Song

It's spring again. Bohag. Once more, the air is full of the sounds of dhol and pepa, once more, lilting Bihu songs gladden the heart of even the most hardened cynic. Once more, the streets of the city are full of people dressed in their best, going from one Bihu pandal to another, listening to their favourite singers, watching lissome young girls dance joyously to the enticing beats that their handsome partners thrum out through horn and drum, cymbal and song.

Yes, it's Bohag. The month of joy, a time of celebration. The kuli calls out endlessly to its soulmate far into the balmy nights. Setting aside their usual shyness, cascades of kopou bloom boldly, as busy bees hum happily around this sudden abundance of beauty.

It's been several years since I've come back to the city in time for Rongali Bihu. My life in England—Scotland, actually—is full and fulfilling, but living under grey skies and weak, watery sunshine, I've yearned, often, for the brilliant blue and gold of the Bohag firmament, the warmth of the spring sun on winter-chilled skin, the touch of the warm breeze that is so like a lover's caress. I've been sunlight-deprived and hadn't known it, till I found myself once more in my birthplace during Rongali Bihu.

Yes, I have laughed and sung, danced and been happy in this season. It's amazing, isn't it, that the whole city celebrates spring with such abandon? The sap rose in my veins, too, though I am well past my youth. I'd yearned for Varun's presence near me as I had gone from Bihutoli to Bihutoli with friends and family, taking in the songs and the singers, the dances and the dancers, sharing joy and bonhomie, love and laughter. But Varun is far away, across several oceans, too busy with his work to come back for a month's holiday to his homeland. He calls every day, though, wanting to know what I have been doing, whom I have met, what is life like in the land of my birth now. I told him, casually, that I saw you last night. Just as casually, he asked if we had talked. No, I said truthfully across the static that had suddenly thrummed through the wires, we had not. Indeed, I am not even very sure that you'd seen me at all.

When Seema and Ranjit had invited me to their house for a Bihu gathering, I had no inkling that you would be there. I'd been glad that they had remembered me. 'You'll meet lots of the old college gang,' Seema had promised me. 'Surajit, Dhananjay, Rekha, Shamim, Bobbi, Achintya, Runjun—yes, they're all coming. They're looking forward to meeting you again. It's been a long time, hasn't it, since we all got together again?' She had not mentioned that you would be there as well.

Perhaps she had forgotten? But no, how could that be? Anyone who'd known either of us during that time can't fail to remember you when they talk to me now. And vice versa. A couple, right through our late teens, to our twenties. We were perfectly matched, down to our very names that fitted each other's so euphoniously… Rashmi and Riddhiman, that was us. If Riddhiman was near, Rashmi could never be too far away. If Rashmi's laugh was heard, one could be sure that Riddhiman had said something funny.

I was your inspiration, you said, all through those years when our lives, our waking hours, almost all our waking thoughts were as inextricably intermingled as the waters of the Luit are with the sandbanks that dot its expanse. The poetry you wrote, the songs that you sang, were all for me, you said. And I, basking in the glow of your attention, loving it when you looked straight down at me in the audience as your velvet voice soared rapturously over the crowd, I believed every word that you said.

But ... being somebody's inspiration, like Petrarch's Laura. Is that ever enough?

It was amazing that when I saw you last night, I still felt a frisson. It was a thrill of—what? It wasn't love, no, nothing like what I'd felt during our years together in college, when the mere sight of you across the room was enough for me to break out in goose pimples. But I certainly felt—well, *something*. How could I not, after all those afternoons spent under flaming Krishnosura trees in bloom, or evenings by the side of the Luit, watching the vast river go quietly by, never letting us know its great strength, its power ...

You were singing of the Luit when I saw you last night. Seema had had a small stage built at one end of her large lawn, and you were there, almost as I remembered you. From that distance, across the garden, you still looked as though you were performing at one of those college festivals, the ones where you'd always been such a major attraction. Surrounded by tablas and guitars, harmonium and now even an electronic keyboard, you looked as you had ten years ago, when I last saw you. Strong. Romantic. Vulnerable. And achingly handsome.

Every girl's dream come true, in fact.

But dreams are uni-dimensional, life is not. Life has many dimensions, has it not, many facets.

Oh, of course I'd heard, over the past fifteen years since I left the country, about you. Bits and pieces from people who came to visit us in Scotland, or from friends and relatives when I came home on holiday. Nothing much, just that you were still here, in the town of our youth, working. And also singing. Not professionally—your job didn't leave you time for that—but on occasion, at friends' places or at Bihutolis. But nobody had told me of the change in you. Not in your appearance, but in your voice. It had always been your best characteristic, your voice, better even than your six-foot frame and perfectly chiselled features. So often, as we sat on some park bench holding hands while you talked, I used to close my eyes and my mind to the sense of what you were saying, and let the sound of your voice resonate through my entire being, even as the bright Bohag sunshine had wafted the fragrance of spring flowers down to us.

But if I had not actually seen you last night, I would not have believed that it was you singing. It has changed, your voice. It no longer strikes a chord in some deep part of my soul. Last night, I did not feel myself being lifted on a wave of melody, responding to your voice, totally in consonance with your mood.

Perhaps it is not your voice that has changed, but I…

You were singing that old Bhupen Hazarika song which had always been one of your favourites, and mine.

Soisobotey, dhemalitey,
Tomarey omola monot aasey,
Bohag mahor Luit khonit,
Duyo satura monot aasey…

I remember it all…
The fun, the frolics of our childhood

Our dips in the Luit during the month of Bohag,
The first blush of the shy dawn of youth
When I had said,
That without you, I would kill myself.

My entrance had been noticed by many of my old friends. Their greetings were warm, their smiles affectionate. But there was something—some wariness. I noticed some of them glancing quickly at the stage, then back at me. Of course it was after more than a decade, a full fifteen years, that they were seeing me in the same place as you. Rashmi and Riddhiman. How could they take one's name without the other's? And yet it was no longer legitimate, no longer permissible to do so.

People were everywhere, here to celebrate the coming of spring. You continued to sing, while many who crowded the lawns hummed along with you. Your voice rose with passion as you sang of the storm that created havoc in the spring of your life.

You left me for another...
Leaving behind the monarch of your heart,
You went with the prince of wealth
Chanting of riches, you left,
Shaped by the love of wealth,
In that storm.

How many times in the past had I heard you singing just this song, how many times had I been moved by the lines!

But last night, they had seemed to be imbued with a special significance. I could see people looking at me covertly as you sang those lines. Suddenly, it had dawned on me. To all those people who knew me on the lawn, and were looking out of the sides of their eyes at me, and, most important, to you, I had been—I am!—a betrayer! The song that you were even then singing paralleled, in their eyes, our lives fifteen years ago. No doubt for you, too, the song had become, the story of our lives.

The shock of it had made me stumble to a chair under a rosy radhasura tree, and sit down. Yes, of course, I was the one who had left behind a youthful love, and gone to the land of riches, hadn't I? I was the one who had not waited for my beloved to get himself a job, and had suddenly married, instead, an NRI, a man older to me by several years, a man who could provide for me in a way that you, Riddhiman, could never hope to.

But it was never like that. Never. I have never betrayed you. To betray a love would be to betray oneself. How can I explain to you?

Do I even need to?

Yes, I realize, I need to explain. To you—and also to myself. Not because I feel guilty, or anything like that, you understand. But seeing that you, and others, think of me as a betrayer… I feel the need to revisit the past. You may think, and persuade yourself, that I had betrayed you. It is probably easier for you to believe that of me. But you know, deep down, that it wasn't really like that, don't you?

Many of my old friends were around last night. They talked warmly to me, and were as friendly as though we had last met just fifteen days ago, not fifteen years. We made light conversation, even as my mind was seething with thoughts about you, about us. Runjun, Rita, Shamim, Dhananjay—they were all brought up to me by Seema, with a 'Guess who's here!'

'You look well, Rashmi,' they had said, every one of them. 'And we're so proud of you. Of your achievements—we read about them in the papers. What about your husband—where is he? He hasn't come? What a pity... He must be very busy, especially after that award he got recently; he's doing such excellent work. Truly.'

You repeated the stanza about the storm that entered your life, a storm that carried me away from you. 'He's never married, you know,' said Runjun, misinterpreting my look towards the stage.

I made a careful answer. 'Oh really? What a pity...' Or something like that. There had been no accusation in Runjun's voice, none at all. Yet I had felt something—a twinge of guilt. This was quickly replaced by anger, then sadness.

It's not my fault that you've not married. I never asked you not to. In fact, I remember clearly, I wanted you to be happy. I still do. I had seen the rainbow in my sky, and I had wanted one for you, too.

The storm that entered your life. Yes, it was a stormy time, a difficult time. We had graduated from college at the same time, you with English, I with Chemistry. I had applied to, and got admission into IIT Delhi, for postgraduate studies. You had wanted to go to Delhi to study, too, but hadn't got admission anywhere. You had tried in various places, in vain. Desperate, you had looked around for a job. You had sat for umpteen examinations, tried joining the Civil Services, tried the banking services—it had been three years of frustration for you.

We had, naturally, kept in touch over that time. But my new life, my new studies, were stimulating, exciting, challenging. Besides, there was the guilt that I felt. Guilt that I was doing well, you were not. Was it because I am a woman that I felt this guilt? Possibly. For years, I had looked up to you, hero-worshipped you, your poetry, and your music. But now I was doing something which I was good at, and excelling at it.

Sometimes, after reading your letters, I felt that it was wrong of me to excel, whereas you, the man in my life even at that point, were going through such an agonizing time. You wanted to earn your livelihood. Charmingly, you wanted to support me for life. But things weren't shaping up that way. Sometimes, I even caught myself pitying you. Can a woman marry a man she pities?

And in any case, Varun came into my life soon afterwards.

Varun. How can I describe him? You have labelled him a rich man. Well, 'rich' is a relative term. Yes, he was rich from the point of view of an unemployed, struggling young man. But Varun was no millionaire when I met him. Nor are we wealthy, even today.

He is a doctor, Riddhiman. You know that, don't you? But not a practicing one. He does cancer research. His work focuses specifically on a kind of leukaemia that attacks young children. Physically, he is nowhere near as impressive as you. He is shorter, slighter. His hair is steel-grey now, the black almost eclipsed by the white. Decades of study have stooped his shoulders a bit. Is he good-looking? Honestly, Riddhiman, after all these years together, I really don't know. To me, of course, he is much more than merely handsome.

His intellect was what attracted me first to him. He has a brilliant mind, and I have always admired intelligence. But he had another quality that completely bowled me over. He is the most humane person I have ever met. His work, his life, is dedicated to erasing a particular kind of disease. Could anything be more inspiring?

His family stays in Delhi. We got to know each other gradually, during his visits to this country. I began to look forward to his phone calls, his visits. Our conversations were wonderful. We talked endlessly about many things, ranging from science and society, to the mundane happenings that added meaning to our lives.

With you, I had always been in the role of the listener. You were the brilliant speaker, and I was the enthralled audience. Could you blame me, Riddhiman, for preferring his company to yours as the days went by? He listened to what I had to say, my opinions, my deepest thoughts, mindful always of the tone of my voice, the nuances of my gestures, with the deepest courtesy and unfailing attention.

Varun is a decade older than I am. He, too, has had a past relationship with another woman, an Irish lady who is a software engineer. A live-in relationship, but they were not married. She did not want children; he did. They are still great friends. She has become my friend, as well. I look on her as a kind of elder sister. And no, I do not feel in the least bit threatened by her.

Varun knows all about you. About how far our relationship stretches back in time, about how once you were the centre of my universe, about how I gradually outgrew you.

For that's what happened, Riddhiman. I outgrew you. You remained as you were, while I wanted more. As my horizons expanded, I wanted a man by my side who would be my companion in that new world that I was seeing before me. Was I wrong to do that? No, I don't think so. Shouldn't all of us have the right to a choice, at every point of our lives? I made mine when I married Varun.

Your voice, rougher now than when I last heard it, continued singing in Seema's garden.

Suddenly, after a long time
I saw you again
The gold of your jewellery glistened from afar...

I, too, remember that occasion. It was ten years ago. I had come home with Varun. It was not the first time that we had come on leave. But I remember that I was particularly happy at that time. No, not for the gold that you saw on me. But because things were going well. I had just completed my Ph.D. in Biochemistry from a very well-known British university, and landed a challenging job there. I was looking forward to it. Of course the pay was good. But would you believe it, Riddhiman, when I say that the pay was not the reason I was happy? No, I was happy because I would be part of a team working at the cutting edge of science. Genetic modification, that kind of thing. At last, I was beginning to feel that I would be contributing something truly valuable to humanity.

I wonder if you have ever felt like that, Riddhiman? The glow that you saw around me that day, ten years ago, was not the glow of gold, but the effulgence of happiness. Because I am happy, Riddhiman, more truly happy than I ever was with you. Even when your voice washed over me in the Bohag of our youth, there was, in spite of my joy, always a niggling feeling in my mind. Poetry is all very fine, and music is, too, but what about the other things that make up life? I was a science student, and my mind has always moved along very literal lines. But when I look through an electron microscope at the microcosm of life, when I read about the things that some of my fellow scientists have done recently, I feel the power of poetry surging through my being in a way that I never did feel with you. After all the years spent in research, I have a couple of scientific patents to my name now—and Riddhiman, for me that is music much sweeter than any of the songs that you ever sang for me…

But of course you've never understood, have you? When I went to your house fifteen years ago to tell you, as gently as possible, that it was over between us, all you could think of was that I had betrayed you. Possibly, that's how you feel even today. Certainly, last night when sang that song, you had cast me in your mind as a betrayer.

Why is it that when a woman leaves a relationship, she is branded a betrayer, one who sells out for money? Of course money is any important part of any relationship. It's only in our college days that we imagine that we can live on love and fresh air. Love wilts very quickly without lucre, we all know that now, don't we? But even then, money is not everything.

Last night, as I watched you sing that stanza, a sudden realization had dawned on me. You had refused to accept the fact that I'd left you, all those years ago, because I'd fallen deeply in love with another man. Instead, you'd persisted in believing that it was the lure of gold that had ensnared me.

Was that, I wonder now, because to acknowledge the truth would have been a blow to your ego? Better, isn't it, to cast me in the mould of betrayer, than face the fact that you couldn't keep pace with me? That I left you for a man who was more suited to me? Better for me, even?

If you think, my love
That without you
I shall kill myself
It's a mistake you are making
It's a false dream…
Living, I want to build a place
Where the worth of a man is more
Even though somewhat, than gold.

Well, good for you. I never asked you to kill yourself—I just wanted us to be friends. Build a just society, why don't you?

When I come home, I see guns where flowers used to be, I see the power of money where love used to be, I see conspicuous consumption where simplicity used to be. Sing a song of justice, why don't you, but remember there are many ways of measuring the worth of a man. Or a woman. Not just the poet's way. Not just the scientist's way. But a bit of both, and then some. And all of us have to tread the paths that are most suited to us.

You had looked straight in my direction when you sang that last stanza. I had looked back, steadily. But had you actually seen me? I don't know... it was dark under the tree where I was sitting. I came away without meeting you at all.

It is better so. I am sending this to you by post. By the time it reaches you, I will be gone. Back to Varun, back to our daughter Anita, to our home, to my laboratories, to my friends and my colleagues.

It is cold in Scotland now. Spring comes later there than it does here. And Bohag, with its fragrant breezes and Bihu melodies, Bohag does not come at all. But it will still be Bohag for you when you read this letter. And if some of the meaning of this festival of love, of renewal, still remains in your mind, I ask you to think of me in friendship from now onwards.

And then, perhaps, in some other Bohag, under some other Bihu sky, we can meet again, in companionship and in joy.

The Revenge of Annapurna

THERE'S THAT RESTLESSNESS ABOUT HIM AGAIN TONIGHT.

So. All right.

I know my face has pursed up as soon as I notice it, but there's little I can do to prevent that. In any case, he is not looking at me. Nobody is, even though we are sitting around the dining table, facing each other. Everybody is concentrating on the food that I am serving out to them. Like Annapurna herself, goddess of plenty. She who is the symbol of prosperity and abundance. She who is revered, and worshipped in all households. For of course food, and plenty of it, is what is central to our lives, isn't it? Without food, without nourishment, nothing would be. Not thoughts, not ideas, not emotions, not existence. Not even love.

Love. *And what about Annapurna's love life, then?* I carry the thought in my mind even as I ladle out the daal without onions to Ma because it is Saturday, the day she doesn't touch meat or fish or even onions and garlic. To Deuta, I carefully slide out the large roundel of rohu fish, along with the tenga. They look at their plates, content. Bablu wants the chicken thigh, so I turn and give him that, unpursing my face as I look at his bright eyes. And to him …

But he waves aside the ladle as I approach with the tureen of fish tenga. His fingers drum on the table, and he loosens his collar. His eyes slide sideways to look out of the window, to the dark, moonless night, and then back again to the room. He is careful not to meet my gaze, though.

Annapurna. What do we know of her, anyway? Was she desired, lusted after? Or was she ok with being the harbinger of abundance, the deity to whom even Shiva, her mendicant husband, held out his bowl in supplication?

I never begin on my food until the others have been fed. Like Annapurna, I will not touch a morsel until my devotees have full bellies. Well, perhaps 'devotee' is not really the right word. On the other hand, maybe it is. They are certainly fans of my cooking, Ma and Deuta and Bablu. And he? Bablu's father, whose name I cannot take because he is my husband? Even in my thoughts, I refer to him as Bablu's father. I have never called him by his actual name, the one he is known by in this house, and outside. Abhishekh. Abhishekh Barua, the acclaimed novelist, the path-breaking short story-writer… And the poet who brings a frisson to every heart. For me, within these domestic walls, he is Bablu's father.

'That was really good, Bowari,' says Deuta, beaming. I am known to the elders by this appellation. Bowari, daughter-in-law. I am a designation. Annapurna-like in my ability to serve up meals that please them all, and keep order in the house, and around the table, and in the kitchen. 'That bit of outenga was really tasty.' He points to the slice of elephant apple, now sucked dry of juice, at the side of the shining brass kahi that has served as his dinner plate for decades now.

I smile at him, serene. I am confident that none of the thoughts storming through my head show on my face. 'The fish was fresh,' I say softly, to indicate modestly that it is the quality of the fish rather than my culinary abilities that have made the dish so tasty. Not that I believe it, really. I know I am a good cook. A fabulous one, even. Other women ensnare and charm with beauty, with wit, with brains, with their sexuality. Me, it's my ability to turn the most mundane dish into ambrosia that makes all look at me adoringly. Correction. Most people, not all. No, not all, by any means. I glance sideways at him as he sits there, his fingers drumming moodily on the table, his eyes sliding out and then back again. He is debating something, no doubt. Perhaps he does not know what the outcome of that debate will be, though I do. Oh yes, I do.

I turn my attention, which had wavered momentarily, back to the table. I revel in it, this skill of mine that makes people look at me with devotion and love, even. Ma adds, the smile in her voice reflecting the happiness in her face, 'I hope you have kept a bit of that fish for me, Bowari. I'll have it for lunch tomorrow...'

'But why should you have stale food, Ma?' I ask. The end of my sador has slipped, revealing more of my head than what I normally show before Deuta. I pull it up in a movement that has become automatic for me now. 'I will make a fresh bowl for you, for all of you tomorrow.' I glance around the table, including him in the sweep of my eyes. But as always, he refuses to meet my glance.

This, too, is power, then. This inability of his to meet my gaze, it's my triumph, too. Trying to keep the exultation from my voice, modulating it with some difficultly to its usual softness, I ask him solicitously, 'You've not had the chicken, the fish... try it...'

He just shakes his head, not even saying anything. He still keeps looking out of the window, though.

Oh yes, I know how this evening will end for him, all right. But I look around, satisfied that none of that knowledge is showing on my face. Ma looks at me, and says, 'You haven't eaten a thing, have you Bowari? As usual. Well, you can, now. We are done.'

I nod, and put the last of the food on my plate. They don't wait for me as I eat. Ma, Deuta, Bablu ... they push back their chairs and go to wash their hands. Only he waits, silent still, for me to finish. He always was a courteous man, at least in some respects. In the superficial things.

I know this irks him, the fact that I eat after everybody else has finished. But there's nothing he can do about it. One can battle injustice, evil, badness. But how can one battle a sense of duty, and just plain *goodness?*

We sit in silence as I finish my meal. I am a leisurely eater at the best of times. Today, I delight in prolonging the meal, taking a sip of water between almost every mouthful to spin it out. Finally, after I finish the last spoonful of payox, I am done.

I still have work to do in the kitchen. By the time that is finished, he has gone to his place. I go to what I still call in my mind 'our room', and get ready for bed.

~

Of course it is not our room any more. It hasn't been for many years now. I sleep alone in this vast bed that was part of my dowry. He has already gone to the room above this one. That is his room. He is after all a famous writer, and he needs his space, his privacy. It is full of books and papers and dictionaries and files and a computer. I have hardly ever been there. Even in the early years, even before that single bed was put into the room, I was not welcome there. For many years now, I have not entered that place. I don't even want to, any more.

But then I can see what's happening there, above my head, can't I? Why do I need to go up there when I can see it all? I hear his steps pacing up and down. This is one of those old half-timbered houses, the ones that are called 'Assam Type'. The floors are made of wood, too. Sounds are magnified. And after all these nights alone, after all these years of anguish and humiliation, listening to him in the room above me, I have learnt to read the meaning of every sound that seeps down to me. True, I cannot see. But I can hear, and I can intuit.

He would be astonished to know how I can read the sound of his steps. It is a language that he is unaware he is 'speaking'. Tonight, there is that debate within him as he moves restlessly around.

God. I can't stand it anymore. Shall I call her? What's the point? I want her, not some mechanical amplification of her voice. Her warmth, her softness, her arching body against mine… her whispers, the fragrance of her.

It's foggy outside. And cold. It's December, after all. Not safe to make that trip. So many accidents happen, one reads about them all the time. And then… we had decided to break it off. We had decided it wasn't fair on her, on me, on the family, to continue meeting like this. I had told her I was setting her free… she could meet and mingle and eventually maybe even settle down with somebody. She wants children. And some cloak of legitimacy to give them. Understandable… and that's not something I'll be able to give them, will I?

But. God, this agony. If I call her, maybe the sound of her voice itself will be enough to see me through this night. Or maybe not. It'll just be one more knife…

Oh yes, I can hear his thoughts just as clearly as though he has spoken them out. It's as though I am inside his head.

The pacing stops. He's sitting down on that large chair now. Yes, I can hear him reach out to the cigarettes on the table. The sound of the match striking the box. I can feel him drag on the stick, feel the smoke burning down to the gut. There is momentary relief in this nicotine rush. I see the tremor in his fingers quieten; the turmoil in his mind begins to coil down to a quiescence.

No, not tonight. Not ever again. Not through these pounding miles upon miles of hilly road. I have made that journey enough times, God knows, but I have never got a sense of its distance. It has always been in the dark, with the lights of the Scorpio tunnelling a path through the darkness. All I have been able to feel during those journeys has been the pounding in my head. Thoughts, the will, everything is stilled when I make that journey. I am on auto-pilot. It's a totally bodily thing. My whole body is concentrated just getting there, getting the Scorpio to its destination.

There are deep forests on both sides of the road. Oh yes I know that. Wild animals roam the road on which no traffic ventures at that hour. I have seen elephants there, as the herds cross at the elephant corridor halfway up the hill. It climbs higher and higher, the road, getting narrower and narrower, but I have never given the dangers of the road a thought. And there are guns too in those jungles, guns that bristle and threaten to bring down the unwary traveller journeying alone, that too on this deep moonless night.

No, never again, though. I have Bablu to think of. And his mother. It's not her fault, this thing of mine. What is it, what can I call this wild, untameable, un-thing that takes over every pore of mine on nights such as this? And then takes me to her, as she lies, waiting, knowing I am at the last bend of the road now? She hears the car, sees the headlamps through the curtains of her hillside home.

The deep forest behind the cottage is dark and silent when she opens the door. The old woman who lives with her has melted away to some discreet place, leaving the house for her and for me. I see her framed against the light each time, her shape perfect, her eyes gleaming with the passion they see reflected in mine.

There are never words spoken at that time between us. In spite of the long drive, I can never wait.

And then, later, the journey back home, at dawn. I go down the hill road much more quietly than I came up, each time. The sun rises to my right as I get back to the valley. Its serenity is a reflection of the peace that is finally in my limbs, my soul. A peace that will last for a few days, a few weeks, before the restlessness takes over again, and then I have to make the journey once more.

But no, that's all over. No more. Not again. We owe that to ourselves, to the people around us.

Oh yes, I know exactly what he's thinking. I can visualize everything. She is usually in her nightclothes when she opens the door, diaphanous stuff, deep cut and short, that is nothing like what I wear to bed. But then I am a wife. I live in a joint family. I am Annapurna, the keeper of the granary, the bhoral of plenty of this house. I do not need to cajole with silken skin and hair like the monsoon clouds that rest on the mountain tops behind her house. She still needs to entice and tempt with virginal breasts, rose-tipped. My nourishing mammaries are ample, my childbearing hips and strong thighs wide and comfort-giving. She, on the other hand, needs slimness to draw him to her. Her power against mine, mine against hers.

I give him fifteen minutes, thirty at the most, before he gives in.

As I wait for the effects of the nicotine rush to die down, I begin to think of the time it started. Not that our marriage was anything as passionate as this other relationship, ever. Can desire and a need that cannot be denied pound through a man's veins in the same way if the woman before him sits demurely draped in domesticity? Can lust become a madness that sinks every sane thought in the mind, can it become an all-consuming thirst that rages through every cell, not to be denied, if the woman sits there with sendur in her hair, legitimately his, to be taken right then, if he so wishes? Can, indeed, a woman chosen by parents and family ever be an object of lust in the same way a woman forbidden to him, a woman with silken hill skin and monsoon hair? No. Of course she cannot.

Still, there was a liking, if not lust. There was kindness, and compassion, if not a wild hunger. There was a recognition of the importance of domestic concerns. Bablu was born. He was—is—a considerate man in every other way, and he saw to it that I got every care, that every material need of mine was fulfilled.

Maybe it would have continued like this, calm and tranquil, content and even happy, for ever. There would perhaps have been little patches of time when either one of us would wonder if this was all, if this was what poets wrote about, and singers described, when they talked of love. Where, then, was the melody of the deep-throated veena that throbbed with passion on full-moon nights? Where were the heights of ecstasy that the poet described so convincingly in his sonnets? But then, once more we would be caught up in domestic concerns, and the momentary discontent would vanish. Building a house, making a home, getting on with our lives, seeing Bablu through school and college, keeping Ma and Deuta happy and comfortable ... these would be the multiple axes around which our lives would revolve. There would be respect between us, a mutual affection, and perhaps even caringness. But no fire. Oh no. Not even, gradually, a spark.

But then he is a writer. A poet. A different breed it seems, from the rest of us uncreative humanity. Oh yes, I say this with irony, with bitterness even. Oh yes, I know all about how poets and writers are supposed to be seers. The show the rest of us the way to the future, they light up the path ahead. And so, then, is that the reason we give them this license? 'Ah, he's a poet. He is different.'

And so, then, if he is different, what about this person, this Annapurna at home?

At first, though, I was not Annapurna. At first, indeed, I did not even suspect. Where did he meet her, this hill maiden with the moonlight skin and the monsoon hair? I do not know, and it is not even important. He would sometimes, in any case, go away for days at a time, in those years. Before he met her, he would always tell me where he was going, and why.

'I'll be at that Rest House right inside the Reserved Forest. I have to finish that novella for the Puja Special, you know. University is closed now, but if I'm here there will be so many other demands on my time, I won't be able to concentrate on finishing it. Don't tell anybody where I am. If you need me, I can be reached at this number. You'll take care, won't you?'

I was proud, in those days, to be his accomplice. I was the person who guarded the flame of his creativity, protected it from the baser demands of quotidian life. Even his colleagues from the university where he worked, even, indeed, his parents, were not privy to that knowledge. I felt proud.

So proud, indeed, that I was not even aware when my power waned, and hers began to wax. Like the moon's pull on the water, she drew him to her. He started to spend his nights in the study. In the beginning I thought nothing of it, for he often worked late there while I slept. The day the single bed was taken to the room, though, I knew that it was over. Oh, not legally. But certainly, emotionally.

~

I remember very clearly the night these journeys started. I was not yet able to get into the room, and into his mind then. He had just come back that very day from an absence of seven days. 'Finishing a novel', he had muttered as he had packed before leaving a week ago. But it hadn't been like before, and he had not been able to look me in the eye as he had said it.

He had not told me where he was going. Seven days during which I did not know where he was. He had neglected to tell me that. Or was it deliberate? In any case, I did not ask. Why should I? Let him tell me of his own free will. Otherwise ... And I would certainly never let him see how it was affecting me. No, never.

He had arrived in the evening. I had looked at him, making sure that he didn't realize I was doing that. I saw to it that he got all the comforts as usual. Hot snacks on his return, ginger chai, fresh towels in the bathroom, the geyser turned on so that he wouldn't have to wait for his shower after his dusty drive. I was just beginning, at that time, to morph into Annapurna.

A few hours later, after dinner, I woke up to the sound of the Scorpio. I went to the window, in time to see the taillights move down the driveway and out of the gate, into the night. I rushed into the study. Of course he wasn't there. I didn't bother to look around the other rooms. Yes, he had gone, through the misty darkness. Did he miss her so much then, this woman whom I was now sure had been with him over the last seven nights?

Did he want to smell the fragrance of her, taste the sweetness of her so much, that he could not even wait till daybreak before rushing off like that?

I hadn't slept at all that night. I had lain awake, straining at the darkness outside. Just before dawn, as the first rosy streaks began to give a hint of its coming in the east, I began to see him. A small house, a cottage, in front of a bank of tall, dark trees. There was a little stream between the cottage and the trees. And inside, too, I saw, that night, for the first time. The girl, with her slanted eyes and high cheekboned, perfectly oval face, her moonlight skin and monsoon hair. And he, looking at her with sated eyes as he got ready to leave. To come back to me, waiting here, like some demanding domestic monster, a female Bakasura who must be appeased.

When he returned a few hours later, I was ready. I had thought it all through. Well, not thought, not really, not like that. I am not so much a brain person as I am an instinctive one. I feel, rather than think things through. I intuit. It was my instincts that told me how best I should go about it, so that I could survive. Not simply survive, no, that's not really the word. But live with dignity. And triumph over him.

I take care never to come face-to-face with him when he returns from these mad journeys. I don't want to see that look in his eyes, the look that speaks of how he had her right there on the living-room floor as soon as he reached her house, and then again, later, before returning, on her bed. I make sure to stay out of his way for the day. It's not difficult. He's always inside his study at that time. He doesn't sleep though. Well, not much. I see him sitting at his table, writing, reflecting, sometimes even smiling. Mostly he's writing though.

In the beginning, I used to wonder: does he need her to fuel his art? Is this passion, this wild abandon, something that has to happen before he can set down the songs of his heart onto paper? It's true that as his involvement with the mountain girl grew stronger, his fame as a writer grew greater. People heaped praises on him. He was invited to lit. fests, to conferences, where he was lauded and feted. Garlands were heaped around his neck, ceremonial scarves were placed with honour on his shoulders.

People said, 'He knows the language of the heart!' 'He is the poet of the modern love story!' They exclaimed, 'What an understanding of passion he has!' They looked at me with admiration and envy, as the undeniable muse of those poems. I would smile, Annapurna-like, and say nothing. And Annapurna, the persona, became mine. She was—is—my salvation.

I became so perfect a domestic goddess that I became Annapurna herself. As he grew more and more distant, more and more famous as a writer, and his journeys to the mountains grew more desperate, I too nurtured perfection in the domestic sphere. My home began to run on the axis that was me. Everything spun around me. Without me, it was obvious that things would grind to a standstill. Oh, of course, it was his salary from the university that kept the home fires burning. But it was I who saw to it that he got his ginger chai at his elbow just as he emerged from the haze of writing yet another poem about his mountain beauty. It was I who saw to it that his clothes befitted his stature now, as one of the country's leading poets. Eri silk kurtas in cream, teamed with a muga seleng bordered with deep maroon floral patterns. Or a paat silk kurta with tiny black butis along the front, and a Bodo scarf to match it. I did it all unobtrusively, shopping for them in his size, and getting the maids to place the packets on the single bed in his study.

As Annapurna, I was satisfied that he wore them and was photographed in them. So what if it was not me of whom he asked, 'How do I look, sweetheart' as he turned this way and that? Let her tell him he looks good. It's I, after all, who make him look good. That is enough, more than enough, for me.

People come and look with envy around the perfectly appointed house, at the contentment on my parents-in-law's faces. I am praised by them, compliments are showered on me.

'You are looking well, Aita,' says Sheila, the neighbour whom everybody avoids because of her poison tongue, as she looks at Ma. But with me she is all sugar and honey. Why not? After all it's my freshly baked brownies she's munching with her Darjeeling tea, brought to her in the single-cup pot.

'It's all Bowari's doing,' beams Ma. I am used to getting these kinds of compliments, right in my face, these days. Of course, what she says is true. I take care of them in ways that few would be able to. Medicines on time, check-ups at the appointed hours, meals with all their favourite foods on the dot. The car ready for them when they want to go somewhere. Their relatives and friends made much of when they visit. Their daughters welcomed warmly, and laden with gifts when they leave again for their marital homes. When Deuta fell and broke his hip, it was I who single-handedly nursed him back to health. It was I who held him as he hobbled around on his walker. When Ma's asthma grows troublesome, it is I who bring her the nebulizer, and wait up with her till she breathes easier.

No wonder they tell their daughters, in my hearing, 'Bowari is a saint. A saint, I am telling you. It's because of her that we are alive, and well ... All this comfort in our old age must be the result of some good deed of ours in our previous life ...'

It's all simple enough, really. Not rocket science. People are so easy to please, actually. A few minutes of study about what their buttons are, and there we are. I can have them eating out of my hands.

Inside the house, I am Annapurna. I am she around whom this world revolves. As my power grows here, he moves more and more into himself. His own parents, his son, are closer to me than to him. It has taken me three years, but I have achieved what I set out to do.

~

Today, when I hear you start the Scorpio and rush up the mountain, I can smile. Yes, go on, go up. But in the end, it is I who holds the reins of your life. You pelt up the mountain, desperation in every cell of your body. But in the end, you will have to come back. Because I am Annapurna, a goddess and a saint. Who can belittle a goddess, who can battle against a saint? Nobody. Certainly not you.

It's easy enough to catch a man, I want to tell the girl with the moonlight skin and monsoon hair. Not difficult at all, if you set your mind to it. What is difficult is to sustain the passion, keep the relationship going. Your body will be ravaged, oh yes it will, by that beast, Time. Your wiles, your enticements, will stale. You will become familiar, commonplace, ordinary. Your quickening breath will fail to excite, the circle of your arms will constrict.

No, I don't hate you, not at all. Why should I? I see the end drawing near for you, my little sister. And then, as I had always known I would, I, Annapurna, will win.

A Long Drive

SHE NEEDED A DRINK OF WATER. THE SUN WAS HOT IN THE skies. She had forgotten to factor in that it was already late February. And of course she had forgotten to bring a bottle of water. Perhaps, she thought, looking out through the tinted glasses of the hired car, they would pass a shop in one of the little townlets that they were crossing. Each one stocked bottled water these days. Bisleri? Whatever. Some would be fake. But she needed that water. The dryness of the late winter was getting to her, even though she was inside a car.

She looked at the backpack beside her. It sat there like an extra passenger between her and the man. A sentinel. A chaperone between them. He had wanted to keep it in the front seat, but she had been the one who had insisted, 'No no keep it here. There's enough space, isn't there? Besides, it has your camera, you said. You might want it. The view of the river from the bridge is quite spectacular.'

She wondered if it had bottled water. It probably did. He was an NRI. A Non Resident Indian who did not trust the hygiene or purity of the bottles available at roadside shops and dhabas. An NRI who would make sure, even in the home of his parents which he had left ten, twelve years ago, that the water was 'safe'. Probably he would even rinse his plate with bottled water before sitting down to pick delicately at the food placed before him. She knew a man who had done that once at a dinner at her parents' house. Her parents had been mortified, but they had taken it in their stride. It was something that NRIs did, especially those who came in from some Western 'advanced' country. Their immune system, nurtured painstakingly over the years by the germs and filth of their own country, had become delicate in those sterile environments. Yes, her parents had accepted what the man had done, and had even invited him several other times to their home. Not she, though. The anger and humiliation she had felt had not gone away. She had made it a point not to be present when he had come to their home again.

Yes, of course he would have a bottle. It wasn't in any of the side pouches though. Would he keep it inside the backpack, along with his expensive camera then? Probably not. In any case, she would not ask him. For some reason that she would not analyze or understand, she felt it would be being unnecessarily submissive to him, to his perceived 'superior' NRI ways, if she asked him if he had remembered to carry a bottle of water. No, she would just buy one on the way.

They had been introduced to each other by her friend Mimli, at that party. Mimli, her friend from way back, Mimli, now married to the richest man in town. So rich that he had been touched several times for 'donations', she had heard, by people who lived by the gun. In their town, that was the yardstick of wealth—being touched by gun-toting youths for money. Mimli had happily left her schoolteacher's job, and become a lady of leisure. From their college days itself, Mimli had wanted to be what they called, in those days, 'the hostess with the mostest', and now in their city, she was definitely that. She put all her energy, all her talents, into these 'events', as she liked to call them, while her husband looked indulgently on, feeling, no doubt, that he was getting good value for the money she spent on these gatherings.

Mimli liked to 'pair' people. A single man or woman sitting without an 'opposite number' at any of her parties was anathema to her. If she knew that a single man—even one who was temporarily single because his girlfriend or wife could not make it that day—was going to be there, she made sure that there was a single woman, too, to 'partner' him. She liked things to be neat. Joba was single, too, so it was a double bonus that she could get her friend to come and add symmetry as well as interest to the gathering.

'Deepak,' Mimli had told her on the phone. 'He's here from that state up there... what's it, Wisconsin? Minnesota? Whatever. You'll like him.'

'I will?' Joba had asked.

Mimli had known what that dry tone had implied. 'No no, he's not typical at all. Not that "Hey, I am now of a higher caste than any of you because I live outside the country" type. And yes, of course, it's nice that you will make up the sixth woman. How odd it would be if there were six men and five women. You know I have a kind of OCD about that.'

And because Mimli was her best friend, and good fun as well, and because she had nothing much to do after work on that Saturday anyway, she had gone to the party that evening. Deepak was duly introduced to her. She had expected somebody florid, tending to plumpness, a somewhat large person. But Deepak was not large, not tall, not pink-cheeked. He was mild-mannered, too, and never once used the words 'back home' that evening, at least not within her earshot. And though she watched him, hawk-eyed, as he took his plate from the sideboard to help himself to the buffet laid out on the terrace, he did not, to the best of her knowledge, rinse it with bottled water.

He had come the day after the next to the bank. She had been surprised, and, for a few seconds, disoriented. It was Monday morning, and a mad rush as usual. She had quite forgotten Mimli's party, and its guests. He must have seen the blankness in her look, or rather, the professionalism— the 'How may I help you' look she reserved for customers. Though after her promotions, her job did not really let her meet too many customers these days.

'Deepak', he said. 'Deepak Barua. We met at Mimli's party...'

She was immediately embarrassed, but tried not to show it. 'Of course, of course, certainly I remember,' she gushed, over-compensatingly.

'I asked for you ... the girl at the front desk showed the way to your cubicle.'

'Yes ... do sit down. Tea?' What could he want, she wondered. Why was he here?

It was soon made clear. 'You did mention that you worked here, and your bank deals in foreign exchange. I need to change some dollars ...'

'Of course ...' She busied herself, doing what was necessary. Forms, signatures, ID proofs. Passports. She noticed his date of birth. He was forty-two. Four years older than her. He looked older than that. She had thought him to be in his mid-forties, maybe because there was something, an air of sadness about him, which made him look older than he was.

'How much? I mean, how much do you wish to exchange? And how would you like it, what denominations ... ?'

He looked thoughtful. 'I'm not too sure. I need a large-ish amount because Ma is in hospital, due to be released tomorrow. But I don't really know how much ...'

She rearranged her thoughts. 'Oh, I'm so sorry to hear that,' she said. 'Hope she is better?'

'It was an operation. Yes, she's going to be okay.' He hesitated, then said, 'Maybe three thousand dollars? Around two lakh rupees? That should cover it, I suppose…'

'You can always come back to me if you need more… here's my card. Give me a call, and I'll handle it for you if you need anything in this department.'

She didn't make small talk, nor did he expect her to, it seemed. She went out to the main door with him to see him off, because after all he was Mimli's friend. But her smile was professional. He lingered for a few seconds on the steps. Rameswar was standing nearby with his gun, looking harmless to her eyes. But not to Deepak's, apparently, because he said, 'So much security. It's necessary, I guess.'

'Oh yes,' she said, remembering the heists and the demands and the extortion notes that were so much a part of life here. 'You must have heard about it all. We do need some protection from those extortionists.'

He nodded, and looked around. All right, he hadn't yet complained of the dust and the 'dirry' drains and overflowing dustbins of her city, so in her estimation that placed him a couple of notches above the usual NRIs she met. Suddenly she felt protective. These NRIs were so naïve, so innocent. They were unused to the complicated lives that people led here, especially now with all this violence around. She eyed his briefcase, and asked, 'How are you going back? With all that money, cash, in your bag…'

'No, I have a car, it's all right,' he said, turning around to look at her. He was standing two steps below her, and his eyes were level with hers. They looked faintly amused, as though he knew exactly what she was thinking. He turned away again, and said, 'Thank you so much for this. I appreciate it.'

'It's my job…' she shrugged.

'But you made it much easier, no waiting around, sitting in comfort and sipping that excellent Assam tea.' He smiled and said, 'Let me buy you a coffee? As a token of appreciation?'

She laughed. 'I'm on duty. And it's not really safe to move around coffee shops with your bag bulging with cash.'

'No I meant later,' he said, smiling. 'After work. Well, dinner would be better really. I've heard so much about that new Asomiya restaurant, I've been wanting to try it out…'

There was something disarming about the way he said it, something that was much milder than the usual invitations from men. It was open-ended, and didn't convey the idea that she was committing to something much larger by agreeing to be bought some dinner.

At the restaurant that evening, he didn't ask her about her home and family, but listened to what she had to say about her job with interest.

'Such a difference from the banks I remember of the time when I left the country. The private banks were just coming in, we were stuck with the nationalized ones.'

'Ours is one of the largest private banks in the country,' she said proudly. She loved her job. It had been one of the main anchors in her life after… Her mind shied away from the thought and the memories, quickly.

And it was pleasant. He had loved the bilahi pitika, the roasted, mashed and herbed tomatoes, and of course the various kinds of fish, cooked in an assortment of ways. With sesame, or simply roasted on bamboo slivers, or with mustard. She had asked about his mother, who lived with his sister nearby. Independent and happy. But she'd had to have a knee replacement surgery, because her arthritis was acting up. She had refused, at first, any financial help, because after all, his father had left her well provided for, and she got the government family pension every month anyway. But he had insisted.

'It's the least I can do, isn't it?' he asked, his gaze outside, away from Joba's. 'Money. It's a poor compensation for absence, especially when it's not needed. Still, that's all I can do, really.' But she saw the look in his eyes, and was, suddenly, moved.

Of course she had asked Mimli about him after he had left that bank that day. 'Tell me about Deepak, is it ok if I go to dinner with him? I mean I don't want to, if he's married or engaged or something, even though it's only dinner. Still…'

'Divorced. He's divorced, Joba. Unattached, if that's what you're asking.'

'Yes, it is. Not that I foresee any attachment down the line, you understand. But I don't want added complications. A dragon-wife breathing fire at me, when I hardly know the guy. But he's nice. Good to have as a friend. He's not been the typical NRI at all so far.'

Mimli had laughed, having heard Joba's tirades against the flocks of NRIs who had arrived, like migratory birds, every autumn, to leave again when the weather turned warmer. 'They think they're so much better than us, just listen to them, just see their body language…'

'You're prejudiced, Joba,' her friends had told her, gently mocking. 'You can't generalize. Of course some are like that, there's no denying it. But not all…' But Joba had been unconvinced.

'Good,' Mimli had agreed. 'Yes, he's a wonderful person, Deepak. And a friend is always nice, isn't it?'

'You must let me take you out,' Joba said now, watching him pay the bill. She stopped herself from adding, 'in return.' He was fumbling with currency notes that had become unfamiliar to him by now. And this shop did not accept credit cards. She quelled her bankerly urge to take over the monetary transaction, and urged, instead, 'Dinner, somewhere ...'

In the end, they had decided on this. They had agreed, both of them, mutually, to go out together, for the day. He had heard about the many dhabas and resorts that had come up on the other side of the river, but had found nobody to go with. Everybody was so busy. And so, this February Sunday, here they were, in the hired car, two almost-strangers, out for the day.

Now that they were out of the city, everything looked green. Unbelievably so. And so many shades of it. She tried to codify them as they passed the trees and shrubs bursting with fresh spring greenery. The older leaves on the large-leaved trees were emerald green. The undergrowth was moss green. Banana plants grew wild, their leaves, what else, banana-leaf green. She smiled, then became conscious of the fact that she was not alone. Quickly, she looked sidelong at him. But he was looking out of his window, his gaze riveted to the scenery outside. They were inside one of those sudden patches of deep forest that occurred unexpectedly all around them. The light on his face was a cool green tint. There was a smell of growing things, of something that was life-giving.

'How green it is here,' he said, almost to himself. 'I had forgotten. It's a defining feature of our land, isn't it? *Xeuji xeuji*

xeuji O, xeuji dhoroni dhuniya,' he said, quoting the poet. '*Green, green, how beautiful is this green earth...*' He turned to look at her, half-smiling. But she noticed, again, his eyes. Once more, she was moved.

Why had he left his home, then, if he loved it so much? Or was it just a case of distance lending enchantment? She would have asked him, but he interrupted her: 'Rontu, Rontu, stop! Please! Daab! They are selling daab... I'm parched. Aren't you?' he asked Joba, turning to her, the sadness in his eyes now replaced by a childish excitement.

They chose their tender coconuts from the pile beside the vendor, then watched him as he sliced off the tops expertly, inserted a straw and handed them over. The water inside was cool, sweet, tinged with that slight salinity that refreshed. She smiled as she watched Deepak's excitement, the way he took pictures on his cellphone, as the vendor went through the familiar ritual. Time and distance had made these things unfamiliar to him. She found it endearing, and was surprised at herself for her reaction.

'It's the best thirst quencher, isn't it?' Deepak asked, in between sucking at the pink-and-white striped straw. 'I wouldn't mind another. What about you?' She nodded. 'Rontu, one more for you?' Rontu, the hired driver of their rented car, nodded and came up to where they were standing. Without comment, he drank up.

The vendor sliced open the nuts after they had finished and fashioned scoops out of the sliced tops so that they could eat the soft, slippery flesh, too. It was filling, cool and quite amazingly tasty.

She watched, a little uneasy, as Deepak took out his wallet to pay. It was plump, full of notes and cards. He was still living, she thought, in the land that the poet had described. *Green, green, how beautiful…* Nobody showed full wallets in strange places these days. It was too dangerous. Everybody had cellphones, who knew who was watching? They would tell some of their friends up ahead, and then there would be holdups, demands, all kinds of things. They would be divested of whatever cash and valuables they had. But he, living outside this country, would not know. She made up her mind to tell him about being careful. Later, when they were alone, with no third pair of ears listening.

They had planned it so that they could lunch at the Red River Resort. It was just a little past one when they reached the picturesque collection of bamboo huts on the low rise above the vastness of the river. They ordered their food.

'If you order the khorika, it will take a little time,' said the thin boy with ears that stuck out from his skull. He looked efficient, as he wrote down their order. There was an innocence in his eyes that Joba rarely saw in boys his age in the city.

She looked at Deepak, 'The skewered fish, barbecued on live coals is nice. You should have it. Hope it's worth the wait.'

He replied, 'It's fine by me…'

'It's ok, we can wait,' she told the boy.

They waited for their beers to arrive, then wandered down to the edge of the compound, tankards in their hands. There were benches here from which they could look down at the river below. Sandbanks dotted its blue expanse. It was edged on both sides with white sand. It looked quiescent, a peaceful blue expanse of water, stretching harmlessly from the eastern horizon to the west. The chugging boats on it looked like mosquitoes from this distance.

'How peaceful it is here...' he said, his voice soft. The sound of the kuli, bird of spring, calling out behind them only accentuated the quiet.

'In July, August, this river bursts its banks. Eats away the shores, gobbles up villages, towns, people, animals. This peace is deceptive, you know.' She looked at him, aware that her mind was going into its familiar churn again. She had thought she had put it away, at least for this day trip. She closed her eyes, and willed those images of burning vehicles, screaming people, charred bodies, to go back into their cage in her mind. She breathed deeply, as she had been taught to, by the counsellor.

He didn't seem to have noticed her momentary discomfort, or the way she had been on the verge of hyperventilating again. He had taken out his camera, a complicated-looking gadget, and was fixing lenses and things onto it. Soon, Deepak was busy clicking the river, their surroundings, the flowers around them and the collection of little huts behind.

He looked at the hibiscus shrub a little distance away. 'There's your namesake,' he said, looking at her and smiling. He took a sip of his beer and focussed on the red flowers. 'Joba. The goddess loves them, doesn't she? Kamakhya, Ma Kali, Ma Durga...'

She was surprised. 'You remember,' she said, her voice a statement, not a question.

He didn't reply, but concentrated on taking pictures.

Suddenly, she wanted to know more about him. His town, his work. His divorce. His life there, in the US. Was he lonely, living wifeless? Or did he have somebody else in his life now? She was about to ask, 'Tell me about your life in that other country.' It was on the tip of her tongue. But she bit it off, quickly, before it could be uttered. Because then she would have to reciprocate. He would ask her, perhaps out of nothing else but simple politeness, 'Tell me about your late husband.' Because he must know that she was a widow. Because surely Mimli had told him about her. Perhaps he had asked his mother, his sister, about this woman he was going to spend the day with. And of course everybody in her city knew about it. A sudden widow, three years ago, at the age of thirty-five. After all, theirs was in many ways, in spite of its rapid growth, a small town. Everybody knew everybody else, or rather, about everybody else.

No, she wouldn't ask him. She wouldn't risk having to reply to his reciprocal questions.

He got up and went to the hibiscus bush. The ground below it was scattered with some of the bright red flowers, still fresh. He picked up one, and brought it to her. Without a word, he held it out, smiling.

Surprise made her laugh out loud. She took the flower and looked at its grooved petals, its large pistil and stamens, and realized that she was holding this flower after a very long time.

'Joba,' he said, though it was unclear to her whether he was referring to her, or the flower. 'What a pretty name.'

Suddenly, she felt a loosening of the bands that always, these days, constricted her chest. 'It's also called Shoeflower, you know,' she said, laughing. 'Better to be Joba, for the flower and also for me, than being called by that name, no?'

She put the flower behind her ear, and gave exaggerated poses as he clicked her from various angles. They laughed together as they looked at the pictures that he showed her, bringing the camera closer, sitting beside her on the bench. She was beginning to feel that she had known him for a while, that he was a friend from at least a decade ago, if not exactly her childhood. It was the laughter, she supposed.

'In school, we were taught dissection on this, in our botany classes. Plant dissection. Shoeflower. We actually polished our shoes with it. Or tried to. Let's see now…' He picked up another red flower from the ground. But he was wearing sneakers and so was she.

'Try it on my bag,' she offered. 'It's leather.' He took it and began to rub the flower on the maroon surface of the bag. Nothing much happened, except that the flower got crushed, and the bag had damp stains.

'Oh sorry, I hope those stains go…' he said contritely. 'Here, use my handkerchief.'

He was nice, she thought, rubbing the bag with it. The dampness vanished. 'Maybe it's looking a little shinier,' she said, doubtfully.

'Let's try my wallet,' he said, pulling it out from his pocket.

She remembered.

'I meant to tell you…you know, you must be careful with your wallet.' He paused in his rubbing, and looked at her. He knew there would be more to come. 'In front of strangers, don't take out a wallet as full as that. Like you did at that daab seller's. Times, they are not good. There is greed everywhere. And everybody has a cellphone, of course.'

He looked at her. There was sadness in his eyes. 'Ah. It's come to that, has it, in this land,' he said, softly.

She nodded. Once more, the images threatened to come out of their cage. But she looked steadfastly at him as she said, 'Yes. And worse. What we do usually is keep a small amount in a purse or wallet, and take that out. The rest we keep in another place in our bags, in another wallet.'

He looked at her, about to say something. But before he could do so, the boy who had taken their orders came down to them. 'More beer, saar?' he asked.

'How much longer for the lunch?' she asked.

'Almost ready, Baideo...just a little while more...yes, I'll bring some more beer, and maybe some snacks if you wish.'

They walked around the place, gradually becoming at ease. But their talk skirted the personal. They kept it light. The time passed pleasantly. It was cooler here than in the city, with the fresh breeze blowing in from the river below. The sun on their faces was softer, too.

Lunch was later than they had thought it would be. Dusk came early in this eastern part of the country, and this was just past winter, when the sun became a sinking red ball at five. But the food was delicious.

'Worth the wait, I think,' said Deepak, smiling. He certainly seemed to relish the khorika. She was glad.

It was almost dusk by the time they finished. The post-lunch coffee, too, had been late in arriving. There had been a few other guests around, but now they were alone in their little bamboo hut. The breeze was much cooler, and Joba took out the pullover from her bag. Deepak didn't seem to need one. She remembered that he had come from a much colder climate. Talking to him hadn't been like her idea of talking to an NRI at all. How prejudiced she had been, based on her experiences with just a few people.

Deepak paid for their three lunches—Rontu had had his inside, in the dining hall. They started on the journey back, talking much more animatedly now than they had while coming out. Without saying anything, he put his bag in the front seat. Joba noticed, but said nothing.

Now that it was darkening, the road by which they had come was much more deserted. A small scattering of people were on it; most seeming to be hurrying. The villages that they passed were dark and not nearly as friendly looking as they had seemed while coming out. Joba shivered. She drew her sweater close, but it wasn't only the chill that was bothering her.

She remembered the deep forest that they had passed on their way out. It would be pitch dark there. She wished Rontu was not quite so taciturn. He had barely spoken to them the entire journey. She often hired cars for the day, for work, and the drivers were invariably friendly and ready to talk, garrulous even. This one was different. It made her uneasy.

They passed the place where they'd had the daab in the morning. There was nobody there, no sign that four or five people had been at that spot, selling the green coconuts. Even the heap of green husks had been cleared away.

Behind them, to the east, the moon rose, silvering the path ahead. She was a little relieved. But in no time, they were within the darkness of the sudden forest that she remembered. She resisted the urge to tell Rontu to speed up and dash past that dark patch. There was something ominous about it. She tried to relax. She realized she was being a bad companion. Deepak had talked off and on, but he seemed to have caught on that something that was not quite right with her. This bit, she knew, would last about twenty minutes. Fifteen, if they sped up. With an effort, she spoke again, 'This bit is somewhat... spooky... isn't it?' Her voice sounded edgy. She tried to keep the memories within their cage. But they were straining at the gates, baring their fangs, slobbering at her.

Oh God. When would this end?

In the darkness, she realized that he had turned to look at her. Gently, he put his hand on her shoulder. In a quiet voice, he said, 'It's all right. Just a little bit more, then we'll be out in the open again. In the moonlight. That will be nice, won't it?'

That was all he said, but something about his tone, his eyes, told her that he knew. Well, of course he would, once he'd been told about her husband, Borun. That bomb blast three years ago on a busy flyover in the heart of their city had caught the attention of the world. There had been deaths, people had been maimed. Many had lost limbs, putting an end to any hope of a normal life later. Little children had been orphaned. Parents had lost their children. She was not the only one who had been widowed in that instant.

Borun had just parked his car at the side of the road, and had been about to get out, when the blast had flung him many metres away. His body had been charred, his clothes had caught fire. Death, they said, had been instantaneous—he had been dead before his body hit the ground.

If Borun had left home a few minutes earlier, or if she had been able to keep him at home for a few minutes more, he would be alive today. If she had insisted that he have another cup of coffee before going to work, he would be alive today. Who had died, who had been maimed, who had escaped by a whisker—it was all totally random. And she, she had been picked for widowhood at thirty-five, totally randomly.

Within a week, she had miscarried. The doctors had done all they could, but her body had just not been able to carry on. For three months, she had carried Borun's child in her womb. And now that he was gone, he had taken the child along with him.

Yes, he would know about her. Her back story, as they said. She looked towards him, his face lit up occasionally by the faint glow from the dashboard. She became aware that tears were streaming down her face. But there was nothing she could say, not even 'I'm sorry for being such a bad companion. This was supposed to be a fun outing.'

He kept his hand on hers, even when they emerged out into the moonlight-silvered road outside. It was comforting. A good touch, gentle. There was humanity in his touch, kindness and empathy. Fellow feeling. She was grateful.

She realized, gradually, that the car was slowing down. She was aware, also, of Deepak's awareness of that same fact. His hand tightened on hers.

The road ahead curved to the left, along a dark hill. The silver thread ahead was darkened by its shadow. She could not see beyond, to where the road became invisible. But there was something, something that was not quite right. Her uneasiness grew. All of them who lived here in these valleys had had their senses honed by the innumerable tragedies that had fallen on them over the years, decades, of violence. While their conscious thoughts remained unaware, their subconscious caught indefinable signals that jangled alarms in their minds.

And then, suddenly, ahead of them, she saw it. A roadblock. In any case, the driver was slowing down. But he had been slowing down from a few minutes before, hadn't he? So he knew. And so, he was an informer. And those people in the resort where they had lunched. Had they, too, been part of it then? Delayed them, so that it would be dark and lonely on this stretch of road when they reached it?

She wanted to scream, but stifled the urge. She took away her hand, and brought it to her mouth. Deepak didn't say anything, but he sat up. He too was looking ahead.

'Block,' said the driver unnecessarily as the car stopped. His voice was edged with some emotion. Excitement, rather than nervousness.

Things happened very quickly after that. The two men who were standing near it left the barrier, and banged on the closed windows at the back. They had handkerchiefs tied across their faces. Only their eyes were visible above them. 'Don't ...' began Deepak, but Rontu had already pressed the button that rolled the windows down automatically. The guns in their hands glinted in the moonlight.

'Out,' said the man next to her. He opened the door from outside—the driver must have unlocked everything—and gestured that she should step out.

'No, wait,' she heard Deepak say behind her as she began to get out. 'Let her remain inside. It's me you want, I'm sure. I'm coming out.'

'Both of you. We want both of you, come out,' the man's voice was harsh.

They stood outside the car. She noticed the coolness outside. One of the men took the rucksack from the front seat and slung it across his own shoulder. He did not bother to look at the contents. The other one pointed the gun at Deepak and said, 'Your wallet. Watch. Quick.'

So this was going to be a robbery, plain and simple. Thank God. Relief came in timid little waves to Joba even as she responded to the other person's demand that she hand over her own bag to them. Not a kidnapping, like so many others across the land. No ideological battle with them as pawns. No extortions and demand notes. Just a simple law-and-order aberration.

The man was looking at Deepak's wallet with a glint in his eyes. With some difficulty because of its thickness, he pushed it into his own pocket. He gesticulated that Deepak should turn out his pockets. Silently, he did as he was told. There was nothing there.

'Cellphones.'

'Inside my knapsack,' said Deepak.

'In my bag,' echoed Joba. She hoped that they wouldn't ask her to turn out the pockets of her jeans. Not that there was anything there, except her handkerchief. Still. It would be a command that she would have to obey, and it would add to the feeling of helplessness that she was already drowning in.

'Er,' he said. His voice, she noticed, was still quite normal. 'I have some cards there, in my wallet. And a couple of photographs. Pictures. They will be of no use to you, even the cards. They don't work here. Can I have them back please?' He was speaking in the language of the land, Asomiya, without any NRI accent. 'And in her bag... she has some things... just take the money, and leave the rest behind, please?'

But they were not having any of it. It was as if he hadn't spoken at all. She remembered the cards, the cash in her own bag now. Keys. No pictures, nothing of that kind. But she realized that this was twice that he had spoken up for her already.

The men were already getting ready to leave. 'No going to the police,' they warned. 'There will be consequences if you do.'

Both men looked at the driver, still seated in the car. Joba thought she saw some message flash from the man beside her to the man behind the wheel. Was it her imagination? A trick of the moonlight? She didn't think so. The driver seemed very calm, in any case. But then so were they, the victims. A holdup, and she was not even screaming. Not that it would have helped, of course. There was no other soul within sight or earshot, no cars, no trucks even.

And then they were gone. Just like that, they melted into the shadows of the hill beside them. Their glinting guns, their flashing eyes merged with the darkness. Only the bamboo barricade remained.

Both of them were silent as they got into the car again. The driver went out and hauled the flimsy bamboo barricade aside. Perhaps he could have rushed into it, if he had wished, and broken through, and then speeded away to safety, thought Joba, dispassionately, watching him deal with the barricade so effortlessly now. As though he had done this many times before. But no, she thought immediately. She remembered the guns. It was better this way. Better the inconvenience of a robbery than a shootout.

'Are you all right?' he asked her, quietly, as they waited for the driver to get back.

She nodded, then realized he would not be able to see inside the shadowed car. 'Yes. Don't worry. I'm fine. And you ... ?'

'Yes.'

She remembered that the driver had a cellphone. But she saw no point in asking him for it. Who would she call? The police? Better to go home and then report it.

They began to move on again. And suddenly, without warning, as though some dam had burst, great waves of anger came rushing into her mind. Anger against the robbers, who had been so sure that they could get away with it. Anger against this driver, who was no doubt part of the gang. And anger against the perpetrators of that blast of three years ago, who had snuffed out so many lives so casually.

She looked at the back of the driver's head. Let him think he was secure. In this dark land where incidents like this were so commonplace, his confidence was not misplaced. But she would go home, go to the police, and make sure that he would be put behind bars. Yes, there would be consequences. Threats. Money would change hands. Bribes. But she was armed, too. Empowered by education, strengthened by grief, toughened by a need to redress.

'You are an unusual woman,' said the man beside her, quietly, as though he had read her mind.

She smiled. It felt good to do so. 'And you are an unusual NRI', she said, beginning to laugh.

He laughed back. 'I'm seeing this through,' he said, quietly again. 'I can delay my going back. No, I'm not going to run away. I want to see the end of this,' he said in English, lowering his voice even more, so that the driver would not hear.

She looked at him, still smiling.

Ahead, the road stretched out, silver-bright with possibility.

Author's Note

THIS COLLECTION OF THIRTEEN SHORT STORIES HAS HAD A very slow growth. Over the years, these stories were written in the intervals between my other works of fiction and while toiling over translation work. They came to me with an urgency that would not wait in the wings and made me set aside whatever work I was currently engaged in.

These stories were totally independent of whatever writing I was currently occupied with. Several of them were inspired by real-life incidents and characters, but they are not biography or history. They are, unquestionably, fiction. The characters and incidents that insisted on coming out onto the pages are from my imagination, though they have roots in real life in some way: a word heard here, an incident witnessed there, a riveting expression on a person's face, an observed relationship ... These have all been triggers, over the years, which led me to the stories.

Some of these have already appeared, in other avatars, in various journals. For this collection, though, they have all changed, some more than others. This was inevitable, because with the passage of time, my own perspective, my own understanding of human nature, has undergone alteration. Some of the stories have also been translated into other languages, including my own mother tongue, Assamese.

'A Full Night's Thievery', in its original version, appeared in the online journal *Northeast Review*. 'The Tabla Player', much shorter then, was published in *Pratibha India* and 'The Rings' won a prize in a short-story competition organized by *The Telegraph*, Kolkata. I was delighted to have the chance to meet Khushwant Singh, the judge, at the prize distribution ceremony in Delhi. 'The Reckoning' and 'Homecoming' have both appeared in the online journal, *Pratilipi*. 'The Journey' was published in the *South Asian Review*, while 'Spring Song' first appeared in *Indian Literature*. Each of these stories has been layered and reworked extensively for this collection, while the others are entirely new.

Without the encouragement of so many, these stories would not have seen the light of day. Though the lack of space prohibits my listing all, here are some of the people to whom I am indebted.

Thank you, firstly, Rupam, Rittique, Proma and Rona, for your steady support and unobtrusive care.

Preeti Gill, once my editor, is now also my close friend, confidante, agent and companion over many mountains of momos and oceans of fish tenga. Thank you Preeti for your faith in me over the years, and your patience in seeing things through.

Dhirendra Nath Bezboruah, retired Editor of *The Sentinel*, gave me the confidence to write years ago. Those middles that you encouraged me to put down just grew and grew till they became short fiction, some of which you published in your Sunday section. Thank you, Dhirenda, for giving me that space.

Renuka Chatterjee commissioned this collection for Speaking Tiger. Though we have never met, we have often 'talked' via email. Thank you for it all!

Shalini Krishan edited these stories with much sensitivity and understanding, a sharp eye, and pertinent suggestions. Thank you, Shalini!

And lastly, to all the readers who have been with me over the years, whose comments, encouragements, disagreements, love, empathy and annoyance have all inspired me greatly... I value your feedback greatly. Just as a musician needs an auditorium of Rasikas to spur her on, so too, you, my family of readers, have been of great importance in my life. Thank you!

Changing Equation in Asia-Pacific and ASEAN

Mukesh Kumar Singh

PRASHANT PUBLISHING HOUSE
DELHI-110094

Published by :
Prashant Publishing House
C-34, 28 Foota Road, Gali-3,
West Karwal Nagar, Delhi-110094
Phone : 011-22963970, Mob. : 9810396373
e-mail.: prashantpublishinghouse@gmail.com

Changing Equation in Asia-Pacific and ASEAN

Reserved
First Published 2014

ISBN 978-93-80565-45-3

PRINTED IN INDIA
Published by Mr. R.K. Jha M/s Prashant Publishing House and Published at H.S. Offset House Press, Delhi.

Preface

At present, ASEAN is not tied to any Great Power military alliance and an no longer be dragged into any balance of power game as in the Cold War. Thus, ASEAN has considerable choices and scope to maneuver in the regional game.

China's consistent strategic objective is to become a powerful political, economic and military state in the world, first and foremost in Asia-Pacific. To realize this goal, China on the one hand seeks to develop cooperative relations with all countries, especially the United States and other Great Powers, just as it takes advantage of other countries' constraints and difficulties to enhance its own role in the region. Southeast Asia is perceived as China's traditional "backyard" and ASEAN is an important competing object that China needs to win over in order to strengthen its position and create a counterbalance to the other Great Powers in Asia-Pacific.

Beijing did not take too seriously ASEAN's growing role initially. Instead, it anticipated a greater role for the UN Security Council and a multipolar world when the Cold War ended. Within the Asian context, China saw the United States, Russia, Japan, and itself as the critical players, but not ASEAN, as it was deemed largely a subregional grouping with an inward-looking orientation. That began to change in the mid-1990s as Beijing both recognized and indeed appreciated the role that ASEAN could play. This became even more apparent with the expansion of the original ASEAN-6 to the Greater ASEAN of Ten by the decade's end.

It is further hoped that the book will prove to be of immense value to teachers, students and researchers.

—Editor

Contents

Contents

1

Balance of Power in Asia-Pacific in the Post-Cold War Era

BALANCE OF POWER IN ASIA-PACIFIC

Behind the collapse of the Soviet Union and the disappearance of the four-decade-long Cold War structure, the entire nature of the geopolitical landscape in the Asia-Pacific region has dramatically changed. The bipolar equilibrium of the two superpowers broke down. As a result, regional players have commenced *a new game of balance of power*.

One of the main features of the regional strategic chessboard is the emergence of a new balance of power. The question of just how a balance of power is formed and what direction this new balance is moving in remains complicated, unpredictable, and even arguable. Nevertheless, it is likely characterized as an evolution in which no major conflict occurs, and the new power equation appears *as a flexible five-power equilibrium* in which no single power becomes a hegemon, while the United States and China play dominant roles. The relationships among the five Great Powers in the region (United States, China, Japan, Russia and India) are now geared to *both cooperation and competition,* instead of collusion and confrontation.

Under these circumstances, how should the future role of an expanding ASEAN, as middle-sized game-players in the Asia-Pacific region, be viewed and assessed? In other words, how will the new correlation of forces affect the interests and strategic posture of the states of Southeast Asia? Answering these questions would undoubtedly help identify various policy options that can best serve the benefits of ASEAN. This is of significant importance for ASEAN states, especially as we enter a new century.

The purpose of this chapter is to look into and understand a variety of factors, particularly the relationship between the United States and China, and how it affects the rallying of forces and the shaping of a new balance of power in the Asia-Pacific. Based on this, an attempt is made here to arrive at a critical evaluation of ASEAN's current posture, the problems that may arise, and the policy options taken by ASEAN that can contribute to the strengthening of its role and position.

The subject of the research is addressed in three parts. Part one deals with the concept of balance of power and the present balance of power in Asia-Pacific in the post-Cold War era. Part two concentrates on assessments of the US-China relationship, the trends of its future evolution, and its effects on the rallying of forces in the region. All ideas and observations relating to ASEAN's role and posture, its opportunities and challenges, as well as its strategic options in a new regional game, are contained in the final part of this paper.

PERCEPTION OF BALANCE OF POWER

In general, there are two main theoretical schools of international relations: *realism* and *liberalism*. *Realism* identifies the entire system of state relations based on criteria such as strength, power, geopolitics, geostrategy and the correlation of forces largely among Great Powers. *Liberalism* emphasizes other factors, such as economic interdependence, "soft" sources of power, and the role of international institutions and multilateralism.

According to many scholars, while various approaches could be considered supplementary, realism is the more dominant theoretical tradition since the policies of Great Powers and their relations have so far strongly influenced international affairs. Moreover, the regional and multilateral institutions would not be able to function without the participation of Great Powers.

The theory on balance of power is associated with realism and remains the most fundamental framework for understanding international relations. The concept of balance of power has historically been used to explain the actions of states in an insecure environment. The system was first formed and operationalized among the applied though debate on it continues.

Balance of Power: Meaning

Balance of power is perceived *as the basic concept in the relations among states*. Modern theory on balance of power is connected to the Newtonian conception of an universe in equilibrium. The substance of this theory is: *Under normal circumstances, all states always seek to maximize their power and international positions through various methods and techniques, and because of the adjustments of the "invisible hand", no one gains hegemony and an equilibrium in the international relations systems is maintained.* This definition suggests a mechanism in which any attempt by any state to expand its power and attain dominance or hegemony that would allow it to impose its will on the other states will be resisted. No state, therefore, will be in a position to determine the fate of others.

Thus, a state of equilibrium in the international relations system is one in which no state becomes an absolute dominant power; more powerful states, in spite of pursuing various strategic interests, are satisfied with the existing territorial, adjustments may take place, no powerful state (or group of states) seeks to change the system fundamentally, as it would not yield additional benefits commensurate with the anticipated costs.

Consequently, the Great Powers have frequently supported the balance of power system throughout history, because they have both greater capacity to influence outcomes and the largest stake in the established order. In effect, balance of power mirrors the Great Powers' compromises on the distribution of benefits and spheres of influence in the world on the basis of their correlation of forces.

Rules of the Diversion

The aim of countervailing power is the protection of each state's security and the system in which these states exist as a whole. Therefore, the way to ensure each state's security is to prevent the emergence of any preponderant state that would lead to an upset of the existing status of equilibrium.

As Wolfer puts it, in balance of power terms, these rules can be stated in the following manner:

(a) Watch a potential adversary's power and match it.

(b) Ally oneself with a weaker state to restore the balance of power.

(c) Abandon such alliances when the balance has been restored and the common danger has passed.

(d) Regard national security interests as permanent; alliances must therefore change when a new threat rises.

(e) *Do not treat defeated states harshly through punitive peace treaties (today's adversary may be tomorrow's ally).*

Change of Balance

An international system is not maintained in a state of stable equilibrium when important shifts in the array of forces among states occur. There are two basic elements leading to the attempts to change the balance of power system:

- Differential growth in political, military and technological power that creates a change in the array of forces among states.
- Shifts in states' domestic political coalitions may necessitate redefinition of their "national interests" and foreign policies.

An equilibrium can be altered if there is a shift in political, military and technological capabilities of states and, as a result, *the expected benefits exceed the expected costs of bringing about a change in the system.* Victorious state or states would create the new peace settlements and status quo reflecting the redistribution of power in the system. The hegemonic wars in this view included the Thirty Years War from 1618-1648, the wars of King Louis XIV from 1667-1713, the Napoleonic Wars from 1792-1814, World War I from 1914-1918 and World War II from 1939-1945. However, resolution of crises is still possible through peaceful adjustment of the systemic disequilibrium, by compromises or moderation of the ambitions of emerging Great Powers. Essentially, it is the sharing of costs and benefits in keeping the status quo among the existing Great Powers.

The determinants of whether or not to create and maintain the international balance of power are the cost-benefit calculations that a state (or states) will make in the determination to change the existing equilibrium. The material environment (e.g., economic growth, demographic change, military technologies, communications and transportation conditions), the international system structures, and "internal" factors (e.g., leadership personalities, national identities, political-economic interests of groups and others in the society) provide incentives or disincentives for a state to attempt to change the international system.

Meaning of Implement a Balance of Power Policy

As J. Spanier explains, all states are very concerned about their strength or power for survival. To prevent an attack, a state must be *as powerful as potential aggressors; a disproportion of power may tempt another state. A balance of power is thus a prerequisite for each state's security.* When the balance is disturbed, the tendency is to take responsive action to return to a position of equilibrium. If states disregard the operational rule that power must be counterbalanced, they place their own security in jeopardy.

As Kissinger argues, *the balance of power serves to restrict the ability of states to dominate each other and to limit the scope of conflicts.* Kissinger views the balance of power not as an automatic mechanism, but instead as one of two possible outcomes of a situation in which states are obliged to deal with each other. One state can become so powerful that it dominates the others, or else the "pretensions" of the most aggressive member of the international community are kept in check by chosen by prudent leaders.

Harmán, when studying the significance of theory on balance of power, asserts that *prudent states do not amass more enemies than they can effectively counter or handle at any one time. If states must deal with two or three adversaries, it would be wiser to concentrate on the strongest one by isolating and separating it from the others*. This principle is called the "conservation of enemies".

Chessmen on the New Strategic Chessboard

On the international strategic chessboard, the ranks of "chessmen" are classified by geopolitical, demographic, economic, military and traditional criteria in which geopolitics has significant importance. Generally, two ranks are identified: the first rank comprises *Great Powers,* whose scope of interests and capability of intervention reaches out beyond their borders. The second rank is comprised of *Middle and Small Powers,* which do not have (or have only a very few) of these roles to act, while the Middle and Small Powers are acted upon.

The "chessmen" positioned on the strategic chessboard in the Asia-Pacific are ranked as follows:

- *First* is a group of Great Powers that includes the United States, China, Japan, Russia and India. These are the chief game players in the strategic chessboard. Their positions, however, are not necessarily equal to one another:
    - The United States is currently the single superpower having political, economic and military might, and global influence.
    - China is an emerging power with an increasingly important voice in the regional economy and greater political influence in the Asia-Pacific. -Japan is an economic power whose political and military stature are not commensurate with its economic abilities.

- Russia's international prestige declined sharply after the collapse of the Soviet Union. In spite of this, however, Russia still has a strong military force, including nuclear weapons.
- India is now exercising its clout mainly in the South Asian region and is also viewed as a rising power.

- *Second* is a group of Middle Powers. These countries do not have great influence on the developments in the region, but they play an important role in balancing power, as they occupy strategic geopolitical positions and are the Korea, and Vietnam.
- *Third* are Small Powers (Laos, Cambodia, Singapore) and some very small states like Brunei (with a population of 300,000 people), and the Marshall Islands (with a population of 40,000 people). Those countries can only make worthwhile stands when they are engaged in alliances or alignments with other actors.
- *In addition*, some scholars of liberalism have flirted with the idea that new transnational actors, such as international and regional organizations, NGOs and multinational corporations, are gradually playing a greater role in international affairs.

TREND OF CHANGE IN AUTHORITY EQUATIONS

The US economy has recently gained advantages in technology, productivity and competitiveness, and the country is likely to continue as the unique global power for several decades to come. Brzezinski holds that the United States is not only the first as well as the only truly global superpower, but is also likely to be the very last. In the coming years, no single power is likely to reach the level of 30% of the world's GDP that the United States sustained throughout much of the twentieth superpower with the capacity to intervene in every part of globe in the post-Cold War world.

However, the United States is also facing severe competition with other contenders, namely Western Europe, Japan and a rising China. At the current rate, the US economy's share of the world economy will decline to about 20% of world GDP by 2010, and Asia's share of world output is predicted to grow to exceed 70% of North America's and Europe's output combined.

China is on the road to superpower status by the first decades of the twenty-first century. As projected by the World Bank in its recent report on China in 2020, if China can sustain economic growth rates of 7-8% per year, China's GDP on a purchasing power parity basis would reach $3.3 trillion in 2015. This would be about 27 percent of US GDP in that year, and roughly equal to the US GDP in 1966. China would then become the world's largest economy in terms of total GNP by 2020.

An economically powerful China would no doubt introduce faster changes in the power equation in the Asia-Pacific. Paul Dibb observes that China's influence will grow over the next decade or two as its economic strength develops. China is not a status quo power: it seeks a greater role for itself in world affairs and it does not fully accept the legitimacy of the present international order.

It should not be overlooked, however, that China has some problems that might make its future uncertain. The most serious problems arise from the transition of its political and economic system. In this, the possibility of economic failure might lead China to adopt a more assertive and hostile foreign policy. Because of this, some scholars argue that China can only become a regional, not a global, dominant power in the future.

Japan is now undergoing a period of serious structural crisis. However, the Japanese economy has enormous potential, and it is unlikely that it will see the turbulence that occurred in the 1970s. Nevertheless, Japan will need a longer time to revive its economy and to undertake necessary large-scale reforms.

Russia currently faces many difficulties and has few prospects for improvement in the next few years. However, Russia is a large country situated in both Europe and Asia. Its territory has substantial natural resources, and its economy has great potential. Russia also retains a very large nuclear arsenal and extensive transformation succeeds, Russia will regain its Great Power status.

India currently exerts its influence only in South Asia. India's GDP is the sixth largest in the world in terms of purchasing power parity, and its economic reforms promise a much more successful economy in the long run which, unlike China's, is based on an established judicial and financial system. In May 1998, India carried out nuclear tests, joining the Great Powers' nuclear club. It will unquestionably remain the most powerful South Asian state in the long run.

In brief, the trends of change in the power equation in Asia-Pacific in the coming decades are: the United States maintains supremacy as the single superpower, and China strives to develop into one of the leading Great Powers with the capacity to challenge the supremacy of the United States in the Asia-Pacific region. These two Great Powers are situated at a higher level than the others. Behind them, Japan and Russia also have important voices in regional affairs, while India will emerge as a regional power.

Rivalry for Globe of Influence among Great Powers

The United States continues to be the predominant power that wants to keep the status quo in Asia. After the disintegration of the Soviet Union, the United States is of hostile powers that could dominate Asia and alter the power equation in the region.

However, the United States today must adapt to a very different reality in the relationship among Great Powers. In the past, China was once allied with the Soviet Union against the United States, only to later align itself with the United States against the Soviet Union. But China has now become the No.1 contender of the United States in the Asia-Pacific. Dibb goes further and identifies that China is the one power with the potential to contend with the United States for leadership in the twenty-first century.

Japan's growing desire to reduce its dependence on the United States and play a greater political role in regional issues has complicated its relationship with the United States. In fact, it has become an increasingly fierce economic competitor. Russia has also readjusted its strategy, displaying a "more independent" relationship with the United States, and has dramatically improved its relations with China and Japan. Under these circumstances, the United States advocates a policy of carrying out a mixture of containment and collaboration with these powers. The US policy on obvious. The continued deployment of 100,000 US military troops in the Asia-Pacific region (the same level of deployment as in Europe) as well as the intensification of security ties with Japan are targeted in this regard.

China's strength is expected to grow further within a few decades, in line with its economic modernization. Its central objective is to strive to become a superpower. China's relationship with the United States remains a primary concern, as China badly needs capital and technologies for economic development and the achievement of great power status in the twenty-first century. In the eyes of the Chinese, the United States is considered both an important partner as well as a tough contender, especially in Asia-Pacific and Southeast Asia.

At this point, China's first priority is devoted to cooperation with the United States. Coupled with the above requirements, China is also making rapid strides to improve its relations with Russia, building up a "strategic partnership" aimed at taking countervailing measures to its relations with the United States. With regard to Japan, China seeks ways to pursue a policy of both containment and cooperation, in particular, grasping at opportunities to attract Japanese capital and technology.

Japan has a long-term interest in developing into a political power commensurate with its economic might, first and foremost in Asia-Pacific. Recognizing new regional and global developments, Japan has recently placed emphasis on pursuing a strategy on "turning back to Asia" with a view to scrambling for, or at least consolidating, its role in Asia and having a more balanced position in the US-China-Japan-Russia strategic quadrangle.

Chalmers Johnson is of the view that Japan is moving towards a disengagement from the United States, and is at least seriously considering orienting its foreign policy "around East Asia and the United Nations." To this end, Japan on the one hand continues to enhance closer bilateral relations with the United States, but on more equal basis. On the other hand, it is expanding its economic-political engagement with China in order to both exploit the vast market and constrict China's influence. It also attaches importance to making necessary "arrangements" with Russia, which is seen as the weakest edge of Japan's relations with Great Powers. Japan also promotes its traditional cooperation with Southeast Asian states (ASEAN).

Soviet Union. Since the end of the Cold War, Russia has emphasized the importance of maintaining constructive relations with China, Japan, and other states in the region. Russia is intensifying its efforts to make a rapprochement with China, establishing the "strategic partnership towards the twenty-first century."

At the same time, Russia is markedly improving its relations with Japan, which has strong economic potential and direct impact on Russia's security. If the territorial disputes are resolved, the Russia-Japan relationship could move even closer, especially in the economic-commercial areas. In addition, Russia continues its traditional ties and maintains political, economic and military cooperation with India.

India's long-term goal is to overcome the economic and political constraints that have limited its influence outside South Asia and to become a qualified regional power. In order to cope with the danger of increased Chinese presence in the region, including the Indian Ocean, India is developing nuclear weapons capable of deterring China and enhancing its military cooperation with Russia (though not as the same level as with the Soviet Union). From trade-investment and strategic perspectives, an improved and stable relationship with the United States is inevitably most beneficial for India.

Prediction for a New Balance of Power

During the Cold War, peace and stability in the Asia-Pacific were closely connected and determined by either tension or détente between the Soviet Union and the United States, and by the readjustments in strategic triangular relationships among the United States, the Soviet Union, and China. Nevertheless, unlike in Europe, a distinct polarization had taken place in the region by the end of the 1960s and early 1970s, when China split from the Soviet Union and antagonized it (e.g., the Sino-Soviet border clashes in 1969). The balance of power game played by the United States, the Soviet Union, and China began from that time, though China remained relatively weak compared with the other two sides of the triangle.

Since the end of the Cold War, Asia-Pacific has experienced profound changes that have strongly affected the strategic power equation as well as the gathering of forces among regional states. The evolvement of the correlation of forces and the Great Powers' rivalries constitute major factors shaping the balance of power and institutions in the region's international relations system. The key point here is that for the first time in centuries, *the prospect for peace and stability in the region will depend more on Asian countries than on external powers.*

What direction will the new balance of power tend to follow in the next few years? As Kissinger observes, the relations of the principal Asian nations to each other nineteenth century. Any significant increase in strength by one of them is almost certain to evoke an offsetting maneuver by the others. Calder takes a similar view that the balance of power being formed in Asia-Pacific is almost in the same shape of Europe from the middle of seventeenth century up to World War II.

Dibb describes how the former two-power balance is now being replaced by a five-power balance that has different characteristics: *a) The actors no longer need to be equal in power, like the Soviet Union and the United States were before. b) The actors no longer need to be equal in military power, including strategic nuclear deterrents like nuclear missiles. c) The bilateral relationships among five great powers need not be equal to one another. d) The actors' own spheres of influence are not completely divided as they were in the two-power balance. e) The rule of the game is not necessarily that of a zero-sum game. f) There will be no new alliances, but only alignments on specific policy issues (e.g., arms control, environment, trade, human rights).*

Powers' interests, the alignments among themselves and their alignments with the middle and small countries are in a state of flux. In sum, the five-power balance is a structural equilibrium in which no rank is provided, military strength is unequal, and the spheres of influence are intertwined. This will lead to setting up an open system providing information on steps taken by opponents in the strategic chessboard and responses to any danger of upsetting the equilibrium. In other words, this is a system of coordination on checks and balances among states.

In such a situation, *the middle and small countries are able to further strengthen their positions and to have more choices and bargaining counters in the balance of power game.*

THE US-CHINA RELATIONSHIP ITS EFFECTS ON THE AUTHORITY EQUATION IN ASIA-PACIFIC

Since the establishment of the People's Republic of China (1949) until the collapse of the Soviet Union (1991), US-China relations have had ups and downs closely linked to profound changes occurring in the world, in the relationship among Great Powers, and in the internal affairs of respective countries. Many historians and international relations researchers share identical views on the *three major factors governing US-China relations over the last five decades, i.e. strategic, ideological, and domestic factors.*

Planned Factors

China: The People's Republic of China came into being during the existence of the US-Soviet "bipolar" world. In the Great Powers' equation, China was a weaker state in comparison to the United States and the Soviet Union; economically it was even weaker than Japan and Western Europe. Despite this, China still enjoyed a degree of international influence. If China were to align with either side, the power equation would inevitably change.

By recognizing its geostrategic advantages and disadvantages, China constantly gave top priority to balancing strategies vis-a-vis the United States and the Soviet Union throughout the "bipolar" era.

To realize its strategic goal, China engaged once in alignment with the Soviet Union against the United States and once in "strategic coordination" with the United States against the Soviet Union. It then maintained "well-balanced" relations with both the United States and the Soviet Union. According to Kissinger, what China seeks from the United States is a strategic relationship to balance neighbours it considers to be both powerful and covetous.

The United States: The United States has essential interests in Asia, though it is neither an Asian state nor a state bordering China. However, the United States can not protect these interests without "coordination" or "participation" from China. China is a vast land and the most populous nation in the world, situated in the centre of the Asian mainland.

Furthermore, it has the capability of generating enormous challenges for the United States and other Great Powers. Ross holds that in an emerging multipolar environment, the United States may well find China a useful partner in maintaining a regional balance of power or in deterring regional conflict.

This is based on two perceptions: China is both a potential adversary (because, except for China, no other power in Asia is expected to challenge the superpower supremacy of the United States), and an important partner in solving regional and global issues. In 1943, Roosevelt envisioned China as one of the world's "four policemen" and thought that it would show the greatest relative increase in stature among the Great Powers. At the same time, the United States has been most important to China's political stability and economic modernization, for with the exception of the US, none of the other powers, including

Japan, Russia and India, can pose a direct threat to its security and development.

Ideological Factors

The history of US-China relations has shown that the ideological differences between the Unites States and China over issues of political regimes, structural social organizations, cultural traditions, religions, and perceptions of democracy and human rights have continued as factors influencing foreign policy-making processes and ways of handling bilateral and multilateral relations. As Harding argues, many Chinese Communist leaders had a lifelong aversion to capitalism and imperialism and saw the Unites States as the principal embodiment of both evils in cultural presence in China as a dangerous intervention in its internal affairs and are worried that the United States is again trying to damage China's international image. Conversely, many Americans considered any variety of communism repugnant and regarded Chinese communism as even more brutal than its Soviet counterpart.

However, *ideological differences are not* the fundamentals that determine the nature of US-China relations. In fact, this relationship has seen wide fluctuations of tension and détente since 1972, and the overall trend is moving towards the easing of strained relations and the setting up of a "strategic partnership." During the last fifty years, although both the United States and China have on several occasions altered their strategies, China's consistent national interest has been to make itself into a Great Power having a worthy stature in international relations. On the other hand, the objective of the United States in this regard has been to contain China from rising into a powerful state that will change the power equation in the region.

Household Factors

For many decades, all markedly important events occurring in the political-social lives of the two countries have contributed considerably to the fluctuations of US-China relations. The years 1989-1996 were marked by continuous frictions in the bilateral relations between the two countries, as both countries internally experienced many conflicting decision-making debates.

According to Harding, there were two rounds of serious debates about the national priorities and policies vis-a-vis China in the United States in the first half of 1990s with two tendencies. One emphasized the pursuit of containment policy, while the other emphasized "comprehensive engagement."

These two tendencies struggled against one another, and as a result, the China policy carried out by the Clinton administration in the first term was viewed as lacking clarity. As Steve Teles and Robert Sutter argue in their book *After the Cold War*, US policy towards China is buffeted by the pressures of domestic politics, making in the aftermath of the Cold War.

Concurrently, heated internal debate on the policy vis-a-vis the United States was also taking place in China between "conservative" and "radical" factions within the civilian and military branches. The conservatives were concerned about the US "containment" policy, while the radicals advocated overcoming difficulties and avoiding confrontation with the United States in order to create favourable international conditions for China's entry into the twenty-first century.

The political, economic and social turbulence, especially the profound changes produced by economic reforms in China that culminated in the Tiananmen Square incident (June 1989), pushed US-China relations into a disruptive period. More obstacles for the US-China relationship were created by congressional lobbyists, the MFN debates, nuclear nonproliferation groups, and activities taken by interest groups such as those concerned with human rights.

US-China Planned Similarities

In the next ten to twenty years, both the United States and China should give top priority to economic growth, market expansion, and scientific-technological invention, especially in high-tech and military industries in order to improve their national strength. Proceeding from these identical strategies, the two countries need to maintain peace and stability, build up long-term cooperative relations, and refrain from provoking direct military conflicts that could jeopardize the security and economic development of either country.

The United States and China need to cooperate with one another to prevent potential flash-points from causing major turbulence in the region or in the world, and to deal with global issues such as arms control, environment, narcotics, population, energy and food production and distribution.

Furthermore, the United States and China need to share the common ground by using the Great Powers' mechanism in international organizations and multilateral forums to control the world situation, particularly the P5 (permanent representatives) in the UN Security Council and the "Nuclear Powers" Club.

US-China Planned Differences

The United States seeks to maintain the world order it wants, while China opposes US supremacy and wants to establish a multipolar order. Over the last several decades, the prevention of any newly emerging superpower that could conceivably challenge the position of the US unique has been an unswerving objective of the United States in the Asia-Pacific.

This objective, however, runs counter to China's goal. This is the fundamental contradiction between the United States and China, and it will dictate the direction of all US-China relations in the coming decades. The United States and China are not only two Great Powers but are also two large economies in the world. Their relations are not only closely interlinked, but are also filled with potential elements that may lead to considerable conflict over the issues of national interests, economic institutions, and levels of development.

For instance, according to US statistics, the United States had a $49.7 billion trade deficit with China in 1997, second only to the US trade deficit with Japan. Moreover, China's 1996 exports to the United States increased by 21.4% over the agencies have indicated that in the near future China could easily replace Japan as the country with the largest trade surplus with the United States. These differences tend to exacerbate problems related to Chinese protectionism, textiles, trade deficits, infringement of intellectual property rights (American manufacturers lose $2 billion per year from IPR piracy in China) and conditions for Chinese membership in the World Trade Organization (WTO).

Taiwan also continues to be a sensitive issue in the US-China relationship. How to tackle the Taiwan issue? What will the "Taiwanese regime" be? After the handing-over of Hong Kong in 1997 and Macao in 1999, China's next step is to reunite Taiwan leaving open the possibility of using force if Taiwan unilaterally declares independence. China's formula is "One China, Two Political Systems". However, the Taiwanese voters elected President Chen Shui-bian, a pro-independence leader of the Democratic Progress Party, in the March 2000 Elections creates a situation fraught with danger which risks a clash between the United States and China.

For these reasons, Taiwan remains a hurdle that can easily flare up in US-China relations. Harry Harding also shares the view that many uncertainties surround the Sino-American relations.

These two East and West cultures and civilizations greatly differ from each other. With its economic, scientific-technological and military advantages, the United States has achieved tremendous expansion of both "soft power" and its superpower stature. China on the other hand, as one of the earliest civilization, is very sensitive to the influence of "external cultures" and acts to protect its national cultural traditions. In another dimension, China also seeks to expand its own cultural clout by different ways and means, especially through the well-organized ethnic Chinese networks all over the world.

PREDICTION FOR US-CHINA RELATIONS

The future of US-China relations is difficult to predict, as all the important conditions are in a state of flux. Nevertheless, various assessments have been made on trends of its development. The realists generally offer a "pessimistic" view about the future of cooperation with China, as they believe that it will rise to change the existing power equation and challenge the US world leadership status. Their view rests on the assumption that US conflicts with China in the future are inevitable.

The liberal thinkers see the prospects for US-China cooperation as "optimistic." Their argument is that all economies, including those of the United States and China, are closely intertwined in an increasingly globalized world, and that regional and global multilateral institutions are becoming more important. Therefore, many global issues in international relations in the post-Cold War era will be solved not only by the United States, but with China and the other Great Powers. Engaging and binding China to common rules will therefore help limit China's actions from harming the interests of the United States and other countries.

As analysed above, the US-China relationship is a complicated one governed by various factors, but it clearly shows that a balance of power strategy is the most decisive factor affecting the future development of their relationship. In fifteen or twenty years to come, there may be three following scenarios:

Argument

China becomes a more powerful state. The clashes between the United States and China intensify. The "contain China" calculations in the US policy escalate. This outcome leads to confrontation between the two countries and the world enters into the "US-China Cold War" era. Neither the United States nor China is desirous of this scenario in the foreseeable future, as the two countries will be forced into a new arms race, jeopardizing the priority given to economic development and protection of Great Power status. Kissinger argues that a policy of confrontation with China risks America's isolation in Asia. No Asian country would want to or could afford to be supportive of America, and in such circumstances the vast majority of

Asian nations would dissociate themselves from America. In addition, what has happened in the relations between the two countries in the "post-Tiananmen" period indicates that confrontation and tension are not the optimum, since both sides have to pay a price for their losses (though China certainly has to pay more). Due to their strategic differences, however, some potential elements may lead to this scenario in the future.

In their book *The Coming Conflict with China*, Richard Bernstein and Ross Munro assert that in spite of common interests in a number of issues, the United States and China will eventually be adversaries, because a stronger China will upset the power equilibrium in Asia-Pacific and place US vital interests in jeopardy. Robert Scalapino believes that there is a real prospect of a strongly nationalist China with ample military power emerging within a decade or so. Furthermore, according to only to become globally preeminent, but even just regionally predominant. Is a collision between the United States and China therefore, inevitable?

Agreement

China becomes stronger, but the two countries share more common interests in dealing with differences and coordinating international political-economic activities. US-China relations enter into a framework of long-term stable cooperation and avoidance of direct military confrontation. With this scenario, the United States and China establish an international order in which they both play dominant roles. The solutions to many current transnational issues require collective and cooperation from both countries. These include hot points, crises, regional territorial disputes, and other global issues such as nuclear nonproliferation, the environment, food security, terrorism and narcotics.

However, the sustainability of this scenario is very low, as the two countries widely differ in their strategic interests and sociopolitical systems and the volatility of China's internal affairs is unpredictable. Although a "strategic partnership" is China relations cannot determine the other Great Powers' relationships.

Mixture

The United States and China are not likely to face a compelling need for a geostrategic alliance, nor can they easily overcome their ideological and cultural differences. In fact, the two countries pursue varied strategic policies, taking advantage of bilateral ties to counterbalance their relationships with other Great Powers. *This relationship undoubtedly fluctuates between strain and relaxation, cooperation and confrontation, but does not converge onto a destructive collision course.*

Based on the nature of US-China relations, as well as the trends of balance of power shaped in the region, it is anticipated that *this third scenario is the most likely to come about. Alternately, the third and the second scenarios simultaneously take place on specific issues at specific times. The first scenario is unlike to be seen.*

EFFECTS ON OTHER GREAT POWERS' POSITION

The United States, China, and the other Great Powers do not want to see this scenario occur, as they all will be placed in a very difficult situation in dealing with one another. However, if this case should come about, *the process of rallying forces will be followed by two blocks, with one block comprised of the United States and its allies, the other block comprised of China and its allies, and with the rest in between the two sides.* Specifically:

- Polarization is in place, with the United States and Japan on the one side (based on US-Japan Security Pact), and China and Russia on the other.
- China seeks alliances with other Asian nations (based on cultural and religious similarities), which may lead to a loose coalition between China and India and Japan (the US-Japan Security Pact to be nullified by China) to limit US influence in the region.

When China becomes more powerful and more aggressive, other Great Powers may ally with the United States to curb China's ambitions.

Regarding options taken in dealing with the United States and China, two hypotheses can be put forward:

- Russia, Japan, and India improve their relations with both the United States and China, thus making *a concert of power*. Coordination among Great Powers is formulated in solving regional and international issues in which the United States and China play leading roles.
- After the establishment of strategic partnerships, the United States and China attach less importance to their relations with other Great Powers or even compromise on each others' interests. The consequent gradual decline of the role played by Japan, Russia, and India in the strategies of the United States and China therefore compel them to regroup to struggle for their balanced interests.

As the US-China relationship is largely driven by a mixture of cooperation and competition, both countries must attach greater importance to broadening their relations with external forces so that other countries will have more policy choices that conform to their own interests.

Effects on Middle and Small Powers' Status

The Middle and Small Powers often have less opportunity to act rather than be acted upon by the adjustments of Great Powers' strategies in complicated international relations. In Asia, the relations of neighbouring countries with China and the status of its relations with other Great Powers.

Middle and Small Powers in dealing with Great Powers:

- To ally or align with one single Great Power and rely on security, political, and economic protections from that Power.
- To participate in the games, but keep balanced relations with all Great Powers.
- To stay out of the games and keep neutral like Finland and Switzerland (the mode called "Finlandization").

Because of the widely diversified interests of all countries, there is a variety of behaviors. In view of many fundamental changes in the world today (e.g., the existence of multipower balance, growing globalization, highly interdependent conditions), *alignment is likely to be seen instead of the classical alliance, and no nation is likely to stay outside or be "neutral."*

Dibb observes that in these uncertain circumstances, Middle Powers in the region are likely to view their own interests as best served by preserving an equilibrium among Great Powers. He cites Amitav Acharya, who notes that the ASEAN states' preferred approach to regional order seems to lie in the maintenance of a regional mechanisms remain critical to the prospects for regional order in the post-Cold War era. The Middle Powers are likely to feel threatened by the domination of the Asia-Pacific region by any one Great Power, and to regard some measures of checks and balances on each by the other as the condition of their own security. According to Dibb, *all the Middle and Small Powers in the region seek ways to avoid tendencies of either a keen rivalry or confrontation or a concert of Great Powers,* because these scenarios leave them less space for maneuver.

It is anticipated therefore that whatever US-China relations develop, *Middle and Small Powers naturally opt to participate in the balance of power game, maintaining balanced relations with the Great Powers, especially with the United States and China on the one hand, and regrouping themselves to raise counterweights in dealing with those Great Powers on the other.*

EFFECTS OF US-CHINA RELATIONS ON THE BEARING OF ASEAN COUNTRIES

ASEAN is an association comprised of all ten Southeast Asian nations that are not regarded as powerful states having dominant influence on developments in Asia-Pacific or in the world as a whole. However, ASEAN captures an important position in Great Powers' strategies as *ASEAN states are ranked Middle Powers (some of them have become newly industrialized countries) and are geographically situated in sensitive areas in the region.* Brzezinski argues that these Middle Powers are "geopolitical pivots" that have very significant political and cultural consequences for more active neighbouring geostrategic players. Moreover, the landscape in Southeast Asia today is strikingly different from that of the Cold War period. For the first time since 1945, Southeast Asia is a relatively peaceful and stable region, where a state of confrontation in the relationships

All ASEAN states are now actively involved in a regional integration process for the benefit of their own development, and the association has emerged as a noticeable political and economic centre in Asia-Pacific.

In spite of new challenges posed by ASEAN's expansion, its remarkable achievements recorded in all fields over the past three decades are undeniable, and up to now ASEAN has basically preserved its solidarity, cohesion, regional self-reliance and self-resistance identities. ASEAN is also a unique regional organization in a developing world, which successfully attracts all major Centres and Great Powers to engage in regional political, security, economic forums.

For that reason, *ASEAN asserts itself as an indispensable element in the establishment of a new balance of power and regional order in Asia-Pacific in the post-Cold War era.*

Some are of the view that ASEAN's position in the regional strategic chessboard is no longer considered as important as before, when "certain arrangements" were directly made by Great Powers. Even so, it is obvious that the international game today is entirely changing. If all chessmen had to entrust their fates to one general on the board during the Cold War, they are now in mixed positions. Every chessman, even a pawn, has its own soul, fate, and moves on the board, though growing international posture, ASEAN's role will be increasingly enhanced.

Location of ASEAN in the US Asia-Pacific Strategy

Stemming from the strategic requirements of the United States as well as ASEAN's political role and economic dynamism,

ASEAN constitutes a considerable element in the US policy vis-a-vis Asia-Pacific, particularly in the context of the higher priority given to this region and China's rise as a new power. Furthermore, this region is also capturing increased attention from other Great Powers.

Given these considerations, the United States wants to see a continued prosperous and American-influenced Southeast Asia serving the political and economic interests of the United States in the region and becoming a counterweight to China and Japan so as not allow these countries to control the region and modify the balance of power. Economically, ASEAN is viewed as an attractive potential market with enormous trade and investment opportunities (the region consists of 500 million people and a total GDP of $600-1000 billion), and the United States has great interest in promoting economic ties with ASEAN.

Accordingly, the Unites States has reaffirmed its continued commitment to the region, applauding ASEAN's position economically and politically, and has encouraged ASEAN to be a driving force in building up regional security mechanisms. Recently, the United States has devoted further attention in assisting those ASEAN countries affected by economic crises in overcoming difficulties, thus preventing the danger of spreading regional disturbances, and limiting the negative impacts on the US economy.

Position of ASEAN in China's Asia-Pacific Approach

China's consistent strategic objective is to become a powerful political, economic and military state in the world, first and foremost in Asia-Pacific. To realize this goal, China on the one hand seeks to develop cooperative relations with all countries, especially the United States and other Great Powers, just as it takes advantage of other countries' constraints and difficulties to enhance its own role in the region. Southeast Asia is perceived as China's traditional "backyard" and ASEAN is an important competing object that China needs to win over in order to strengthen its position and create a counterbalance to the other Great Powers in Asia-Pacific.

Over the last few years, China's ties with the Southeast Asian states have been continuously fostered and developed into full-fledged partnership, while China's relations with other Great Powers have been complicated. Remarkably, China has undertaken a series of activities aimed at consolidating and building up a comprehensive cooperation programs in political, economic, security, military, cultural fields for the twenty-first century, marking a new milestone in the China-ASEAN relationship.

However, China has reaffirmed on several occasions since 1991 its claim to sovereignty of the Spratly Islands, and has projected military forces there (adoption of state law on territorial waters in 1992; proclamations of basic lines in 1996; economic special exclusive zones and continental shelves with an area of over 3.5 million square kilometers; construction of structures in Mischief Reef; a ban on fishing in the Spratly Islands). Some scholars have argued that China has taken advantage of US preoccupation with European affairs to vigorously expand its own role in Asia and Southeast Asia.

ASEAN's opportunities and challenges originate from its position on the regional strategic chessboard.

CONSTRUCTIVE CONDITIONS AND OPPORTUNITIES FOR ASEAN

From a balance of power perspective, ASEAN states currently enjoy fundamentally favourable conditions for the implementation of their foreign policies. With the end of the Cold War, peace and development have prevailed in the international relations in the region. Great Powers, namely the United States, China, Japan, Russia and India, have been willing to compromise and seek coordination, creating a relatively balanced and stable framework of their relations. All these factors have contributed to an ongoing favourable environment. Moreover, the Great Powers' possession of nuclear weapons constitutes, to some extent, a deterrent balance in the region. In the next fifteen to twenty years, China still needs to maintain stable international relations, especially with Great

Powers and its neighbours, to realize its four modernizations (i.e., agriculture, industry, culture and military). The political and economic advances that ASEAN has made over the last thirty years, as well as the international prestige, have helped lay solid foundations for ASEAN's future.

At present, ASEAN is not tied to any Great Power military alliance and an no longer be dragged into any balance of power game as in the Cold War. *Thus, ASEAN has considerable choices and scope to maneuver in the regional game.*

Difficulties and Challenge for ASEAN

The first challenge is ASEAN's inescapable "security dilemma." The security of ASEAN is closely linked to that of the Asia-Pacific region and to the global policy considerations of the Great Powers. As a consequence of its geography and historical background, any single gesture made by ASEAN in its relations with the United States or other Great Powers is understandably very "sensitive" to China, just as any further improvement in ASEAN's relations with China is understandably very "sensitive" to the United States, Japan and other Great Powers.

Faced with unceasing fluctuations of the array of forces among Great Powers and unpredictable complexities while the Asia-Pacific region still lacks region-wide comprehensive cooperation and security mechanisms to regulate potential rivalries, how to build a more balanced relations with Great Powers and to limit their shoulders in the conduct of international relations.

The second challenge is ASEAN's ability to "manage" sources of conflict with Great Powers. While other regions were able to develop peacefully after World War II, the ASEAN states had to face the sufferings and consequences of continued wars and conflicts. Besides that, the sources of conflict that existed in the region remain unsolved, as illustrated by various forms of territorial and natural resource disputes, and differences on levels of economic, historical, cultural and religious development. The crucial challenge for ASEAN therefore lies in its ability to manage these sources of conflict without the possibility of provocation from Great Powers, and to restrain the conjuncture of being affected, controlled, or even imposed upon with a "rule of the game" by Great Powers.

The third challenge is the question of the Indochinese peninsula, which is tacitly understood as the "sensitive" zone of Southeast Asia. For the Southeast Asian region, Indochina is of great geostrategic importance and often draws the Great Powers' special attention. This fact is demonstrated by those complexities of Great Powers' deep involvement throughout the Cold War period.

This is a difficult math for both the Southeast Asian mainlanders and islanders in seeking a policy on balance of power among Great Powers for the common sake of the association.

THE MAKING OF CALCULATED DECISIONS BY ASEAN IN A NEW CHESS GAME

The policy options taken by ASEAN originate from its strategic interests and position in the interactions with other players, especially the Unites States and China.

1 *The desirable as well as the basic and long-term goal of ASEAN* is to see an Asia-Pacific region of peace, stability, and harmonious settlement of disputes and differences, where international laws and cooperation for mutual prosperity abide.

2 In a period of transition from the old regional order to a new one with many.

T*he optimal interests of Middle Powers like ASEAN states are guaranteed by a relative equilibrium among Great Powers.* History has shown that conflicts or confrontations among Great Powers with the compelling involvement of other countries are a catastrophe for the region. Furthermore, a concert of Great Powers is also viewed as a circumstance unfavourable for Middle and Small Powers. As Dibb suggests, a situation of "moderate rivalry" among Great Powers provides the best conditions for the Middle Powers.

The pursuit of balance of power strategy among Great Powers in general and between the United States and China in particular will generate more flexibility for ASEAN in carrying out its foreign policy. This will allow it to avoid dependence on any single Great Power, as well as being stranded in the power struggles among Great Powers. This will enable ASEAN to maximize benefits by both taking "cooperation opportunities" with Great Powers and exploiting the Great Powers' differences.

The building up of multilateral institutions aimed at engaging all big and small states in working out codes of conduct in the region will help limit the "scope of negative responses" to be taken by Great Powers, especially those who have ambitions to regional or global hegemony. Dibb is convinced that it is only be able to face the twenty-first century with greater confidence and that Great Powers can be encouraged to work within a peaceful regional order.

The approach to region-wide "cooperative security" being pursued by ASEAN is part of these arrangements and in fact ASEAN has already been a considerable factor in the establishment of a new security order and balance of power in the region.

2

Changing the China-ASEAN Relations

CHANGING BALANCE OF LIMITED POWER

It is hard to argue with the view from Beijing that the benefits of Chinese aid, such as economic and infrastructural development, will improve standards of living among Nepalis and thus reduce tensions that might otherwise give rise to argument.

At the same time, the benefits of Chinese aid may also increase inequalities and divisions, both between local Nepali communities and between Nepalis and Chinese incomers. Given the scale of Chinese investments and development in Nepal, there is considerable risk that this sizeable injection of resources will upset the balance of local power and interests, which may lead to violence.

In September 2011, there was a bomb attack on a Chinese food factory in the Narsingh district of the Terai. This was reportedly carried out by the Janatantrik Tera-Madhesi Mukti Party, an armed militia battling for the independence of the Terai, which aims to expel Chinese and 'non-indigenous' populations from the region. It is the first attack against Chinese industry in the region, but it is feared there may be more to follow given the proliferation of Chinese entrepreneurs in the Terai, especially in the construction, textile and hotel industries. The risk of violence arising from the influx of Chinese companies into Nepal is likely to become a growing concern for peace and security from the Viewpoint of Beijing, as well as from Kathmandu.

CHANGING STABILITY OF INFLUENCE WITH THE WEST

China's growing role in Nepal does not just shift the balance of power and influence *vis-à-vis* India, it also affects the role and influence of Western powers, including their ability to influence the peace process. In Nepal, as in other developing countries, China's increased support for the government means that it becomes less dependent upon Western aid. This may diminish Western leverage to persuade the Nepali Government to address some of the more difficult aspects of the argument, which Western analysts believe must be addressed for peace to be sustainable. Such aspects include the human rights abuses carried out by all sides during the war. These are due to be addressed by a Truth and Reconciliation Commission, but this commission has yet to be set up. If human rights abuses are not dealt with, then impunity will become entrenched; and impunity is often an underlying driver of argument.

Western strategy makers need to be aware of this changing international context and of the implications for their own strategies for peace and development in Nepal. If the approach of Western donors is perceived to be overly prescriptive and/ or conditional – as some contend with regard to issues like integration and security sector reform – this may push the Nepali Government to seek support from other sources. The likelihood is that the Government will turn to states like China that generally provide what the Government requests – often hardware rather than 'software' – and provide it with no strings attached. This may affect the democratic quality of the systems that emerge, and it is a particular concern in areas like the security and justice sectors, where weak governance can lead to violence and insecurity.

The implication in this case is that China's growing role in Nepal is freeing the GoN from pressure to comply with

Western standards of good governance and human rights. China's increased aid to the Nepali Government means that the 'donor marketplace' is expanding. By offering an alternative model of support to the traditional Western donors, China (and India) are introducing more competition into this marketplace. This weakens the bargaining position of Western donors since it means that the Nepali Government has more options regarding from whom it would like to receive development assistance and with what, if any, strings attached.

It is hard to predict what will be the implications for peace and argument of an expanded donor marketplace in Nepal. It would be naïve to suggest that the agendas of Western donors are wholly benign in contrast to those of China or India. All external actors that engage in Nepal, as in other developing countries, do so based on a calculus of different interests: economic, security, developmental and geostrategic. So it does not automatically follow that a decline in the influence of Western donors will increase the prospect of argument in Nepal.

It is also important to keep in mind the basic role and agency of Nepalis themselves. The focus of this study is upon external actors, notably China, and how their engagement affects peace and argument in Nepal. The role of foreign powers in Nepal is highly significant, as this report demonstrates, especially in light of shifting balances of power and influence *vis-à-vis* the government in Kathmandu. However, ultimately it is the Nepali people who will determine whether there is a return to widespread violent argument or if sustainable peace can be secured.

What the research findings and analysis contained in this report do suggest is that strategy makers in the West, in China and in Kathmandu need to engage proactively with the changing realities; and they need to consider what it means for their policies and practice in support of peace and stability. For Western actors, the expansion of the donor marketplace means that the tools of conditionality they have used in the past to support peacebuilding will become less effective. This suggests that not just new tools, but new multi-lateral approaches, will be required if Western donors are to support peace in Nepal and in other argument-affected states.

Altering Stability of Influence with India

Another concern expressed was that China's growing role and influence may provoke India into a response that threatens Nepal's peace. This is based on the assumption that India considers Nepal as being within its sphere of influence and so will regard China's increasing engagement as a threat. According to such views, New Delhi is apprehensive that China's expansion into Nepal is part of a wider plan to contain and encircle India. One Indian analyst reports "a substantial amount of concern among the Indian establishment. The Chinese are making inroads across South Asia". According to this analysis, Chinese infrastructural developments in Nepal, combined with the build-up of its military capabilities in Tibet, will enable the PLA to deploy rapidly to India's borders.

Various recent events are attributed to Indian concern about China's growing role in Nepal. The petrol shortage in Nepal in early 2011 was seen by some as engineered by New Delhi in reaction to the then Government's proximity to Beijing. India also remains closely involved in Nepal's politics and reportedly it has stepped up its micromanagement of Nepali politicians to counter Chinese influence. There was a notorious controversy in late 2010 when a recording was leaked of a man with a Chinese accent offering US$6.9 million to a Maoist party leader to bribe 50 Nepali members of parliament to support a Maoist government. This affair was portrayed in India as evidence of China's meddling in Nepali politics. However, the recording has not been verified, nor the identity of the Chinese speaker, and it is suspected in some quarters that the whole incident was an Indian propaganda exercise. Whatever the reality, these incidents indicate increased tensions between the two powers over Nepal. India's concerns about China's proximity to Kathmandu are compounded by its distrust of the Maoists – despite New Delhi's instrumental role in bringing them into the political process in 2005. The fact that the UCPN-M party still debates whether India should be considered as 'national enemy number one' illustrates that the distrust and antagonism between New Delhi and Nepal's Maoists is mutual. That said, different factions within the Maoist party are perceived to have different views about Nepal's neighbours. Thus Prachanda is regarded as being relatively pro-Beijing, while Baburam Bhattarai is considered to be more sympathetic to New Delhi. The appointment of Bhattarai as Nepal's Prime Minister in August 2011 was thus viewed in India as a reassuring development. Furthermore, the fact that Bhattarai made his first official visit to New Delhi rather than to Beijing, unlike his predecessor, may presage a swing back towards the traditional balance of power.

Another cause for concern in New Delhi has been that the Maoist regime in Nepal could lend support to Maoist rebels in India, the Naxalites. There have been rumours of Naxalites receiving military training from Nepal's Maoists, and in 2010 the Indian Ambassador lodged a protest with the GoN over "organised training" of Naxalites in Maoist camps in Nepal. However, no evidence has been provided to substantiate this allegation, and most analysts consider a connection between Nepal's Maoists and India's Naxalites to be far-fetched.

China and India are seen to have adopted different approaches to Nepal: Beijing playing a strategic 'long-game', whereas India's approach is regarded as more tactical and short-term. India's tactics include alleged attempts to obstruct and undermine key aspects of the CPA, including the constitution and integration processes. Certainly there are suggestions that Indian manoeuvring has undermined Western attempts to support the peace process. The alleged obstructionism reflects Indian concern that the integration of Maoist combatants will weaken its special relationship with the Nepalese Army. There is a risk that such tactics – or at least the perception of them – will increase disillusionment with Nepal's peace process and may lead to its ultimate collapse. If China's growing role provokes India to intensify its involvement in Nepal's politics, this risks aggravating divisions among Nepali political leaders, destabilising the political situation and further delaying the implementation of the CPA. Indian concerns about China's expansion into its sphere of influence, allied to its distrust of the Maoists, have the potential to provoke a response that could disrupt the peace process and destabilise Nepal. However, Beijing appears well aware of India's sensitivity given the historic privileged relationship between Delhi and Kathmandu. Thus far, it has been careful not to overplay its hand; indeed it has on occasion urged the Nepali Government to work at restoring its relationship with New Delhi. Furthermore, the preceding analysis suggests that China's increased engagement in Nepal, and the shift in the relative influence of the two powers, may lead to a net gain in terms of peace and stability. If India is seen to have a destabilising influence on Nepal's peace process while China has a broadly stabilising influence, then China's increasing engagement should have a positive effect in terms of peace and stability.

ASEAN ENGAGES CHINA

The ASEAN nations have always viewed China with both suspicion and some cautious optimism. Their threat perceptions are influenced by history, geography, and cultural factors. In the former sense, being small states vis-à-vis China, they have always harboured a suspicion of their giant northern neighbor for two reasons. One is historical precedent, in particular Beijing's past support of the insurgent movements in their countries; the other is uncertainty about how China will use its power in regional affairs. China's preponderance and its growing weight in the post-Cold War era create additional concerns. Territorial disputes in the South China Sea and China's military modernization programs, together with perceived U.S. drawdown of forces have further heightened the sense of insecurity. But ASEAN countries also recognize that, given their limited capabilities, they need to live with China, and one way of ensuring that China will act responsibly is to encourage greater integration between China and the region, thus increasing the stakes. Indeed, ASEAN has been pragmatic enough to recognize the importance of engagement rather than confrontation and hence adopted a strategy that aims at integrating China gradually into a regional web of economic interdependence, political dialogue, and security dialogue processes. They also reject the strategy of containment as the best way to deal with a rising China.

ASEAN's active engagement of China played a critical role in removing suspicions and encouraged Beijing to full participation in the regional multilateral security arrangement. Specifcally, three outstanding issues of particular concern to the Southeast Asian states were to be addressed: potential economic competition coming from China, territorial disputes, and lack of transparency in China's defence spending. Beijing began to address these concerns, winning ASEAN's confidence in the process.

There is no question that the ARF has performed a critical role in exposing and socializing China to the ideas of cooperative security, multilateralism, consultation and dialogue, consensus-building, and noncoercive ways of settling disputes. Beijing's early concerns fell in four areas: that the regional forum would be dominated by the United States or otherwise could provide the justification for Washington to intervene in the region's affairs; concern over the internationalization of territorial disputes; concern that the Taiwan issue might be brought on the table, hence interfering China's internal affairs; and concern that China would be pressured to display greater military transparency.

ASEAN has been instrumental in engaging China and sensitizing Beijing to the values of the so-called ASEAN Way. This process has served to change China's perceptions of its interests and its policy choice preferences, leading to more moderate behaviour as contrasted to its earlier assertive posture.

Over time, through participation in various ASEAN-led multilateral dialogues, China has moved from its early suspicion and resistance to gradual acceptance and embrace of the idea of cooperative security and multilateralism. However, China's interpretation of multilateralism is a rather limited one, in that it is considered to be a supplement, rather than a replacement of the traditional bilateral approach. It also has resisted the more formal institutionalization of the ARF, as desired by the western countries. Beijing's comfort level clearly has increased with the understanding that ASEAN will remain in the driver's seat, and the forum will not touch on issues of vital importance to China.

Indeed, while ASEAN could be credited with socializing China to the concept of multilateralism, one must acknowledge that the multilateralism Beijing embraces remains conditional, selective, and largely a way to counter U.S. power politics. State sovereignty is still the core of Chinese foreign policy and on fundamental issues such as territorial disputes and Taiwan, China's positions continue to be more realpolitik than receptive of multilateralism. What China pursues remains a notion of multipolarity, in which it will be recognized as an important actor. For ASEAN, this remains an issue to be reckoned with, but for the time being at least, Beijing is trying to reassure its southeastern neighbours.

The 1997 financial crisis significantly weakened ASEAN's position. However, continued uncertainty in Sino-U.S. relations and their perceived competition for influence and primacy in Asia have given ASEAN some leverage, in so far as China's diplomacy is concerned. This has enabled the organization to remain in the driver's seat in regional security arrangements such as the ARF.

At the same time, ASEAN also is reluctant to join U.S.-led military alliances due to ethnic sensitivity, as Southeast Asia is home to a large Islamic population. At a time when Beijing's relations with Tokyo also are experiencing difficulties, the value for Beijing of a better relationship with ASEAN has increased steadily. Beginning in the second half of the 1990s, the two sides moved to develop a number of institutionalized mechanisms to deepen bilateral relations, including the ASEAN+1, among others. In 2003, China and ASEAN signed the Joint Declaration on Strategic Partnership for Peace and Prosperity.

The Prevarication Strategy

International Relations theories long have debated the policy options of states facing an emerging power or hegemon. They invariably would either choose to balance (internally and/or externally) against the dominant power or bandwagon with that power. The latter is divided further into bandwagoning because of fear or bandwagoning for profits. In recent discussions, a new concept of hedging has emerged as yet another policy option for states facing uncertain international security environments. Denny Roy has further characterized the ASEAN strategy of hedging as "low-intensity balancing" that both seeks U.S. support and works with China. They encourage the United States to maintain a military presence in the region and provide support and base access but decline to form formal military alliances with Washington.

In Southeast Asia, hedging has been a particularly useful strategy for the region's small powers to manoeuvre among major powers to secure their interests. According to Robert Ross, the continental ASEAN and maritime ASEAN member states would have different attitudes toward China. The new ASEAN, which consists of Vietnam, Laos, Cambodia, and Myanmar, for instance, has special relationships with China due to history, geographical proximity, as well as unsettled issues.

Wherever possible, ASEAN member states try not to be forced to choose sides, but opt for developing and maintaining good working relationships with as many major powers as possible. They all recognize the inevitability of China's rise and see in it both opportunities and challenges. In a certain way, ASEAN states realize that they cannot by themselves form an effective alliance to check China's rise; but neither do they want to ally themselves with external powers such as the United States for fear of provoking China. In addition to engagement with China, they therefore also seek to persuade the United States to stay engaged in the region to balance China's rise and to develop a network involving all major regional powers so they have stakes in regional order.

As pointed out above, since the end of the Cold War, ASEAN has pursued a dual-strategy of retaining U.S. security involvement in the region, including a military presence, and engaging China in diplomatic-political terms and expanding economic ties. While all member states recognize the importance of continued U.S. security involvement in the region, they also are concerned with Washington's penchant for unilateral use of force, in particular after the September 11, 2001 (9/11), terrorist attacks on the United States. Regarding China, ASEAN members have tried to refrain from identifying China as a threat; rather they talk about challenges and concerns, and their chosen strategy remains that of engagement rather than isolation, let alone containment. However, ASEAN also has reservations and appears uncertain about what a rising China will mean for them.

If one could argue that ideology, overseas Chinese living in Southeast Asia, economic competition, and territorial disputes are the four key elements that could affect China-ASEAN relations, then it is clear that the first two, by and large, have been addressed, with the latter two constituting the remaining major challenges. But even here, the implications may be different for ASEAN member states; the more developed may see less of economic competition in a rising China but more opportunities; countries that have territorial disputes with China may view Beijing's policies and activities more suspiciously. This may explain why ASEAN member states have adopted different approaches, and applied the hedging strategies with varying degrees, in their handling of China. For instance, some look for closer U.S. ties, while others seek greater engagement with China; still others, living in China's shadow, are making the best of their situations.

Although China has developed extensive ties with ASEAN on political and economic fronts, Beijing also has maintained close relationships with specific member states, which remain essential in China's regional diplomacy, especially where territorial disputes are concerned. At the same time, it should also be understood that ASEAN itself has yet to develop its own identity apart from agreements on general principles and processes. Each member state has unique historical experiences dealing with China, with varying threat perceptions regarding China's rise, and has adopted different strategies in its respective China policy. ASEAN countries' threat perceptions of China vary depending on history, geography, and the extent and nature of unresolved disputes.

SINO-MYANMAR RELATIONS

Myanmar was one of the primary countries to recognise the People's Republic of China in 1949. But the relations had suffered set back in the 1960s when anti-Chinese riots broke out in Yangon. One observer has briefly divided the China-Myanmar relations since diplomatic recognition in 1949 until today into the following phases: "first, ambivalent peaceful coexistence: 1949-1961; second, temporary setback: 1962-1970; third, improving relationship: 1971-1988; fourth, closer entente since 1989".

The US and its European allies imposed broad sanctions on Myanmar when the military Junta of Myanmar cracked down on the pro-democracy activists across Myanmar in 1988. It created a void in Myanmar's foreign relations and China stepped in to fill up the void. It is alleged that despite the sanctions, China provided Myanmar with aid and weapons and strengthened existing trade ties. It is also opined that China provides broad diplomatic support to Myanmar's military government. However, Sino-Myanmar relations suffered a blow in August, 2009, when 30,000-50,000 ethnic Chinese, who had emigrated to Myanmar and are mainly traders, fled back to China following a crack down on the Myanmar National Democratic Alliance Army (MNDAA) in Kokang. MNDAA is a predominately ethnic Chinese militia group in the Kokang region of the Shan State, Myanmar. Media reports stated that about 1500 Kokang militiamen also retreated to China following the conflict. This incident was a shock to Beijing.

Myanmar is strategically very important for China. Myanmar provides China critical access to the Indian Ocean.

The maritime aspect is very significant and gives Sino-Myanmar relations a strategic angle, not only for imports of natural resources (mainly oil and gas) and exports from landlocked southwestern Chinese provinces, but also "potentially for military bases or listening posts". Over time, China has built naval facilities, radars and signal-intelligence (SIGINT) posts along the Myanmarese coast and in Coco Islands. Media reports suggest that China is assisting Myanmar to modernise, improve and militarise naval port facilities in the Bay of Bengal at Akyab (Sittwe), Kyaukpyu and Mergui, and constructed a major naval base on Hainggyi Island near the Irrawaddy River delta.

According to an editorial published in the state controlled newspaper in Yangon, The New Light of Myanmar, bilateral cooperation between the two countries has expanded in various sectors, especially in the agriculture, hydropower, industrial, mining, oil and gas sectors and infrastructural building industry in the recent years. According to Chinese official statistics, China-Myanmar bilateral trade amounted to US$ 2.6 billion in 2008, which is 26.4 percent higher than in the year before. Until the year 2008, China's contracted investment in Myanmar amounted US$ 1.33 billion. Today, China is officially Myanmar's third-largest trading partner (after Singapore and Thailand) and the largest foreign investor.

Sino-Myanmar defence cooperation is also burgeoning. China is a major supplier of Myanmar's military hardware and training. According to various sources, in recent years Beijing has provided billions of dollars in military assistance to Yangon, including fighter, ground-attack and transport aircraft; tanks and armoured personnel carriers; naval vessels and surface-to-air missiles. Chinese Vice President Xi Jinping, during his recent visit to Myanmar, met with Than Shwe, Chairman of the State Peace and Development Council of Myanmar and both leaders pledged to improve traditional friendship of the two countries.

Despite the recent developments and positive trends in the Sino-Myanmar relations, observers have often labeled the entente as "uneven, asymmetrical, but nevertheless reciprocal and mutually beneficial". The Sino-Myanmar strategic entente and economic relations are regarded as "a marriage of convenience".

SINO-PAKISTAN RELATIONS

Since establishing diplomatic relations in 1951, China and Pakistan have enjoyed a close and mutually beneficial relationship. Pakistan was one of the first countries to recognise the People's Republic of China and to break ties with Republic of China, based in Taiwan. Sino-Pakistan relations have evolved amid the period of Beijing's international isolation in the 1960s and early 1970s. Sino-Pak cooperation ranges from economic, military and technical exchanges to supporting each other at various global forums.

Many believe that Sino-Indian rift in the 1960s also played a critical role in bringing China and Pakistan closer. Today, rise of India is unsettling for Pakistan and is also equally discomforting for China. This reminds us of the age old adage: enemy's enemy is my friend! "A strong China means a strong Pakistan," said the Pakistani President Asif Ali Zardari when he visited China in October, 2008. It was his maiden foreign trip after he came to power in 2008.

Many analysts term Sino-Pak relations as "all-weather friendship". Trade and commerce between China and Pakistan are growing rapidly. Trade between the two countries was about US$ 7 billion in 2008, and both sides have a target to soar bilateral trade to US$ 15 billion by 2011. In recent years, Chinese investment in Pakistan has grown, with Beijing investing in heavy engineering, power generation, and mining and telecommunication sectors in Pakistan.

China and Pakistan have a strong strategic alliance. China is helping Pakistan to build a deepwater sea port in Gwadar, in Baluchistan Province. Apart from its economic value, analysts believe, the port has significant strategic importance. It can be militarised in the future, "providing China with a base to defend Persian Gulf oil shipping lanes. India regards the port with discomfort". The port has been a major concern for India.

India believes that the Gwadar port would become the westernmost 'pearl' in China's "string of pearls" strategy.

Sino-Pak military cooperation is also witnessing an upward trend. Very recently, China (on July 31, 2009) delivered the first of the four state-of-the-art F-22P frigates to its "all-weather ally" Pakistan in accordance with contracts signed between the countries four years ago. The Sino-Pak relations reached a new height when news came out that China has agreed to sell 36 J-10B fighter jets to Pakistan. The Chinese J-10 aircraft are known to be one of the most advanced weapon systems made in China. Pakistan will be the first country to receive technologically advanced J-10B Chinese combat aircraft. This arms deal indicates the depth of the strategic alliance between China and Pakistan. China has also offered Pakistan military assistance to fight terrorist activities in Pakistan. China and Pakistan have been jointly conducting R&D in the defence sector for many years. For instance, in January 1990, Pakistan and China formally agreed to jointly design, develop and manufacture MBT-2000 *Al Khalid* tanks for Pakistan army.

SINO-INDIA RELATIONS

"President Hu and we also discussed our mutual interest in security and stability of Afghanistan and Pakistan. And neither country can or should be used as a base for terrorism, and we agreed to cooperate more on meeting this goal, including bringing about more stable, peaceful relations in all of South Asia." (Joint Press Statement by President Obama and President Hu of China in Beijing, China.)

The joint statement issued by President Obama and President Hu during Obama's visit to the China has raised concerns in India regarding the future role of China in South Asia. Obama's calling for a greater Chinese role in South Asia has caused raised-eyebrows in the Indian political and strategic arena. Many analysts believe the joint statement was meant to accord China an important role in Indo-Pak relations. This development is contrary to New Delhi's official position that the India-Pakistan relationship is exclusively bilateral. It would be quite interesting to watch how this development shapes the course of Sino-Indian relations in the coming days.

The Indian State of Arunachal Pradesh remains the bone of contention between the two countries. When Indian Prime Minister Manmohan Singh made his maiden visit to Arunachal Pradesh as Prime Minister in January 2008, he proclaimed the disputed state as "our land of the rising sun." The Chinese government quickly expressed its protest over Manmohan's claim. In a recent move, the Indian Government has endorsed raising four new mountain divisions of the Indian Army along the 4,056 km long disputed Line of Actual Control between India and China.

According to Indian media report, Indian Army Chief General Deepak Kapoor in a seminar in December 2009 in Army Training Command, based in Shimla, India, stated that Indian army is revising its war doctrine for Pakistan and China. The Times of India, an influential Indian national daily, on December 2009 reported that Indian army is bringing about changes in its war doctrine to face challenges of a "possible two-front-war with Pakistan and China", along with a host of other fourth generation warfare strategy reformulations. This is a significant development in the South Asian security realm and only exacerbates Indo-China tensions. Pakistani Army Chief, General Ashfaq Parvez Kayani, responded sharply terming the Indian move as "an adventurous and dangerous path, the consequences of which could be both unintended and uncontrollable." We are yet to hear Chinese reactions to Indian Army Chief's statement. Sino-India maritime competition is leaving a footprint on the relationship between the two countries. China is extending and establishing maritime cooperation with South and Southeast Asian states with a view to securing its foreign oil and trade routes. It is China's realisation that maintaining formidable maritime cooperation with Pakistan, Sri Lanka, Myanmar, Bangladesh, Thailand and Cambodia through investment and port development is essential to establish Chinese influence in the Indian Ocean, Strait of Malacca and the South China Sea. Therefore, China has taken up the 'String of Pearls' strategy quite seriously and it has become a major concern for India. There is a growing fear in India that the Chinese "Pearl" ports would be used for military means in the future to curtail Indian maritime influence in the region.

India bounced back in 2007. During that year, Indian navy, along with the navies of the US, Australia, Japan and Singapore, conducted a massive naval exercise, codenamed "Malabar-07-2", in the Bay of Bengal. Thirty-four ships and submarines of these five countries took part in the six-day war game. Two aircraft carriers of the US navy - USS Nimitz and USS Kitty Hawk joined India's only aircraft carrier, the INS Viraat, in the drill. According to Indian navy spokesman Captain Vinay Garg, this drill was perhaps the biggest ever peace-time joint naval exercise in Asia. While Indian Defence Minister A.K. Antony told that there was no military alignment, many analysts believed the exercise was an attempt by these countries (including India) to contain China's growing presence in the Indian Ocean. China registered its concerns over the war games.

Both China and India have great power ambitions. Both are on the fast track to development and are in competition with each other. Despite the suspicion and competition, Indo-China cooperation in various sectors is also being witnessed. India-China trade has burgeoned from US$ 2 billion in 2000 to an expected US$ 60 billion in 2010, exceeding the trade between India and the United States.

THE CHANGING FACE OF CHINESE DIPLOMACY

One of the most curious and underexamined features of the evolving North Korean nuclear crisis is the active and leading role played by China in the last nine months. Breaking with years of traditional Chinese passivity on global-security challenges, Beijing has helped to walk both Pyongyang and Washington back from the brink, surprising even China's critics.

Chinese diplomats were instrumental in bringing about a first round of tripartite discussions and six-party talks. Since then, senior Chinese officials have shuttled between Pyongyang and Washington to maintain momentum for the next round. Beijing has also used coercive measures such as a reported temporary suspension of oil supplies, an "inspection" of a North Korean ship in a Chinese port and shifting troop deployments on the China-North Korean border.

Beijing's consistent efforts to resolve the North Korean nuclear subject is one of many indications of a broader evolution in China's diplomacy. In recent years, Beijing's foreign policy has begun to reflect a more sophisticated, confident and, at times, constructive and proactive approach toward regional and global affairs.

For many previous decades until the mid-1990s, China regularly criticized the structure of the international system and complained that other powers colluded against its interests. Beijing now increasingly appears to be embracing the current constellation of international institutions, rules and norms as a means through which to promote and pursue its national interests. China is now working within the international system as opposed to criticizing and challenging it.

Evidence of the changes in Chinese diplomacy abound. China has expanded the breadth and depth of its bilateral relations, joined numerous regional and international agreements and increased the quality of its participation in multilateral organizations. Beijing's embrace of multilateral institutions represents one of the most dramatic shifts in its foreign relations. In the early 1990s, China was wary of such forums as venues that would criticize and constrain China. Beijing now views participation as a means to shape international rules, improve relations with neighbouring countries (especially in Southeast Asia) and limit what it perceives as undue U.S. global influence.

In East Asia, China has actively engaged the Association of Southeast Asian Nations and the Asean Regional Forum. Beijing has taken a series of calculated steps to reassure Asean states that China's rise doesn't threaten their economic and security interests. In 2001, China proposed the establishment of a China-Asean Free Trade Area, the first of its kind. To allay regional fears about its territorial ambitions, China also agreed to a Declaration on a Code of Conduct for the island disputes in the South China Sea. And Beijing most recently signed the Treaty of Amity and Cooperation, one of the first non-Asean states to take this step, signaling its acceptance of their norms of conflict resolution.

Elsewhere in the region, China led the establishment of a multilateral organization focused on regional security in Central Asia, known as the Shanghai Cooperation Organization. The group now has six members who cooperate on border demilitarization, counter terrorism and trade.

Beyond Asia, China initiated an annual meeting with the European Union in 1998 and recently approached the North Atlantic Treaty Organization about starting an annual dialogue on strategic perceptions and regional security threats. This effort stands in stark contrast to China's traditionally critical approach to U.S.-led security alliances. In the U.N. Security Council, China voted in favour of the November 2002 U.N. Resolution 1441 on weapons inspections in Iraq. This was only the second time since China joined the U.N. in 1971 that it supported a Security Council resolution of the U.N. Charter, which authorizes the use of force. Through the 1990s, while it generally did not block U.N. action, China abstained on similar votes, including during the first Gulf War. More recently, China has voted in support of resolutions relating to the rebuilding of Iraq.

Over the past 10 years, China has sign several key arms control and nonproliferation treaties. Beijing has also subjectd numerous domestic export control laws in an effort to enforce these new nonproliferation commitments. While differences in interpretation of the regimes and problems with implementing controls on sensitive technology exports continue, the overall trend is encouraging. China has also actively addressed numerous territorial disputes that historically soured its regional relations. Since 1991, it has resolved disputes with Laos, Russia, Vietnam, Kazakhstan, Kyrgyzstan and Tajikistan. In these settlements, China often received less than half of the disputed areas. In addition, China has instituted troop reductions and confidence-building measures on border security with key neighbours such as India and Russia.

Likewise, the execution of China's diplomacy has become more sophisticated, as Beijing seeks to shape world opinion. At an individual level, China's third and fourth generation of leaders have sought to personalize China's diplomacy by traveling abroad far more than previous leaders.

More broadly, China has subjectd well over a dozen "white papers" outlining the government's official position on domestic and international policy subjects. The Foreign Ministry's and State Council's Web pages include an impressive trove of basic data on Chinese positions, new policy developments and official statements. Perhaps most surprising, Chinese officials have started providing the international press with Western-style "background briefings" before and after most important diplomatic events.

Within the last few years, and especially since September 11, 2001, even more dramatic shifts have occurred in China's thinking about its role in the international system. Influential Chinese analysts have begun advocating that China abandon its long-held victim mentality and instead promote the adoption of a "great-power mentality."

An important manifestation of these ideas is that Chinese strategists increasingly see their interests as more akin to most important powers and less associated with those of developing nations. This change alone represents a significant perceptual shift from the 1990s, when many Chinese still viewed their nation as disenfranchised by globalization, the other most important powers, and multilateral forums. Reflecting this change, President Hu Jintao was the first Chinese leader to attend a dialogue meeting of the Group of Eight leading nations this past summer.

Chinese diplomats and political leaders now talk about "shared global responsibilities" and improving cooperation among "great powers" (which includes China) to combat global security threats. This thinking stands in stark contrast to China's previously narrow view of its national interests, its identity as a most important power and its role in the international community.

A final, most important element of China's new thinking is a recent, if grudging, acceptance that the world is for the moment unipolar and that U.S. preponderance will persist for decades. Although Chinese leaders publicly tout multipolarization as the trend of the times (and condemn American unilateralism), Chinese analysts also acknowledge that their country cannot (and will not) challenge U.S. global dominance anytime soon.

While all these trends are important, China still faces serious obstacles to becoming a high-profile, much less a dominant, player in the international community. Even as the country's diplomacy becomes more active, Chinese leaders need to grapple with severe political, social and economic challenges. China's new diplomacy presents Asian and American leaders with both opportunities and challenges. China's active participation in international institutions creates more chances to elicit its assistance on key subjects. Recent examples of this trend include U.S.-China cooperation on counterterrorism, counternarcotics and nonproliferation.

However, policy makers should remember that even as China becomes more engaged, it is also growing more adept at using its foreign policy and foreign relations to serve Chinese interests. Today's China is certainly smarter and more sophisticated — but not necessarily kinder or gentler. Beijing's new skills may at times frustrate Washington's objectives, as China is potentially becoming better equipped to challenge the policies of the U.S. and its allies. China's ability to consistently outmaneuver the U.S. at the U.N. Human Rights Commission in recent years should serve as a wake-up call.

China is dissatisfied with some features of the international system, such as U.S. preponderance and especially the status of Taiwan. Washington should remain aware of these frustrations and shape its ties with Asian nations in a way that recognizes the reality of China's expanding regional role. China is rapidly emerging as the engine of growth in Asia, which affords it increasing influence and leverage. Washington needs to pay consistent attention to managing relations with regional friends and allies, if it hopes to maintain its pull.

A longer-term task for the entire international group of people is to ensure that China's new diplomacy is consistent with regional stability and security. China's top political leaders have deemed the next 20 years a strategic opportunity to develop their country. An opening exists for the international community as well, and policy makers should use it wisely, to manage China's emergence as a diplomatic power.

CHINA'S SHIFTING RELATIONSHIP WITH ASEAN

The history of China and its Southeast Asian neighbours during the Cold War years was one of both amity and animosity. Indonesia (April 1950) and Burma (June 1950) were among the first few countries to recognize the People's Republic of China (PRC). From the early 1950s until the mid-1960s, Beijing enjoyed an especially warm relationship with Jakarta, most prominently displayed in the 1955 Bandung Conference of Asian-African Countries and continued during much of President Sukarno's reign. Beijing also maintained a close relationship with the fellow communist regime in North Vietnam and rendered significant support to its causes against France and the United States from the 1950s to the 1970s, including sizable material and human assistance.

But China's relationships with many Southeast Asia's noncommunist states were decidedly estranged. Concerns over potential threats from communism led some of them to participate in and form alliance-like regional organizations (Southeast Asian Treaty Organization or SEATO, 1954-77; the Five-Power Defence Arrangements or FPDA, 1971-) with external powers—the United States in particular—to protect their interests. There were deep suspicions over China's motives and activities, especially as they related to the large number of overseas Chinese residing in these countries. Beijing's public support of the communist insurgents in the region only reinforced their perceptions and heightened their fears. Not surprisingly, many of them did not establish diplomatic relations with Beijing until the mid-1970s (Thailand, Malaysia, and the Philippines). Others only normalized ties with China in the 1990s (Singapore and Indonesia).

The Sino-U.S. rapprochement in the early 1970s led to the establishment of diplomatic ties between China and a number of ASEAN states. The emerging Chinese-ASEAN cooperation in the late 1970s ironically was prompted largely by their shared concerns over Vietnam's growing assertiveness and its attempt to establish hegemony in Indochina, in particular in the aftermath of its invasion of neighbouring Cambodia. Thailand, being on the frontline of the Cambodian conflict, sought to develop security ties with China. China also coordinated with ASEAN in seeking a political settlement of the Cambodian issue and supported the latter's position that the Cambodian coalition government headed by Prince Sihanouk, not the Hanoi-backed Heng Samrin regime, should represent Phnom Penh in the United Nations (UN).

During the 1980s, Chinese policy toward Southeast Asia began to undergo important changes in two critical areas. Beijing started to place state-to-state relationships in precedence over ideological ties by halting its support to communist insurgence movements in the region. In 1989, it also passed laws on Chinese citizenship requiring overseas Chinese to adopt citizenship of their countries of residence. By taking these two important measures, major irritants effectively were removed from China's bilateral relationships with a number of Southeast Asian countries. Beijing now seemed more than ever eager to court better relationships with its Southern neighbours, and this has paved the way for improvement of political ties.

Beijing's official contact with ASEAN as a group began in July 1991 when Chinese Foreign Minister Qian Qichen was invited to attend the opening ceremony of the 24th ASEAN Foreign Ministers' Meeting. Since then China has attended each ASEAN Foreign Ministers' Meeting consecutively. In 1994,

China participated in the ASEAN Regional Forum (ARF) and became a consultative dialogue partner of ASEAN. This status was elevated in 1996, when China became a full dialogue partner with ASEAN. In December 1997, Chinese President Jiang Zemin and ASEAN leaders held their first ever summit in Malaysia and issued a joint statement announcing their decision to establish a partnership of good neighborliness and mutual trust between China and ASEAN oriented toward the 21st century. In October 2003, China and ASEAN signed the "Joint Declaration of the PRC and ASEAN State Leaders—A Strategic Partnership for Peace and Prosperity."

The emerging China-ASEAN ties were influenced by a number of developments at the time. One was Beijing's efforts, in the wake of the Tiananmen incident, in particular in response to the sanctions imposed by the West, to break the isolation. Southeast Asian countries, given their relative reticence regarding the June 4 Incident, became targets of the Chinese diplomatic good neighborly policy. Beijing and Jakarta restored, and China and Singapore established, diplomatic relations in 1990. Chinese Premier Li Peng visited Indonesia, the Philippines, Malaysia, and Laos as part of that diplomatic endeavor. A second reason was to sustain the cooperation between the two in the wake of the Cambodian settlement, in which China played a constructive role in the resolution of the dispute and had been in close consultation with ASEAN in the 1980s. But most important of all was Beijing's changing perception of its security environment and the relative place of Southeast Asia in its post-Cold War security policy. This resulted in the successful management of the territorial disputes in the South China Sea, Beijing's reassurance to ASEAN of its benign intentions and its acceptance of multilateralism and cooperative security, and China's growing economic ties with ASEAN.

ORGANIZATION TERRITORIAL DISPUTES

To ensure a conducive environment for economic development required strengthening relations and/ or mending fences with China's neighbours, including the Southeast Asian states. Disputes over the Spratly Islands began to emerge in the 1980s, especially after the signing of the United Nations Convention on the Law of the Sea (UNCLOS) in 1982. The reported rich deposits of maritime resources, including oil and natural gas, led to scrambling for atolls and islets in the South China Sea and disputes among six claimants—Brunei, China, Malaysia, Philippines, Taiwan, and Vietnam. While Beijing sought to improve relations with ASEAN, its assertiveness in sovereignty claims almost derailed such efforts. This was most evident in China's handling of the territorial disputes in the South China Sea, especially its occasional display of military might. The construction of shelters on the disputed Mischief Reef also was seen by some of the contenders as an act of aggressiveness. In addition to strengthening its claims to the disputed territories, China's South China Sea policy also was a refection of its growing interest and ambitions in extending its influence, and as a result, greater efforts in developing a navy that could go beyond coastal defence.

Chinese assertiveness in its claims over the Spratly Islands was informed both by its strong sense of sovereignty and territorial integrity, and more pragmatic economic security considerations, including securing a peaceful external environment for economic development and protecting the country's economic interests, including protecting its land, air space, and its territorial waters. The growing attention to maritime interests and the cultivation of a "conception of sea as territory" (*haiyang guotuguan*) refected both a recognition of the potential of maritime resources for national economic development and a realization that China must enhance its ability to protect its perceived maritime territories. One Chinese analyst suggested:

> To make sure that such [maritime] resources are fully tapped and utilized, China needs to ensure the security of its maritime economic activities. A strong naval defence is essential to reducing the threat posed by sea-borne smuggling and piracy to China's tariff incomes, ocean fishery, and marine transportation.

According to Chinese sources, of the more than 3 million square km of territorial waters China claims as its own, an area of more than 800,000 square km within China's traditional maritime boundaries has been illegally delineated into the domain of other nations, with 410,000 square km taken by the Philippines, 270,000 by Malaysia, 70,000 by Vietnam, 50,000 by Indonesia, and the remainder by Brunei.... With rapid economic growth, China will be in greater and greater need of energy. The 3 million square km of national marine territory is where the Chinese nation's descendants pin their hopes.

This had prompted calls for exercising one's own rights under UNCLOS that provides legitimacy for such claims. One Chinese naval offcer contended: "From a national viewpoint, the Convention allows each country to utilize the ocean according to its own needs and gain its own individual ocean rights and interests, and it supplies a legal framework." This call for more assertive sovereignty claims was understandably prompted by the fact that other claimant states reportedly already were operating 120 oil wells that could extract between 30 and 50 million tons of crude oil, which was almost one-third of China's annual extraction and surpassed China's South China Sea oil production by 40 times. The loss to China was therefore enormous.

China became a net oil importer in 1993. The need for energy to fuel economic development could create instability as countries in the region compete for energy resources, which in turn could exacerbate the already touchy territorial disputes in the South China Sea. China's ongoing naval development can be seen, apart from the Taiwan scenario, as a direct response to energy shortages and the need to be able to assert claims over territories believed to contain much needed energy reserves. For these reasons, the Chinese Navy had been given the task of broadening the traditional mission of coastal defence to that of force projection into the South China Sea and beyond. Two important factors probably explain the rising importance of maritime security to China. One is that maritime routes are becoming essential to China's growing international trade; it increasingly depends on the seaborne resources that go through the key chokepoints in Southeast Asia. With about 85 percent of its trade being transported by sea, including an estimated 50 percent of its oil imports transiting the Strait of Malacca, Beijing understandably is keen on developing its force projection capability, if for nothing else than to protect critical sea lanes. The other reason is the potential offshore oil and mineral deposits, which are crucial resources to China's economic development in the coming decades.

China claims complete sovereignty over the entire Spratly Island groups that are partly or in whole also claimed by Brunei, Malaysia, the Philippines, Taiwan, and Vietnam, and over Paracel, a claim that also is contended by Vietnam. In February 1992, China's National People's Congress (NPC), the country's putative legislature, passed the Law of Territorial Waters and Contiguous Zone that claims complete control and asserts that it will resort to the use of force to protect its territories. The controversial law, together with reported Chinese People's Liberation Army (PLA) construction of an airstrip on the Woody Island, struck the ASEAN states as showing assertive Chinese intentions toward the entire South China Sea. An internal document in China argued at the time that, given the country's increasing demands for resources and the decreasing resource bases at home, the importance of the Spratly Island groups in terms of their potential oil and mineral reserves was becoming greater and, indeed, might provide the only survival space for China.

The island groups also sit on important SLOCs and therefore are strategically significant. Chinese control over the area means that they will be able not only to enhance their power projection capabilities but also to exert tremendous leverage over countries that rely on these SLOCs for their imports of key industrial resources such as oil. In other words, the ability or the perceived ability to disrupt normal transportation can cause great uncertainty and economic fallout. China already had engaged in two military clashes with Vietnam (1974, 1988) and was slowly but steadily increasing its presence in the South China

Sea. The Chinese leaders, meanwhile, were trying to assure the neighbours by expressing willingness to discuss joint exploration and development efforts with other claimant states and shelve the sovereignty issue.

However, Beijing continued to assert its exclusive sovereignty over the disputed territories in the South China Sea even as it advocated shelving the question of sovereignty. This was demonstrated by the revelation of its occupation of the Mischief Reef in February 1995, where the PLA built concrete constructs and shelters. There were competing explanations as to China's intention in occupying the reef, and the Chinese themselves explained that the structure built would be used for fishermen regardless of nationalities. Nonetheless the Philippines were alarmed.

The Mischief incident effectively raised ASEAN's concern over China's assertiveness and galvanized the organization into action. Until 1995, ASEAN had taken no public position on the South China Sea disputes. In March 1995, ASEAN for the first time publicly called for all parties to the dispute to adhere to the spirit and letter of the 1992 Manila Declaration on the South China Sea. The issue subsequently was placed on the agenda of the ARF despite Chinese objection. Member states converged on the idea of the code of conduct, refecting the principles the group had always adhered to—nonforceful settlement of disputes, norm-building, and confidence-building measures (CBMs). ASEAN itself first adopted principles of behaviour among member states and then presented a united front vis-à-vis China. The approach was driven by two considerations. The first was to develop consensus among members, since not all of them lay claims to the disputed territories and as they each had a different relationship with China; secondly, it was hoped that a code of conduct, should it be accepted by Beijing, would constrain China, a stronger power in the disputes, to refrain from the use of force.

However, even as member states were contem-plating unifed approaches toward the South China Sea disputes, some also sought to strike separate deals/understandings with Beijing.

Malaysia, for one, accepted China's preference for bilateral negotiation. What also was significant was Malaysian Prime Minister Mahathir's call for external powers to stay out of the disputes, effectively ruling out possible intervention by the United States, something Manila was keen on securing. Indeed, the Philippines sought U.S. support and signed a Visiting Forces Agreement with Washington in February 1998, 7 years after it had evicted American forces from its naval and air force bases. Meanwhile, the Philippines also engaged in bilateral discussion with China, resulting in a Joint Statement on PRC-RP Consultation on the South China Sea and on Other Areas of Cooperation in August 1995.

On November 4, 2002, ASEAN and China signed the Declaration on the Conduct of Parties in the South China Sea, a major milestone in China-ASEAN relations, concerning how the claimant countries to the territorial disputes would resolve them. While ASEAN was not able to get Beijing committed to a code of conduct, which would be a more stringent measure, the declaration at least obliged China to pursue a multilateral approach to the issue, a shift from the bilateralism that it had preferred. It also was symbolic in that China had appeared to be accepting ASEAN's preference for norms and regulation of the dispute. Specifcally, the Declaration commits the signatory parties: to exercise self-restraint in the conduct of activities that would complicate or escalate disputes and affect peace and stability including, among others, refraining from action of inhabiting on the presently uninhabited islands, reefs, shoals, cays, and other features and to handle their differences in a constructive manner.

What motivated Beijing to adopt a more moderate approach to the territorial disputes was a growing concern over the Taiwan independence issue, and hence the need to secure ASEAN support for its unifcation policy; the risk of pushing the small Southeast Asian countries to the United States, resulting in greater ASEAN-U.S. military cooperation that could allow U.S. access to military facilities in the region, hence posing a greater threat to Chinese security interests, especially where the Taiwan contingency was concerned; and China's own lack of power projection capability that could help enforce its claims effectively. These considerations led to changes in managing territorial disputes, moving away from more confrontational and militaristic approaches to ones that emphasize dialogue and promote joint exploration and development, without in any way giving up its claim to sovereignty over the disputed territories in the South China Sea.

The more moderate stance was meant to defate growing alarm over Chinese aggressiveness, especially in the context of the 1995-96 Chinese missile exercises in the Taiwan Strait, rather than a fundamental change of the conception of sovereignty. Indeed, if anything, western analysts suggest that Beijing may be engaged in a slow-intensity conflict where it steadily strengthens its hold on, and extends its reach to, disputed maritime territories.

Beijing also negotiated separate codes of conduct with Vietnam and the Philippines. Between 1992 and 2000, seven rounds of negotiation took place between China and Vietnam. In December 1999, Beijing and Hanoi signed a Land Border Treaty, which subsequently was ratifed by the two countries' parliaments in 2000. On December 25, 2000, China and Vietnam signed the Agreement on the Delimitation of the Territorial Seas, Exclusive Economic Zones, and Continental Shelves in the Gulf of Tonkin and the Agreement on Fishery Cooperation in the Beibu Gulf. Both agreements subsequently were ratifed by the two countries' legislatures in 2004.

In March 2005, national oil companies from China, the Philippines, and Vietnam signed a landmark agreement to conduct joint prospecting for oil and gas in the South China Sea. On the one hand, this is considered to be a major breakthrough, especially based on the idea of shelving territorial disputes and seeking joint exploitation and development. However, there also are concerns, from the ASEAN perspective, over China's "divide and rule" tactic that is establishing its dominance effectively in the region and undermining the organization's unity in dealing with the rising power. Furthermore, the territorial disputes continue to resurface from time to time, with occasional clashes resulti·g in casualties and detention, or otherwise property damages. A July 1999 run-in between a Chinese fshing boat and the Philippine Navy ended in the former's sinking. Similar incidents occurred in January 2000, when Philippine naval patrol personnel boarded Chinese fishing boats, touching off protests and warnings from Beijing. Chinese media also point out that Vietnam continues to encroach on Chinese territorial integrity in the South China Sea by setting up telephone networks on atolls and islets currently under Vietnamese occupation. These activities are seen as efforts to establish *fait accompli* to strengthen Hanoi's leverage in future negotiations.

CHINA RISING POWER IN SOUTH ASIA

Beijing did not take too seriously ASEAN's growing role initially. Instead, it anticipated a greater role for the UN Security Council and a multipolar world when the Cold War ended. Within the Asian context, China saw the United States, Russia, Japan, and itself as the critical players, but not ASEAN, as it was deemed largely a subregional grouping with an inward-looking orientation. That began to change in the mid-1990s as Beijing both recognized and indeed appreciated the role that ASEAN could play. This became even more apparent with the expansion of the original ASEAN-6 to the Greater ASEAN of Ten by the decade's end.

Chinese analysts have characterized ASEAN's evolving regional role as evolving in four phases. In the first phase, which began in the late 1970s largely in response to Vietnam's invasion of Cambodia (and hence a direct threat to Thailand's security), the organization's major efforts were expended on seeking a peaceful solution of the Cambodian issue by engaging extra-regional powers. The Paris Agreement, to which ASEAN made a significant contribution, gave the organization a high profile in the international diplomatic arena and provided it with greater interest and the confidence to participate in and influence Southeast Asian affairs. The second phase began in the early 1990s and focused mostly on ASEAN's effort to engage major powers in the development of a regional security dialogue that aimed at both socializing China to the benefit of multilateralism and cooperative security and keeping the other major powers engaged in the region's security to prevent the emergence of a power vacuum and hence invitation for competition. Through the Post-Ministerial Meetings, dialogues, and the establishment of the ARF, the group succeeded in bringing all major powers under the framework of a security dialogue that was subject to the ASEAN Way of gradualism, consensus-building, and nonuse of force in dispute settlement.

The third phase was characterized by ASEAN's continuing pursuit of multichannel, multilevel security dialogues that involved the Asia-Europe meeting (ASEM), ASEAN+1 and 3, and the organization's own plan toward greater integration, including the ASEAN FTA. The current phase involves ASEAN's efforts to move beyond Southeast Asia to launch a region-wide political forum that would include all major East Asian powers. Initially the brain-child of Malaysian Prime Minister Mahathir, the East Asia Summit was formally held in Kuala Lumpur in December 2005, but with the participation of Australia, India, and New Zealand, in addition to the originally conceived participating countries.

Over the years, ASEAN has debated, explored, and developed various strategies of dealing with major powers. These strategies have been applied during different periods, depending on specific security circumstances of the time. Essentially, three approaches have been especially emphasized. One is the Non-Aligned Movement (NAM) approach promoted by Indonesia. This would be an effort to exclude major power interference in ASEAN's internal affairs. At the same time, it would sustain Jakarta's position within the organization. The second approach is favored by Malaysia, which advocates neutrality in two ways. One is noninterference and nonaggression in interstate relations to avoid being involved in great power conflicts; the other is to secure major powers' pledges not to intervene in Southeast Asian affairs, hence allowing the region to maintain autonomy and neutrality. The third is balancing, promoted by Singapore, between great powers. Singapore recognizes that major powers all have important interests in the region, therefore it is unrealistic to exclude their involvement. But efforts can be made to prevent one particular power from dominating the entire region.

The ASEAN Way of informality and noninterference in domestic affairs has served as the guiding principle in its approach to regional affairs. While this approach has served the organization well and provided a comfort level for member states to interact with each other without having to accept binding decisions, it is now facing increasing challenges. The tendency to hold meetings, talk, and sign documents but to be slow in implementation has begun to constrain ASEAN's ability to address real issues.

Beijing increasingly has viewed ASEAN as an important power centre in Asia. This is largely due to ASEAN's skillful diplomacy of balancing all the major powers, hence enhancing its own leverage. This is possible because major powers essentially have balanced out one another, with no one able to dominate. Finally, ASEAN itself since 1997 has sought to consolidate and achieve economic integration (ASEAN Economic Community) by 2015, with security and social community to follow. It hosted the first East Asia Summit in December 2005, and has over the years developed various ASEAN+1/3 meetings, with the ASEM playing a facilitating role in promoting regionalism.

At the same time, it should also be noted that ASEAN still harbours some suspicions toward China and likely will continue to resort to strategies of hedging or balancing through expanded ties with other external powers. In recent years, ASEAN member states have expanded their military cooperation greatly with the United States. Japan has been very active in regaining its influence in Southeast Asia and has offered a large economic aid package to the region. India also is actively engaging with ASEAN on greater economic, political, and military contacts.

Finally, the East Asia Summit, originally billed as an exclusive regional event, had its inaugural meeting attended by Australia, India, and New Zealand, in addition to the ASEAN+3 countries. While a realpolitik assessment of these developments would alarm Beijing, as extra-regional forces would dilute China's own influence, Chinese officials and analysts seem not to be bothered by ASEAN's efforts to knit complex and overlapping arrangements and relationships with itself as the coordinating core.

Indeed, a major Chinese report on ASEAN recommended that Beijing respect ASEAN's position, including some member states' growing military ties with the United States; acknowledge and respect that the United States has legitimate interests in the region; and actually encourage better ASEAN-U.S. cooperation, especially in the context of fighting terrorism. In that context, U.S. deployment of military forces, dispatching of special force advisors, and specific arrangements for base access should not be viewed as targeted at China.

Nonetheless, Chinese analysts are monitoring these developments closely. The post-9/11 U.S. policy adjustment toward Southeast Asia could have a significant impact on issues of territorial disputes in the South China Sea, SLOCs, the cohesion of ASEAN as a group, and could cause domestic turmoil in some member states. Since 9/11, the United States has strengthened its military presence in the region and resumed and intensifed joint military exercises with a number of ASEAN member states, ostensibly aimed at fighting global terrorism. Meanwhile, the U.S. position on territorial disputes in the South China Sea has shifted from neutrality and nonintervention to "positive" mediation, with greater emphasis on freedom of navigation, including escorts.

What is most significant is a U.S. proposal for joint patrol of the Malacca Strait with the "Regional Maritime Security Initiative." While the proposal has been turned down by the three Strait countries—Malaysia, Singapore, and Indonesia—there has since been more cooperation between the United States and the regional militaries. For China, stable and uninterrupted supplies of oil through the Malacca Strait is critical to its economic security, and control by foreign powers could seriously undermine Chinese security interests.

Another issue of potential concern is Taiwan's activities in ASEAN countries. For various reasons, most of them economic, ASEAN has maintained rather close ties with Taipei. In fact, Taiwan has nine times the investment in the region than does China, and Taiwan was most active in the early to mid-1990s in pushing for more official contacts through "vacation diplomacy" and "golf diplomacy," among other tactics. Lee Hsien Loong's visit to Taiwan in the summer of 2004—billed as "private"—just before he became Singapore's prime minister triggered strong reactions from China, including cancellation of previously scheduled bilateral meetings and visits by Singaporean ministers. Managing such incidents requires delicate diplomacy as much as it demands a resolute stance on an issue for which China has no room for negotiation.

CHINA AND INDIA AS DRIVERS OF REGIONAL GROWTH

There is little doubt that China's rapidly growing exports to countries outside of Asia-Pacific in Asia has generated equally rapid growth in imports by China from other Asian and Pacific countries, not just from its neighbours in East Asia but also from Australia, India and Indonesia. According to Perlez (2003), Japan's current "recovery is being driven by a surge in exports to China. Australia's healthy economy is being kept that way by Chinese investments in liquid natural gas products. China is now South Korea's largest trading partner... In Indonesia, Malaysia and the Philippines (and to a lesser extent in Thailand)... China's main interest is to scoop up what it can for its modernization. Indonesians call this new relationship with Beijing as 'feeding the dragon.'" Although India is by far the largest (and rapidly growing) market in South Asia, it is yet to have a major impact on the trade of its neighbours in South Asia in spite of the creation of the South Asian Preferential Trade Area (SAPTA) in 1997. To a significant extent, this reflects the hostile relations between India and the next largest market in South Asia, viz. Pakistan. Pakistan is yet to grant a most favoured nation status to India. Unless the relations between the two normalize, the prospects of SAPTA are not bright. However, India-Sri Lanka bilateral trade and investment have grown rapidly since the conclusion of a free trade agreement between the two became operational in March 2000. Recent signs of a warming of Indo- Pakistani relations, if they lead to their normalization, could make India the engine of growth for South Asia, as China already is in the Asia-Pacific region.

Foreign Direct Investment

China receives a much larger flow of net foreign direct investment (projected at $57 billion in 2003) than India's (under $4 billion in 2001-02). In Srinivasan (2002), I discussed some of the reasons for this difference. In short, as Luce and Kynge (2003) succinctly point out, "whether it is China's cheaper, more reliable power supply or the more rapid turn around at its ports, China remains an incalculably better environment for most manufacturing than India, which is slowly waking up to this." This environment and the bureaucratic obstacles at all levels of government in India in large part explain the huge flow of FDI to China relative to India. The Indian government has recognized FDI as key for achieving the Tenth Plan target of 8% annual growth and appointed a steering committee on FDI in 2001. It reported in 2002 with several recommendations for making India more attractive as a destination for FDI.

Exchange Rates and Foreign Reserves

Although China's trade surplus with the United States has been growing, its overall trade surplus is modest since it is running a growing trade deficit with Asia-Pacific countries that offsets in large part its trade surplus with the US. The economic logic that only a country's overall trade and current account balances have economic significance and not its bilateral balances with any one or a subset of trading partners, has never been understood by politicians anywhere, and in particular, in the US. As Japanese trade surpluses created an anti-Japan backlash in the eighties, it is now China's turn to be at the receiving end of US pressure. China has accumulated a substantial (projected at $383 billion by the end of 2003) foreign exchange reserves, exceeding its annual imports. India has done the same—its reserves, around $92 billion at the end of 2003, exceed by a substantial margin the likely imports of $60 billion. The issues of the appropriate level of reserves, and whether both countries have accumulated far too much relative to what would be needed to smooth volatility in export earnings and import expenditures and to contain any potential financial crisis like the one experienced by East Asia in 19975. Since neither the renminbi nor the rupee is convertible on capital account and capital controls are in place in both countries, prima facie the probability of an exchange rate crisis of the type experienced by countries with open capital account and fully convertible currencies is very low. This is not to say, of course, that a balance of payments crisis (BOP) that makes the prevailing exchange rate unsustainable cannot arise—after all, despite capital controls and an inconvertible (on capital account) rupee, India experienced a severe BOP crisis in 1991, which resulted in the devaluation of the rupee and other policy changes. Still, given that partial insurance from other sources of external funds (e.g., from the IMF) is in principle available, should self-insurance through reserves be pushed as far as the current level of reserves in China and India seem to have done?

Any attempt to determine the appropriate level of reserves has to be based on an analysis of the appropriate exchange rate regime for either country, and the related issue of whether the benefits from integration with the global financial markets outweigh the costs. Without doing such an analysis myself, let me cite Kenneth Rogoff of Harvard, the former Economic Councillor and Director, Research Department of the IMF, on the issue:

My interpretation of the evidence not just from Asia but from the whole world, from Europe's experience, from floating rates, from the Bretton Woods system, is that policy makers vastly overrate the risks of having volatile exchange rates and vastly underrate the indirect costs that can come from all the policies that they have to try to suppress them. Certainly I wouldn't say that India has gone too far at the moment in accumulating reserves, it has a very strong position but I think all the countries in Asia are reaching a point when they have to start asking the question how much is enough, that basically a lot of the reserves that the Asian economies are accumulating—even outside of Japan—we are talking about close to a trillion dollars, are basically low interest rate loans from the emerging markets to United States and Europe, and this is very costly. There are opportunity costs to the domestic economy. How much is enough and at what point should one risk letting the exchange rate appreciate. Knowing the multilateral aspects of it, I realize that there are some outside the IMF who call for greater flexibility in Asian currencies in order to strengthen demand from the rest of the world. I think that is an issue worth considering but it is not the one I want to focus on. From the Asian economies' own perspective, and this is true for India, it is true for China, it is true for virtually all the countries in the region, moving to a regime of greater flexibility would be something that is advisable, would not bring the cost many policy makers fear, and in fact would allow the economies to reduce the level of recession and that would have many positive growth effects (Rogoff 2003). Rogoff's conclusion does not imply that US pressure on China to revalue the renminbi was justified or that India should also let its rupee appreciate, but only that greater flexibility in exchange rates would be appropriate in both countries.

The Indian exchange rate regime is one of managed float (although Rogoff prefers to characterize it as a crawling peg), and it does allow some flexibility. It is possible to argue that the Indian central bank (i.e., Reserve Bank of India) has inappropriately intervened to prevent the rupee from appreciating, and this has cost the Indian economy in terms of foregone growth. But this is an argument that the flexibility inherent in the managed float regime has not been utilized appropriately. It is not the same as arguing that India should immediately make the rupee fully convertible and adopt a regime of clean float. The latter argument is not persuasive for the simple reason that domestic financial sector reforms are incomplete, and it is risky to open the capital account under the circumstances. In any case, there is no country in the world, developed or developing, that allows a clean float of its currency. On the other hand, there are long term benefits from a convertible currency and by credibly committing to a fully convertible rupee for at a not too distant and specified future date, the pressure to complete the financial sector reforms by that date would become significant. What about China? Again, the problems in the financial sector, particularly the overhang of NPLs are serious, and an immediate revaluation might worsen the problem. Besides, it has not been established by anyone, least of all by the US Treasury, that the current renminbi-dollar exchange rate is too far from a long-run equilibrium rate. If it is not, and China moves to a floating regime, that US Treasury might find, to its surprise, that the exchange rate does not move from its current level! Unfortunately, China is likely to succumb to the pressure to revalue if newspaper reports (*Financial Times*, February 10, 2004) are to be believed.

It is not unlikely that if India's reserves continue to climb, and outsourcing gathers further momentum, there would be charges of "currency manipulation" against Indian authorities, as the Chinese are currently being charged with. China and India should cooperate in resisting such accusations and pressures and decide on their exchange rate policies in their own interests. Finally, as Rogoff rightly points out, by continuing to accumulate reserves in terms of US dollar assets, China, India and other Asian countries are financing US current account deficits. As Alan Beattie (2003) points out: "In theory, Asians' role in financing the US current account deficit could give them enormous economic or even political leverage, since a sudden shortfall in capital inflows would spark a slide in the dollar and possibly a sharp rise in interest rates." But he rightly concludes that: "A wholesale flight from the dollar, if it drove up interest rates and forced the US into a rapid tightening of consumers' belts, would also hurt one of the principle buyers of Asia's exports." Chinese and Indian policy makers are sophisticated enough to realize this and can be expected to slow the accumulation of reserves, if appropriate, and allow greater exchange rate flexibility in due course.

INDIA FALLING BEHIND CHINA IN SOUTH ASIAN DIPLOMACY

India has always been a local superpower, being by far the largest country within South Asia, and is, in fact, the only one in the group that borders every other South Asian country except Afghanistan, which shares a border with Pakistan. But India's economic performance was stunted by years of state control of the kind now prevalent in Iran. Over the past 15 years, however, economic growth has been strong, enabling the country to have a much greater diplomatic reach than at any time since the 1950s when India briefly emerged as the leader of those countries that were being de-colonized by the European powers. Given this situation, it ought to have been the case that New Delhi would be preeminent in its own backyard. Instead, over the past two decades, India has lost the status of being the lead player in any South Asian country barring Bhutan, a country with which it still has a treaty relationship. In almost the entire region, China has overtaken India in that intangible quality - influence - especially in Nepal and Sri Lanka, while Beijing's existing alliances with Pakistan and Bangladesh are growing stronger.

This is not due to a lack of quality within India's diplomatic service. Instead, the Indian Foreign Service (IFS) has produced a modern corps of skilled diplomats, many experts in different regions of the world, and eager to do more to advance their country's interests. The wall they face is the ambivalence that has become second nature to the country's top policy makers, both within the political crust as well as the administrative backup. Phrases such as "going all the way" and "going for the kill" are inelegant. Yet they represent a reality that is that sometimes a country has to formulate and then determinedly implement a clear policy to be carried out till success is achieved.

In South Asia, such a quality was recently displayed by President Percy Mahinda Rajapaksa of Sri Lanka. He succeeded in wiping out the terrorist group known as the Liberation Tigers of Tamil Eelam (LTTE) where, over the past three decades, all his predecessors had failed. Unlike them, President Rajapaksa did not heed (well-meaning but disastrous) advice to slow down his offensive or agree to a cease-fire, the latter being a device that the LTTE used since 1987 to gain time to recover after having lost the initiative in the field. Once the LTTE recovered its strength, the ceasefire would be abandoned. This point was repeatedly made by Rajapaksa to the peacemakers who clustered around him, especially in the final months of the brief, brutal war against the LTTE that began with his coming to office in 2005.

Once India, because of political considerations such as the need to avoid alienating the country's sizable Tamil population, refused to give the Sri Lankan army equipment, Rajapaksa turned to Pakistan and China. Both countries opened their warehouses to him, and so built up immense capital both within Sri Lanka's Sinhala most importantity as well as the country's policy establishment. Rajapaksa showed none of the half-heartedness that has characterized so much of Indian policy and, as a result, emerged a winner. In the case of India, the desire to win brownie points with key international players (by heeding their sometimes incorrect advice) as well as an aversion to risk ensured that much of Indian diplomacy was too watered down to be effective. This is especially the case in its immediate neighbourhood.

This on-again, off-again excellence can be seen in Indian diplomatic policy towards Pakistan especially in regard to the long-term pattern of instituting confidence building measures (CBM) being followed - usually after a mass terror attack - with strong rhetoric and a withdrawal of contact. The reality is that in the case of Pakistan, conventional war may have ceased to be an option. This is because the Pakistan army has itself lost control of many of the jihadis that it has trained, equipped and funded for so long.

Instead of reducing the risk of a terror attack, going after the Pakistan military would inflame a large segment of the Pakistani population thus making them susceptible to recruitment in the ongoing jihad against India. Given that situation, it may have been preferable for Indian policymakers to publicly resort to a conventional war except in the case of a conflict started by Pakistan, an unlikely possibility. The military option would work only if (a) the Pakistan army controls the jihadi networks and (b) is comprehensively defeated in battle. Neither condition exists.

A "No War" declaration by India would remove the Pakistani military establishment's most frequently used excuse to station more than 60 percent of its army along the India border, even as the force is engaged in a life-and-death struggle with the Pakistan Taliban. Instead, even though New Delhi has no intention of going to war, the prospect of one is deliberately kept open especially after terror strikes such as Mumbai 11/26-28. Thus, the benefits of India's "No War" declaration are denied, while the other side is aware that the mock-aggressive posture is a bluff and hence will not change its behaviour as a result of the threat.

A glaring example of how promoting the idea that India would go to war over Pakistani provocations has hurt New Delhi can be seen in the 2002 standoff with Pakistan in the mountains separating the two. Ostensibly to scare the international community into putting pressure on Pakistan to call off its Kashmir jihad, the then-Vajpayee government mobilized two Indian army strike corps on the border, keeping them and their support units on a hair-trigger alert for the greater part of the year. Aware that the Indians were bluffing, the Pakistan government refused to budge from its policy of helping jihadists active in Kashmir. The long Indian army mobilization created a perception of regional instability that affected India's status as a safe investment destination even as it exhausted the elite army units on the front line. Given the information that India would not attack, the 2002 mobilization came at a horrendous cost and no benefit. In a system where posturing comes easily to the higher levels of the Indian policy establishment, Prime Minister Manmohan Singh has thus far resisted jingoism and has made it evident that India would not be stampeded into military action. In the case of Sri Lanka, the policy was to intensify conflict until victory. What is needed is a clear policy that is carried out effectively, not a zig-zag routine that confuses the international community and results in a loss of credibility for India.

Military sales can become an effective instrument of diplomacy, were they deployed by India. Within the region, including in Sri Lanka and Nepal, the military is a significant component of the policy process, often the crucial player. Because of New Delhi's longstanding policy of not permitting foreign military sales save for exceptional situations, China has been provided an opportunity to fill the gap. Had Bangladesh, Nepal and Sri Lanka been more reliant on Indian equipment and training for their armed forces, New Delhi would have been in a much stronger position to influence policy in those places than it is today. Instead, the "weapons gap" isincreasingly being filled by China.

The mantra of "non-alignment" has in most instances become a cover for lack of action. Even during the period of the Cold War, when India suffered many of the consequences of being seen as a Soviet ally, not a single Soviet soldier was ever stationed in India or trained here, nor did any Indian soldier undertake any sort of mission in the USSR. In contrast, there are regular exchanges of U.S. and Indian soldiers and joint training exercises have become routine. The warming of ties is because there is a natural fit between the two sides. India has a significant pool of trained (and trainable) manpower, while the United States has abundant stocks of equipment that could be transferred to New Delhi rather than mothballed or left under-utilized. This is especially the case with naval vessels, where India is now being made to pay $3 billion for a secondhand

Russian aircraft carrier that it is finding it difficult to float and move at the same time.

Progress in U.S.-India military to military relatives has been slow and is still far below its potential in substantial part because of the wariness of the Indian establishment over China's reaction. Compare this with Pakistan which has built up close military ties with both China and the United States, its friendship with one not affecting the other. In the military field, the choice is between going with the United States or going alone, because a military alliance with China is not an option. Beijing sees New Delhi as a potential competitor and has repeatedly shown through its actions its commitment to a strategic policy that inhibits the growth of Indian power. Unfortunately, in this case, Indian ambivalence is now being matched by the United States under the Obama administration, which has downgraded ties with India to a level much below that set under President George W. Bush. It seems inevitable, however, that both countries will, hopefully within the present presidential term, awaken to the need for a partnership that can ensure that Asia does not fall under the sway of any single power.

The persistent Indian ambivalence in policy was visible in Sri Lanka, where India simultaneously called for a cease-fire while backing the unity of the island nation. As a consequence of simultaneously conveying two contradictory messages, neither the Tamil nor the Sinhala zealots have anything other than distaste for India, while the abundant provision of military supplies has led the Sri Lankan military towards becoming as close to Beijing as are their counterparts in Pakistan.

In Nepal, after first helping to get King Gyanendra to abdicate, New Delhi threw its support behind the Maoists, who promptly reacted by threatening to scrap the India-Nepal agreement and replace it with a similar deal with China. After its embrace of the Maoists, which ended only after their tilt to Beijing became manifest (by the end of 2008), no other Nepali party is willing to trust New Delhi and see it as a reliable partner, even the once-friendly Nepali Congress. Meanwhile, in a show of deft footwork, Chinese diplomats have been active in Kathmandu renewing ties with the non-Maoist parties that today run the government (after the departure of the Maoists), so as to accelerate the growth of PRC influence in Nepal.

Today, there are almost as many radical training camps located within Bangladesh as there in Pakistan, camps whose specific purpose is to replenish the stream of jihadis into India. Yet, unlike in the case of Pakistan, the Indian government is not posturing as if was is likely. A hostile Pakistan, an unfriendly Bangladesh, and Nepal and Sri Lanka heading towards the PRC. These are the wages of a diplomacy that refuses to go for the jugular in the pursuit of objectives, but almost invariably crafts a compromise that gives much less geopolitical benefit. India presents an example of how a most important power that avoids a clear policy line or a better deployment of its assets gives way to the other who is ruthless and willing to complete the marathon rather than slow down and stop before the finish line. Such a policy is the delight of politicians and anathema to statesmen, who understand the need for not just vision, but for will and perseverance.

CHINA-ASEAN FREE TRADE AREA

A major development in China-ASEAN relations since the end of the Cold War is perhaps the growing economic interdependence between the two. Indeed, two-way trade has been growing at a rate of 20 percent for the last decade and reached over U.S. $100 billion in 2004, a year ahead of a previously set target. It further registered a 23 percent increase in 2005, reaching $130.4 billion. ASEAN member states have benefted from China's spectacular economic growth as the Asian giant's growing demands also generate economic benefits for the region as a whole. For instance, in 2004, ASEAN had a roughly $20 billion trade surplus with China, while China's other major trading partners all sustained sizable defcits. Chinese analysts have divided the evolution of China-ASEAN economic relations into two phases. The first one, from 1991, when Chinese Foreign Minister Qian Qichen was invited to attend the 24th ASEAN Foreign Ministers meeting, to 2001 when Chinese Premier Zhu Rongji proposed a China-ASEAN free trade area, saw the two sides expand and deepen bilateral trade ties. The second phase began in November 2002, with the signing of the China-ASEAN Framework Agreement on Comprehensive Economic Cooperation moving toward regional economic integration. Over the years, China and ASEAN have institutionalized 48 regular mechanisms to facilitate closer economic cooperation. Prominent among them is the highest political mechanism—ASEAN+1, launched in 1997. In addition, there are five working groups: the China-ASEAN Senior Officials meeting, the China-ASEAN Joint Cooperation Committee, ASEAN-China Joint Committee on Economic and Trade Cooperation, ASEAN-China Joint Committee on Science and Technology (July 1994), and the ASEAN Beijing Committee. The two sides also have identified five key areas for cooperation—agriculture, information and communication technologies, human resource development, the Mekong River Development, and mutual investment.

At the eighth ASEAN summit in Phnom Penh, Cambodia, in November 2002, China and ASEAN signed the Framework Agreement on Comprehensive Economic Cooperation. If and when implemented, it would constitute a common market of 1.7 billion people, with a combined gross domestic product (GDP) of U.S.$1.5-2 trillion. The two sides sought to establish a free trade area (FTA) within 10 years, first with the original ASEAN-6 by 2010, followed by the entire ASEAN-10 by 2015. The initiative largely came from China, as it recognized ASEAN member states' concerns over China's growing economy and its crowding-out effect on investment fows into Southeast Asia and increasing economic competition. After Premier Zhu proposed the FTA idea, an ASEAN-China Expert Group on Economic Cooperation was established to study Zhu's proposal, as well as the impact of China's World Trade Organization (WTO) entry in 2001. It also is a response to the 1997 Asian financial crisis and hence the need for a more regional approach to future economic challenges. Cooperation also includes the

Mekong River Basin development project that has been supported by the Asian Development Bank and the endorsement by ASEAN of a U.S.$2.5 billion Trans-Asian railway joining Kunming and Singapore.

While there are many economic reasons for greater integration, some analysts also point to the strategic rationale for developing an FTA, especially from China's perspective. To begin with, such an arrangement could facilitate a more peaceful regional security environment critical to China's continued economic rise. Second, it addresses concerns in the region over China's growing power by more closely integrating itself with ASEAN, hence increasing the costs of conflicts. Chinese analysts suggest that the CAFTA should be viewed from a strategic perspective and as part of its peaceful rise. Geo-economics and greater economic interactions with ASEAN would support these objectives. To preempt Taiwan's strategy to buy its way into Southeast Asia, China should pay greater attention to the development of its southwestern region (Yunnan and Guangxi in particular) to develop and strengthen economic ties with the ASEAN countries.

Third, by taking the lead in forming an FTA, China also hopes to play a more prominent role as the region's centre of economic growth. Fourth, by investing more in the region and allowing a certain degree of self-discrimination—as in the form of the so-called "Early Harvest Program," giving ASEAN states preferential treatment on agricultural products in terms of tariff reduction and market access—Beijing seeks to address the perceived "China threat," not in the security area but in the context of economic competition. And fnally, by entering a rules-based free trade arrangement, China also wants to demonstrate its acceptance of multilateralism and respect for norms and rules. ASEAN member states for their own reasons sought to partake in China's dynamic economic growth; at least not to be left behind. An FTA also could energize other external powers to seek similar arrangements, therefore opening up more opportunities in the areas of trade and foreign direct investment (FDI).

While China-ASEAN trade has registered rapid growth over the last decade, both rank fifth as each other's trading partners, after intra-ASEAN, Japan, the United States, and the European Union (EU). Future developments will depend on how both could complement, rather than compete, in labour-intensive manufacturing sectors and increase investment in each other. ASEAN countries recognize the opportunities that a growing China provides, but they also are worried over the long-term impact of a stronger China competing with them for foreign direct investment and replacing them as the manufacturer of labour-intensive consumer products. There remain serious concerns that China may compete and crowd out ASEAN in terms of foreign direct investment, replace ASEAN states as a manufacturing base, and hence cause severe economic downturn in the ASEAN countries less capable of competition and with little room for adjustment.

To address these concerns, China in particular needs to make a greater investment in ASEAN, potentially in the energy and resource-based sectors, to raise two-way trade volumes further, as well as to generate a larger market as is supposed to be provided by the CAFTA. However, investment negotiations between the two still face major hurdles. For instance, during 1995-2004, Chinese investment ($1 billion) in ASEAN amounted to only 0.4 percent of the total. This compares poorly with EU-15 ($68.5 billion, 28.3 percent), the United States ($42.3 billion, 17.5 percent), and Japan ($32 billion, 13.3 percent). It even is lower significantly than Taiwan's investment in the region ($8.9 billion, 3.6 percent). At the same time, China has replaced Southeast Asia as the destination of FDI. Beijing also needs to manage potentially contentious issues such as the Mekong River project that has economic, ecological, and environmental impacts on downstream Southeast Asian countries.

The CAFTA has generated much interest in other extra-regional powers that seek FTAs with ASEAN. The United States proposed the Enterprise for ASEAN Initiative (EAI) that would enable member states to establish FTAs along the line of the U.S.-Singapore FTA. Japan also issued the "Joint

Declaration of the Leaders of ASEAN and Japan on the Comprehensive Economic Partnership" on November 5, 2002, in Phnom Penh. At the 2003 ASEAN+1 summit held in Tokyo, Japanese Prime Minister Junichiro Koizumi pledged $3 billion in new aid. With CAFTA, ASEAN+1, and other regional forums, including the East Asia Summit in December 2005, there is what some would call the trend toward regionalism with shared markets, growing economic interdependence, and even shared ideas on what a regional security architecture should look like.

China-ASEAN relations have evolved from enmity and suspicion to amity and greater cooperation on a broad range of issues. Having established a strategic partnership for peace and prosperity, the two sides are working toward building a stable, long-term relationship for the future. In addition to the state-to-state security and economic ties since reform started in the late 1970s, the Chinese Communist Party (CCP) has sought to establish and expand ties with political parties in Southeast Asia. Today, the CCP has official relations with 39 political parties in the region, and the rationale and objectives are to promote mutual understanding, learning, economic success, and governance, regardless of ideologies. This is a far cry from the 1960s and 1970s when the CCP supported indigenous communist parties as part of a strategy to fan revolution in the region to topple ruling governments.

Beijing's efforts to assure its neighbours through the so-called new diplomacy have paid off in winning confidence from its Southeast Asian neighbours, if not completely erasing disputes between them. The 1997 Asian financial crisis was a turning point. Chinese responses to the crisis, including its pledges of $1 billion to help Thailand and not to devaluate the Renminbi, won good will in ASEAN. Beijing also emerged more confdent of its own potential leadership role in the region, although it remains deferential to ASEAN. China began to publish a defence white paper in 1998. Now published every 2 years, the document also has moved from mere exposition of general principles to some elementary explanations of defence budgets, modernization programs, and doctrinal issues. While still far from ideal, at least some modest steps have been made to enhance transparency. China also put forward the "New Security Concept" (NSC) at the ARF Inter-Sessional Support Group (ISG) on Confidence-Building Measures that it co-hosted with the Philippines in Beijing, March 1997. The NSC emphasizes cooperative security, confidence-building, peaceful resolution of disputes, and multilateral dialogue. In November 2004, China hosted the first ARF Security Policy Conference in Beijing. Within a decade, growing interdependence and skillful Chinese diplomacy have sustained a steady improvement and rising comfort level between China and ASEAN, allowing Beijing to exercise greater influence in the region.

China and ASEAN also are expanding areas of cooperation, in particular in the nontraditional security areas, including securing SLOCs, antiterrorism, and antipiracy; ecological issues related to the Greater Mekong River project and other environmental issues; responses to the severe acute respiratory syndrome (SARS) outbreak, for instance, the first China-ASEAN summit on SARS; transnational organized crimes; and money laundering. Chinese Premier Wen Jiabao has proposed *mulin, anlin, fulin* to ASEAN ["friendly neighbours—peaceful coexistence, regional stability, and harmony"; "secure neighbours—regional peace and stability through dialogue, negotiation to resolve disputes," and "rich neighbours"—develop, deepen regional and subregional economic cooperation, and promote regional integration].

3

Substantiation from Asia-Pacific Markets

Fama (1969) introduced well-known efficient market hypothesis (EMH) with three forms: strong form, semi-strong form and weak form. Stock prices at any time fully reflect all available information in the strong form, all public available information in the semi-strong form and historical information in the weak form of EMH. Two important implications of EMH are that future stock prices are unpredictable and expected stock returns can only be determined by rational asset pricing models.

Evidence from empirical studies has suggested that stock prices do not always accurately reflect available information. In particularly, research in experimental psychology has suggested that *"most people overreact to unexpected and dramatic news"* (Debondt and Thaler (1985)). Motivated by this, Debondt and Thaler (1985) develop the overreaction hypothesis which suggests: *"Extreme movements in stock prices will be followed by subsequent price movements in the opposite direction"*, and *"The more extreme the initial price movement, the greater will be the subsequent adjustment"* (Debondt and Thaler (1985)). The overreaction hypothesis implies a violation of weak form of EMH, i.e. future stock prices cannot be predicted from past stock prices. A great number of studies have assessed whether short-term price movements in the opposite direction or price reversals occur following one-day extreme price movement. Some notable papers in this area include Brown, Harlow, and Tinic (1988, 1993), Atkins and Dyl (1990), Bremer and Sweeney (1991, 1996), Cox and Peterson (1994), Park (1995) and Bremer *et al.* (1997). Stock prices are generally found to be reversed following one-day sharp declines. Exceptional case is Cox and Peterson (1994), whose study finds that abnormal returns of longer term (4 days to 20 days) are negative after a large one-day decline.

This paper aims to expand the overreaction literature by examining whether the price reversals occur in the short-term period i.e. three days and longer term period i.e. up to twenty days following the large one-day price changes in Asia-Pacific markets over the period 2001 to 2005. The sample is firms of three different markets, i.e. 100 firms comprising the ASX 100 index, 300 firms included in the Nikkei 300 and 33 firms trading on the Ho Chi Minh City Securities Trading Centre (HCMC STC). Wong (1997) also examined price reversals in Asia-Pacific markets, however, in his paper, only market indexes such as All Ordinaries Index and Nikkei 225 Index were taken into accounts. His finding is that stock prices tend to rise (fall) after a large one-day increase (decease), in other words, this is inconsistent with Debondt and Thaler's overreaction hypothesis. Our study utilizes individual firm data. Therefore, the study answers the questions of whether the results obtained from the same markets are different by using different types of dataset and how the price patterns following large price changes differ from country to country.

Our approach distinguishes itself from exiting ones in a major way. This study applies the method developed by MacKinlay and Richardson (1991), using GMM to estimate the expected stock returns as described by the CAPM. GMM is chosen for its many advantages. It is a general estimator which encompasses many standard econometric estimators including OLS, instrumental variables (IVs), and maximum likelihood. Not only that GMM is valid under weaker assumptions about the normality of data distribution, but it also has the potential to improve the estimation since it allows serially correlated residuals and conditional dependency of residuals on the factors. Our results indicate short - term reversal patterns across Asia-Pacific markets.

INVESTIGATES THE BEHAVIOUR OF STOCK RETURN

Data

The study investigates the behaviour of stock return on days after large price change for firms of three different markets in the Asia-Pacific region. The daily returns are computed based on the closing price of each trading day. If two successive closing prices are not available, the daily returns are also not recorded. The sample period extends from January 20001 to December 2005.

Methodology

Our approach to investigate whether there are predictable patterns of stock returns after large price changes is simple and similar to that of Brown, Harlow, and Tinic (1993), Atkins and Dyl (1990), Bremer and Sweeney (1991), Cox and Peterson (1994), Park (1995), Bremer *et al.* (1997) and Wong (1997). Two measurements for large price changes are examined.

The first measure considers all daily rates of returns that were greater/ less than or equal to pre-specify *trigger values* over the five-year period from January 2001 to December 2005 as *"large"* price increase/decrease events. Consistent with Bremer and Sweeney (1991), Cox and Peterson (1994), Park (1995) and Bremer *et al.* (1997), the triggers values are (+/-) 10 percent for Australian and Japanese markets. For Vietnamese market, the trigger values are lower at (+/-) 4 percent since HCMC STC applies narrow daily price limits of (+/-) 5 percent. As explained by Atkins and Dyl (1990) and Bremer *et al.* (1997), such events are largely caused by unexpected, new information pertinent to the value of the stock i.e. unexpected operating results, or unanticipated government decisions. These events provide good opportunity to assess whether stock prices fairly reflect unexpected, new information or overreact to such information.

As of Wong (1997), the second measure utilizes dynamic trigger values based upon firm's expected return and volatility. Define all daily rates of returns that were significantly greater/ less than their sample mean returns at around 2.5 percent level as large price increases ($R_{it} > \mu_i + 2\sigma_i$) /decreases ($R_{it} < \mu_i - 2\sigma_i$). Sample mean return μ_i and sample standard deviation σ_i of stock i are estimated over the period from 2001 to 2005.

Following Bremer and Sweeney (1991) and Cox and Peterson (1994), only one event per day is allowed in order to minimize correlation across sample. The event observations are ordered first by date and then alphabetically by stock name. If a date has more than one event, only the observation appearing first in the ordering sort for that date is retained. Table 3 shows the number of large price changes across three markets measured using pre-specified trigger values and dynamic trigger values. Event samples "3" in the table indicate the final event samples appropriate for analyzing abnormal returns.

EXPERIENTIAL FINDINGS

Abnormal returns following large price changes that are greater/less than pre-specified trigger values, the frequency of price continuations and price reversals occur on days 1, 2, and 3 and days 1-3, 1-5, 1-10 and 1-20 following the day of large price changes. The triggers values are (+/-) 10 percent for Australian and Japanese markets and 4 percent for Vietnamese market. In general, the results across three markets indicate higher frequency of price reversals than for price continuations over the short term period, i.e., three days following the large price changes.

The average cumulative abnormal returns around 20 days of 10% or greater price decrease, calculated using unrestricted CAPM model. The figure shows that cumulative abnormal returns keep falling on day 1 after the large price decrease in Australia and Japan markets. In these two markets, price reversals occur on days 2 and 3. Price reversals occur immediately on day 1 and continue to day 3 after large price decline in Vietnam market. The figure also shows that price reversals persist in longer term up to 20 days in Australia, whereas price tends to decline over the 20 days period in Vietnam and there is no clear return pattern during day 20 days following large price decrease in Japan.

The presents mean abnormal returns of large stock price decreases and increases over the five-year period from January 2001 to December 2005.

The mean abnormal returns are -14.6807 percent, -12.2346 percent and -4.1637 percent on the day of large price decrease (i.e. day 0) in Australia, Japan and Vietnam markets respectively, measured using the unrestricted CAPM model, and of similar magnitude using the market model. The mean abnormal returns are positive for day 2 and day 3 of the three trading days following the day of the large price decrease in Australia and Japan, and positive for these three days in Vietnam. Significantly positive mean abnormal returns are observed on day 2 in Australia and day 1 in Vietnam, as indicated by two-tailed test. The clearest evidence of short-term price reversal is seen in Vietnam market where average cumulative abnormal return for three days following large price decline (CAR1-3) is 0.5727 percent and statistically significant. CAR1-3 in Australia and Japan markets are 0.9020 percent and -0.0281 percent, respectively, and both are statistically insignificant. With respect to longer-term, the average cumulative abnormal returns over days 1 through 20 (CAR1-20) are 2.6399 percent, -0.2279 percent and -1.0717 percent, respectively in the three markets. We interpret these cross-country results as mixed evidence on the price reversal and overreaction hypothesis over the longer term period.

The average cumulative abnormal returns around 20 days of 10% or greater price increase. The abnormal returns are calculated using unrestricted CAPM model. Following the rise on event day, cumulative abnormal returns decrease on days 1 and 2; days 1, 2 and 3; and days 2 and 3 in Australia, Japan and Vietnam markets, respectively. Over the longer term, stock price increases significantly in Australia, whereas decline slightly in Japan and Vietnam over the 20 days period following the large price advance.

The mean abnormal returns are 13.8499 percent, 11.9320 percent and 3.9259 percent on the day of the large price advance in Australia, Japan and Vietnam markets respectively, measured using the unrestricted CAPM model. The mean abnormal returns are negative for day 1 and day 2 in Australia market; day 2 and day 3 in Vietnam market; and three trading days following the initial large price increase in Japan market. Significantly negative mean abnormal returns are evident on day 1 and day 2 in Japan market. Among three markets, Japan shows strongest evidence of short term price reversal where total abnormal return over days 1-3 (CAR1-3) is -1.1187 percent and statistically significant. Over the longer term, price reversals are evident in Japan market with significant and negative CAR1-5 and in Vietnam market with significant and negative CAR 1-5 and CAR 1-10. In contrast, there is no evidence in support of longer term price reversal in Australia market. This market shows significant price continuation, i.e. cumulative abnormal return of 3.5471 percent over 20 days period after large price increase.

The frequency of price continuations and price reversals occur on days 1, 2, and 3 and days 1-3, 1-5, 1-10 and 1-20 following the day of large price increases () /decreases (). Similar to results from pre-specified trigger values, the results based on dynamic trigger values across three markets show higher frequency of price reversals than for price continuations over the short term period.

The average cumulative abnormal returns for the period from 20 days before to 20 days after the day of initial price decline, calculated using unrestricted CAPM model. The figure shows clear short-term patterns of price reversals across the three markets. Cumulative abnormal returns rise immediately from day 1 to day 3 in Australia and Vietnam and on day 1 and day 2 in Japan. The price patterns from day 4 through day 20 quite differ from market to market. The mean abnormal returns are -4.4453 percent, -5.5064 percent and -3.7591 percent on the day of large price decrease (i.e. day 0) in Australia, Japan and Vietnam markets respectively, measured using the unrestricted CAPM model. Average cumulative abnormal return for three days following large price decline (CAR1-3) are positive and significant in three markets. This evidence on short term price reversals therefore supports the overreaction hypothesis.

The average cumulative abnormal returns around 20 days of 10% or greater price increase. Cumulative abnormal returns fall immediately from day 1 to day 3 in three markets, indicating clear short-term patterns of price reversals.

The mean abnormal returns are 4.5862 percent, 5.8811 percent and 3.6710 percent on the day of the large price advance in Australia, Japan and Vietnam markets respectively, measured using the unrestricted CAPM model. The mean abnormal returns are negative for days 1, 2 and 3 of the three trading days following the initial large price increase in three markets. Total abnormal returns over days 1-3 (CAR1-3) are significant and negative. These results indicate significant short term price reversals that are supportive of the overreaction hypothesis.

We discussed abnormal return patterns using two measurements of large price changes. In general, both measurements provide evidence in supportive of the price reversals and overreaction hypothesis in the short term period, i.e. three days period. The measure of large price changes based on dynamic trigger values provide stronger evidence of short-term price reversals than such measure based on pre-specified trigger values. This suggests that firm specific characteristics play a significant role in explaining the price reversals.

Compared with previous literature, for the cases of price pattern following larger price decreases, our study0is consistent with Atkins and Dyl (1990), Bremer and Sweeney (1991), Cox and Peterson (1994), and Bremer *et al.* (1997), i.e. stock price is short-term reversed after large one-day price decreases.

Our results based on individual firms are in contrast to Wong's (1997) findings based on market indices, though utilizing similar dynamic measure of large price changes. For the cases of large price increases, our results indicate CAR 1-10 and CAR 1-20 are negative and significant in Australia and Japan, whereas in Wong's paper, these figures are found to be positive in the same markets. Similarly, for the cases of large price decreases, we find positive CAR 1-10 in Australia and Japan which are associated with negative values according to Wong's results.

The differences between results obtained from dynamic measures of large price changes and statically pre-specified measures of large price changes, and between results obtained from dynamic measures based on individual firms and such measures based on overall market indices as discussed above suggest that the dynamic measures based on individual firms provide most consistent evidence across markets which are supportive of short-term price reversals and overreaction hypothesis.

Financial Significance

The economic significance, i.e. whether opportunities for investors to earn excess profit from the observed patterns exist. The average cumulative abnormal return for ten trading days following large price decrease (CAR 1-10) is 1.8618 percent in Australia, and CAR 1-3 is 0.5727 percent in Vietnam. These values are statistically significant which may offer opportunities for contrarian investors.

Consider two investment strategies for investors in Australian stock market over the six-year period from January 2000 to December 2005 as follows. The first strategy is passive management, i.e., buy and hold the All Ordinaries Index over five years from 2001 to 2005. By following this strategy, the profit before transaction cost is 46.9%, i.e., buying All-Ords at 3205.4 on first trading day of 2001 and selling at 4708.8 on last trading day of 2005.

The second strategy is active management. We periodically invest the same amount that otherwise is invested in passive funds, in any stock whose return equals to, or falls bellow the trigger, i.e. 10 percent, and selling all the same stocks ten trading days later. Over the five years period, this strategy can be repeated 45 times out of 68 trading days that the stock price falls bellow the trigger value. The return on every 1 Australian Dollar of initial investment before transaction costs is: , withthe cumulative abnormal return for ten trading days following the initial price decrease. Clearly, the profit from active strategy is less than that of passive management.

Similar results are obtained for Vietnamese market. The evidence across countries indicates that although there are evident of price reversals, they are not worthy to exploit. This is consistent with the EMH. To investigate whether market conditions affect the magnitude of price reversals, we examine the cumulative abnormal returns following large price changes in bear period, i.e., the period that market experiences stock declining, and bull period, the period that market experiences stock advancing. The bear periods are from January 2001 to March 2003 in Australia and Japan and from July 2001 to October 2003 in Vietnam. The remaining periods are bull periods in those markets. In Australian market, the magnitude of price reversals following large price decreases in bear period is larger than that in bull period, i.e. CAR 1-10 are 2.7313 percent and 0.0436 percent in bear and bull period, respectively. Whereas, in Vietnamese market, the magnitude of price reversals following large price decreases in bear period is less than that in bull period, i.e. CAR 1-3 are 0.4404 percent and 0.6493 percent in bear and bull period, respectively. The different results between two markets indicate that market conditions may not explain the magnitude of price reversals.

4

India, Pakistan and Afghanistan: A New Measurement to the Provincial Disagreement

The stalled Indo-Pak peace process has beckoned well neither for India nor for Pakistan nor for peace in South Asian region, in which Afghanistan has found a place as a member of South Asian Association for Regional Cooperation. In this critical juncture it appears imminent that India and Pakistan must shun suspicions and resume the dialogue process at higher level and resolve or at least moderate contentious issues. It is undoubtedly a long and arduous process, but it must begin now without any loss of precious time. Besides India and Pakistan, other players like Russia, US, Iran and China need to be involved in any conflict resolution process in Afghanistan. One of the ideas that makes round recently is to return Afghanistan to its traditional policy of neutrality. Whatever may be resolution process the fact remains that the gap in relations between these two nuclear weapon possessing countries created by mistrust and suspicion will provide the terrorist organizations and other similar elements occasion to further realize their agenda and take the South Asian players into ride with serious implications not only for the region but for the world as a whole.

Afghanistan The opinion polls in Afghanistan conducted in December 2009 and revealed this month have shown India as the most favourable country among the people particularly in aspects of initiating development measures. This development is not liked well by many regional players. Pakistan's policy of keeping India out of the solution format of the Afghan turmoil and its discomfiture particularly at Pakistan-US deliberations about India's influence in its neighbourhood is well known.

The recent reiteration of Pakistan of 'thousand years of war' with India in Pak controlled Kashmir has brought into the forefront the deep tensions in the South Asian politics. The likely Afghan scenario after the withdrawal of NATO forces in 2012 and the strategies of various players in the region has further complicated the geopolitical matrix of the region.

According to the poll conducted by the Afghan Centre for Socio Economic and Opinion Research 71 per cent of 1534 respondents in 43 Afghan locations have overwhelmingly welcomed India's role in developmental activities in Afghanistan. India has already committed $ 1.2 billion in Afghanistan in terms of building bridges, roads, and schools and other developmental activities and also in training Afghan police. These Indian activities have been viewed with suspicion by Pakistan. India is the largest regional donor in Afghanistan. The poll has registered support of only 2 per cent in the context of Pakistan's supportive role in Afghanistan. Surprisingly the Taliban has secured 3 per cent of votes, one per cent higher than Pakistan. The Gallup poll with regard to reconstruction of the war-torn country, conducted in November last year, too has overwhelmingly indicated this trend. As per the poll India secures 56 per cent of votes, while Pakistan 30 per cent. The series of attacks on Kabul on 18 January 2010 while President Hamid Karzai was administering oath to 14 ministers in the presidential palace have reflected the open discontent of groups against the elected Karzai government. Reportedly, the attacks were more aimed at displaying the militant groups' discomfiture, among others, at the government's getting close to New Delhi.

It is common knowledge that Pakistan has openly declared its reservation over India's activities in Afghanistan. It has viewed Hamid Karzai's friendly gesture towards India with suspicion. According to Pak analyst Rasul Bakhsh Rais, "There is a degree of disappointment with him (Karzai), in particular over the way he has provided Afghanistan as a playing field for India." Another development that further added, or at least helped maintain the tense relation was the speech of Pakistan President Asif Ali Zardari in Pak controlled Kashmir.

Addressing a joint session of its assembly and the Kashmir Council, Zardari almost reiterated Zulfikar Ali Bhutto's theory that Pakistan will wedge thousands years war with India in Kashmir. He attempted to moderate it by saying the war will be on the level of ideas. Describing Kashmir as the jugular vein of Pakistan, he said, "Soon the time will come when the world will take important decisions regarding Kashmir."

However, the statement did unnerve New Delhi which has repeatedly complained against Pakistan's inaction against terrorist elements in its controlled Kashmir and other parts of Pakistan. India has argued that these groups have a determined policy to destabilize India. Some recent developments have impacted Pakistan's policy towards India. Pakistan has long suspected India's hand in playing havoc in Balochistan. In fact, the inclusion of Balochistan word in the joint statement of India and Pakistan in Sharm-el-Sheikh in Egypt in July 2009 has provided Pakistan ammunition to accuse Indian agencies for playing devious role in Pakistan's troubled region. The statement by Indian Army Chief in December 2009 that India is ready to continue a two-front war simultaneously against Pakistan and China has further ruffled the feathers of Pakistan as to the true intentions of India, which is militarily more powerful. Furthermore, the volatile situation in Pakistan, the surge in terror activities, the rising imbalance in policy approaches of army and civilian government exacerbate this vulnerability factor in Pakistan, which has already fought four wars with India.

In the context of Afghanistan the likely withdrawal of US led NATO forces by 2012 will create a vacuum to be contested by various powers to fill in. Pakistan apprehends India getting an upper hand in this game. This apprehension may likely motivate Pakistan to follow a more complicated policy in terms of using elements under its control towards India and Afghanistan. It is true that Afghanistan has miles to go to have semblance of stability, and a transparent and effective governance system but the already set pace for a democratic governance in the trouble-torn can be considered a good start. Hence, in this background it appears more an imperative for the regional powers like India and Pakistan to coordinate their policies to stabilize the region. The fact remains unless there is peace between India and Pakistan, and unless there is evolution of a common approach on the sensitive issues, the region will likely remain unstable and violent. The terrorist organizations like Lashkar-e-Taiba have not hidden their agenda to trigger a conflict between India and Pakistan by using devious means.

THE INDIA AND PAKISTAN DIMENSION IN ASEAN SECURITY

On behalf of the International Security Research and Outreach Programme (ISROP) of the Department of Foreign Affairs and International Trade Canada (DFAIT), and with additional sponsorship from IDRC, DND and CSIS, the Graduate School of Public and International Affairs (GSPIA) of the University of Ottawa held a one day workshop entitled "South Asia Security: The India-Pakistan Dimension." The workshop was held at the University of Ottawa on 27 April, 2009. This is a full report of the workshop. This report will discuss the main points raised during the workshop in a thematic manner. As the workshop was conducted under the Chatham House Rules, this report will not attribute specific points to individual speakers.

Participation

The workshop was opened by The Hon. Allan Rock, President of the University of Ottawa. The principal speakers at the workshop were ten experts on regional affairs, with three Canadian discussants also presenting. The regional affairs experts were (in alphabetical order, by last name):

- Pervaiz Iqbal Cheema (National Defence University, Pakistan);
- Lisa Curtis (Heritage Foundation, USA)
- Mohan Guruswamy (Centre for Policy Analysis, India):
- Rifaat Hussein (Quaid-i-Azam University, Pakistan);
- Lalit Mansingh (former Foreign Secretary, India);
- Talat Masood (Lt. General, retired, Pakistan);
- Amitabh Mattoo (Jawaharlal Nehru University, India);
- Raja Menon (Rear Admiral, retired, India);
- Shuja Nawaz (Atlantic Council, Pakistan and USA); and
- Arun Prakash (Admiral, retired, and former Chair of the Chiefs of Staff Committee, India).

The discussants were (in alphabetical order, by last name):

- Paul Evans (University of British Columbia);
- T.V. Paul (McGill University); and
- Julian Schofield (Concordia University).

The workshop host was Mr. Greg Giokas (DFAIT) and the workshop was moderated by Peter Jones (GSPIA, University of Ottawa). Attendees came from several Government of Canada departments and agencies, including DFAIT, IDRC, DND, PCO, CSIS-Academic Outreach, Public Safety, CIDA, and others.

THEMATIC POINTS

Timing and Context

Participants noted that the discussion was happening at a critical time. It was acknowledged that, in the South Asia context, there is often the sense of timeliness and high stakes. Nevertheless, the uniqueness of the current situation was described by regional participants as a convergence of signals emanating especially from Pakistan that highlight the acute need for discussion and cooperation. The Mumbai bombing of November 2008, and the impending Indian election in May 2009, meant that the Composite Dialogue had been suspended and high-level contacts between the two countries, at either the official or the Track Two level, had since been few. Moreover, the deteriorating situation in Pakistan added new tension to the regional situation.

It was widely agreed that these elements make such contacts both more difficult and more necessary. With the Indian election fast approaching, participants felt that an opportunity may be presenting itself to explore ideas as to ways in which India can engage the region through a re-vamped foreign policy. In that context, the workshop sponsors and the GSPIA were commended for taking the initiative to bring the meeting together. The workshop was also considered timely by Canadian participants who welcomed the discussion as an opportunity to inform analysis on the region and policy innovation as South Asia becomes an increasing focus for Canada.

Mumbai Bombing

On the Indian side, a view was raised that the Mumbai attack was a "turning point," especially when taken in the context of the series of attacks over the past few years, such as the attack on the Indian Parliament. Even though it was contended that India had shown restraint in its reactions, such an attack in the future will place extraordinary pressure on the Indian Government to react much more forcefully (though it was noted that this does not necessarily mean that India will react with force, as such).

On this point, Indian participants fielded several questions regarding the possible outcomes of escalated attacks in the future. It was acknowledged that the massive media coverage in India over the several days of the Mumbai attack, and the great loss of life, has meant that Indian public opinion is now roused to such an extent that no Government will be able to "shrug off" future attacks as part of the normal cycle of relations. It is therefore incumbent upon Pakistan to show much greater determination to tackle extremism and terrorism than it has to date. Views were also expressed to the effect that elements of the Government of Pakistan were in some ways complicit in the attack, even if the Pakistani Government as a whole may not have sanctioned the action. Moreover, many of the Indian participants remained of the view that Pakistan has not really renounced terror as a possible instrument of policy.

Participants from Pakistan acknowledged that India had demonstrated restraint in its response to Mumbai, but expressed the view that there was no proof that any elements of the Government of Pakistan were involved in the attack. It was noted that evidence is required and this has not been forthcoming. It was further noted by many that intensive cooperation is underway between the authorities in both countries to investigate the attack, and this is a very positive outcome.

On the broader question of Pakistan's use of terror as an instrument of policy, several Pakistani participants noted that many of the terror groups are far beyond the Government's control and are acting on the basis of historic grievances which India must do her part to help resolve. That said, there was recognition by the participants from Pakistan that previous Pakistani Governments had developed unhealthy relationships with extremist groups. These have hurt Pakistan as much as they have hurt India and there is a determination in Islamabad to change these relationships.

The attack was framed by one participant as evidence of the ability of terrorism to quickly and unpredictably overtake policy on bilateral issues. It was noted that, immediately following the attack, rather than implement the mechanisms developed over the course of the Composite Dialogue for cooperation in the event of a terrorist strike, the countries engaged in a "blame game". While understandable, this response undermines the accomplishments of the Dialogue. It also indicates that the political situation has not yet reached a point whereby the political will exists in a crisis to follow the path of bilateral cooperation and dialogue that the parties have agreed.

It was noted that Indian officials have stated that the Composite Dialogue will not resume until the attack in Mumbai has been thoroughly investigated with the full cooperation of

Pakistan and a ruling on the matter has been released. Concern was expressed on both sides over the possible consequences of this stance. Such investigations in the past have lasted several years. This has been the case even when significant state resources are dedicated to the investigation and all parties offer their full cooperation. There was a sense, voiced especially on the Pakistani side, that such an approach will subject the dialogue to an unacceptable delay.

Pakistan's Internal Security

Turning to Pakistan's internal situation, workshop participants from Pakistan acknowledged, and shared, the concerns expressed by the other participants. However, it was noted that Pakistan's Army remains essentially loyal and the Government is now facing the insurgencies underway across the country with renewed determination. In response to particular concerns over the fighting underway at the time of the workshop itself, a discussant noted that the Swat valley is "a long way" from Islamabad, in practical and political terms, if not geographically.

Other participants were not so sanguine and expressed considerable fear over the future of Pakistan as a stable state. These fears are accentuated by Pakistan's nuclear status. One Indian participant noted the fear of a "nuclear Somalia" on India's doorstep. Others expressed concern that the growing power of the insurgents was such that, even if they did not take over the Pakistani state, they would make of Pakistan a quasi-failed state which would simply bleed out over time. The concern was also expressed that the strengthening of Pakistani extremists could exert a negative influence on India's own "communal fault-lines" and bolster those Indian groups inclined to the same path, thereby encouraging greater practical cooperation between extremist elements in the two countries. Turning specifically to the issue of how Pakistan would fight the insurgency, several workshop participants noted repeatedly that "90 percent" of Pakistan's Army is "facing the wrong way" – that is, it is deployed and prepared for a conventional war with India and not taking any part in the real threat facing

Pakistan: the insurgency. Pakistani participants noted a reluctance on the part of the Army to fight against fellow Muslims and tribesmen. This was not accepted by most workshops participants, who noted that the Pakistani police were also Muslims and seemed to be willing to fight the insurgents. In response, the Pakistani participants also noted that, even though India claims that China is supposedly India's main enemy, some 70 percent of India's Army is facing Pakistan.

Apart from the debate over the intentions of India's military strategy, one Indian participant highlighted the need for India to think seriously about how to create incentive structures, engage moderates, and eliminate jihadis in Pakistan. Several Indian participants noted that while the above-listed initiatives are necessary, it is unclear to Indian officials who should be engaged in Pakistan, both because the official power structure is unfamiliar (given the role of the military) and because there is little sense of who are, in fact, the "moderates". A further challenge lies in determining what kind of Pakistan is envisioned by interested parties. In sum, this discussion revealed considerable disquiet. While some felt that the situation is characterised in an overly dramatic fashion, most were not of this view. But few could think of ways that outsiders could dramatically assist Pakistan – this is a fight that Islamabad will have to wage itself. The Pakistani participants acknowledged this, but argued that pressures on Pakistan to take steps that will serve outside agendas (especially in Afghanistan) are not helpful.

AFGHANISTAN AND ASEAN AFTER "9/11"

Afghanistan has been a historical gateway to South Asia and a playingcum- killing field for imperialistic great games in the region. Its security problems demonstrate only too graphically and tragically how national and human insecurity can in fact intersect and feed off each other. The terrorist attacks on US targets on 11 September 2001 ("9/11") provoked a massive US-led attack on the Taliban regime of Afghanistan. In discussing the implications of that, Samina Ahmed argues that continued conflict in Afghanistan will destabilize South Asia. Conversely, a pacified Afghanistan will promote regional stability, reduce the threat of terrorism in the region and create trade opportunities with Central Asian neighbours. Although the US-led coalition overthrew the Taliban, it has found it difficult to achieve the follow-up goal of eradicating the threat of terrorism through political, economic and social reconstruction. Afghanistan's Transitional Administration faces multiple challenges: alienated ethnic actors contest its legitimacy; warlords still control their territories; infighting prevails over rule of law; and the slow pace of reconstruction is hampering reconciliation. National and regional security are threatened by the reluctance of international forces to expand their security presence beyond Kabul. As a consequence, the peace is fragile and, if conflict resumes, terrorism will return with it. Also, the unchecked war economy (involving drugs and arms trade) strengthens warlords and militias compared with the central government. India and Pakistan must refrain from interfering in Afghanistan's reconstruction to promote their own agendas, Ahmed urges. It is in the security interest of both to lobby for greater international reconstruction assistance. Non-intervention by neighbours in Afghanistan's affairs would enhance the prospects for peace and deprive extremists of support.

Mohammed Ayoob argues that, in its war on terrorism, Washington has attempted to untie the knot of Islamic extremism that has been at the centre of Pakistani–Afghan relations for years. It has recorded two modest successes: the establishment of an interim Afghan government with a moderate leader, and General Pervez Musharraf's pledge to break Pakistani-based terror groups and pull away from the theocratic state. But South-West Asia is still threatened by instability. Further conflict and fragmentation in Afghanistan could have ripple effects. Moreover, Afghan stability looks elusive: the government does not have control beyond Kabul; the strategic interests of external neighbours are at odds and they have different favourite clients; the warlords are benefiting from strife; the government has less resources and it is also unpopular because of the ban on poppy cultivation and the drug trade. With Afghanistan and Pakistan in unrest, Ayoob concludes that the United States needs support from India and Iran as the only responsible powers with capabilities and interest in South-West Asia's stability.

The subject, Amin Saikal agrees that "9/11" and the US response to it have had a profound impact on the political and strategic landscape of Central, West and South Asia, altering key geopolitical configurations in the area. The Taliban and al-Qaida have been replaced by a US-supported coalition, Pakistan has switched sides to join the United States, India has upped the ante with Pakistan over "crossborder terrorism" in the light of the US war on terror, Afghanistan and the Central Asian republics have been transformed into US footholds, Iran is encircled by US forces, and political Islam has been put on the defensive. In this fluid situation the United States and its allies have to choose either to remain fully engaged in Afghanistan for 5–10 years or to risk its falling into renewed fragmentation. The United States is ambiva- lent about engaging in nation-building in Afghanistan, Pakistan and Central Asia. Yet this is necessary to stabilize Central, West and South Asia. The United States will need to adopt multilateralism in order to do this.

For a Brighter Tomorrow

The volume ends with two possible roadmaps for a better, more prosperous and peaceful South Asia. The pivot is the historic animosity between India and Pakistan.

Samina Yasmeen postulates that the negative mythology of "the other" provides the context for perceptions and decision-making between India and Pakistan. This has permeated the relationship since independence, and has been aggravated by three wars and the continuing rivalry over Kashmir. The symmetrical negative imagery pervades the two civil societies as well. Education (for example, history books), the media and cultural elements such as movies contribute to a "shared consciousness" that rests upon and fuels the demonization of the other. Yasmeen distinguishes between hawkish/orthodox and moderate schools of thought in both countries, and identifies the moderate tendencies throughout the turbulent relationship. Nevertheless, the orthodox perception of the relationship as a zero-sum conflict has influenced decision-making on the process of nuclearization as well as the missile race. Hawkish leaders in both countries have used the other country's difficulties and problems to tilt the balance in their favour. While recommending continuing efforts for moderation within and between the two countries, such as the Gujral Doctrine and Lahore agreement, Yasmeen suggests that, among external actors, the United States is better placed to play a short-term role as the facilitating superpower, while the United Nations should play a longerterm part, addressing the root causes of instability such as poverty, population growth rates, environmental degradation and the AIDS epidemic.

India's former High Commissioner (ambassador) to Pakistan, Gopalaswami Parthasarathy, reminds us that the conflict in Afghanistan has spilled over into Pakistan, the Taliban and its supporters have not been eliminated, and the Indian and Pakistani armies are still facing each other in Kashmir. But he argues that the nuclear dimension is exaggerated, being less threatening than the West thinks. For practical purposes, the two defence forces have known of each other's nuclear capability for a decade. Despite the persistent volatility, there are positive trends in the relationship between India and Pakistan, including the Lahore Summit (1999) and progress towards economic integration. It is now necessary to create the conditions for moving from conflict to cooperation. Parthasarathy compares the situation to that of Ireland and the United Kingdom over Northern Ireland, conciliated in part because they are both members of the European Union. He hopes that the vision statement from Lahore – of an economic union in South Asia by 2020 – will be implemented, because economic links and integration will facilitate conflict resolution. Mistrust must be reduced in populations – by people-topeople contact (tourism and exchange programmes), the media, trade and the promotion of cultural understanding – and also between governments, for example through agreements on a set of confidence-building measures for both nuclear and conventional weapons. It is important to create a climate conducive to bilateral dialogue. The SAARC summits in Lahore and Kathmandu show that positive development is possible, and that neither party gains by remaining hostage to the mistrust and animosity of the past.

In sum, the facts of geography have given the seven countries of South Asia a shared history and will ensure a common destiny. Neither enmity nor friendship, neither poverty nor prosperity, is predestined. With mutual and international goodwill, with the mustering of the necessary political will, and with the adoption of mutually conciliatory, marketfriendly and pro-growth policies, the peoples and governments of South Asia could as yet take their fate back into their own hands and rediscover the greatness and the glory that once were theirs.

INDIA AND PAKISTAN-NUCLEAR STATES IN DISAGREEMENT

When the British withdrew from the Indian subcontinent after the second world war, it was divided, primarily on religious grounds, into the two states of India and Pakistan. At that time Kashmir was included in India, but the issue of which state it should belong to has been contested ever since, largely because Kashmir's population is predominantly Muslim. In 1947 a United Nations resolution called for a referendum in Kashmir to settle the issue on the basis of what the people wanted. It was, however never carried out and it is generally assumed that the reason for this is because the Indian government feared the popular vote would support unification with Pakistan on religious grounds. Many in Kashmir campaign for independence, a position that neither India nor Pakistan supports.

Around 30,000 people have died in Kashmir in the last 11 years. What happens in Kashmir is at the heart of the continuing tension between India and Pakistan. The possibility of the world's first direct war between two nuclear-armed states occurring is very real. The history of the conflict over Kashmir is well documented with three India/Pakistan wars taking place since 1947. But this time it would be with both sides having access to nuclear weapons. Since the attack on the Indian Parliament building in December 2001, the tension and rhetoric have grown considerably. India accused Pakistan of supporting terrorist groups. Pakistan, in turn, pledges its support for Kashmiri freedom fighters. One state's terrorist is another's freedom fighter. Since the attack in December, Pakistan has arrested around 1500 'militants' and banned five groups, two said to be sectarian, one pro-Taliban and two who have been fighting Indian rule in Kashmir. However, Gen Musharraf has pledged continued support for Kashmir.

Many people living along the border close to Kashmir have fled the area due to the large military presence being built up by both sides. From the end of 2001 there were clashes virtually every night in that border region, with sometimes one or two people being shot. There are claims that large numbers of military silos have been destroyed. In an atmosphere of increased tension and sabre-rattling rhetoric on both sides, this led to the situation in May 2002 where upwards of a million troops were gathered near the border. Any mistake or small incident runs the risk of setting off something far, far worse.

The Current Situation

All this, of course, is fuelled by the continuing rhetoric on both sides. Officials in both countries claimed that they would not use nuclear weapons first, but they seem remarkably keen to use them second. Given the proximity of the two states, it is clear that millions of their own people would die along with millions of their nearest neighbours. India has said that it would not use nuclear weapons first, while Pakistan has clearly stated that it would. Whilst a 'no first use' policy is an important step towards disarmament, it is all too often used as an excuse to build a large 'second use' capacity. Eventually, of course, the 'second use' becomes indistinguishable from the 'first use'. As the tension mounts, the temptation grows to get your retaliation in first. But what are the immediate reasons for the current increasing tension and the risk of war? India appears to be escalating events but its argument is that it is following the lead of the US and the west by zero tolerance of terrorist attacks. It has identified what it sees as terrorists being harboured by another state so it threatens military retaliation.

Both sides have had internal problems as well. In Pakistan, Musharraf has been promising a democratic election ever since the army took control, but there has been only a referendum. Though it was boycotted by many political parties, Musharraf claimed it as a mandate for him to continue. Meanwhile in India, the ruling BJP has lost every state election for over a year, so now uses the well-known tactic of uniting the country against an outside 'threat'. Whatever the reasons for the tensions, the crucial aim is to avoid the devastation of nuclear war.

The British Prime Minister, Tony Blair, visited the region in January 2002 to try to persuade both sides that a war was not a good idea. This took place against the background of the bombing in Afghanistan, in which Britain was an enthusiastic participant. His approach raised concerns about Western hypocrisy, as if war is fine for some countries but not others. The sincerity of Blair's mission was also in question after it transpired that his plea for peace preceded two British trade missions to Delhi in February, both designed to sell weapons to India. Defexpo is an arms fair whose promotional material pushes the weaponry on sale, with everything from small arms to missile systems. India and Pakistan have long been valuable markets for British arms manufacturers. So this arms fair, combined with the resumption of arms sales to Pakistan, as a result of its support for the war in Afghanistan, means that Britain will be arming both sides in any future war. This is, of course, not unique. A similar thing happened during the Iraq-Iran war.

So, what's the answer? The situation in south Asia shows the importance of nuclear disarmament. A war even with conventional weapons would be an appalling waste of life. But this would be turned into a complete disaster on an unimaginable scale if nuclear weapons were used. In the short term there must be more diplomatic language and there must be proper international negotiations at the UN to resolve the problem of Kashmir. Our own politicians could do more to help. How can the British Government's attempts to calm the situation be taken seriously when the Defence Minister, Geoff Hoon, appears on television saying that he would use nuclear weapons against any state if necessary? In the long term, the declared nuclear weapon states (NWS)-US, UK, France, Russia and China-must carry out their obligations under the nuclear Non-Proliferation Treaty (NPT) and get rid of their nuclear weapons. The NPT was drawn up in 1968, giving the definition of a NWS as one that tested nuclear weapons before then. Because India was preparing its nuclear programme at that time, it would not sign. Because India would not sign, neither would Pakistan. Therefore, they cannot sign the NPT as NWS and, since the nuclear testing by both sides in 1998, they cannot sign as non-nuclear weapon states. The NWS made statements at the time of the tests saying how appalled they were at this development. But after 11 September, the US lifted sanctions imposed on both sides, in order to boost its coalition in the 'War on Terrorism'.

If the NWS put the words of the NPT into action, they would be in a position to push India and Pakistan to sign the NPT themselves. After all, part of the excuse given by India and Pakistan for the 1998 nuclear tests was that those nuclear weapon states had done nothing about their NPT commitments, so if nuclear weapons were good enough for them...

Both sides need to be persuaded that nuclear weapons make the world a more dangerous, not a safer, place and to take a step back and realise that peaceful resolutions to conflict are the best way forward. This should happen through the UN. But the UN also needs to look at the continuing nuclear policies of the NWS. There are peace activists in both India and Pakistan working hard to get their views across. Their work has been particularly difficult since the nuclear tests carried out by both countries in 1998. They have the entire might of the government and military propaganda machine ranged against them. We should do all we can to support them.

INDIA-PAKISTAN JOINT PRESS STATEMENT, 6 JANUARY 2004

In a dramatic development on the sidelines of the twelfth SAARC Summit in Islamabad in January 2004, India and Pakistan agreed to resume an official-level dialogue after a three-year hiatus. The Joint Statement of 6 January 2004 also noted that Delhi agreed to settle Kashmir 'to the satisfaction of both sides', and that Islamabad would not permit 'any territory under Pakistan's control to be used to support terrorism in any manner'. On 18 February 2004, after three days of official-level 'talks on talks' in Islamabad, India and Pakistan agreed to resume their bilateral 'composite dialogue' in May– June 2004, soon after the Indian general elections. This is to take the form of a 'composite dialogue' on eight issues, including two—on 'peace and security, including CBMs' and 'Jammu and Kashmir'— at the Foreign Secretary-level. The two foreign ministers are to meet in August 2004 to review progress. Both Delhi and Islamabad had strong motivations to reach an accord during the SAARC Summit. For Vajpayee, a personal desire for a stable bilateral relationship with Pakistan—his third and final peace effort—had been initiated with his 'hand of friendship' speech in Srinagar in April 2003, and buttressed by approaching general elections in April 2004; for Musharraf, two assassination attempts within eleven days in December 2003 had led to a renewed vigour to fight terrorism of all kinds, along with the increasing radicalization of domestic politics. Vajpayee's rising popularity, seen by the results of the Indian assembly elections in November 2003, also boosted Islamabad's view that it would be advisable to deal with Vajpayee himself. In addition, American pressure on Islamabad to end cross-border infiltration into Indianadministered Kashmir, and to a lesser extent on India—to begin an official-level dialogue with

Pakistan— may also have played a part in the success of bilateral diplomacy on the sidelines of the multilateral summit. Even if the United States had facilitated such a dialogue, it would have been advisable to have maintained this in a low-key manner, for fear of undermining the fledgling peace process.

CURRENT AMERICAN ENGAGEMENT WITH INDIA AND PAKISTAN

In the post-11 September security environment, American relations with Delhi and Islamabad have strengthened considerably, placing it in a unique position of trust by two traditionally antagonistic nuclear-armed states. But the content of the two sets of 'dehyphenated' diplomatic relationships—stressing the absence of any inter-relationship—are quite different and complex.

Current Indo-American ties are fairly broad-based and comprehensive, with the prospect of developing into a strategic relationship in the medium term. If the United States 'tilted' towards Islamabad in the 1971 India-Pakistan war, it clearly 'tilted' towards Delhi in the 1999 Kargil conflict. A relatively high level of joint military exercises, growing naval cooperation, and high-level political and traderelated relations continue to take place between Delhi and Washington. This has not been adversely affected by Delhi's refusal in mid-July 2003 to send troops to Iraq—at the behest of the United States—in the absence of a UN mandate or UN forces command. In January 2004, a joint agreement on a 'quartet' of issues—cooperation in high technology fields, civilian nuclear and space programmes, and discussions on missile defence—provided the framework for significantly enhanced strategic relations. While this may appear related to an American requirement to counter China in the medium term, it is extremely unlikely that Delhi will acquiesce to such a role for some very good reasons—the most important being that both countries share a long land border.

In marked contrast, American relations with Islamabad appear to be more focused on the war on terror and on countering nuclear proliferation. Within Pakistan's highly charged and volatile politics, there are legitimate concerns over Musharraf's personal safety—exacerbated by the two assassination attempts. His reputation and influence is increasingly under question in the light of the proliferation activities of key scientists in the nuclear-weapons establishment. They are expected to decline further when he retires as Army Chief at the end of the year, even though he continues as President until 2007.

However, the United States also sees Pakistan as a major source of Islamic radicalism. On several occasions, the United States has had to stress to Islamabad the need to counter terrorism in Afghanistan, and its related aspects in Indian-administered Kashmir and the activities of Islamist extremist groups operating in Pakistan. In November 2003, Musharraf re-banned several Islamist extremist groups. In one of his strongest statements against extremism, Musharraf—in his first address to the joint sitting of parliament on 17 January 2004—appealed to the Pakistani nation 'to wage *jehad* against extremism'. Nonetheless, Islamabad is clearly Washington's closest ally in the war on terror, through the provision of considerable intelligence and logistical support to its Afghanistan operations. In March 2004, Pakistani paramilitary and armed forces carried out their first major operation against Al-Qaedalinked militants in the tribal areas of Wana in South Waziristan, loosely controlled by Islamabad. In recognition of this support, the United States granted Pakistan the status of 'major non-NATO ally' in March 2004, subject to Congressional approval. Although this appeared to be largely, though not wholly, symbolic, to provide additional support for Musharraf under trying conditions, Delhi expressed pique at not being informed earlier. This also increased Islamabad's prospects for acquiring American military equipment, ammunition and defence R&D cooperation—all of which had been previously denied.

Prospects for the Future

In view of the nature and extent of diplomatic relations with both Delhi and Islamabad, there are attempts to encourage a sustained American foreign policy engagement in the region.

Instead of current American foreign policy fixation on what is essentially 'crisis management', a more activist role in conflict resolution in South Asia is advocated. In October 2003, for example, an American Independent Task Force on India and South Asia—co-sponsored by the Council on Foreign Relations and the Asia Society—urged Congress and the Bush Administration to make South Asia a high foreign policy priority. It warned that if this did not take place, the United States could face crises in the region that would pose major threats to American national security. Although some members of the Task Force felt that American foreign policy did not go far enough in view of the dangers of another India-Pakistan conflict— and therefore urged a more active stance, including putting forward American ideas about a Kashmir settlement— this was not its formal conclusion. Instead, it felt that there should be 'more forward-leaning and sustained United States engagement. There should be a long-term American diplomatic effort to assist—not to mediate or arbitrate—India and Pakistan's intermittent efforts to bridge their differences'.

Despite highly successful American facilitation between India and Pakistan in the recent past— formally ending the Kargil conflict, easing tensions during the border confrontation, and helping initiate an official-level dialogue between the two countries—Delhi remains disinclined to accept an Americanmandated resolution of the Kashmir dispute. It continues to feel quite strongly that this remains a bilateral issue, as stated in the Simla declaration of 2 July 1972. This stated that both countries agreed to 'settle their differences by peaceful means through bilateral negotiations or by any other peaceful means mutually agreed upon between them'. Emphasis on the implementation of the Simla Agreement—in letter and spirit—was reiterated in the Lahore Declaration of 21 February 1999. The India-Pakistan Joint Press Statement of 6 January 2004 also noted the bilateral nature of the dialogue which is required to resolve the disputes between the two countries, including Kashmir. In a wide-ranging interview with *India Today* in January 2004, Vajpayee clearly indicated this when he stated that the United States had been making genuine efforts to promote peace in the subcontinent— 'as friend, not mediator'. In effect, a resolution of the Kashmir dispute needs to emanate from the governments and people of India and Pakistan, if it is to lead to a meaningful and lasting settlement. However, the United States can play an extremely useful role in the following issues, but it needs to be done quietly in the background.

Assist the fledgling India-Pakistan peace process. For the peace process to be tangible, it needs to be understood as a long-term process, as there are no quick solutions. However, it is fraught with problems and difficulties. If it is not to break down—as has happened so often in the past—it needs to be carefully managed by both Delhi and Islamabad, with assistance from the United States. The key, therefore, will be to sustain the dialogue against disruption. The United States could assist by facilitating communication and promoting dialogue.

Share ideas on nuclear-related issues. Much more needs to be done to enhance bilateral nuclear stability. The United States could assist by sharing ideas on various technical issues, such as the drafting of a bilateral agreement on the advanced notification of ballistic missile flight tests or the establishment of nuclear risk reduction centres for the mutual notification of nuclear accidents or unauthorized or unexplained nuclear incidents—both of which have been agreed to in the Lahore MoU of February 1999. Also, nuclear deterrence in both countries needs to be made more stable, with far greater understanding and thinking on critical issues, such as nuclear doctrine, force development, command and control, deployment and readiness, survivability and nuclear safety.

Prepare for the disruption of diplomatic communication between India and Pakistan. In a worst case scenario, the disruption of bilateral diplomatic communication in the future may not easily lend itself to American facilitation as in the past. This may require the conduct of immediate 'back channel' negotiations between the Indian and Pakistani governments—with senior and trusted representatives of the two leaders. The United States could assist in setting the groundwork for such 'back channel' diplomacy amidst the current thaw in India-Pakistan relations.

AFGHANISTAN–PAKISTAN RELATIONS

Afghanistan–Pakistan relations began in 1949 after British India was partitioned into the Republic of India and the Islamic Republic of Pakistan. Afghanistan and Pakistan are usually described as inseparable states due to their historical, religious, cultural, linguistic, and ethnic ties, as well as their multiple trade and economic ties. Both neighbouring states are Islamic republics and part of the South Asian Association for Regional Cooperation. However, the relationship between the two has been affected by the Durand Line, the issues of Pashtunistan and Balochistan, the 1980s Soviet war, the rise of the Taliban, the 2001-present war in Afghanistan, and Afghanistan's relations with India and Shia Iran.

Southern and eastern Afghanistan is predominately a Pashto-speaking region, like the adjacent Khyber-Pakhtunkhwa, Federally Administered Tribal Areas, and northern Balochistan in Pakistan. This entire area is inhabited by the indigenous Pashtuns who belong to different Pashtun tribes. The Pashtuns have lived in this region for thousands of years, since at least the 1st millennium BC.

The Durand Line

The Afghan government does not recognize the Durand Line as the official border between the two states, claiming that the Durand Line Agreement has been void in the past due to violations by Pakistan as well as other reasons. Pakistan, on the other side, issued a warning to Afghanistan that it would not "tolerate any violations of its borders". Relations have continued to be strained, as several top Afghan officials stated that they are weary of Pakistan's negative influence in the country. The Afghan government usually accuses Pakistan of using its intelligence agency, the Inter-Services Intelligence (ISI), in aiding the Taliban militants. Pakistan has denied the allegations but has said it does not have full control of the actions of the ISI. Relations became even more strained as the

United States supports an Afghan invasion of rogue tribal regions.

Other Contemporary Issues

Following the Soviet invasion of Afghanistan in 1979, the Pakistani government played a vital role in supporting the Mujahideen and assisting Afghan refugees. Pakistan absorbed an estimated 3 million refugees and provided shelter, education, and places to work. After the Soviet withdrawal in February 1989, Pakistan, with cooperation from the world community, continued to provide extensive support for displaced Afghans. In 1999, the United States provided approximately $70 million in humanitarian assistance to Afghanistan and Afghan refugees in Pakistan, mainly through multilateral organizations and Non-governmental organizations (NGOs).

Pakistani strategists view Afghanistan as providing "strategic depth" in the event of a war with neighbouring India. In the event that the Indian Army crosses into Pakistan, the Pakistan Army would temporary locate supplies in Afghanistan and prepare for a counter-offensive.

Furthermore, many Pakistanis see in Afghanistan and Afghans a common bond based on religion, history, culture, language and ethnic ties. At various times, Pakistan backed the mujahideen against the Soviets, mujahideen against each other and the Taliban against the Iranian-backed Northern Alliance. The overthrow of the Taliban regime in November 2001 has seen somewhat strained relations between Afghanistan and Pakistan.

The present Karzai administration in Kabul feels that the remnants of the former Taliban government are being supported by factions within Pakistan for the same above reasons. However, Pakistan has said the government cannot control all elements of its intelligence agency, the ISI, which several countries accuse of contributing to instability in Afghanistan. In 2006 Afghan President Hamid Karzai warned that "Iran and Pakistan and others are not fooling anyone" when it come to interfering in his country.

"If they don't stop, the consequences will be ... that the region will suffer with us equally. In the past we have suffered alone; this time everybody will suffer with us.... Any effort to divide Afghanistan ethnically or weaken it will create the same thing in the neighbouring countries. All the countries in the neighborhood have the same ethnic groups that we have, so they should know that it is a different ball game this time." —Hamid Karzai, *February 17, 2006*

Afghan-Pak Transit Trade Agreement

In October 2010, Afghanistan and Pakistan finally inked together the long-awaited Afghan-Pak Transit Trade Agreement (APTTA) between the two states. The landmark agreement was signed by Pakistani Commerce Minister Makhdoom Amin Fahim and Anwar ul-Haq Ahady, Afghan Ministry of Commerce. The ceremony was attended by Richard Holbrooke, U.S. Special Representative for Afghanistan and Pakistan, and a number of foreign ambassadors, Afghan parliamentarians and senior officials.

In July 2010, a Memorandum of understanding (MoU) was reached between the two states, which was observed by U.S. Secretary of State Hillary Clinton. It would allow each nation's shipping trucks into the others; Afghan container trucks will be allowed to drive through Pakistan to the Wagah border with India, including to the port cities of Karachi and Gwadar. Also in July 2010, the two states signed a Memorandum of Understanding agreeing the construction of rail tracks in Afghanistan to connect with Pakistan Railways (PR). Work on the proposed project is set to start in the next four months, which has been in the making since at least 2005. In November 2010, the two states formed a joint chamber of commerce to expande trade relations and solve the problems traders face. The APTTA agreement is to take affect in February 2011.

Relationship between Pakistan and Afghanistan

A poll showed that Afghans rated India as the most favourable country, while Pakistan was the least favoured country with only 2% popularity.

AN ECOLOGICAL CRITIQUE OF PAKISTAN'S ENERGY POLICY

The most fundamental concern with Pakistan's current energy policy trajectory stems from how success is being defined by the government. There is a perception that somehow reaching our energy extraction potential is necessarily a positive indicator of development. Such definitional mistakes have led to major environmental policy concerns in yesteryears. For example, during the early decades of the twentieth century the Bureau of Reclamation in the United States had defined "conservation" of resources as harnessing every kilowatt of energy that flowed through a river. There was a perception that not harnessing such energy and letting the water flow to the ocean was "wastage." The bureau has since then realized that conservation is not synonymous with extraction but rather efficient usage of resources with minimal impact on the systems that sustain those resources in the first place.

Here are some specific metrics that appear to be misleading energy policy-makers in Pakistan, based on a recent presentation by the country's senior energy advisor to the Prime Minister:

Per capita consumption is low: Use of unrefined macro-indicator planning is pervasive in Pakistan and the country continues to consider consumption as a direct indicator of success. While there may be some correlation between higher consumption and industrial success, using this as a metric creates perverse incentives for excessive energy usage that might even be wasted. Therefore in benchmarking performance against regional economic competitors the use of "per capita consumption" is highly misleading. Indeed, if per capita consumption is low that could also be considered a measure of success in terms of efficiency of processes. For example Morocco has a lower per capita energy consumption of 372 kilograms of oil equivalent per person per year (kgoe) than Pakistan's metric of 471(kgoe). However, Morocco has a better performance than Pakistan on the human development index as well as in terms of industrialization indicators. Instead of using consumption as a metric of success, development indicators in terms of industrial output per units of investment should be used as metrics of success to prevent errant policies that artificially increase consumption.

Efficiency defined in terms of units of energy per GDP: Aggregate economic metrics such as the gross domestic product (GDP) are useful to some degree in providing a very rough gauge of economic activity in a country. However, the use of such indicators for benchmarking energy policy can again lead to skewed outcomes. For example, the Pakistani government continues to define efficiency of energy in terms of energy input divided by GDP (also referred to as energy intensity), when most countries have moved to more refined measures that take into account the climate and sectoral mix of the country in question. For example, countries in extreme climates may have a much higher energy intensity due to energy consumption for heating or air conditioning. At the same time, some countries may have a much higher contribution of the service sector than of high-energy industry in promoting GDP which would lead to low energy intensity. The ultimate policy goal from an environmental perspective should be to achieve a mix of low energy-intensive economic growth sectors. A measurement of efficiency should be based on an evaluation of how much energy is being used to produce a given industrial output or useful end product (such as lumens of light for domestic usage) and how much is being lost or wasted.

Supply-side policies driven by GDP growth targets: The aforementioned metrics of energy ultimately lead to a set of policies that have tunnel vision towards economic growth without considering whether such growth is sustainable. To make matters worse, GDP growth targets are set and then existing energy usage ratios are used to calculate what amount of energy would be required to meet those growth targets. In one set of scenarios developed for the government, conservation was the last policy scenario considered in which a modest 9% reduction through reduced demand and 15% technical savings for power generation were assumed. However, there is little attempt by policymakers to focus on how demand might be altered and made more efficient to meet the existing supply constraints. This supply-side approach stifles innovation towards environmental consciousness or energy conservation while leading to massive investments in new energy generation capacity at the expense of ecological factors. *Skewed cost-benefit analyses:* Policymakers are often presented cost-benefit analysis in a stylized objective fashion when in fact the embedded assumption in such analyses can reveal enormous inconsistencies and a departure from ecological constraints. For example, usage of high discount rates being used to calculate the benefits of environmentally beneficial projects such as solar and wind may render them uncompetitive in terms of cost even if they are likely to be more secure in the long-run. Also, there are assumptions about energy imports being more expensive than domestic production because of existing regulatory constraints. However, if the cost of production, including environmental impact are calculated, imports will not necessarily be more expensive than domestic production. This is clearly the case with natural gas imports from Central Asia being more economical as well as having much less aggregate environmental impact in project development and air pollution concerns than local coal mines. While the security of energy supplies is a vital argument against imports, geopolitical circumstances are moving towards greater interdependence between countries on matters of energy as discussed later in this essay.

INDIA, PAKISTAN, AND AMERICAN NUCLEAR DIPLOMACY

India's nuclear tests at Pokhran on May 11, 1998, stunned the world—including American intelligence and policy officials. Pakistan's response, five nuclear weapons detonated in the Baluchistan desert, confirmed officially that the two military rivals were now also nuclear powers. In one of the most populous regions of the world, bitter adversaries in the midst of along-standing and hot war over Kashmir each achieved proven destructive power reaching well beyond their contiguous territories or the region as a whole.... How do we account for the sobering reality that nuclear tests conducted on the Indian subcontinent in mid-May 1998 were neither predicted nor prevented by U.S. policy-makers or intelligence officials? The specifics of the tests aside, the India-Pakistan case is instructive as an example of the failure of the instruments of U.S. statecraft to dissuade states from acquiring active nuclear forces. It also is a microcosm of the growing complexity of U.S. regional relations which will require far more nuanced and sophisticated forms of diplomatic and intelligence operations reaching well beyond engagement only of governments or heads of state.

Unlike the other cases examined in the course of the Study Group's project (North Korea, Iran, and Libya), the United States was intricately involved in discussions with the governments of both India and Pakistan at the time of the nuclear tests and had for decades been seeking nuclear restraint from both parties, using a mixture of carrots and sticks. That such efforts failed to alter nuclear ambitions significantly, including reaching any agreement to postpone or certainly to abandon plans to conduct tests, speaks to possible misjudgments made by both the U.S. policy and intelligence communities about how the U.S. could best wield influence in the region. At the same time, the case puts into question whether the U.S. ever had the influence it thought it had to persuade states that had repeatedly expressed the conviction that nuclear capabilities were vital to their national interest and the willingness, at least rhetorically, to do so regardless of the costs. Does this mean that the various U.S. attempts to halt nuclearization in the region were largely quixotic? A key difficulty of assessing the impact of U.S. nonproliferation policy on South Asia is that the objectives sought by policymakers changed repeatedly over time. To understand whether U.S. nonproliferation policies succeeded or failed in South Asia, it is important to recognize that these policies have not been fixed and constant over the years. In his introductory remarks to the Study Group, a lead speaker described four stages of U.S. nonproliferation efforts in South Asia, and each of these stages had different goals and different policies. In the first stage (1970s-1980s), U.S. policy was focused on persuading countries not to seek nuclear weapons and on getting them to sign onto the NPT. In many ways, the United States succeeded during this stage, despite the fact that India and Pakistan never signed the treaty. After India's initial test in 1974, it never publicly declared itself a nuclear weapons state: as an undeclared power, it achieved its desired security objective while preserving the global nuclear regime. Study Group participants noted that nonproliferation policies worked for 24 years thereafter—not a small achievement.

These policies limited nuclear escalation on the Indian subcontinent, and they may have contributed to ensuring the credibility of the NPT. As one senior official put it, "In 1974 there were key countries like Japan, many advanced countries, that had really not yet decided whether to have nuclear weapons or to join the NPT. I think that if at that time India and Pakistan had pursued active, overt nuclear weapons programs, it would have been very, very difficult to persuade a lot of these countries to join the NPT." During the second stage (1990s–1998), according to this expert, "we had realized that it was simply unrealistic to expect to roll back these capabilities."

The policy goal of this period was to try to convince the Indians and Pakistanis to be satisfied with untested, undeclared nuclear capability. Einhorn added that in private discussions, U.S. officials had stopped pressing India to join the NPT. Clearly, for many of the reasons described above, however, U.S. policies failed to prevent India and Pakistan from testing nuclear weapons. In the face of a perceived existential threat, both India and Pakistan defied world opinion, forming, along with Israel and now North Korea, a special category of non-NPT-sanctioned nuclear weapons states. Given the conditions that compelled India and Pakistan to test, many have suggested that nuclearization was inevitable or at least unpreventable. Regardless of whether it could have been prevented in theory, it seems clear that, with the policy tools and bureaucratic conditions available to the United States at the time, an outcome of failure was understandable. The third period of American policy began with the tests in May 1998 and lasted until 9/11. After the 1998 tests, the policy goal of the United States was to persuade India and Pakistan to accept limitations on their programs. While a concerted effort was launched under Strobe Talbott at the end of the Clinton administration to convince India to agree to limitations, the timing of these efforts was ill-fated. As one senior official in the Study Group noted, events—including the Kargil episode, the plane hijacking to Kandahar, the Musharraf coup, and the fall of the BJP government—made the prospect of nuclear limitations very unlikely.

In the final and most recent period (from 9/11 to the present), the U.S. agenda was refocused on preventing terrorists from acquiring access to nuclear weapons. This new focus allowed the United States to make a distinction between India, which had been a responsible caretaker of its nuclear capability, and Pakistan, which had been a major proliferator, not least as a result of the A.Q. Khan nuclear supply network, two of whose retired scientists reportedly met with Osama bin Laden. In addition, U.S. policy in South Asia emphasized avoiding regional conflict and on installing protections on nuclear facilities and materials. Aside from the 10-month conflict between India and Pakistan in late 2001 and early 2002, these two objectives have so far been successful.

The Decision-Making Process

In any given period, certain incompatibilities, if not outright contradictions, have arisen among the goals the U.S. sought in South Asia. For example, during the Soviet occupation of Afghanistan and again after the Taliban seized power in the 1990s and began harboring Al Qaeda terrorists, the American preoccupation with Pakistan shifted squarely from nonproliferation to combating terrorism. During the Reagan administration, for example, State Department officials were called upon each year to testify in Congress that, against all evidence and available intelligence, Pakistan could be "certified" to not be engaged in certain proscribed nuclear weapons activities so as to avoid triggering congressionally-mandated sanctions.

Shifting preoccupations were accompanied by commensurate shifts in the level and type of policy and intelligence resources devoted to the region, elevating some officials and agencies while subordinating others at different times. On the whole, however, it was the consensus of the study group that nonproliferation objectives were repeatedly overtaken by other priorities, first in Pakistan and later in India. Combined with the freewheeling use of sanctions imposed by both the Executive and Legislative branches, such policies were often perceived by the respective regimes as ill-conceived and high handed. Sanctions, in particular, seem to have impinged on critical leverage the U.S. needed to sustain an effective strategy to stem regional nuclearization.

The insufficiency of high-level policy attention accorded the region or to the internal dynamics of each state compounded the likelihood that American diplomacy would fail. As one Study Group participant noted, South Asian proliferation issues typically garnered the attention of Principals only in conjunction with more pressing high-level events, such as a state visit to Washington or a major flashpoint like Kargil. This was not because concerns about proliferation in South Asia remained within the purview of a few policy or intelligence specialists, as might have been the case in other, more remote areas of the world. To the contrary, developments on the subcontinent involved key players across several government agencies, including the National Security Council, the State Department, and the intelligence community; only the Defence Department remained a second-tier player.

The tension in the U.S. government between regional bureaus and functional bureaus which had an interest in South Asian nuclearization was a common feature of policy deliberations, as is typically the case with issues that cut cross traditional bureau-cratic alignments. South Asia was dubbed by one Study Group member as the "theme park for the functional bureaus." Two participants argued that regional experts who see themselves as responsible for maintaining the overall relationship of the U.S. with key states are likely to be better equipped to manage the inevitably competing priorities which can arise in diplomatic and security affairs. This is not so for functionalists, who, some argued, pursue singular agendas can prove costly to other urgent objectives and the larger relationship. Thus, it was argued, while regional bureaus can be informed by functional specialists, regional specialists are an inherently better choice to manage the complexities of diplomatic and security relationships.

This view invited strong opposition, especially from a veteran non-proliferation diplomat who countered that it is essential and indeed routine for functional specialists to work closely with and learn from regional experts. The idea that there is an inherent dichotomy between the two is not just patently false but a hindrance to effective policymaking. Several participants noted, in turn, that it is the skill and attention of senior officials— undersecretaries and above—that is essential in balancing vital interests while preventing unnecessary internecine domestic rivalries.

Participants identified additional institutional alignments in the decision-making process that affected the design and choice of U.S.-South Asia policy options. The realignment of military commands that led to splitting India into the Pacific Command while leaving Pakistan in Central Command, it was argued, complicated efforts to sustain an accurate strategic vision which could take the entire region and its complex interests into account. On the policy side, the decision to move Afghanistan and the rest of South Asia from its traditional Near East/South Asia office in the National Security Council into the East Asia office in 2001 also was said to prompt confusion over portfolios and bureaucratic alignments in a way that may have interfered with policy-formulation— especially with respect to Afghanistan, but also in the region as a whole. Study Group participants generally agreed that the team that was pulled together by Deputy Secretary of State Strobe Talbott to work toward nuclear limitations in South Asia after the 1998 tests serves as a good example of team work and trans-agency cooperation that is needed to tackle such inherently interdisciplinary challenges. Talbott's group included individuals from the intelligence community, State, Defence, Treasury, and other agencies. It was, remarked one former intelligence official, "an example of [an] informal mechanism that was not part of the national security apparatus that played a very important role." In addition, meetings convened by Assistant Secretary Inderfurth during the Kargil Crisis also were said to have brought the intelligence and policy communities together in a productive way. Study Group members noted that both of these instances were the result the thoughtful planning by certain individuals, however, and not standard or enduring organizational procedure.

The group also addressed the role of the ambassadors to Delhi and Islamabad in advancing American interests in the region, particularly after the 1998 tests. During the early Bush 2 Administration, for example, one participant remarked that "the tail of events was wagging the dog of the bureaucracy."

Ambassador Wendy Chamberlin, while serving in Pakistan after 9/11, was perceived by one observer as having to spend too much time pitted in competition with her counterpart in India, Ambassador Robert Blackwill, to get the attention of senior decision-makers. Blackwill and his aide, Ashley Tellis, participants agreed, were strong advocates of an improved U.S.-India relationship and made a very strong case to this effect. Indeed, the decision to appoint such powerful bureaucratic players both signaled and in turn strengthened the growing bond between the United States and India in recent years. The competition of ambassadors for attention in Washington both reflects the relative scarcity of interest in these countries as well as a failure to engage in efforts based on a genuine strategic consensus.

INDIA, PAKISTAN AND NUCLEAR WEAPONS: A WAY OUT OF THE QUAGMIRE

The non-proliferation bottle breaks

Nuclear weapons have burst onto the international scene once again with the recent nuclear tests by India and Pakistan, and thus their entrance into the *"nuclear club."* With tensions mounting in the disputed area of Kashmir, the prospect of war leading to a nuclear exchange cannot be discounted. Senator Daniel Moynihan, former U.S. Ambassador to India has warned that *"the world is on the edge of nuclear warfare."*

The tests have broken the non-proliferation bottle and could legitimize and accelerate the acquisition of nuclear weapons in Asia and the Middle East. Already, Israel is known to possess nuclear weapons. Iran is approaching a nuclear capability and is receiving assistance in missile technology.

Sanctions will not Work

A major diplomatic effort is required to prevent the deployment of nuclear weapons on Indian and Pakistani missiles, to prevent the India-Pakistan conflict breaking out into a nuclear war and to roll back the nuclear weapons policies in the region. However, the approach taken by Western states, led by the U.S., of punishing India and Pakistan economically for conducting the tests, will not work. This was clearly demonstrated by their decision to test despite U.S. legislation mandating economic sanctions if a non-nuclear country tested, and in the case of Pakistan, despite direct communications from President Clinton prior to the testing.

Sanctions will only heighten nationalistic sentiment in both India and Pakistan because they will be perceived as hypocritical and directed by rich developed countries against poor developing countries. The U.S., France, U.K., Russia and China have conducted over 2000 nuclear explosion tests without official sanction, and the U.S., in particular, continues to test its nuclear weapons by alternative high tech means such as "sub-critical" experiments, fusion research and super-computer simulations. A major reason prompting India to test is the absolute refusal of the nuclear weapon States to implement their obligation under the Non-Proliferation Treaty (NPT), recently reaffirmed by the International Court of Justice, to negotiate for the elimination of nuclear weapons.

"¼ the refusal of the nuclear weapon states to consider the elimination of nuclear weapons...continues to be the single biggest

threat to international peace and security¼ It is because of the continuing threat posed to India by the deployment of nuclear weapons¼ that we have been forced to carry out these tests." – Indian Press Statement, May 15, 1998

Instead the nuclear weapon States maintain a collective stockpile of over 20,000 nuclear weapons, many of them still on alert and ready to be fired at a moment's notice. President Clinton recently issued new nuclear guidelines in a Presidential Decision Directive which made no commitment to nuclear disarmament but instead reaffirmed the indefinite possession of nuclear weapons and their threat of use including a first-use policy.

At the May 1998 meeting in Geneva of Parties to the NPT, appeals by non-nuclear weapon States to the nuclear weapon States to make progress towards nuclear disarmament fell on deaf ears. The nuclear breakout of India and Pakistan was thus no surprise, and is just the beginning of further proliferation unless there is progress toward nuclear disarmament.

A Purely Regional Approach will not Work

India has clearly stated that the primary reasons for going nuclear are not the India - Pakistan conflict but much wider security concerns. Naresh Chandra, Indian Ambassador to the US stated that *"It would be very wrong to see these tests which we conducted in the India-Pakistan context...What we did was not Pakistan specific."*

In press statements following the tests, India has cited the following major concerns:

* loop holes in the Comprehensive Test Ban Treaty which allow the nuclear weapon States to continue testing through *"experiments described as sub-critical or hydronuclear"*.
* lack of progress on negotiations leading to the elimination of nuclear weapons.
* threats to India from the deployment of nuclear weapons by other states.

India-Pakistan talks on confidence building measures relating to their nuclear weapons and on the Kashmir conflict would definitely help. However, such talks could not roll back their nuclear policies because they would not address the major reasons for India's nuclear breakout as cited above.

INDIA'S EMBATTLED SECURITY ENVIRONMENT

India's embattled security environment today has crystallized as a result of Indian foreign policy failures to take charge of India's neighborhood as a regional power and further still India's failures to use her political and economic leverages to ensure that the external intrusive powers in South Asia respect her strategic sensitivities. These policy failures have been more noticeable in the last five years. India's political and policy establishments in different political dispensations have yet to recognize that diplomacy not backed by muscular power and muscular power not backed by adroit diplomacy end in failure and embattled security environment. South Asia in the case of India highlights this dictum. India has lacked the will to use power to ensure a stable South Asia security environment.

India to be admitted in the global strategic calculus would need first to conclusively demonstrate that it does not shy away or is meek and feeble in ordering her own regional strategic environment as the predominant power in South Asia. India has yet to demonstrate that conclusively to the global strategic community. The recent crises in South Asia have found India wanting in this direction. Significantly noticeable was that in the wake of Mumbai 9/11, it was regrettable to observe the Indian Government counting on the United States to politically coerce Pakistan on India's behalf.

With General Elections due in April 2009, the present Indian Government is incapable of exploring fresh policy options to reorder its embattled security environment which has arisen from its own acts of foreign policy omissions and commissions. A new political dispensation, if it comes into power should ponder over fresh policy options to reinforce India's regional power weight and standing. If the same political dispensation returns to power, it would have a lot to answer on its foreign policy failures and would be well advised too to ponder afresh in light of the flaws that have constantly stood pointed out in this Author's Papers in the last five years. This chapter therefore reviews India's policies in South Asia and options to bring to order its embattled security environment, not by advantage of hindsight, but as a reinforcement of what has been asserted by this Author in his earlier Papers. In that light this Paper offers the following perspectives and policy options that India should adopt to ensure that India's strategic sensitivities as a regional power are respected both by the external intrusive powers in South Asia and by South Asian countries themselves:

- India's Regional Power Status Impeded by United States and China: Use India's Comprehensive Strategic Leverages
- Pakistan: India's Policy should Rest on National Security Imperatives and Not Dancing with the Wolves
- Afghanistan: India's Priorities to Assist Nation Building Not Military Involvement
- Bangladesh's Political Stability: India's Strategic Imperative
- Nepal: India Must Contain Enlarging Chinese Penetration under Maoist Government
- Sri Lanka: India's National Security Interests Should Predominate Over Domestic Political Compulsions
- Bhutan: Imperatives for India's Assistance in Capacity Building of Defensive Capabilities
- India's War Preparedness: A Pressing Strategic Imperative
- India's Options to Re-Order Her Embattled Strategic Environment

PAKISTAN, CHINA UNDERPIN INDIA'S SECURITY DOCTRINE

Any national security doctrine of India has to cater to the possibility of threats from two sources-China and Pakistan.

The threat from China was rated high until 1988 because of the unresolved border dispute between the two countries, the clandestine military and nuclear assistance given by the Chinese government to the Pakistani armed forces in order to keep the Indian security forces preoccupied on two fronts, and the support extended by the Chinese intelligence agencies to the tribal insurgent groups of India's Northeast.

The border dispute led to a war between the two countries in 1962. Between 1967 and 1979, many of these insurgent groups went to Yunnan in China via north Myanmar and were trained and armed by the Chinese intelligence. The visit of Rajiv Gandhi, the then Indian prime minister, to China in 1988 and his meeting with Deng Xiaoping set in motion the process of improving bilateral relations. In 1988 and thereafter, the two countries agreed on a number of confidence-building measures, set up a joint working group to discuss the border problem on a sustained basis and decided not to let the pending border dispute come in the way of an improvement in relations in the economic, cultural and other fields.

The Chinese intelligence, which had already started reducing its clandestine assistance to the tribal insurgent groups from 1979, totally stopped it after 1988. Despite this, China continues to pre-occupy the attention of India's national security managers due to the following reasons:

The very slow progress of the talks on the border issue, giving rise to misgivings that Beijing probably wants to keep this issue alive till it has totally pacified Tibet to its satisfaction. Though there is no more unrest in Tibet, which has been developing economically, the Dalai Lama still enjoys a large following there. The Chinese are determined that when the present Dalai Lama dies, his successor will be a man of their choice. They appreciate that this could give rise to serious unrest, which could be exploited by the Tibetan Diaspora in India and elsewhere. By keeping the border issue alive, China wants to retain a pressure point which it can exploit should India show reluctance to keep the Tibetan refugees under control.

In national security matters, the Chinese, unlike the Indians, work on a long-term basis and try to develop today options that they may need years hence should circumstances so warrant. For example, China's continued clandestine assistance to Pakistan in the military nuclear field and in the acquisition of a missile-based delivery capability. Even as Beijing was entering into an agreement with Rajiv Gandhi on improving bilateral relations, it was secretly entering an agreement with Islamabad for assistance in the missile field. Another example is China's decision in 2001 to assist Pakistan in the construction of the Gwadar port on the Balochistan coast, which will reduce Pakistan's present dependence on Karachi port, which is within easy reach of the Indian navy, and give the Pakistani navy a greater operational flexibility. The threat from Pakistan, meanwhile, has always remained and will continue to remain of a very high order due to the following reasons:

- Pakistan's inability to reconcile itself to the loss of Jammu and Kashmir and its obsessive urge to gain control of this territory by hook or by crook.
- Its equally obsessive urge to avenge its defeat at the hands of India in 1971 and its loss of the then East Pakistan.
- The predominant role of the revenge-seeking Pakistani army in its national security management, with practically no role for an elected political leadership in this matter.
- Its refusal to work for a reduction of tension and for the improvement of relations in other fields until a negotiated solution could be found to the Kashmir question.
- The complexes and the feelings of insecurity from which the Pakistan army suffers vis-a-vis its Indian counterpart.
- The role of the pan-Islamic extremist elements in moulding perceptions towards India, whether in the civil society or in the national security apparatus.

Its 1971 defeat at the hands of India brought home to Pakistan the ground reality that it could never hope to achieve its territorial objective through a conventional war on India. It therefore embarked on a policy of waging a proxy war through the use of terrorism as a weapon against the Indian state.

Pakistan had been using terrorism against the Indian state since 1956 when the Naga insurgency broke out. Whereas its use of terrorism against India before 1971 was a defensive measure to keep the Indian security forces preoccupied with internal security duties so that they could not pose a threat to it, its use after 1971 was an aggressive measure having the dual objective of continuing to keep the Indian security forces bleeding and preoccupied with internal security duties and achieving its strategic objective of annexing Jammu and Kashmir without the direct use of its army in a conventional war.

Until Pakistan achieved a military nuclear capability in the late 1980s, which was subsequently openly demonstrated in the Chagai nuclear tests of 1998, it kept its proxy war restricted to the training and arming of Indian separatist groups, whether in Punjab or Kashmir, which had taken to arms against the government of India due to various grievances.

The acquisition of the military nuclear capability made the Pakistani military leadership conclude that the possibility of an Indian-imposed conventional war in retaliation for its proxy war had been reduced considerably, if not largely eliminated, and hence it could further escalate its proxy war by training, arming and infiltrating into India its own nationals under the guise of jihadi volunteers from different pan-Islamic organizations to intensify the jihad against India. Until 1995, the role of these mercenaries was largely confined to Jammu and Kashmir, but since then Pakistan's Inter-Services Intelligence has been using them in other parts of India too.

Pakistan looks on its nuclear arsenal and its missile delivery capability not as a weapon of deterrence to deter India from using its nuclear capability against it, but as a weapon of intimidation to prevent India from retaliating against it through its armed forces for its proxy war and as a weapon of psychological pressure by creating fears of a possible nuclear holocaust and thereby moving the rest of the world, particularly the US, to exercise pressure on India on the Jammu and Kashmir issue.

Its consistent refusal to subscribe to the no first use of nuclear weapons declaration and its repeated reiteration of its readiness to make first use of its nuclear weapons to prevent the Indian army from over-running its large cities and crushing its army are part of its intimidatory tactics.

The nuclear threat from Pakistan is compounded by the presence of pan-Islamic jihadi elements which justify the use of the weapons of mass destruction to protect Islam, if necessary. The possibility of the nuclearization of terrorism originating from the terrorist hub of Pakistan is a matter of great concern not only to India, but also to the international community as a whole, confronted with the threat of pan-Islamic jihadi terrorism. Since President General Pervez Musharraf seized power on October 12, 1999, Pakistan has embarked on a policy of over-projecting its nuclear and missile capability in order to reassure its own population of the adequacy of its capability and to intimidate India and prevent a retaliatory conventional strike against its proxy war.

GLOBALIZATION IMPACT ON THREAT PERCEPTIONS IN INDIA, PAKISTAN AND CHINA

For the purpose of this book, South Asia has been taken to cover India, Afghanistan, Pakistan, Bangladesh, Sri Lanka, Nepal, Bhutan and the Maldives. Even though China is not considered a part of South Asia, it has common borders with some of the countries of the region and their threat perceptions are influenced by the China factor. There cannot, therefore, be any meaningful discussion on this subject without a reference to this factor. South Asia, as defined above, covers only about 10 per cent of the total land area of the Asian continent, but about 40 per cent of Asia's total population and between 45 and 50 per cent of Asia's Muslim population live in this area.

Many analysts in India, including this writer, make a distinction between the Indian sub-continent and South Asia. When they talk of the Indian sub-continent, they have in mind India, Pakistan, Bangladesh, Nepal and Bhutan. Of these, India, Pakistan and Bangladesh constituted one political entity before the British left the sub-continent in 1947. Pakistan was born in 1947 through the partition of the British India and Bangladesh was born in 1971 through the partition of Pakistan after a war of liberation waged by the Bengalis of the then East Pakistan, with Indian assistance.

Indian analysts, who talk of the Indian sub-continent, wish to keep in mind, in their analyses, the common historical, political, religious and cultural heritage of these three countries. The term sub-continent is used less and less in Pakistan and Bangladesh.

The political leadership and the policy-makers in these two countries do not wish to be reminded of this common heritage. Any highlighting of this common heritage by Indian analysts is viewed by them with suspicion—— as indicating a hidden desire to reverse history and undo the 1947 partition. They, therefore, talk only of South Asia and have, for all practical purposes, banished any reference to the sub-continent from their strategic discourse.

This has to be kept in mind since complexes arising from sub-continental memories tend to influence their mind-set and threat perceptions and have stood in the way of the progress of globalization in this area. They view any Indian enthusiasm for globalization as a concealed attempt towards political and economic re-subcontinentalisation.

The threat perceptions of the countries of South Asia are influenced and will continue to be influenced in the short and medium terms by four factors:

- The India factor.
- The China factor.
- The Pakistan factor.
- The non-State actors factor.

The India Factor

The India factor has had an impact on the threat perceptions of all the countries of this region except Afghanistan and the Maldives. This arises due to the following reasons:

- Asymmetry in size, human and material resources and economic and military potential.
- Perceived Indian willingness/tendency to assert its national interests even if they be detrimental to those of the neighbours. Examples: India's role in the creation of Bangladesh, alleged Indian support to the Tamils of Sri Lanka.
- Perceived Indian encouragement of its political favourites in the countries of the region. Examples: India's alleged soft corner for the opposition Awami League in Bangladesh and for the democratic forces in Nepal.
- Continuing differences relating to territory (Kashmir with Pakistan) and utilization of water resources (Pakistan and Bangladesh).

The other countries, except Afghanistan and the Maldives, tend to guard themselves against these factors by avoiding too close economic linkages with India, which comes in the way of the region as a whole benefiting from the fruits of globalization, by developing economic and military linkages with China and by supporting Chinese aspirations for a role in regional organizations such as the SAARC as an observer.

Pakistan and Bangladesh embarked on a policy of liberalization of their economies before India. Despite this, their economic development has not been as satisfactory as they would have like it to be. Amongst the reasons, one could cite the bad internal security situation, which keeps foreign investors away despite a favourable policy framework; political instability due to periodic interventions by the Army in politics; inadequate investment in a modern education system due to the diversion of the limited resources to meet military and strategic needs; and failure to diversify the economy. Pakistan's economy continues to be largely a three-commodity (cotton and cotton textiles, leather goods and sports articles) and one-port (Karachi) economy. Bangladesh's economy continues to be largely textiles, jute and raw materials dependent.

Though India embarked on the liberalization of its economy only from 1991 onwards, its economy has made impressive progress freeing it from its past dependence on traditional goods such as textiles, tea etc. India's rapid diversification and development of its economy have been facilitated by the facts that democracy has taken firm roots in the country; that its internal security problems, though serious, are confined to areas in which the foreign investors are presently not interested; and that its founding fathers had shown foresight in investing heavily on a modern education system, including institutes of excellence in technology, which have significantly contributed to its emergence as a leading Information Technology (IT) power.

Complexes and concerns arising from the India factor continue to come in the way of the normalization of trade relations between Pakistan and India, the improvement in the trade relations between India and Bangladesh and progress towards the integration of the economies of the region through appropriate institutional and policy frameworks. Political factors continue to receive priority over economic and prejudices and fears continue to rule out pragmatism.

However, economic realities ultimately have a way of asserting themselves. One could already see a beginning of it in Pakistan. Its rulers and policy-makers have realized that a favourable policy frame-work and wide-ranging reforms alone will not attract foreign investors. They also need a market and consumers large enough to make their investments adequately profitable. Pakistan does not provide such a market and such a reservoir of consumers. Unless the foreign investors perceive the sub-continent as a whole as a single economic entity and market and are able to sell their products anywhere within this entity, they are reluctant to invest in Pakistan or Bangladesh alone, without guarantees of access to the Indian market.

The realization of this ground reality has already brought about a significant change in Pakistan's policy since Gen. Pervez Musharraf came to power in October, 1999. While continuing to oppose the normalization of economic relations with India till the differences over Jammu & Kashmir (J&K) are settled, he has made an exception in respect of energy supplies. He is prepared now to allow the foreign investors investing heavily in the construction of oil and gas pipelines to Pakistan from Iran or Turkmenistan to cater to the requirements of the Indian market too in order to make their investments adequately profitable. Significantly, even the religious fundamentalist parties, who continue to insist on a policy of "Kashmir first and the rest later", have not objected to what Gen. Musharraf describes as the stand-alone exception. If this exception materializes and if the benefits of it are felt by the Pakistani people, this will become more and more a rule than a mere exception.

Such a realization is yet to come about in Bangladesh. The trade relations between India and Bangladesh are not as restricted as those between India and Pakistan. There is a much, much freer flow of trade between the two countries. While encouraging a greater flow of trade with China, Bangladesh continues to prevent pragmatism, profitability and mutual benefits from having a free play to contribute to a rapid expansion of the bilateral economic relations with India.

Four examples could be cited as illustrations of the Bangladesh attitude:

- It refuses to sell its surplus gas to India on the ostensible ground that it wants to conserve it for its future use. At the same time, it has reportedly entered into negotiations with China for selling it through a pipeline to China via Myanmar.
- It refuses to grant transit rights to India to facilitate the movement of Indian goods to India's northeast.
- It has been reluctant to permit a pipeline to bring gas from the Arakan area of Myanmar to India pass through Bangladesh territory.

- During the period from July to December, 2005, the value of Chinese exports to Bangladesh amounted to US $ 1.03 billion and Chinese imports from Bangladesh only US $ 27.9 million. During the same period, the value of Indian exports to Bangladesh amounted to US $ 820 million and imports from Bangladesh to US $ 105 million. India's imports from Bangladesh are still small, but they are four times the value of Chinese imports from Bangladesh. Chinese exports to Bangladesh are nearly 25 per cent more than those of India. And yet, while Bangladesh nurses a grudge against India on the ground that it has allegedly been dumping its goods in Bangladesh and has not been buying enough from there, it does not voice a similar grievance against China.

Feelings of insecurity, an aggressive inferiority complex, and a Me-too syndrome continue to influence policy-making in Pakistan. What India does, it must do too. What India gets, it must get too. One saw an example of this syndrome in action during the recent visit of President George Bush to India and Pakistan, when, during Mr. Bush's talks in Islamabad, Gen. Musharraf reportedly pleaded with him to reach with Pakistan an agreement on co-operation in the development of civilian nuclear energy similar to the agreement offered to India. Mr. Bush had to point out to him that the needs and circumstances of the two countries are different.

These factors——feelings of insecurity, the inferiority complex and the Me-too syndrome—will continue to influence the Pakistani mind-set and policy-making in the short and medium terms. Though there has been progress in the identification and implementation of confidence-building measures and in the promotion of people-to-people contacts, the relationship between the two countries will continue to be fragile and the exploitation of the opportunities for beneficial co-operation provided by globalization will be slow.

While Pakistan's longing for the acquisition of J&K and its painful memories of 1971 could explain its attitude to India, no convincing explanation is possible for the behaviour of

Bangladesh. While there are differences between India and Bangladesh over the utilization of river waters, there are no major differences over territory compared to the Kashmir issue with Pakistan and Bangladesh has no negative memories of India's military might in action against it. The anti-Indian reflexes in Bangladesh are largely confined to the present ruling formation headed by Begum Khalida Zia and are not shared by the opposition headed by the Awami League, which was in the forefront of its independence struggle.

India-Bangladesh relations will continue to zigzag—— improving when the Awami League is in power and stagnating, if not declining, when the Bangladesh National Party comes to power. Globalization has not made any significant difference to this zigzag and is unlikely to do so in the short and medium terms.

5

China-South Asia Political Relations

"Peaceful co-existence" is the main principle in China-South Asia relations. The fundamentals of this principles are i) mutual equality, ii) non-interference in each other's internal affairs, iii) mutual respect to territorial integrity, iv) cooperation against hegemonism and power politics, and v) mutual accommodation and benefit (Wang Hongwei, 2005). In view of the colonial and feudal background, the main principle and fundamentals of China-South Asia ties are progressive. If one closely examines the natural and spiritual realities that persist between China and South Asia, the main principle and fundamentals of their ties can not truly be more than egalitarian.

China and South Asia are linked by land and water, mountains and rivers. Unlike East Asia and South East Asia and China, Chinese and most of South Asian ties are contiguous, more natural and comprehensive. Mountains pass through and major rivers flow down to China and South Asia from the Tibet Autonomous Region (TAR) of China. Now, it is science and technology that is poised to harness snow and water for larger benefits of the people. In China and South Asia, it has yet remained a geo-political as well as ecological truism that link maintained by mountains and rivers are more stable than opportunistic alliances offered by nuclear power.

Another basic articulation of China-South Asia relations is Buddhism. Gautam Buddha, who was born and had acquired knowledge about the ultimate truth in South Asia, very much lives life-size every where in China. The civilization of China and South Asia thus holds common source of inspiration with a profound degree of continuity. As Buddhism does not stand as an anti-thesis for any other religion, it helps to create an internal capacity to absorb, acculturate and assimilate in both China and South Asia. In short, geo-politically charged neighborhood in an intense natural and spiritual sense is what stands out in China-South Asia relations.

China's politics till the recent past was concentrated on its east coast of the Taiwan Straits. Asia as a whole ranked relatively low in its security agenda since creation of the People's Republic of China. But the Cold War era did not leave China untouched. Tibet in particular conditioned China in formulation of its South Asia policy and to the stability in its frontier regions. The tenets of this policy were: Peace at the south-west border region of China. Efficient signing of border treaty with the neighbouring countries was part of this policy to ensure peace along China's long border.

The Tibetan question. This question raised by the external forces had made China acutely sensitive of its national integration and domestic stability. Chinese policy recognized Tibetan separatism as having serious implications for the national integration and domestic stability. It also recognized that the forces supporting the Tibetan separatism were working by proxy, and many aspects of the separatist moves were utterly non-transparent. So trying its best to correctly understand the external as well as internal features of Tibetan question, and appreciating highly those neighbouring countries and organizations who did not allow Tibetan separatists to engage in activities and also did not permit outside powers to support such activities on their soil, China's South Asia Policy tried proactively hard to work at the two inter-related fronts at the same time-discouraging the separatist elements and, praising and encouraging those countries and organizations who did not support and did not provide any ground to support the Tibetan separatism.

Independent relations with South Asian states. China was aware of the unequal interstate relations that do not allow development of cordial and trustily ties between them. Difference in size, power and interpretation of agreements had affected relations between states in South Asia. During the Cold War years, the dominating trend in the interstate relations was exploitation and gains at the cost of other, and a tendency to have "sphere of influence." Exchange and cooperation between China and a number of small South Asian states was not liked by India. But China continued to cultivate ties with small South Asian countries independently. It supported independence of these countries, and their independent decision making. After 1962 border war with India, the importance of independence of the countries in South Asia-particularly of those small and non-nuclear power countries-had increased for China. China realized that only unilaterally wishing for cooperation might not be wise and realistic.

Therefore in view of a Chinese analyst, "It is undeniable, ...after the 1962 border war, China's policy toward Nepal might have reflected, to some extent, a strategy in which China supported Nepal, along with other small countries in South Asia, to check India's influence" (Hua Han, 2005). Despite so, China provided unflinching support to late King Birendra's proposal to declare Nepal a "Zone of Peace" in mid 1970s. It was indicative of China's firmer conviction that the indigenous will and ability of neighbouring small states in South Asia to independently conduct their foreign and defence affairs together with its independent foreign policy and self-defence strategy was more important and conducive for peace and stability of China's frontier regions than mere lonely Chinese efforts directed at the same.

It was this sense of working together which had been the driving force for China to reciprocally commit to the independence of the small South Asian states. Whatever financial, material and military assistance China has provided to these countries were corollary of the said policy. The United States of America (the US) has ever been at the centre stage whether it was the end of the bi-polar Cold War, 9/11 terrorist attacks and the subsequent US campaign against terrorism, and now the US campaign for democracy. It is the only power which could put troops in Iraq and Afghanistan at the same time and spend enough money to rebuild the economies. Indeed, despite the euphoria for multi-lateralism after the end of Cold War, the South Asian countries were "gravely relying on the assistance and loans provided by the World Bank and developed countries, which in turn resulted in the heavy burden of foreign debts and shortage of foreign exchange reserves and investment capital.

After 9/11, the new strategic development (beginning of the US offensive in Afghanistan) changed the security environment in Asia. US military presence in Uzbekistan and Afghanistan and the new military relationship of the US with Pakistan and India completed the US military involvement in the whole of the Asian continent. Until then South Asia was a gap between the US involvement in West Asia and East Asia. After the US completed its Asian military expansion by filling the gaps left by collapse of Soviet Union under its "war against terror" planning, it felt a need to address another gap which its own larger military involvement had created. The felt US need was primarily due to genuine domestic concerns. The felt need this time was democracy.

For China and the US "the week that changed the world" in February, 1972 when President Nixon visited China had a clear American objective, and that was "to transform the two-power world of the Cold War into a triangle then to manage the triangle in such a way that we would be closer to each of the contenders than they were to each other, thereby maximizing our options". With the disappearance of the Soviet Union, one of the two-power world, despite the initial instability and uncertainty, the US and China appear to move into a maturing stage, and carry out responsibilities particularly in Asia-Pacific region. The following statements of President Bush and Premier Wen confirm how they viewed their role in relation to each other.

Welcoming Chinese Premier Wen Jiabao at the White House on December 9, 2003, President George Bush of the United States of America described the US and China as "partners in diplomacy working to meet the dangers of 21st century." He further added: "As our two nations work constructively across areas of common interest, we are candid about our disagreements. The growing strength and maturity of our relationship allows us to discuss our differences, whether over economic issues, Taiwan, Tibet, or human rights and religious freedom, in a spirit of mutual understanding and respect." Replying to President Bush on the occasion, Chinese Premier Wen said, "Our cooperation in a wide range of areas such as counterterrorism, economy, trade and international and regional issues has effectively safeguarded our mutual interests and promoted peace, stability and prosperity in the Asia Pacific region and the world at large."

The key policy statements above from President Bush and Premier Wen, beyond any doubt, eloquently establishes the importance of Sino-US relationship for the Asia-Pacific region and the world at large over and above the bilateral ties existing between the two great countries. In the period ahead where agenda for democracy is pushed to the front, China-US ties may loose glitters; and China may face all the blames for being a "communist" state. And specifically in the context of South Asia, where the majority belongs to the poor and level of interstate cooperation is low, it is for the people and states of the South Asia to decide either for China-inspired peace with independence and self-governed development or for the US-inspired peace with global democracy and development. Whatever the choice the people and states of South Asia make, the decision of Thirteenth Dhaka SAARC summit to associate China and Japan with SAARC was indeed a very welcome unprecedented geopolitical development. The constructive role played by the small SAARC members in this decision making will certainly help fruitfully maximize comparative advantage of SAARC member's vis-à-vis the new partners (China and Japan).

South Asian states are poor. One major reason for such a condition is they do not have an effective good neighborly policy between themselves. At times certain state's behaviour suggests that it wants to live without neighbours. Mahatma Gandhi has provided an example of a good neighborly policy. In his words of wisdom, "One who serves his neighbours serves all the world."

Since 1978 when the modernization and reform process started, economic growth in China has averaged 9.5 percent per year which remains a truly astounding rate. Similarly, foreign trade has expanded at an annual rate of 15 percent over the same period. As for foreign investment China was able to attract $53.2 billion in 2002 as against $52.7 billion for the United States of America. Indeed, the economic transformation has been so rapid that even renowned investment banking firms like Golsdman Sachs predict that China could be the world's largest economy by 2050 with a GDP of $44.4 trillion ahead of the US GDP of $35 trillion and India's GDP of $27 trillion in the same period.

To correct some of the economic divide of a market based economy so that no part of the country remains left out in the great process of economic transformation, the Chinese government is allocating increasing resources including new investment funds from better off provinces in building new physical and social infrastructure and new industrial establishments in the western region. As a part of this strategy the Qinghai-Tibet railway is completed at a cost of $3.16 billion. Similarly, road network in Tibet is being expanded and improved with links to important cities in other provinces.

China's rapid economic growth has its neighbours change their perception on China. The shift from a "China threat" to "China opportunity" theory opens the alternative to explore the benefits that can be draw from the gigantic China's market-leading to deeper and inner natural and spiritual bonds with China. As the immediate neighbours, as many South Asian scholars and experts have wisely suggested, the SAARC members states should take full advantage of China's achievement, especially China's "western development program," which can facilitate a closer economic and trade interaction specially between Tibet, Xingjian, Sichuan and Yunnan and neighbouring South Asian states. Opening of new transport and trade routes and just completed railway line over "the roof of the world" will provide China's western parts with efficient access to neighbouring countries leading to a change in geo-political outlook.

The ultimate test of the South Asian ability will lie with its leaders' determination to practically conduct the principle of peaceful co-existence along with its fundamentals in relationship with China. Hopefully the Himalayan twins as if representing north face and south face of Kailash-China and South Asia-cherish more a vision of working together than a division of sphere of influence.

It was this spirit of working together that had inspired the press release that was issued after the international seminar on SAARC and China. China Study Centre, Nepal organized this seminar on 23 December, 2002 in Kathmandu, the venue of SAARC Secretariat. The press release stated: "Based on the papers presented and comments and observations made during the discussion, the participants of the seminar on SAARC and China ...have come to the following consensus." There is a need for institutionalized dialogue mechanism between SAARC and China. The imperative for good neighbourhood and challenges and opportunities of the 21st century in regard to peace, cooperation and development dictate the needs for bold and speedy action to move forward in this direction. In this connection it is necessary to hold follow-up seminar focusing on the specific of the institutionalized dialogue mechanism between SAARC and China.

The SAARC member states may try to expand and intensify their social and economic interaction with China at sub-regional level. The Track II initiative prepares ground for promoting and complementing official level discussion. It is gratifying to note that Thirteenth SAARC summit at Dhaka in November last has gloriously taken initiative for establishing institutionalized dialogue mechanism between SAARC and China. The SAARC member leaders should be commended for their bold and glorious initiative. It is hoped that they will also ensure speedy actions regarding the paraphernalia of China's institutionalized association with SAARC.

What is expected are upcoming SAARC official meetings at various levels will prepare grounds for the SAARC member states to expand and intensify their social and economic interaction with China at sub-regional level. Various sub-regional groupings within SAARC may find, for example, i) eastern Himalayan resource, ii) western Himalayan resources, iii) transportation links and networks, iv) nature tourism and v) spiritual tourism as important themes for sustainable cooperation to the various sub-regional groups within SAARC.

It has been learned that attempts have been made to organize seminars on China and South Asian Relations in Colombo. Such activities are encouraging as they promote and compliment official level discussion on inter-regional collaborative dialogue between China and South Asian states.

It will be extremely good if the SAARC member states attempts to expand and intensify their social and economic interaction with China at sub-regional level.

A sub-region (based on sub-geographical level-for example, eastern South Asia, western South Asia, and/or function-for example, culture, natural sources or infrastructure) is recognized as a practical mechanism to promote and strengthen SAARC's over all link with China. As more effective, immediate and direct geo-political link between China and South Asia will be through sub-regional grouping of South Asia; members of the South Asian sub-regional grouping will be more dependent on each other to realize the purpose.

Whereas for China, this sort of cooperative arrangement will ensure required stability and peace in the frontier regions, for each South Asian sub-region value will be added to tourism, culture, and physical development which will enhance overall quality of life of its people.

NATIONAL DEFENCE POLICY OF CHINA

China pursues a national defence policy which is purely defensive in nature. China places the protection of national sovereignty, security, territorial integrity, safeguarding of the interests of national development, and the interests of the Chinese people above all else.

China endeavors to build a fortified national defence and strong military forces compatible with national security and development interests, and enrich the country and strengthen the military while building a moderately prosperous society in all aspects. China's national defence policy for the new stage in the new century basically includes: upholding national security and unity, and ensuring the interests of national development; achieving the all-round, coordinated and sustainable development of China's national defence and armed forces; enhancing the performance of the armed forces with informationization as the major measuring criterion; implementing the military strategy of active defence; pursuing a self-defensive nuclear strategy; and fostering a security environment conducive to China's peaceful development. According to the needs of national security and the level of economic and social development, China pursues a three-step development strategy to modernize its national defence and armed forces step by step in a well-planned way.

This strategic framework is defined as follows: Promoting the informationization of China's national defence and armed forces. Taking informationization as the goal of modernization of its national defence and armed forces and in light of its national and military conditions, China actively pushes forward the RMA with Chinese characteristics. It has formulated in a scientific way strategic plans for national defence and armed forces building and strategies for the development of the services and arms, according to which it will lay a solid foundation by 2010, basically accomplish mechanization and make major progress in informationization by 2020, and by and large reach the goal of modernization of national defence and armed forces by the mid-21st century. Overall planning of economic development and national defence building. Sticking to the principle of coordinated development of economy and national defence, China makes overall plans for the use of its national resources and strikes a balance between enriching the country and strengthening the military, so as to ensure that its strategy for national defence and armed forces building is compatible with its strategy for national development. It makes national defence building an organic part of its social and economic development, endeavors to establish scientific mechanisms for the coordinated development of economy and national defence, and thus provides rich resources and sustainable driving force for the modernization of its national defence and armed forces. In national defence building, China makes it a point to take into consideration the needs of economic and social development and insists on having military and civilian purposes compatible with and beneficial to each other, so as to achieve more social benefits in the use of national defence resources in peacetime. Deepening the reform of national defence and armed forces. China is working to adjust and reform the organization, structure and policies of the armed forces, and will advance step by step the modernization of the organizational form and pattern of the armed forces in order to develop by 2020 a complete set of scientific modes of organization, institutions and ways of operation both with Chinese characteristics and in conformity with the laws governing the building of modern armed forces.

China strives to adjust and reform the systems of defence-related industry of science and technology and the procurement of weapons and equipment, and enhance its capacity for independent innovation in R&D of weapons and equipment with better quality and cost-effectiveness. China endeavors to establish and improve the systems of weaponry and equipment research and manufacturing, military personnel training and logistical support that integrate military with civilian purposes and combine military efforts with civilian support.

In addition, China makes an effort to establish and improve a national defence mobilization system that is centralized and unified, well structured, rapid in reaction, and authoritative and efficient. Taking the road of leapfrog development.

Persisting in taking mechanization as the foundation and informationization as focus, China is stepping up the composite development of mechanization and informationization. Persisting in strengthening the military by means of science and technology, China is working to develop new and high-tech weaponry and equipment, carry out the strategic project of training talented people, conduct military training in conditions of informationization, and build a modern logistics system in an all-round way, so as to change the mode of formation of war-fighting capabilities. Persisting in laying stress on priorities, China distinguishes between the primary and the secondary, and refrains from doing certain things, striving to achieve leapfrog development in key areas. China persists in building the armed forces through diligence and thrift, attaching importance to scientific management, in order to make the fullest use of its limited defence resources. China implements a military strategy of active defence. Strategically, it adheres to the principle of featuring defensive operations, self-defence and striking and getting the better of the enemy only after the enemy has started an attack. In response to the new trends in world military developments and the requirements of the national security and development strategy, China has formulated a military strategic guideline of active defence for the new period. This guideline aims at winning local wars in conditions of informationization. It takes into overall consideration the evolution of modern warfare and the major security threats facing China, and prepares for defensive operations under the most difficult and complex circum-stances.

Meeting the requirements of confrontation between war systems in modern warfare and taking integrated joint operations as the basic approach, it is designed to bring the operational strengths of different services and arms into full play, combine offensive operations with defensive operations, give priority to the flexible application of strategies and tactics, seek advantages and avoid disadvantages, and make the best use of our strong points to attack the enemy's weak points. It endeavors to refine the command system for joint operations, the joint training system and the joint support system, optimize the structure and composition of forces, and speed up the building of a combat force structure suitable for winning local wars in conditions of informationization. This guideline lays stress on deterring crises and wars. It works for close coordination between military struggle and political, diplomatic, economic, cultural and legal endeavours, strives to foster a favourable security environment, and takes the initiative to prevent and defuse crises, and deter conflicts and wars. It strictly adheres to a position of self-defence, exercises prudence in the use of force, seeks to effectively control war situations, and strives to reduce the risks and costs of war. It calls for the building of a lean and effective deterrent force and the flexible use of different means of deterrence.

China remains committed to the policy of no first use of nuclear weapons, pursues a self-defensive nuclear strategy, and will never enter into a nuclear arms race with any other country. This guideline focuses on enhancing the capabilities of the armed forces in countering various security threats and accomplishing diversified military tasks.

With the focus of attention on performing the historical missions of the armed forces for the new stage in the new century and with raising the capability to win local wars in conditions of informationization at the core, it works to increase the country's capabilities to maintain maritime, space and electromagnetic space security and to carry out the tasks of counter-terrorism, stability maintenance, emergency rescue and international peacekeeping. It takes military operations other than war (MOOTW) as an important form of applying national military forces, and scientifically makes and executes plans for the development of MOOTW capabilities. China participates in international security cooperation, conducts various forms of military exchanges and promotes the establishment of military confidence-building mechanisms in accordance with this guideline. This guideline adheres to and carries forward the strategic concept of people's war. In accordance with this guideline, China always relies on the people to build national defence and the armed forces, combines a lean standing force with a powerful reserve force, and endeavours to reinforce its national war potential and defence strength.

China is working to set up a mechanism for unified and efficient national defence mobilization, stepping up the mobilization of economy, science and technology, information and transportation, and making improvements in the building of the reserve force. China is striving to make innovations in the content and forms of people's war, exploring new approaches of the people in participating in warfare and support for the front, and developing new strategies and tactics for people's war in conditions of informationization. Moreover, the People's Liberation Army (PLA) subordinates its development to the overall national construction, supports local economic and social development, and consolidates the unity between the PLA and the government, and between the PLA and the people.

THE LIMITS OF CHINESE POWER IN SOUTHEAST ASIA

That China is one of the most powerful states in the world is no longer a contested claim, but cataloguing China's increasing material resources does not in itself demonstrate that China is powerful. Southeast Asia presents an apparently 'easy' case for investigating China's rising power. Given the significant asymmetry of power, if China's power has grown we would expect to see altered preferences and behaviour among these weaker neighbours in response to coercion, persuasion or inducement. Results so far are mixed. While China has been able to harness much of the region's economic energy in a favourable direction, it does not always get its way in territorial and resource conflicts.

In mainland Southeast Asia, China's participation makes feasible region-wide economic development plans for the Greater Mekong Subregion initiative of the Asian Development Bank, drawing international investment for infrastructural projects. These connect the poorer states — Cambodia, Laos and Vietnam

— to the markets of China and Thailand while improving China's access to raw material supplies and ports in the Indian Ocean and East China Sea. These schemes also spur Japanese and American interest and investment in Mekong regionalism. More prominently, China's initiative for an FTA with ASEAN overcame the nagging problem of galvanising an economic integration project. When it came into effect in 2010, the China-ASEAN FTA formed the world's largest free trade area, comprising 1.9 billion consumers and US$4.3 trillion in trade.

Situations in which the pre-existing preferences of other states are unclear or undecided — such as the 1990s debate about whether rising China was a threat — present opportunities for China to influence its neighbours by persuading them that its own narrative is more accurate and certainly more profitable. This campaign, from the mid-1990s, involved an alternative narrative about China's cooperative New Security Idea, and its 'peaceful rise' or 'peaceful development' as it strives for a 'harmonious world.' The message was intended to reassure neighbours that China's resurgence would not threaten their economic or security interests because of its peaceful intentions, limited national capabilities, mutually beneficial development trajectory and pluralist international mindset.

Rhetoric was accompanied by policy action. In Southeast Asia, China negotiated land (though not maritime) border disputes with Vietnam; fully participated in ASEAN institutions; and undertook highly publicised restraint and aid during the 1997 and 2009 financial crises. China's persuasive power encompassed economic inducement. Its China-ASEAN FTA Early Harvest Programmes with some ASEAN countries — the partial lifting of trade barriers on selected goods — is portrayed by Chinese analysts as China 'giving more and taking less', working towards harmony and enrichment of its neighbours.

Yet there are limits to how much policymakers in Southeast Asian states are reassured regarding the China threat. China's power to persuade is rooted in its ability to sustain benign policy action. Apart from efforts to offset some of the adverse effects of Chinese economic competition, China's neighbours are also watching its behaviour in more serious conflicts of interest.

The best way to gauge the change of power into influence is in cases where the powerful actor causes another actor to change policy on a significant subject of disagreement. In the case of China and Southeast Asia, such subjects include policies on Taiwan, defence relations with the US and policies on territorial disputes. On these potential hard cases, it is difficult to find significant changes in Southeast Asian states' policies in response to Chinese actions to date.

Of these, China has expended most effort in the disputes over atolls in the South China Sea. China and ASEAN agreed to a Declaration of Conduct in 2002, committing to peaceful negotiations. Yet the Chinese navy continued manoeuvres to assert its claims, leading to skirmishes with Vietnam and the Philippines. Two months into a Vietnamese concession to develop gas fields off the Vietnamese coast in 2007, BP suspended operations, reportedly as a result of Chinese threats to exclude it from future energy deals in China. In March this year, Chinese naval vessels tried to interrupt oil exploration by the Philippines in waters that Manila considers its own.

At a regional defence ministers' meeting in June 2010, statements suggesting that China now regards the South China Sea as part of its 'core national sovereignty interests' led US Secretary of Defence Robert Gates to warn that the US 'oppose[s] the use of force and action that hinder freedom of navigation.' One month later, Secretary of State Hillary Clinton reiterated US 'national interest' in the peaceful resolution of these multilateral disputes. In September 2010, after the Japanese Coast Guard detained a Chinese fishing trawler for allegedly intruding into Japanese waters, a Sino–Japanese standoff ensued. One direct result was the further strengthening of US interest in China's behaviour in maritime disputes. The Obama administration publicly affirmed that the US-Japan treaty umbrella extends to the Senkaku/Diaoyu Islands and reiterated the importance of peaceful dispute resolution, freedom of navigation and respect for international maritime laws in the

South China Sea. China's behaviour in these disputes constitutes a critical test of its intentions, and its hard line backfired seriously in that it led to a closing of ranks across Southeast Asia, Japan and the US. Beijing's actions lend weight to regional pessimists who are not persuaded of its peaceful rise, and sustained coercive action may prompt its neighbours towards the very containment policies that it wishes to avoid.

So far, there are few good cases of China making Southeast Asian states do what they otherwise did not want to do. Alongside Beijing's successful record of persuasion and inducement, it has shown caution in exerting pressure on its neighbours with the most challenging subjects. The recent backlash in the South China Sea is likely to make Beijing more cautious. China's still limited military capacity provides an important explanation since, particularly in the maritime access and security arena, the presence of the US still serves as a significant deterrent.

CHINA'S MISSTEPS IN SOUTHEAST ASIA

As tensions in the South China Sea ratcheted up in 2010, the United States looked on with growing concern that its strategic and economic interests and those of its friends and allies were being undermined. At the Shangri La Dialogue in June, for instance, Secretary of Defence Robert Gates identified the South China Sea as an "area of growing concern for the United States". Yet it was not until Secretary of State Hillary Clinton raised the subject at the ARF a month later that Asia's long-running sovereignty dispute hit world headlines. Clinton reiterated that freedom of navigation was a vital U.S. interest and that it opposed the use of force to resolve the problem. In a departure from past policy, Clinton suggested that the United States stood ready to facilitate talks on implementing the Declaration on the Conduct of Parties in the South China Sea (DoC), the agreement drawn up by ASEAN in China in 2002 to manage the dispute but which the two sides have singularly failed to implement. linton's comments at the ARF were provoked in part by reference to the South China Sea as a "core interest" by Chinese officials, even though the exact context of their comments remains unclear. The subject first surfaced in April, when it was reported that during a visit to Beijing by Deputy Secretary of State James Steinberg and Asia Director of the National Security Council Jeffrey Bader in March, several senior Chinese officials, including Assistant Minister of Foreign Affairs Cui Tiankai and State Councilor Dai Bingguo (President Hu's point man on foreign affairs), had described the South China Sea a "core interest" the implication being that China would brook no interference from the United States (New York Times, April 23; Washington Post, July 30).

Whether the PRC officials were referring to the South China Sea as a whole including the disputed Paracel and Spratly Islands or just the Exclusive Economic Zone where China has protested the surveillance activities of the US military is uncertain. Beijing has never officially described the sea as a "core interest" and government officials claim that Steinberg and Bader "misinterpreted" comments made at the March meeting (Interviews, Beijing, October). Yet according to Clinton, at the U.S.-China Strategic and Economic Dialogue in May in Beijing, Dai Bingguo repeated that the South China Sea was Beijing's "core interest" (Interview with Greg Sheridan of The Australian, U.S. Department of State, November 8). Reference to the South China Sea as a core interest was interpreted in Washington as elevating the problem on a par with Taiwan and thus an subject over which China was prepared to go to war.

The United States was not the only country to push back against Chinese assertiveness in the South China Sea. Twelve countries raised the subject at the ARF, including the four ASEAN claimants (Vietnam, the Philippines, Malaysia and Brunei) and Indonesia which has an overlapping maritime boundary claim with China near the gas-rich Natuna Islands. Southeast Asia's anxieties were further fuelled by the Sino-Japanese standoff in the East China Sea in September when the Japanese Coast Guard detained a Chinese fishing trawler that had rammed one of its vessels near the disputed Senkaku/Diaoyu Islands. Even Malaysian Prime Minister Najib Razak, the leader of a country that has traditionally downplayed tensions in the South China Sea, described the PRC as "more assertive than ever before" (China Daily, September 29). Singapore Prime Minister Lee Hsien Loong described Clinton's comments as a "useful reminder" of America's role in Asia, a role "which China cannot replace ... because of America's security contributions in maintaining the peace in the region" (Straits Times, September 24).

Since the ARF, the United States, ASEAN and China have all moved to tamp down tensions over the South China Sea. In September, Assistant Secretary of State Kurt Campbell denied that Clinton's comments had been aimed at China or that Washington was "taking sides or stoking tensions" and that the Administration's goal was to "create a more stable, predictable environment". A month later, in recognition of the fact that Clinton's offer to facilitate talks on implementing the DoC was strongly opposed by China and viewed as unfeasible by ASEAN because Beijing would walk away from the agreement if a third party attempted to mediate, Campbell told journalists in Tokyo that it would be inappropriate for the United States to play a direct role in the talks. Washington has more pressing problems to deal with than the South China Sea, though Honolulu-based U.S. Pacific Command continues to monitor developments with concern.

The ASEAN states have had to strike a careful balance: they do wish to be seen as siding with America on the South China Sea, but nor do they want to be perceived as appeasing China. Thus while the 2nd U.S.-ASEAN Summit in New York on September 24 provided another opportunity to discuss the territorial problem, member states softened the language in the final communiqué. Prior to the meeting, a leaked draft had made explicit mention of the South China Sea and the importance of freedom of navigation and non-use of force. The final communiqué, however, merely noted the importance of "regional peace and stability, maritime security, freedom of navigation.... and the peaceful settlement of disputes" (White House, Joint Statement of the 2nd US-ASEAN Leaders Meeting,

September 24). The White House "Read-out" on the luncheon meeting, however, did make explicit mention of freedom of navigation and the non use of force in the South China Sea.

According to Campbell and Bader, Clinton's comments in July have served to move China "back to a more collaborative approach" on the South China Sea (AP, September 19). There is some evidence to support this contention. After the ARF, Chinese officials stopped referring to the South China Sea as a core interest in meetings with their American counterparts, though mainland academics continued to muddy the waters by arguing that sovereignty was, by definition, a core interest and that China had "indisputable sovereignty" over the atolls in the sea (Author interviews, Beijing, October 2010). In recent months, however, Chinese academics have also gone quiet on the subject.

Senior Chinese officials have also sought to play down the subject on visits to Southeast Asia. At the inaugural ASEAN Defence Ministers Meeting-Plus (ADMM-Plus)¯which brought the 10 ASEAN defence ministers and their counterparts from the United States, China, Japan, South Korea, India, Russia, Australia and New Zealand together in Hanoi on October 12 Chinese Defence Minister General Liang Guanglie reacted rather mildly when eight countries raised the South China Sea dispute, even though prior to the meeting he had insisted it was not an appropriate venue to discuss the problem.

During October Chinese Vice Foreign Minister Zhang Zhijun was dispatched to four Southeast Asian countries on a "listening and reassurance" mission, while in November Vice President Xi Jinping Hu's heir apparention a trip to Singapore to mark 20 years of formal diplomatic relations stressed that a "prosperous and stable China does not pose a threat to any country," that Beijing would "continue to undertake its responsibilities for regional peace and development" and in an obvious attempt to counter Yang's statement at the ARF, that "China sees all countries, big and small, as equals" (Straits Times, November 16).

By raising the South China Sea at the ARF and ADMM-Plus, both ASEAN and the United States hoped that Beijing would be forced to recalibrate its position and adopt a more flexible and accommodating stance.

The acid test of this expectation is whether meaningful progress can be achieved over the next 12 months on implementing the DoC. There are cautious grounds for optimism. At the ASEAN-China Summit in October, Premier Wen Jiabao told ASEAN leaders that the PRC was committed to implementing the agreement (Philippine Daily Inquirer, October 30). On December 22-23 the ASEAN-China Joint Working Group on the DoC will meet in Kunming to discuss implementation guidelines, the results of which will be discussed by an ASEAN-China Senior Officials Meeting early in the New Year.

Indonesia took over the rotating ASEAN Chair in December, and Foreign Minister Marty Natelagawa has indicated that meaningful progress on the South China Sea problem will be among Jakarta's "leading priorities" (Straits Times, September 19). Yet acute problems remain in implementing the DoC, including the modalities of the discussions (China objects to ASEAN caucusing on the subject) and the precise definition of "disputed waters."

And although Philippine President Benigno Aquino has called for ASEAN solidarity on the South China Sea, arriving at a consensus will be problematic because membership is made up of claimant and non-claimant states, and some members have close ties to the PRC. Moreover, even though the DoC contains some potentially useful confidence building measures, given that the problem has become overlain by nascent Sino-US maritime rivalry, it remains doubtful whether its implementation will fundamentally change the dynamics of the dispute.

For its part China has been incensed at what it perceives as U.S. collusion with some Southeast Asian states at the ARF. At the time the meeting took place Vietnam occupied the ASEAN chair, and Beijing suspects Hanoi encouraged the United States and other participants to raise the subject so as to "internationalize" the problem. Stepped-up military cooperation between the United States and Vietnam has also raised Beijing's ire, including the repair of a U.S. navy supply ship in April, a visit by the hospital ship USNS Mercy in May, and in August a port call to Danang by the destroyer USS John McCain, the transit through Vietnam's EEZ of the aircraft carrier USS George Washington and high level defence talks between the two countries. Vitriolic commentaries in the PRC press have warned Hanoi of the dangers of becoming a "strategic pawn" of the United States (Global Times, July 28).

As a result, Vietnam continues to pursue multiple strategies with China vis-à-vis the South China Sea dispute. First, it holds regular dialogue with the PRC in an attempt to manage tensions but also assuage Chinese concerns.

In August, for instance, Deputy Defence Minister Nguyen Chi Vinh visited Beijing and reiterated Vietnam's "3 nos" policy: no foreign alliances, no foreign bases and no relationship with another country to be directed at a third (VNA, August 26). Second, Hanoi continues to coax ASEAN to implement the DoC and move forward with a formal Code of Conduct. Third, Vietnam highlights the subject at international forums, including a second most important conference on the South China Sea in Ho Chi Minh City in November.

Fourth, the government has accelerated the modernization of the armed forces, particularly the navy and air force, including an order for 12 SU-30 MKK fighters and six Kilo-class submarines from Russia, the first two of which could be delivered in 2014. Fifth, and most controversially, Vietnam seeks to facilitate the military presence of most important external powers in Southeast Asia.

Thus in October Hanoi and New Delhi agreed to increase the frequency of Indian navy ship visits to Vietnam (PTI, October 13) and, most noteworthy, an announcement by Prime Minister Nguyen Tan Dung that the strategically located former US naval base at Cam Ranh Bay would be opened to foreign navies for repair and re-provisioning, including submarines and aircraft carriers. Dung's announcement thus paves the way for increased US Navy ship visits to Vietnam in the coming years.

After nearly a decade of adroit statecraft, China's diplomatic posturing has substantially drained the reservoir of goodwill it had built up in Southeast Asia, forced ASEAN governments to question anew Beijing's peaceful rise, and pushed regional governments closer to the US. Singapore's Minister Mentor Lee Kuan Yew has spoken of 2010 as marking the beginning of a "decades-long tussle between the US and China for pre-eminence in the Pacific" (Straits Times, October 2). Events this year suggest that tussle will increasingly be played out in Southeast Asia.

CHINA'S UNPLEASANT IN SOUTHEAST ASIA

Most mornings, activity in Phnom Penh all but stops when the morning heat begins to rise. But on that day, the city resembled a festive papal visit to a devoutly Catholic nation. Nearly a hundred thousand Cambodian children lined the streets, many in threadbare school uniforms and waving tiny Cambodian and Chinese flags or small photographs of Jiang's face. The children cheered and screamed for Jiang as his open car toured through the city, chanting as if he were David Beckham or Bono, rather than an elderly politician with thick glasses and an oily, swept-back hairdo. Jiang's route did not take him past one of the city's most important attractions. Only a few blocks from his motorcade, foreign tourists wandered through Tuol Sleng, an old high school that Cambodia's Maoist Khmer Rouge regime had converted into a killing factory in the 1970s. Tens of thousands of Cambodians were brought to Tuol Sleng between 1975 and 1979. Fewer than 10 made it out alive.

During the Khmer Rouge's murderous four-year reign, during which they killed as many as 2 million Cambodians, China served as the regime's most important foreign patron. Beijing sent the Khmer Rouge over 15,000 military advisers and provided the bulk of its external aid. Beijing knew what was going on in Cambodia. Before Jiang's visit, Chinese leaders had actively worked to forestall a special international tribunal for the Khmer Rouge officials still alive. But standing alongside Jiang that day, Cambodian Prime Minister Hun Sen did not mention the Khmer Rouge era or the tribunal. Instead, he praised Jiang's "historic" visit to Phnom Penh and called China's relatives with Cambodia "a precious gift." A beaming Jiang replied that he was "overwhelmed by friendship and joy" and promised that the relationship would become much closer.

Jiang was right. Within five years, China had become probably the most important foreign influence in Cambodia, and Hun Sen shuttled to and from Beijing constantly. Beijing became Cambodia's most important provider of foreign aid, giving Cambodia one of the largest Chinese aid packages of any nation in the world while also forgiving Cambodia's entire debt to China. Chinese language programs quickly dominated downtown Phnom Penh: one Chinese-language school alone drew over 10,000 students. As a result, although older Cambodians who remember the Khmer Rouge remain suspicious of China, their sons and daughters, who once would have headed to Australia, France, or the United States for higher education, now look to universities in Shanghai and Beijing. Chinese newspapers, films, television, and radio have become increasingly popular. Thousands of Chinese businesspeople have moved into Phnom Penh and northern Cambodia, creating entire villages of recent migrants. Chinese tourists descend en masse on the capital. Today, even when the prime minister has concerns about China's influence, he keeps quiet. Cambodia is hardly unique. Since the late 1990s, perceptions of China in Southeast Asia have shifted significantly, so much so that elites and publics in a most importantity of the 10 members of the Association of Southeast Asian Nations (ASEAN) now see China as a constructive actor—and, potentially the preeminent regional power.

China's image transformation has resulted from a range of factors. China has benefited from missteps by the United States and Japan, ranging from the response to the 1997 Asian financial crisis to Washington's post–9-11 focus on counterterrorism in Southeast Asia. But the transformation also stems from a rise in China's "soft power" in Southeast Asia—that is, China's ability to influence Southeast Asian countries by persuasion, rather than coercion. This growing attractiveness is conveyed through various means, including culture, diplomacy, participation in multinational organizations, businesses' actions abroad, and the gravitational pull of China's economic strength.

When Joseph Nye coined the term soft power, he originally used a more limited definition that excluded investment and aid and formal diplomacy—more traditional, harder forms of influence. But in the context of Asia today, both China and its neighbours enunciate a broader idea of soft power, implying all elements outside of the security realm, including investment and aid. Soft power stems from both governments and nongovernment actors—from businesspeople and pop stars and language teachers. Nongovernment actors do not necessarily operate in concert with the state, and no state can be said to have a completely coherent foreign policy. Still, it is possible to identify broad strategies Beijing has enunciated and policy tools it has used that allow nongovernment actors to more effectively wield soft power. Just as us policies between World War II and the end of the cold war made Washington popular in the region and smoothed the way for American soft power, it is these frameworks that today make it easier for Chinese soft-power actors, from language schools to businesspeople, to have a growing impact on the ground.

The Unpleasant Begins

Nineteen ninety-seven provides a convenient date to mark China's soft-power emergence in Southeast Asia. Whether or not Beijing explicitly recognized that the United States and Japan were fumbling their responses to the Asian financial meltdown that began with the Thai baht's collapse and soon spread across the region, China's own reaction proved savvy. Beijing refused to devalue its currency, which would have exacerbated devaluations in Thailand and Indonesia, and portrayed its decision as standing up for other Asian nations. After the crisis, ASEAN Secretary General Rodolfo Severino announced, "China is really emerging from this smelling good."

Since then, Beijing has begun to employ several strategies to boost its soft power in Southeast Asia. In statements and speeches, Chinese leaders enunciate a doctrine of "win-win" relations, highlighting that Southeast Asians can benefit from their relationship with China even as China benefits from its relationship with them. China will not interfere or meddle: foreign nations benefit because China will not make demands on other nations' sovereignty, economic models, governance, or political culture. "We don't believe that human rights should stand above sovereignty," the head of Beijing's premier state think tank says. China implicitly contrasts its "win-win" philosophy with that of the United States, a non-Asian actor that Beijing portrays as disrespectful of sovereignty, imposing a web of sanctions on Southeast Asia and demanding economic and political concessions.

The Chinese have backstopped this "win-win" rhetoric with real initiatives. Over the past five years, China has ended nearly all of its old border disputes and has signed Southeast Asia's Treaty of Amity and Cooperation, a document that commits the signers to mutual respect for a country's sovereignty and equality. Beijing has committed to creating a code of conduct on the South China Sea. It has enthusiastically signed bilateral cooperative agreements with several Asian states. Beijing seems willing to sign these agreements en masse, leaving details to be hammered out later. (In the lawyerly—and democratic—US political system, this type of sign first, talk later diplomacy would be virtually impossible.)

Beijing also has reversed its previous disdain for multilateral organizations, which older Chinese leaders had seen as constraints on China's power. It has not hurt that, as the United States became less interested in multilateralism between the late 1990s and today, China's participation in multilateral groups has made it look better by comparison. Again, Beijing has backed up its changing strategy with real initiatives. As a dialogue partner with ASEAN, China works closely with the organization, trying to strengthen it and, according to Asian diplomats, initiating far more joint projects than other partners, such as Japan or the United States. China's strategy also includes focusing on developing nations whose bilateral relationships with the United States or Japan are faltering. After President Gloria Macapagal-Arroyo pulled Filipino troops out of Iraq in 2004 as part of a deal to win the freedom of a Philippine hostage, the United States cut assistance to Manila. Shortly after, China invited Macapagal-Arroyo for a state visit, and then aggressively wooed Philippine policy makers, offering greater cooperation and aid.

Another most important component of China's appeal to developing nations involves Beijing's portrayal of China as a potential ideal, as a model. China emphasizes top-down control of development and poverty reduction and the sidelining of political improvement for economic improvement. China's model particularly appeals to rulers in authoritarian or semi-authoritarian nations. With the Chinese model, the regime has time to think of ways to co-opt businesspeople and other elites that it needs to keep on its side to remain in power.

Flaking Old Insecurities

Until the past decade, China exerted minimal soft power in Southeast Asia. Following Chinese leader Deng Xiaoping's advice, an insecure Beijing still pursued a defensive foreign policy and focused on rebuilding China's domestic economy from the ravages of the Cultural Revolution. The Chinese public still lacked confidence that Beijing could become a global actor, let alone a regional power. A poll taken by the research organization Horizon Group in 1995 asked Chinese citizens their views of the "most prominent countries in the world": one-third ranked the United States most prominent, with only 13 percent choosing China. The Chinese imperial court's treatment of mainland Southeast Asia as vassal states, and the modern history of Maoist China supporting communists in Thailand, Malaysia, and, most disastrously, Cambodia, left a residue of mistrust in the region. China's limited engagement with Southeast Asia foundered on Beijing's continuing claims to the South China Sea, China's suspicion of ASEAN's multilateral forums, and concern among ASEAN nations that China's continuing economic growth would siphon foreign investment from Southeast Asia. Meanwhile, China's policy tools remained weak. It was not a most important aid donor, its diplomatic corps remained dominated by older envoys, and its public diplomacy was blunt.

In the late 1990s all this began to change. China's breakneck economic growth fostered greater confidence within the Chinese public. By the end of the 1990s, many Chinese urbanites were too young to remember the Cultural Revolution. They no longer shared an inherent distrust of the state's wielding of power and ideology. In 2003, the Horizon Group again polled Chinese citizens. This time, nearly 40 percent picked China as "the most prominent country in the world." America came in a distant second. China's leadership was also becoming more confident. Until the mid-1990s, the generation that had grown up around Mao still dominated China's inner circle. But this generation passed away in the 1980s, or was forcibly retired to make way for younger officials. After the crackdown at Tiananmen Square, the leadership recognized that China could not rely on the United States, but had to develop better relations with its neighbours and become a greater international player.

China recognized, too, that its hard power was still limited. In the mid-1990s, Beijing tried to signal its rising military strength to the world by aggressive moves like sending ships to unoccupied, disputed reefs in the South China Sea. This approach backfired. Provocative military exercises, including missile tests in the Taiwan Strait, frightened neighbouring states and evoked old memories of Chinese military adventurism.

Even as they saw that China's aggressive moves triggered Southeast Asian balancing against Beijing, Chinese leaders could not help but notice another trend. Wang Jisi, director of American studies at the Chinese Academy of Social Sciences in Beijing, one of China's elite think tanks, noted in Chinese publications that America's weakness might be its soft influence, not its unrivaled hard power.

Wang was right. After the finish of the cold war, America had retreated from the world, consumed with its own economic boom, its culture wars, and its political scandals. Significant pluralities of Americans opposed US interventions abroad and called for Washington to slash foreign aid, and the White House listened. Washington cut public diplomacy abroad and merged the United States Information Agency, the main public diplomacy outfit, into the State Department. The Clinton administration sidelined many of the multilateral institutions that America had built after World War II, creating perceptions of the United States as a unilateral actor— a perception that would only increase as the Bush administration eviscerated multilateralism.

Support and Trade Tools

China's economic tools also have become more sophisticated. China's aid has undergone a serious transformation. According to a study by Henry Yep of the National Defence University in Washington, in 2003, China's aid to the Philippines was roughly four times greater than America's, China's aid to Laos was three times greater, its aid to Indonesia was nearly double, and its aid to Cambodia nearly matched US levels. Beijing has revamped its aid programs to better tie assistance to discrete policy goals, including promoting Chinese companies abroad, cultivating important political actors, and bolstering China's benign regional image. In Thailand, for instance, Chinese aid has been used for the kind of lobbying familiar in Washington: to bring important elected Thai politicians to study trips and conferences in China. Beijing has also used funds to purchase surplus Thai agriculture, mollifying Thai farmers worried about the impact of China's free trade agreement with Southeast Asia.

China's embrace of free trade in the region and its promotion of the idea that it will become a most important source of foreign direct investment also bolster its image. In addition to the ASEAN-China Free Trade Agreement, Beijing is negotiating closer bilateral trade ties and economic partnerships with individual Southeast Asian states. By the end of 2006, Southeast Asia's total trade with China probably will eclipse Southeast Asian trade with the United States or Japan. (China-ASEAN total trade in 2005 was roughly $130 billion; US-ASEAN total trade in 2005 was about $150 billion.) By comparison, the United States struggled to complete a bilateral free trade agreement with Thailand.

On visits to the region Chinese leaders set targets for future Chinese investment into Southeast Asia. These targets, usually for five or even ten years in the future, tend to be enormous, and obscure the fact that, at present, Chinese direct investment still lags far behind investment from the United States and other wealthy countries like Japan.

Finally, over the past decade the Chinese government has not only lifted restrictions on migration within China but has also made it vastly easier for Chinese to leave the country for business and tourism. Partly as a result, Chinese migration, often on overstayed short-term visas, is transforming the demographic makeup of northern mainland Southeast Asia, from northern Burma to northern Vietnam. Because of outmigration from Yunnan and other border provinces, ethnic Chinese now dominate entire towns in places like Luang Namtha, in northern Laos. The recent migrants are much more attuned to trends in China than older generations of ethnic Chinese, and they also have created a kind of renminbi zone in northern mainland Southeast Asia, where the Chinese currency serves as a de facto second currency.

Beijing's Fresh Toolbox

As China's engagement with the world has become more sophisticated, its tools of soft power have become more sophisticated as well. In the past decade, China has upgraded its public diplomacy, which has focused on selling the idea that China will not be a threat to other nations. China's public diplomacy efforts reinforce the idea of peaceful development. They include museum exhibits in Malaysia and Singapore to celebrate the 600th anniversary of the voyages of Zheng He, a Chinese admiral who sailed across Asia, encountering but never conquering other nations. Part of this new public diplomacy has been increasing cultural exchanges with Southeast Asia. China has begun hosting overseas scholars, the kind of programming the US State Department has long done. Beijing also has created a Chinese version of the Peace Corps, run by the China Association of Youth Volunteers, to send idealistic young Chinese on long-term volunteer service projects to developing nations like Laos and Burma. China has expanded the international reach of its media as well. It has upgraded the Chinese newswire Xinhua and expanded Xinhua's output in languages other than English and Chinese, and it has expanded and professionalized the international broadcasting of CCTV, Chinese state television.

The new Chinese public diplomacy includes setting up networks of informal business and cultural summits in China designed to bring together Asian opinion leaders. These meetings allow China to subtly emphasize its role as a potential partner for investment and trade and its position as a regional leader. The most prominent include the Boao Forum for Asia, which brings together Asian businesspeople for a Davos-style World Economic Forum-like event; and the ASEAN-China Eminent Persons Group, which unites former statesmen.

As China has upgraded its public diplomacy, it also has invested in improving its diplomatic corps. Over the past 15 years, the Chinese Ministry of Foreign Affairs has begun to retire older, more ideological diplomats, replacing them with a young generation of envoys who speak better English and local languages: one 2005 study suggested that one-half of the country's 4,000 diplomats are under 35. China can keep these diplomats in the region because unlike the United States, which gives its Foreign Service officers leeway to choose where they want to be posted, the Chinese foreign affairs ministry can mandate postings. Top Chinese diplomats in nations like Cambodia or Thailand now often have done three or even four rotations in those countries before rising to the rank of ambassador, building their language skills and developing extensive contacts in the local business and political communities.

Beijing supports its diplomacy through constant visits by senior Chinese officials to Southeast Asia, a short hop from Beijing in contrast with the 20-hour flight from Washington.

According to a recent study of visits by top Chinese and US officials to Thailand and Cambodia in 2004 and 2005, senior Chinese officials made at least twice as many visits to Bangkok and Phnom Penh.

Promotion of Chinese culture and Chinese verbal communication studies are most important components of this public diplomacy. Beijing now funds at least the first year of what it calls Confucius Institutes, Chinese language and culture schools created at leading local universities. Beijing has tried to push instruction in Mandarin and in Chinese culture in overseas primary schools, partly by signing agreements with countries like Thailand to help integrate Chinese into public school curricula, and partly by helping students in poor nations like Cambodia attend private local Chinese-language primary schools. While promoting Chinese studies in other nations, Beijing has tried to lure more foreign students to China. The ministry of education advertises Chinese universities abroad and has boosted financial aid and loosened visa policies for foreign students. After 9-11, in contrast, the United States tightened its student visa policies, making it far harder for students from Southeast Asia to attend school in America. Even students already in the United States have had a harder time. In 2003, Washington announced that all Indonesian men residing in America would have to register with immigration authorities. Many of them simply left. Between 1999 and 2003, the number of Indonesians studying in the United States fell by over 20 percent.

CHINA RISING POWER IN SOUTH ASIA

Beijing did not take too seriously ASEAN's growing role initially. Instead, it anticipated a greater role for the UN Security Council and a multipolar world when the Cold War ended. Within the Asian context, China saw the United States, Russia, Japan, and itself as the critical players, but not ASEAN, as it was deemed largely a subregional grouping with an inward-looking orientation. That began to change in the mid-1990s as Beijing both recognized and indeed appreciated the role that

ASEAN could play. This became even more apparent with the expansion of the original ASEAN-6 to the Greater ASEAN of Ten by the decade's end. Chinese analysts have characterized ASEAN's evolving regional role as evolving in four phases. In the first phase, which began in the late 1970s largely in response to Vietnam's invasion of Cambodia (and hence a direct threat to Thailand's security), the organization's major efforts were expended on seeking a peaceful solution of the Cambodian issue by engaging extra-regional powers. The Paris Agreement, to which ASEAN made a significant contribution, gave the organization a high profile in the international diplomatic arena and provided it with greater interest and the confidence to participate in and influence Southeast Asian affairs.

The second phase began in the early 1990s and focused mostly on ASEAN's effort to engage major powers in the development of a regional security dialogue that aimed at both socializing China to the benefit of multilateralism and cooperative security and keeping the other major powers engaged in the region's security to prevent the emergence of a power vacuum and hence invitation for competition. Through the Post-Ministerial Meetings, dialogues, and the establishment of the ARF, the group succeeded in bringing all major powers under the framework of a security dialogue that was subject to the ASEAN Way of gradualism, consensus-building, and nonuse of force in dispute settlement.

The third phase was characterized by ASEAN's continuing pursuit of multichannel, multilevel security dialogues that involved the Asia-Europe meeting (ASEM), ASEAN+1 and 3, and the organization's own plan toward greater integration, including the ASEAN FTA. The current phase involves ASEAN's efforts to move beyond Southeast Asia to launch a region-wide political forum that would include all major East Asian powers. Initially the brain-child of Malaysian Prime Minister Mahathir, the East Asia Summit was formally held in Kuala Lumpur in December 2005, but with the participation of Australia, India, and New Zealand, in addition to the originally conceived participating countries.

Over the years, ASEAN has debated, explored, and developed various strategies of dealing with major powers. These strategies have been applied during different periods, depending on specific security circumstances of the time. Essentially, three approaches have been especially emphasized. One is the Non-Aligned Movement (NAM) approach promoted by Indonesia. This would be an effort to exclude major power interference in ASEAN's internal affairs. At the same time, it would sustain Jakarta's position within the organization. The second approach is favored by Malaysia, which advocates neutrality in two ways. One is noninterference and nonaggression in interstate relations to avoid being involved in great power conflicts; the other is to secure major powers' pledges not to intervene in Southeast Asian affairs, hence allowing the region to maintain autonomy and neutrality. The third is balancing, promoted by Singapore, between great powers. Singapore recognizes that major powers all have important interests in the region, therefore it is unrealistic to exclude their involvement. But efforts can be made to prevent one particular power from dominating the entire region.

The ASEAN Way of informality and noninterference in domestic affairs has served as the guiding principle in its approach to regional affairs. While this approach has served the organization well and provided a comfort level for member states to interact with each other without having to accept binding decisions, it is now facing increasing challenges. The tendency to hold meetings, talk, and sign documents but to be slow in implementation has begun to constrain ASEAN's ability to address real issues.

Beijing increasingly has viewed ASEAN as an important power centre in Asia. This is largely due to ASEAN's skillful diplomacy of balancing all the major powers, hence enhancing its own leverage. This is possible because major powers essentially have balanced out one another, with no one able to dominate. Finally, ASEAN itself since 1997 has sought to consolidate and achieve economic integration (ASEAN Economic Community) by 2015, with security and social community to follow. It hosted the first East Asia Summit in December 2005, and has over the years developed various ASEAN+1/3 meetings, with the ASEM playing a facilitating role in promoting regionalism.

At the same time, it should also be noted that ASEAN still harbours some suspicions toward China and likely will continue to resort to strategies of hedging or balancing through expanded ties with other external powers. In recent years, ASEAN member states have expanded their military cooperation greatly with the United States. Japan has been very active in regaining its influence in Southeast Asia and has offered a large economic aid package to the region. India also is actively engaging with ASEAN on greater economic, political, and military contacts. Finally, the East Asia Summit, originally billed as an exclusive regional event, had its inaugural meeting attended by Australia, India, and New Zealand, in addition to the ASEAN+3 countries. While a realpolitik assessment of these developments would alarm Beijing, as extra-regional forces would dilute China's own influence, Chinese officials and analysts seem not to be bothered by ASEAN's efforts to knit complex and overlapping arrangements and relationships with itself as the coordinating core.

Indeed, a major Chinese report on ASEAN recommended that Beijing respect ASEAN's position, including some member states' growing military ties with the United States; acknowledge and respect that the United States has legitimate interests in the region; and actually encourage better ASEAN-U.S. cooperation, especially in the context of fighting terrorism. In that context, U.S. deployment of military forces, dispatching of special force advisors, and specific arrangements for base access should not be viewed as targeted at China.

Nonetheless, Chinese analysts are monitoring these developments closely. The post-9/11 U.S. policy adjustment toward Southeast Asia could have a significant impact on issues of territorial disputes in the South China Sea, SLOCs, the cohesion of ASEAN as a group, and could cause domestic turmoil in some member states. Since 9/11, the United States has strengthened its military presence in the region and resumed and intensifed joint military exercises with a number of ASEAN member states, ostensibly aimed at fighting global terrorism. Meanwhile, the U.S. position on territorial disputes in the South China Sea has shifted from neutrality and nonintervention to "positive" mediation, with greater emphasis on freedom of navigation, including escorts.

What is most significant is a U.S. proposal for joint patrol of the Malacca Strait with the "Regional Maritime Security Initiative." While the proposal has been turned down by the three Strait countries—Malaysia, Singapore, and Indonesia—there has since been more cooperation between the United States and the regional militaries. For China, stable and uninterrupted supplies of oil through the Malacca Strait is critical to its economic security, and control by foreign powers could seriously undermine Chinese security interests.

Another issue of potential concern is Taiwan's activities in ASEAN countries. For various reasons, most of them economic, ASEAN has maintained rather close ties with Taipei. In fact, Taiwan has nine times the investment in the region than does China, and Taiwan was most active in the early to mid-1990s in pushing for more official contacts through "vacation diplomacy" and "golf diplomacy," among other tactics. Lee Hsien Loong's visit to Taiwan in the summer of 2004—billed as "private"—just before he became Singapore's prime minister triggered strong reactions from China, including cancellation of previously scheduled bilateral meetings and visits by Singaporean ministers. Managing such incidents requires delicate diplomacy as much as it demands a resolute stance on an issue for which China has no room for negotiation.

CHINA'S SECURITY STRUCTURE UNDER STRESS

On 18 September China announced a three-point policy on fighting international terrorism: i) oppose all forms of terrorism, ii) choose clear targets in operations and avoid civilian casualties, and iii) mobilize the international community through the UN to take permanent counter-measures under international law.

At the APEC Summit in Shanghai the US President expressed satisfaction with the cooperation received from China in the campaign against terrorism. Despite the reservations expressed by Malaysia Prime Minister Mahathir and Indonesia's President Megawati the final APEC Communiqué of 19 October focused on the challenge posed by terrorism. President Bush who had earlier characterized China as a strategic competitor rather than a strategic partner in the language of the Clinton regime now talked about a "constructive and cooperative relationship with China". Bush and Jiang announced "a new partnership for constructing a new world order of peace and stability in the age of terrorism and counter-terrorism". After the meeting with US Secretary of State Powell in Shanghai, Chinese Foreign Minister Tang Jiaxuan echoed the official US view and said on 17 October: Anti-terrorism is the struggle of evil vs. good, the civilized and the barbaric. It is not the struggle between different nations, civilizations and religions." Pleased with this view, Powell stated: "US-China ties have been strengthened by China's response to the US campaign against terrorism". The two sides agreed to have regular high-level consultations on this subject. China agreed to allow the FBI to open an office in Beijing. The US agreed to withdraw some of the sanctions imposed after the military crack down on Tiananmen Demonstrators in 1989. The US-China Business Council was excited by the results of the Bush- Jiang meeting opening even newer avenues of trade and investment.

China's strategic meeting with the US anti-terror campaign was essentially guided by its policy of suppressing the secessionist movement in Xinjiang besides the overall priority it gives to economic growth and therefore to trade with the US. (The volume of China-US trade reached $60 Billion taking the second place after Japan's $64 Billion in 2000.) The Xinjiang Uighur Autonomous Region of China has eight million Uighurs and an equal number of other nationalities including nearly 40 per cent of its population as Hans. Since 1996 the movement for a separate East Turkistan has been in the news. After the riots in Yining in February 1997 the central government of China has pursued what it calls "Strike Hard" *(yanda)* policy.

In fact, from all the independent evidence it seems that the terrorist element is still a minor trend in Xinjiang while several different forces seeking political autonomy within the PRC are very active. The Chinese government has taken a number of measures to promote local languages and culture while opposing religious extremism. It has launched the Western Region Development Program facilitating massive investment including foreign capital in this region. But obviously these measures are not considered adequate by the forces of autonomy until the Uighurs themselves manage the structures of political power. The US had cited Tibet and Xinjiang as cases of human rights violations by the Chinese government in the recent years, which the Chinese government refutes. But after Sept.11 the Chinese government disclosed that it had evidence of Osama bin Laden's Al Qaeda having sent over a thousand militants to join the secessionists in Xinjiang. Among the prisoners taken by the US forces in Afghanistan in November and early December were several hundred Uighurs from China who were reportedly fighting as a part of the Al Qaeda forces. That has provided further evidence for the international link of the Al Qaeda with the secessionist movement in Xinjiang. Whether the new campaign against international terrorism will reinforce Chinese government's 'strike hard' policy or there will be a substantive political response to the autonomy movement in Xinjiang will be closely watched in the coming years.

Thus on several fronts China's security framework came under stress. US troops now were based on China's southern border. The Shanghai Six institution had been weakened. Sino-Russian relationship had to now cope with a new level of US-Russia understanding and Russia's acquiescence with the unilateral abrogation of the ABM Treaty of 1972 by the US. And the US now had a strong link with Pakistan and had a political relationship with India. Japan had joined the Afghan operation with three of its military ships providing logistics support. Over all, US global domination had got a new lease. On the other hand, China may have got the US goodwill with which it can go ahead with its economic policies, may not expect escalation of US support for Taiwan and even though US has not announced support for China's anti-terrorist campaign in Xinjiang, it may acquiesce with it.

The new strategic developments after the beginning of the US offensive in Afghanistan changed the security environment in Asia. US military presence in Uzbekistan and Afghanistan and the new military relationship of the US with Pakistan and India completed the US military involvement in the whole of the Asian continent. Until now South Asia was a gap between the US involvement in West Asia and East Asia. Besides the US military relationship with Israel and the stationing of US troops in Saudi Arabia the Diego Garcia base represented the American military presence in West Asia. The 32 US bases in Okinawa and the presence in South Korea an d the military relationship with Taiwan and the Philippines besides the Seventh Fleet covering the Pacific Ocean maintained the US interests in East Asia. Prior to Sept.11 there were 800 military installations outside the US operated only by the Defence Department. Now the opportunity for a serious presence in South Asia and Central Asia was presented to the US in course of the campaign against terrorism. President George W Bush who had earlier opposed the idea of "US undertaking nation-building role abroad" now himself led the process of expanding the military commitment in Asia. This is bound to have its repercussions within the US and across the globe.

The strategic convergence that US seemed to have with India, China and Russia at this moment may not balance the political divergence that they have in objective terms. US may be seen as building up its relationship with India as a counter to China. After all, Vajpayee's letter to Clinton on the aftermath of India's nuclear tests in May 1998 did point at th e security challenge from India's northern side. But both China and India have realized the costs of their sub-normal relationship in terms of security and its economic consequences. India may not be anxious to become party to a future US strategy of containing China. There are already sharp debates on the issue among the Indian elites most of whom hold the view that India should pursue an independent foreign policy of peace in the tradition of non-alignment and contribute to the democratization of the world order. Hence India has pursued its policy of improving bilateral relations with China. This process was interrupted by the post-Sept.11 developments causing cancellation of Foreign Minister Jaswant Singh's visit to Beijing in October and Premier Zhu Rongji's visit to New Delhi in November. The process of improving Sino-Indian relations may get a facelift with the visit of Zhu Rongji rescheduled for January 2002.But the escalation of tensions between India and Pakistan following the terrorist attacks on the Indian Parliament on December 13 has complicated the situation. China's post-1996 policy of a balanced approach to India and Pakistan which was evident during the Kargil conflict facilitates the growth of Sino-Indian cooperation while maintaining the close relations between China and Pakistan. Whether that will come under review in the event of closer Indo-US relations and escalated Indo-Pak conflict is to be closely watched. During President Musharraf's visit to China in December both sides reaffirmed their close relationship despite changes in international environment. Considering the long term effects of Sino-Indian cooperation on the democratization and stabilization of world security and the need for a peaceful neighbourhood, China's balanced approach to South Asia is likely to continue.

India and Russia have forged close political and military relationship over the years as a resource of mutual political advantage. The Moscow Declaration signed jointly by Prime Minister Vajpayee and President Putin in November focused on fighting international terrorism under UN auspices. China and Russia signed a Treaty of Friendship in July cementing even closer relations than in any earlier point in history.

That was definitely seen as balancing force vis-à-vis the US. Putin and Bush have struck a special relationship to coordinate anti-terrorist campaign and reduce nuclear warheads. Their new understanding was evident during Putin's visit to Bush's ranch in Crawford, Texas. In other words, the new US involvement in Asia has to come to terms with all these parallel relationships and is likely to increase military maneuvers in the continent. The regional efforts for peace and cooperation are a positive aid to the people's movements; they are facing danger of dislocation in the new global campaign led-by the US.

The Subcontinent of South Asia has as a result of this development been plunged into a new wave of turbulence. The region known for its intense poverty and underdevelopment is fast becoming a theatre of a fresh wave of militarization. In the wake of the campaign against terror India and Pakistan have acquired recognition from the West as nuclear states as the sanctions imposed by the US in 1998 have been withdrawn or are in the process of being withdrawn. Both countries will now be able to acquire military supplies from the US. Withdrawal of sanctions is always welcome as they are part of the global hegemonic framework. But the US arms merchants will have a gala time in South Asia now on. The US has also withdrawn sanctions imposed on Pakistan in connection with the violation of missile technology transfer regime and also in reaction to the military coup by General Musharraf in October 1999. The legitimacy that the US has provided to the military ruler of Pakistan in the recent months has severely weakened the movement for restoration of democracy in Pakistan

Require for Political Reply

Now the forces of the fifth world or the world of people's movements for peace and justice have been greatly weakened in Asia as a result of the US-led campaign. We may see in the immediate future stronger repressive measures in Jammu & Kashmir, Xinjiang and Chechnya with active support or acquiescence of the US instead of dialogue and political response to substantive issues of autonomy. The ruling elites of Asian countries including the BJP in India, the authoritarian monarchy in Saudi Arabia, the dictatorships in Central Asia will be strengthened in this process. Pakistan's movement for democracy, in fact the movements for peace and democratic rights of oppressed people all over the world are likely to face greater repression from their regimes in the coming years.

MILITARY CONFLICTS IN THE NEW ERA

The end of the Cold War has added many uncertain factors to the international situation. In our efforts to make a greater contribution to the development of our country and nation during this major historical transition period, we should first gain a clear idea of the following two issues concerning military struggle: One is the need to carefully analyse changes in the international strategic setup in our age and be clear about the tasks of military struggle, with a view to keeping to the correct orientation of the struggle; the other is the need to profoundly grasp the law of military struggle in the new period and provide correct strategic guidance, with a view to gaining a sound grasp of work methods.

Tasks of Military Struggle

In our study of military struggle in the new period, we should first take a look at "major events throughout the world" and gain a clear idea of the features of our age. Marxists believe that an historical era serves to be the foundation of our decisions. Lenin stressed repeatedly that "only when we make a correct assessment of the international environment, or the basic features of our times, can we correctly formulate our own strategies." In an effort to base the situation analysis on the features of our age, we should pay attention not only to the local situation of our neighbouring areas, but also to the strategic setup of the whole world, and not only to changes that have taken place during a recent period, but also to the historical vicissitudes over a considerably long period of time. During the mid-1980s, basing on his correct assessment of the situation then, Comrade Deng Xiaoping vividly summarized the highly complicated international situation into a four-word idea of "East, West, South, and North," with "East and West" referring to the issue of seeking peace, while "South and North" refers to the issue of seeking development. Meanwhile, he also expounded the dialectical relationship between peace and development. This summarization not only identified the major contradictions of today's world, but also analysed the two sides of these contradictions, thus putting forward the idea of seeking peace and development. Centred around the two major themes of peace and development, in recent years, the central authorities have readjusted the country's diplomatic strategy and foreign relations, and have attained major victories in our diplomatic struggles. When trying to gain a correct understanding of peace and development as the features of our age, we need to grasp the following several basic points:

- First, relaxation is the general trend of our age. The force of opposing war and seeking peace is growing on a worldwide scale, and major wars have become avoidable.
- Second, countries under different social systems and with different ideologies are allowed to coexist in our age, though such coexistence is naturally characterized by competition and contention.
- Third, economics and science have become the two major competitive fields in our age, and competition in comprehensive national strength among different countries has taken the forms of both global trade wars and ascendence in the scientific and technological fields.
- Fourth, seeking peace and democracy has become an irresistible general development trend in the human society of our age, and the relationship between East and West has always been characterized by simultaneous confrontation and dialogue.

In short, seeking peace and development is a great banner for mankind in our age. We need to regard it as the basic ground for our observation of the world trend, and also for our resolution of major problems during the future historical period. In today's world, the main forms of military struggle share the following two distinguishing features: One is the shift from violent confrontation to deterrence based on actual strength; the other is the exercise of effective control over war behaviour.

Ever since the time when countries first appeared, war has always been a major way to seek national rights and interests.

The evolution of human history, as well as the rise and decline of countries, are mostly a historical record of war. That is why historians have noted: "War is the normal behaviour of mankind." However, during the past 50 years, in the wake of World War II, considerable changes have taken place in the forms of war, unprecedented, savage intercontinental wars have occurred, and the past nearly half a century has witnessed a sustained period of relative stability. During this period, "cold war" has to a great extent, taken the place of the "hot war" of violent confrontation. Instead of causing worldwide turbulence, the over 200 local wars and armed conflicts that have taken place during this period have been effectively limited to a certain scope and intensity.

Deterrence has become a prominent component of modern national strategy, yet it is not a strategy for staging wars but for avoiding wars. It can be said that every formulator of war strategies will have the same thought: On the one hand, he should try his very best to prevent his country from being drawn into a modern war; and on the other hand, he will also try his utmost to enable his country to win an advantageous strategic position and to realize the ideal of "winning a war without actually going into it." As a result, plans to win wars have been turned into efforts to contain war. Such changes, which have been brought about by the special features of military struggle, are not only a reflection of objective material conditions, but a selection of subjective will and behaviour as well. The former is based on the fact that the military revolution facilitated by scientific and technological advances has provided the objective material means for deterrence; while the latter gives expression to a distillation in the understanding of wars shared by strategists.

Military Strategy in Peacetime

Demands for survival and development constitute the eternal interests of a sovereign country. Today, the space and resources needed for survival and development remain the focus of contention between all countries, and military struggle is a major expression of such contention. The turn of century witnessed extremely acute competitions for survival and development among different countries in the world. Amidst the rapids of such international competitions, we will inevitably encounter severe challenges in our effort to realize the strategic target of "unifying the motherland, promoting the economy, and safeguarding peace." At present, major countries in the world are vying with each other to readjust their own strategies. Under the new strategies, they will:

- Give first priority to the development of science, technology, and the economy
- Enhance their comprehensive national strength
- Strive to occupy a superior strategic position in the next century.

As Chairman Jiang Zemin pointed out in "China's Declaration of the 21st Century," China should first turn itself into a powerful country if it intends to make a greater contribution to both the progress of mankind and world peace. This is the strategic thought of our leaders as well as the voice of all our nationals and comes from the bottom of their hearts. The present relatively stable period of peace is still fraught with many destabilizing factors. The challenges result from competition in comprehensive national strength, which is a pressure in reality, while struggles centering on national reunification, territorial disputes, and arguments over maritime rights and interests may lead to local wars and sudden changes. What merits our special attention is that with the increase in the world's population and the ongoing trend of tighter supplies of natural resources and a relatively smaller space for subsistence, the tasks of military struggle currently facing us have not yet been totally separated from the nature of taking cities and seizing territory.

With the economic growth of the Asia-Pacific region and the future arrival of the Pacific age in the 21st century, hegemonists have stepped up their economic, scientific and technological, cultural, and military infiltration into the Asian-Pacific region, thus giving prominence to a number of hidden contradictions. In our efforts to attain the strategic targets of economic take-off and national rejuvenation, we hope to have a peaceful international environment in order and a stable neighbouring environment; to explore and make use of more resources for the purpose of promoting the economic, scientific, and technological development of the country; to gain greater shares in international markets and successfully practice an export-oriented economic strategy; to arouse the self-confidence and enterprising spirit of our nationals; and to safeguard the integrity of our country and nation. External challenges are unavoidable, and what counts is how we are going to meet the challenges and take countermeasures.

To fulfil the tasks of military struggle in the new period, the most important issues are those of military strength and strategic guidance. In ancient times, military strategy was called the "principles of commanding generals." In modern times, military strategy was summed up as the "art of wars and battles," a belief shared among Napoleon, Clausewitz, von Moltke, and Schlieffen. Contemporary strategists believe, however, that traditional military strategies dealt only with what an army must do during wartime and failed to make clear what they should do during peacetime.

We must be aware that with the rapid development of science and technology in the world today, the issue of the peacetime building and the development of military strength is becoming the focus of attention among military strategists. Defence experts in western countries have stressed that today's military strategy is no longer the "science of military victories." This means that under a longstanding peaceful environment, the emphasis of military strategies has been shifted from wartime to peacetime; and peacetime strategies will not be limited to the planning and guidance of wars, but will also cope with the issue of how to build up and develop military strength during peacetime.

The Military Revolution

The Central Military Commission has put forward a military strategic principle for the new period, which calls for efforts to base military struggle on winning local wars, which employ modern technologies, especially wars under high-tech conditions. Meanwhile, stress has been placed on the need to accelerate the modernization building of our Army, contain and win wars, and fulfil the army's major missions in the military struggle of the new period. This new strategic principle embraces both the realistic employment and the long-term building of military strength. Today, the employment of military strength by major countries generally shares the following features:

- First, they have adopted a prudent approach toward wars and taken steps to avoid wars. When employing military strength, we should act in accordance with the needs of the national strategy; adapt it to the needs of political, economic, and diplomatic struggles; adopt a prudent approach towards wars and take steps to avoid wars; and strive to attain the highest strategic realm of "deflating the enemy's arrogance without actually going to war."
- Second, they have resorted to the demonstration of armed forces. Centering on the experiments of new and high-tech weapons and equipment, they have organized major military exercises and other demonstrative activities concerning major strategies and the direction of campaigns. They have displayed the full status quo of their military strength and the will of sovereign states, in order to attain the goal of deterring the enemy and stabilizing the strategic environments that are beneficial to themselves.
- Third, they have adopted the practice of putting an end to war by means of war. Basing a longer and more stable peaceful environment on deterrent forces is one aspect of the principle of "winning a war without actually going into it." However, because war is the ultimate reason for the existence of an army, we still need to consider the issue of "winning victory in all wars."

We should maintain the modernization and alertness of our military forces at a high level so that we can make rapid responses to contingencies and gain the strategic initiative in any place at any time. To win local wars under high-tech conditions, we need all the more to adhere to the Confucian ideology of "winning victory in a war before actually going into it." If we say that the idea of "winning a war before actually going into it" adhered to by militarists in the past was concerned only with the stage of pre-war preparations, then the idea of "winning a war before actually going into it" held by today's militarists means, more importantly, the design and building of military strength during peacetime. The Americans have claimed that victory in the Gulf War was the outcome of 20 years of hard effort. In a sense, the "20 years of hard effort" refers to the whole process of rebuilding their military strength. In the wake of the Vietnam War, the U.S. Armed Forces suffered from low morale and army building remained in the doldrums. To put an end to such a situation, they carried out a series of reforms in such fields as military theory, military technology, military training, cultivation of military officers, and operational formations. The 20 years of hard effort have brought new life to the armed forces. This is a typical example of "winning a war before actually going into it."

In a local high-tech war, the first battle is the decisive battle, which will decide the outcome of the entire war. Generally speaking, there will no longer be any chance for wearing down the enemy's effective strength. In view of this, experts have pointed out that most victories on future battlefields will not be "decided by the war itself" but "decided by pre-war building." Therefore, to fulfil the tasks of military struggle in the new period, we must plant our feet on the reform and the quality building of our army. To reinforce the quality building of our army, we must persistently carry out theory-trailed policies. A global review tells us that in the past, the blueprints for army building were mostly drawn up on the basis of experience gained in previous wars. Today, they are designed in accordance with the demands of future wars.

What are the demands of future wars? We can only gain a clear idea through theoretical thinking, and can only complete such a design through the theoretical study of science. With the emergence of the technology of "virtual reality," the military theories guiding future wars will be produced in combat laboratories, and the inspection of the "product" quality of the army will also be conducted in combat laboratories. This tremendous change has provided new ideas for military development.

A military revolution is now in the ascendant in today's world. Thoughts on reinforcing the quality building of our army should be conducted against this general background. "After going through the stages of bare-handed battles, cold steel weapons, hot steel weapons, and mechanization, military operations are now entering the information age. These five major military revolutions corresponded with five industrial revolutions." What we need to do now is to study the information war under nuclear deterrence; the well-known scientist Qian Xuesen laid bare the essence of the military revolution with one remark. "The world has entered a period of new military revolution, which is a reflection of social, economic, and scientific and technological changes in the military field. Information technology is the nucleus and foundation of this military revolution."

Information and knowledge have changed the past practice by which military capacities were simply measured by numbers of armoured divisions, wings of the air force, and aircraft carrier combat groups. Today, we also need to count invisible strengths, including:

- Calculation capability
- Volume of telecommunications
- Reliability of information
- Real-time reconnaissance ability.

The well-known scientist Zhu Guangya profoundly pointed out these criteria for judging the quality of today's army. In recent years, our troops have attained considerable results in implementing the military strategic principle of the new period, learning high-tech technologies and knowledge, and in studying wars under high-tech conditions. However, where shall we place the nucleus of high-tech development? Where shall we put the main emphasis of local high-tech wars? A consensus on these issues has yet to be reached throughout the army. People still tend to place greater emphasis on hardware instead of software, and on the present instead of the future. Such a transitional "optical parallax" is hindering us from gaining a correct grasp of major contradictions.

In our consideration of the quality development of our military in the context of a world military revolution, we need to appropriately handle relations between universality and individuality and between generality and particularity. Armies have always had a role in the international arena. Therefore, the modernization building of our army will naturally follow the common law guiding the world's army modernization, yet it also needs to maintain its "Chinese characteristics" at the same time. It should not copy indiscriminately the patterns of Western developed countries, yet cannot cut itself off from the general trend of the military revolution. From the strategic change in its guiding ideology to the formulation of a military strategic principle for the new period, our army can be said to have completed the change in its strategic guidance only, and needs to make further efforts to facilitate a change in its overall building.

In view of this, we have called for the efforts of all officers and men of our army to conduct a conscientious study of

- The new changes taking place in the world's strategic setup since the end of the cold war
- The recent military revolution which is producing a most profound and lasting impact
- New ideas on military development
- "Magic weapons" that can really serve our purpose.

A philosopher once said: "At the back of the tremendous tension of traditions is an inert force of history." During this important cross-century period, we should conform to the trend of our times, renew our military concepts, and accelerate the quality building of our army amid reform, with a view to adapting ourselves to the needs of the military struggle during the new period.

EVALUATING CHINA'S MILITARY STRENGTH

The Department of Defence recently released its long-overdue annual report on China's military power. The document tells us much about how the Democratic Congress and the Obama administration would like to approach relations with China, and not nearly enough about China's military modernization. It suggests we have a Congress that does not take the China challenge seriously and a White House that is uncertain how to tackle it.

The problems started with the 2010 National Defence Authorization Act (NDAA), which revised the 2000 NDAA—the law that requires an annual DOD report to Congress on China's military power—in a number of ways. Most noticeably, the 2010 NDAA changed the report's title from "Military Power of the People's Republic of China" to "Military and Security Developments Involving the People's Republic of China," which obscures the report's purpose by framing China as a passive actor. China's development of an anti-satellite (ASAT) capability, for example, is not a military development involving China; it is a decision by China to enhance its military power.

Also, before the 2010 NDAA, the report's scope included "the tenets and probable development of Chinese grand strategy"; now, Congress has stripped away every mention of "grand strategy." DOD had in the past been instructed to provide analysis of "trends in Chinese strategy that would be designed to establish [China] as the leading political power in the Asia-Pacific region and as a political and military presence in other regions of the world." Now, DOD must report on "trends in Chinese security and military behaviour that would be designed to achieve, or that are inconsistent with," "the goals... shaping Chinese security strategy and military strategy."

Further, since its inception, the report's purpose has been to inform the Senate and House about Chinese military power so that Congress can adequately fund U.S. defence needs; this is why the law requires that the report be submitted by March 1 of each year, long before the NDAA debates take place. But this year, not wanting to anger the Chinese—who have complained about the report year after year—the White House delayed its release, presumably excising declassified information that it deemed too provocative. (The Chinese complained anyway.) By the time the administration released the report to the public, Congress was in recess and the rest of Washington on vacation. Published too late to have the impact that it should on the congressional debate over the 2011 NDAA, and at a time when few members of Congress are likely to comment, the report has failed in its purpose: to inform Congress as it prepares the coming year's defence-spending bill.

It seems that the White House wishes to avoid an open, honest, and public debate about China's military modernization and intentions in Asia. Such a debate might make it more difficult for the administration to pursue a cooperative approach to relations with Beijing. While the recent decisions to wade into the South China Sea territorial disputes and to send the USS George Washington to exercise in the Yellow Sea—both of which elicited strident Chinese objections—suggest that the White House might be abandoning that approach, the report's handling should make outside observers think twice. At best, it suggests a confused China policy; at worst, that the president prefers "business as usual"—or rather, business as in 2009. This president seems most comfortable when he is extending an open hand; he is unlikely to quickly set aside the "strategic reassurance" policy articulated last year. If that means manipulating the public's perceptions of a rising China, then so be it.

The irony of this state of affairs, unfortunately, seems to be lost on this administration. It is Beijing—not any report produced by the Defence Department—that is primarily responsible for how China is perceived. As the new report notes, "the limited transparency in China's military and security affairs enhances uncertainty and increases the potential for misunderstanding and miscalculation." Beijing fails to satisfactorily explain the reasoning behind its aggressive military modernization, thus generating concern and suspicion amongst its neighbours and in the United States.

Unfortunately, the DOD report also fails to adequately explain Chinese military modernization. A close reading reveals that the modernization is robust, and is occurring across all of the service branches. But the report (like its predecessors) does not explain how these developments are related to each other or to Beijing's strategic goals. What role will they play in China's security strategy? In China's military strategy?

For example, this year's report, like last year's, notes that China is developing an aircraft carrier and that its navy has already started training pilots for carrier-borne aviation. But it does not explain that aircraft carriers are the quintessential instrument of military power projection. A nation does not build them if it does not see a need to project air power to distant shores. With Chinese carriers patrolling the seas, Guam, Australia, all of Southeast Asia, and the entirety of India will for the first time be in range of People's Liberation Army tactical aircraft. The 2010 report similarly lacks analysis of the developments in China's missile force. While it mentions the 2nd Artillery Corps's development of an anti-ship ballistic missile (ASBM), few details are provided, and no attempt is made to explain the impact it will have on the U.S. Navy's ability to operate in the Western Pacific. The report is vague about the PLA's overall missile buildup as well. It notes that "China is fielding an array of conventionally armed ballistic missiles [and] ground-and air-launched land-attack cruise missiles... to hold targets at risk throughout the region." But again, there is no explanation of what this might mean for U.S. forces in the region. Can those missiles hit American bases and those of our allies? What kind of damage can they inflict?

Though you wouldn't know it from reading the report, China likely envisions using ASBMs, other ballistic and cruise missiles, future carriers, and other capabilities—including nuclear and quiet conventional attack submarines, cyber-and space-warfare assets, and an integrated air-defence system—in pursuit of its regional goals. Those goals are, in short, to unify Taiwan with the mainland, to settle East and South China Sea disputes in China's favour, and, more broadly, to assert its primacy in the region.

In a Taiwan Strait crisis, for example, the PLA could use its missile force to strike American aircraft carriers in the Western Pacific, and airbases in Japan and potentially on Guam. Strike-group ships that survived could be stalked by multiple, increasingly stealthy submarines. Meanwhile, the now-limited number of tactical aircraft that the U.S. could send to the fight would face a highly sophisticated air-defence system on the Chinese mainland, but only if they could bypass or punch through combat air patrols launched from Chinese carriers in the East China and Philippine Seas. Chinese cyber and space operations would further complicate American efforts to bring force to bear. This would leave China's air force, ground forces, and smaller surface warships to focus their efforts on Taiwan.

This is a relatively straightforward story, and one that the DOD reports have failed to tell over the years. China, thankfully, has a long way to go before it will be able to successfully pull off such an operation. But American forces in Asia are vulnerable, and increasingly so as Chinese military modernization continues. The administration should provide the American people and the U.S. Congress with a full accounting of PLA modernization and Chinese strategic goals, and of how they are linked; armed with such an accounting, Congress would be in a position to fund the military America needs for the Asia-Pacific region. Congress, of course, also has a responsibility to ensure that it is getting the information it requires. Last year's changes to the DOD China report were ill considered and should be revisited. When it comes to China, this administration seems to be pulled in two directions. It spent much of 2009 trying to reassure China that the U.S. welcomes its rise; the White House's handling of the report was one effort in that broader campaign. At the same time, there has been the occasional glimpse of a more confrontational approach to Beijing: Secretary Clinton's Internet-freedom speech, arms sales to Taiwan, Secretary Gates's remarks at the International Institute for Strategic Studies' Asia Security Summit (also known as the Shangri-La Dialogue), and the recent diplomatic contretemps over the South China Sea.

Hopefully, the president is learning that these two approaches need not be mutually exclusive. With an honest recognition that the United States and China share some interests but not others, the president should, sooner or later, settle on the proper course: to cooperate with China on issues where goals intersect, and to vigorously defend those U.S. interests that China threatens. If the two countries can find a way to cooperate on climate change or in international economic forums, they should do so. But Washington should be less concerned with "reassuring" Beijing and more concerned with deterring it from upsetting the American-led international order.

This requires both an unwavering commitment to the security of U.S. allies and partners in Asia—including Taiwan—and the maintenance of an American preponderance of military power in the region. The role of U.S. forces in the Asia-Pacific region should be, first and foremost, to deter Chinese aggression. Absent a robust, resilient force in the region, Beijing will be tempted to resort to force to achieve its goals. And absent an honest public debate in this country about China's rise—a debate the report fails to foster—that robust, resilient force may one day be a thing of the past.

SOUTH ASIA'S MANIFOLD CHALLENGE

The concept of "the international community", if it is to have practical meaning and encapsulate the notion of "solidarity without borders" instead of being an empty slogan, must come to terms with the multitude and gravity of the challenges confronting the peoples and nations of South Asia (Bangladesh, Bhutan, India, Maldives, Nepal, Pakistan and Sri Lanka). The scale of the problems faced in the region and the numbers of people involved are so huge that success or failure in South Asia pose defining challenges to the core mandates of the United Nations as the global arena for problem-solving. South Asia by itself accounts for one-fifth of "We the peoples of the United Nations". Developments in South Asia cut across the major faultlines of the UN system with respect to the challenges of economic development, environmental protection, food and water security, democratic governance and human rights, nuclear war and peace, inter-state and internal conflicts, and new security issues such as AIDS (acquired immune deficiency syndrome) and international terrorism. What happens in South Asia will surely shape the contours of the global community in the decades ahead.

Two of the central purposes of the United Nations as expressed in the UN Charter – to maintain international peace and security and to promote social and economic advancement – make it imperative for the organization to address these issues in South Asia. The United Nations University (UNU), in collaboration with the UN agencies in Japan, organized an international conference in May 2002 on "The United Nations and South Asia". UNU in Tokyo is particularly well suited as a forum for discussing these issues as the major UN agencies are located in its headquarters building in Tokyo, "UN House". The South Asian embassies in Japan offered their support for the conference and collaborated in its organization. The conference was well timed in that 2002 marked the fiftieth anniversary of the establishment of diplomatic relations with Japan by India, Pakistan and Sri Lanka. But it was ill timed in that on that date India and Pakistan were in the middle of the biggest and most tense mobilization of their full military mights along the full length of their border. Yet, by presenting a forum for communication between different actors within the various sectors, the conference helped to alleviate the substantial lack of interaction and thus contributed to improved efforts at addressing the problems in South Asia.

The chapters in this book is revised versions of the papers presented at that conference. Their emphasis is on discussing issues of particular relevance to the region and exploring the potential for improvement in both domestic and international efforts at alleviating the problems of South Asia. If and where appropriate, the role that the United Nations can play in this respect is also underscored.

One of the more interesting features of this volume is the divergence of cultures and writing styles of the scholars and the practitioners (officials, politicians, generals). Academics are addicted to notes, whereas practitioners are allergic to them. Many academics have to be reined in so that their contributions form chapters in a book instead of mini-tomes in themselves, whereas some practitioners have to be coaxed into extending their brief vignettes to a length and intellectual weight suitable for publication by a university press. Two of the UNU's five mandated tasks are to serve as a bridge between the normally isolated worlds of scholarship and policy and to serve as a platform for dialogue. This volume is testimony to the need for dialogue not only between participants from the different nations and societies of a deeply divided region of the world, but also between the different professional cultures in the modern world.

Former prime minister of India, I. K. Gujral, expresses the hope that the recent international interest in South Asia is not temporary and based solely on the threat of terrorism and nuclearization, but rather reflects a realization that the world community cannot be safe or happy unless it involves the billion-plus people of South Asia in the critical decisions regarding peace, security and development. According to Gujral, the most serious current challenge facing South Asia is terrorism. But the fight against terrorism cannot be won by force alone. It is of course necessary to fight the jihadi culture. But, even without jihad, there would still be manifestations of terrorism in all South Asian countries in the form of insurgency movements. Therefore there is an urgent need to address the root causes of terrorism, such as lack of good governance, low levels of human development, and new threats such as drug trafficking and the spread of AIDS. Although the main responsibility for the problems and their resolution lies with the South Asian countries, the region has not been brought into the global developmental mainstream by the international community. The international community needs a peaceful, cooperative and dynamic South Asia; it is in its interest to facilitate this.

Gujral sees great potential for development in South Asia in the fields of science and technology, as well as in traditional industries such as chemicals, pharmaceuticals, heavy industries, steel and electronics. For this potential to be realized, however, regional cooperation is necessary. India, as the leading power, can afford to be accommodative to promote such cooperation. Sartaj Aziz, while calling for a comprehensive programme to reduce poverty in South Asia, also asks for UN action to reduce tension between the region's two nuclear powers. There is an urgent need to accelerate the pace of economic and social progress in the region and to meet the challenges of globalization. The United Nations must assume and discharge its responsibility to focus on the inequalities of the globalization process and regain a leadership role in providing a level playing field.

Nor can the international community continue to overlook the security problems in the region. International assistance is needed to fight terrorism and extremism in the region as well as to stabilize Afghanistan. At the same time, Aziz calls for the United Nations to curb "liberal imperialism", that is, the notion that the so-called "postmodern" world can use force, pre-emptive attack or even deception to violate international boundaries with impunity.

Peace and Security

An immediate concern of the international community is the region's impact on international peace and security. South Asia poses many potential threats to regional and global peace and security: it has two nuclear powers engaged in a major territorial dispute; there are several dominant insurgency conflicts here; terrorism is pronounced; and the refugee situation has the potential to be deeply destabilizing. There are also significant cross-regional linkages with respect to relations with China (one of the five permanent members of the UN Security Council), Central Asia (and Russia beyond), the Middle East and South-East Asia. How can domestic and international efforts at resolving conflicts in the region be improved?

Inter-state Conflict

Since the end of the Cold War, the global pattern of conflict has shifted from inter-state to intra-state conflicts (many of which have transnational regional links), yet one of the remaining potential inter-state conflicts is found in South Asia. The situation is aggravated by the fact that the two potential belligerents are armed with nuclear-armed weapons. Whereas the stability of the nuclear deterrence between the superpowers during the Cold War was itself somewhat suspect, the relationship between Pakistan and India is qualitatively different and even more volatile. The two countries share a long border, which allows little time to decide whether to "use or lose" nuclear weapons in response to a perceived threat. Furthermore, Pakistan and India are involved in a territorial dispute over Kashmir. This dispute has already resulted in two wars between the countries and the possibility of armed conflict has not yet been eliminated. Neither country has second-strike retaliatory capability, which makes both of them more vulnerable to a pre-emptive strike than was the case between the superpowers during the Cold War. South Asia's relationship with and ties to neighbouring countries also have implications for the involvement of the international community in the region. A complicating element is India's disputed border with China, a third nuclear power with tangible interests in the region. Resurgence of Islamic fundamentalism in the region is also a cause for concern for regional stability. The disruptive nature of this potential conflict is exacerbated by domestic political volatility in all South Asian countries. It is imperative for the United Nations to contribute to a de-escalation of this conflict in order to maintain international peace and security. Stephen Cohen cautions that, in light of the failure of past predictions, it is impossible to predict future use of nuclear weapons by India and Pakistan with any confidence. It is likely that the future will look much like the current situation – a stable relationship between China and India and a rocky one between India and Pakistan, but with innate common sense or external mediation preventing an outbreak of nuclear conflict. However, Cohen also acknowledges the large number of political and military variables that might affect possible outcomes with regard to the nuclear future of South Asia, only some of which can be influenced or controlled by outside powers. He offers two suggestions: the international community should assist in managing crises; and security planners in the region should avoid overconfidence in deterrence and keep their arsenals low so as to reduce the scale of the catastrophe if there should be a regional war.

Echoing many of the same themes, Christophe Carle emphasizes that the future security of South Asia depends on the relationship between Pakistan and India; the other security threats of the region pale in comparison. He points to the elements of instability in the subcontinent's nuclear deterrence. Contiguity undermines the development of effective and reliable command and control systems and, with ballistic missiles, decision-making time may be reduced to 5–10 minutes. The nuclearization of South Asia and the inherent volatility of the nuclear equation in the region mean that external actors, particularly the United States, have become increasingly important. Thus South Asian (in)security has been internationalized.

INTRA-STATE CONFLICT AND TRANSNATIONAL LINKAGES

Most of the countries in South Asia have insurgency movements. The level of violence is variable, but several of these conflicts have been classified as high intensity. The separatist Tamil Tiger movement in Sri Lanka is one example, where an ethnic group seeks territorial withdrawal from the state entity. The Kashmir dispute feeds on and exacerbates political instability in both India and Pakistan. India faces further challenges in its northeastern regions. The Maoist movement in Nepal impedes effective government in a similar way, and over the past few years commentators have expressed concern about the possible Talibanization of Pakistan. With these threats to political stability and territorial integrity, South Asia remains a region with a high potential for violence and conflict. How can the international community contribute to the peaceful settlement of these disputes? And what can be done domestically to defuse these conflicts?

Nepal has been much in the news in the past couple of years or so, in part because of the palace massacre of the royal family, but mainly because of the ferocity and intractability of the Maoist insurgency. Lok Raj Baral's chapter illustrates the close link between intra-state and interstate conflicts. He points to the transnational elements of the conflict in Nepal, noting that India is often dragged into domestic issues in Nepal, a landlocked Himalayan kingdom sandwiched between two Asian giants with porous and open borders. Weakened states and enfeebled political institutions and leaderships are increasingly incapable of dealing with domestic crises in South Asia, which, in turn, breed inter-state conflicts. Cross-country migration and refugee flows, as well as the issue of treatment of one's own nationals in neighbouring countries, have the potential to trigger inter-state conflict. Conflicts occur over the exploitation of natural resources such as Nepal's water, and over transit rights for a poor and small country seeking an outlet to the sea for its products. There are also challenges with respect to new security issues such as trafficking in drugs and women.

The insurgency in Sri Lanka has been going on for much longer and is also more ferocious: it is the Tamil Tigers, after all, who introduced and perfected the gruesome art of suicide terrorism. Kingsley de Silva notes that South Asia's record of violence in public life is unusual even compared with other post-colonial states. One special feature is the high number of public figures assassinated. Rajiv Gandhi was killed on Indian soil but in the context of Sri Lanka's bitter civil war. The Kashmir conflict has clearer external factors in its origin than

Sri Lanka's but, once the conflict in Sri Lanka erupted and persisted, it was prolonged largely because of Indian intervention. In the Kashmir conflict, terrorism became a distinctive factor in the mid-1980s. The two principal protagonists remain inflexibly resistant to any change in their attitude on this issue. In Sri Lanka the Tamil movement was transformed from a relatively peaceful one until the 1960s into an extraordinarily violent struggle with regional ramifications in the 1980s. Assassinations and suicide bombings became central means of terror. Once terrorism becomes a major factor in the political struggle, de Silva notes, the prospects of negotiating a settlement become all the more difficult. A similar central trait is the marginalization of the so-called moderates.

It is argued by some that the major locus of international terrorism has shifted to South Asia. Terrorist acts are committed in relation to both internal and inter-state conflicts, and the level of violence is alarming. Allegations are also frequently made that governments may support cross-border terrorism to undermine neighbouring states. The phrase "aid, abet and harbour" terrorists has entered the international policymaking agenda since 11 September 2001. How can terrorism be curbed; how can domestic and international actors work to decrease terrorist violence? Is terrorism a purely security problem with no significant political dimensions? Can the challenge of "political terrorism" be met without addressing the fundamental political issues that may underlie it?

Peacekeeping

If South Asia poses a challenge to international peace and security, it is also true that the region contributes strongly to the UN efforts at peacekeeping. The chapters by Lieutenant General Satish Nambiar and Brigadier-General Syed Roomy must be read in the context of three of the world's top four UN peacekeepers being currently from South Asia: Bangladesh, Pakistan and India. Of the total of 44,715 military observers, civilian police and military troops involved in UN peacekeeping operations (PKOs) in July 2001, 12,590 (28 per cent) were from South Asian countries. As of March 2002, Bangladesh was the biggest contributor to UN PKOs, Pakistan was in second place, India third and Nepal eleventh. What accounts for their continued commitment to UN peace operations in the light of the marked reluctance of some Western countries to accept the burden of UN peacekeeping? South Asian countries contribute with unique and useful skills, for example the Indian army's experience in counter-insurgency operations. Are there wider lessons to be drawn from their experience in peacekeeping operations? One might be improved cooperation on training and perhaps institutional cooperation in the future. In the light of the contributions by South Asia to the United Nations and the size and importance of the region, one may ask also if South Asia has gained the influence in international forums that it ought to have. The generals call for adherence to recommendations from the Brahimi Report on UN Peace Operations, especially that troopcontributing countries must be involved in decision-making on mandates for missions. In addition, though, should South Asia have permanent representation on the Security Council?

CHINA'S POWER SECURITY AND SOUTH ASIAN SEA LANES OF STATEMENT

China's spiraling demand for energy, plus its growing dependence on imported petroleum, have made Beijing increasingly concerned with ensuring the uninterrupted flow of oil at reasonable prices. The Middle East plus North and East Africa provide well over half of China imported oil. Virtually all of that oil moves to China by tanker across the Indian Ocean. Beijing confronts several potential threats to its trans-Indian Ocean oil supply. A confrontation between Iran and the United States could lead — either via sanctions or by military actions — to the restriction of oil shipments through the Strait of Hormuz. An Indian-China conflict might escalate into the naval dimension. India might respond to defeats by the PLA in the Himalayas, or to Chinese support for Pakistan in the context of a "fourth round" between India and Pakistan, by using India's naval supremacy in the Indian Ocean to sever

China's vital oil imports. Then there are scenarios of U.S.-PRC conflict over Taiwan that escalated into U.S. naval blockade of China. None of these contingencies is a high probability, yet military institutions everywhere devote attention to remote but potentially dire scenarios.

In any of these contingencies the ability of PLA-N warships to escort vessels carrying oil from Middle Eastern ports to China might be part of an effort to prevent hostile powers from interfering with delivery of China's oil supply. Development of robust over-land transportation systems between Yunnan and the Bay of Bengal, and between western Xinjiang and Gwadar could substantially strengthen the PLA's ability to sustain intense military operations in the eastern and western Indian Oceans. As a neutral power in a possible U.S.-Iran confrontation, China would enjoy the right under international law to continue trading with both belligerents. But historically neutral powers have often found protection by military force essential to upholding those legal rights. Were China's leaders to conclude PLA-N escort of China's oil commerce across the Indian Ocean necessary, the newly created transport lines via Myanmar and Pakistan could become quite useful. In terms of possible Sino-Indian conflict, the PLA-Navy is substantially superior to the Indian Navy in terms of overall tonnage and ship numbers, but the latter enjoys overwhelming geographical advantages when operating in the Indian Ocean. If the PLA-N could obtain bases on the Indian Ocean littoral (perhaps at Gwadar and Kyaukpyu), and link those forward bases to China by robust road and rail lines, India's geographic advantages would be substantially diminished to the PLA-N's advantage.

Termination

China's omni-directional friendship policy in South Asia is not cant, but serves Chinese interests well. Chinese relations with other South Asia nations will be more robust and stable if India views those ties as non-threatening. A friendly and cooperative relation with India will give China a stronger position in South Asia than would a conflictual Sino-Indian relationship. An economic, diplomatic, and even military partnership between China and India, surrounded by similar partnerships between China and the other South Asian countries — a sort of Asian zone of friendship and cooperation — would maximize Chinese influence in South Asia, and ensure that threats to China did not emanate from that region. China's omni-directional friendship diplomacy toward South Asia is working relatively well. China's broad strategic objective is to persuade India to look benevolently on an open-ended and expanding Chinese economic, political, and military presence in South Asia and the Indian Ocean, to eliminate suspicion in Sino-Indian relations, and to transform India into China's partner. In this way the rise of China in Asia will not lead to Indian efforts to countervail China in coalition with the United States. But the conversion of India to friendship with China is to be done without making concessions to India on the status of Tibet, the Sino-Pakistan strategic link, or by restricting China's expanding military, security, and transportation ties with other South Asian nations.

China's optimal outcome would be open-ended, growing political, economic, and military cooperation between China and all the South Asian countries, with India accepting an open-ended expansion of Chinese influence in that region and learning to live comfortably under China's benevolent protection. India would gradually evolve into a key Chinese partner in South Asia. China's intention, its objective, in South Asia is most definitely not to establish dominance over that region, or draw it into some sort of Chinese sphere of influence. That, however, might be the outcome over a period of twenty or thirty years.

China and the South Asian Equilibrium of Power

China has an interest in maintaining the existing balance of power between India and Pakistan. The existence of a strong and confident Pakistan able and willing to challenge India confers important advantages on China. Politically it hobbles India's efforts to act on the global stage as China's equal. Militarily, it forces India to confront the possibility of a two front war, thereby compelling it to divide its military forces.

This is the geopolitical rationale for China's large and long-standing economic and military assistance to Pakistan. It is *possible* that one reason why Beijing is not in a hurry about resolving the boundary dispute with India is that it would fundamentally ease India's two-front problem, intensifying Indian pressure on Pakistan. China's interest in keeping Pakistan strong was one reason why Beijing endorsed Islamabad's re-engagement with the United States after 9-11. While that re-engagement diminished somewhat the potential utility of Pakistan and Gwadar as a logistics "back door" for China in the event of confrontation with the United States or India, it also brought Pakistan in from a situation of increasingly dangerous isolation. Pakistan's close ties with the Taliban in Afghanistan plus the growing Islamisization of Pakistani politics and the steady deterioration of Pakistan-Western relations since the mid-1990s, posed an increasing danger of Pakistan's isolation, perhaps even designation by the international community as a "rogue state." This would have been a serious blow to China's interests, and to the extent that U.S. re-engagement with Pakistan could move Pakistan in a different direction, it served China's strategic interest in a strong Pakistan that constrains India. U.S. engagement with Pakistan also made development of India-US strategic partnership more difficult, and diffused Indian anger over China's own strong military and nuclear links to Pakistan.

This is not to say that Beijing's interests are served by confrontation between Pakistan and India. Beijing's objective, as noted earlier, is to develop cooperative ties with all the countries of South Asia. Confrontation between Pakistan and India would put Beijing in the unfortunate position of having to choose between Islamabad and New Delhi. Failure to support Pakistan could endanger China's fundamental interest in keeping Pakistan strong and independent of Indian domination, and threaten China's strategic partnership with Pakistan. Alignment with Pakistan, on the other hand, would spoil China's ties with the most important south Asian power, India, and possibly push that power further into alignment with the United

States. In this sense, peace between India and Pakistan is in China's interests.

In the event of Pakistan-Indian confrontation, China will piggy-back on the peace diplomacy of the United States and other powers, adding its voice to efforts to restore peace and the status quo ante as quickly as possible. A Chinese tilt toward Pakistan but well below the level of threatened belligerency on Pakistan's behalf, would be virtually certain, but only in the event that India roused itself and threatened to decisively subordinate Pakistan (perhaps in the aftermath of a nuclear exchange) would Beijing move toward actual co-belligerency on Pakistan's behalf.

CHINA'S SOUTH ASIAN INTERESTS AND POLICIES

China's broad objective in South Asia is to expand multi-dimensional cooperative relations with all the countries of that region. "Multi-dimensional" signifies military ties as well as more innocuous political and economic cooperation. "All" means both India and India's smaller neighbours: Pakistan, Myanmar, Nepal, Sri Lanka, Bangladesh, Bhutan, and the Maldives. India has sometimes objected to China's relations — especially military-security ties — with these countries. Beijing views South Asian countries as "neighbours" with whom it is especially important to have friendly, cooperative ties both to increase China's own economic and political influence and to lessen the ability of potentially hostile powers (currently the U.S.) to injure China's interests.

Economically, China seeks to draw South Asia's resources into China's development drive. India with its fast-growing, industrialized, and relatively affluent economy has become China's strongest economic partner in South Asia. Two-way Sino-Indian trade in 2003 was $7.6 billion, compared to $2.4 billion for Sino-Pakistan, $1.4 billion for Sino-Bangladesh, and $1.1 billion for Sino-Myanmar trade. During their April 2005 meeting, Wen Jiabao and Manmohan Singh agreed to increase trade to $20 billion by 2008. While that amount is paltry compared to China's trade with countries like Japan, Germany,

South Korea, or the United States, it leads China's South Asian trade by far.

The simple fact is that India produces much more that Chinese firms want to purchase than do Pakistan, Bangladesh, or Myanmar — let alone the small countries like Nepal, Bhutan, or the Maldives. In 2003, China imported $1 billion more from India than it exported to it, while Chinese exports to Pakistan were three times the value of China's imports, exports to Bangladesh were forty times the value of China's imports, and exports to Myanmar were over five times the volume of imports. While these figures are based on official statistics and do not reflect smuggling (which is substantial in the case of Myanmar), the broader point is that India simply has more to offer China. From India China imports a wide array of mining and industrial products: steel and iron ore, zinc, aluminum and aluminum products, copper and copper products, acids and alkalines, dyes, colouring, alcohol and other chemical products, rubber, plastics, cotton, wool, thread and yarn, leather, and machinery and machine parts. From Pakistan, in contrast, China buys largely cotton, yarn, and leather.

China also recognizes that in key economic-technological areas it has much to learn from India. Chinese analysts recognize India's world-leadership position in computer software creation and aspire to learn from India in this area, meshing these strengths with China's existing strengths in computer hardware production to help catapult China to world-class-economy status. There are no comparable inducements in the case of the other South Asian countries. Pakistan and Bangladesh offer attractive markets for Chinese consumer goods and machine tools. But the ability of these poor countries to purchase Chinese goods, and to produce things useful to China's booming industry, is limited compared to India's. China has not been able to forge with the South Asian countries a robust foreign energy-for-Chinese-capital-goods swap such as it has engineered with Iran. The exploitation of Bangladesh's natural gas deposits could conceivably overcome this structural imbalance, with Bangladesh entering into an energy for Chinese capital goods swap similar to that characterizing the Sino-Iranian relation. Politically, there are interrupted visits between China and the larger South Asian countries at the minister and vice minister level to "exchange views" on various bilateral, regional, and international subjects. Beijing seeks to engage South Asian governments in dialogue and cooperation on substantive subjects of mutual concern: countering narcotics traffic, smuggling, and terrorism; stabilizing the Karzai government in Afghanistan; or dealing with Tibetan presence and activities in various South Asian countries. Beijing also strives to line up South Asian support on the Taiwan subject: to counter Taiwan efforts to expand ties and to guarantee South Asian neutrality in the event of a U.S.-PRC clash over Taiwan.

Friendship with China is often attractive to smaller South Asian countries living in India's shadow. People in those countries often see ties with China as affirming their independence from India and as a way of gaining bargaining leverage with New Delhi. China's voice in the U.N. Security Council is valued by South Asian governments because of Beijing's occasional willingness to say a few words on behalf of smaller South Asian countries, or even to criticize Washington on behalf of those smaller countries. China has expressed a desire for observer status in the South Asian Association for Regional Cooperation (SAARC) where its ability to offset India will be valued by the other South Asian states.

China views military links as part of the normal repertoire of international cooperation and seeks to expand military ties with South Asian countries. Every year China exchanges with Pakistan, India, Bangladesh, and Myanmar two or three delegations at the deputy chief of staff through defence minister level, or from military regions, military academies, or defence industrial agencies. China has recently attempted to institutionalize exchange of views with the larger South Asian countries in the security / military areas. At the political level, there are periodic discussions of regional security subjects of common concern. Bangladesh, Pakistan, and Myanmar have been preferred and heavy customers for Chinese military equipment. Chinese training, maintenance, and parts have come with equipment purchases. Exchange of intelligence between China and Pakistan and Myanmar is routine, with Yangong providing important electronic listening posts at several points in the Bay of Bengal / Strait of Malacca area. Chinese naval squadrons have made friendly port calls to Pakistani (1985, 1993, 2001), Bangladeshi (1986, 1995), Myanmar (2001), and Indian (1993, 2001) ports. In October 2003, the PLA-Navy conducted its first-ever joint exercises with the Pakistani navy in the East China Sea. The next month it conducted joint exercises in the same region with the Indian Navy. China assists Pakistan's missile development and its nuclear energy efforts. Although China's involvement in the latter is under IAEA supervision, the intrinsic fungibility of nuclear materials and know-how makes it likely there is some spill over to Pakistan's nuclear weapons capabilities.

In the past India, has objected to China's military links with South Asian nations. In 1989, for example, a Nepalese attempt to purchase Chinese weapons and initiate an intelligence exchange agreement with China precipitated severe Indian economic sanctions that forced Kathmandu to abandon the objectionable policies. Given New Dehli's opposition to Sino-South Asian military cooperation, Beijing's insistence on forging such links is testament to its determination to become a multi-dimensional power in the region, and its refusal to cede South Asia to an Indian sphere of influence.

China's response to Indian concerns over China-South Asian military cooperation has been to assert that since China does not have aggressive or malevolent intentions, China's military cooperation with India's neighbours does not threaten India.

If India is concerned about China's military ties with the smaller South Asian nations, Beijing argues, the proper course is to increase mutual trust between China and India via security dialogues and other such venues. Or if New Delhi is unhappy with Chinese military cooperation with India's South Asian neighbours, China is quite willing to expand such cooperation with India itself. There is no valid reason to object to these friendly, cooperative relations, Beijing argues. In fact, such objections manifest "anti-China" sentiments and hostility toward China, which will be answer in kind by China.

The sort of punishment contained in this implied threat was demonstrated during the eighteen months after India's May 1998 nuclear tests that New Delhi had justified as a response to threat from China. After the Indian tests with their China threat justification, Beijing cancelled scheduled sessions of the Joint Working Group on the boundary. Chinese media rhetoric became harsher, even resurrecting charges of Indian "hegemony." Beijing urged Washington and the U.N. Security Council to adopt tough measures against India, and to target mainly India, not Pakistan's "response" to India's tests. Beijing hinted it might shift to a more pro-Pakistan position on Kashmir. Beijing's carrot and stick approach seems to have been fairly successful. India has agreed to open-ended cooperation with China, even while China expands military ties with India's neighbours.

CHINA'S ENERGY SECURITY AND SOUTH ASIAN

China's spiraling demand for energy, plus its growing dependence on imported petroleum, have made Beijing increasingly concerned with ensuring the uninterrupted flow of oil at reasonable prices. The Middle East plus North and East Africa provide well over half of China imported oil. Virtually all of that oil moves to China by tanker across the Indian Ocean. Beijing confronts several potential threats to its trans-Indian Ocean oil supply. A confrontation between Iran and the United States could lead — either via sanctions or by military actions — to the restriction of oil shipments through the Strait of Hormuz. An Indian-China conflict might escalate into the naval dimension. India might respond to defeats by the PLA in the Himalayas, or to Chinese support for Pakistan in the context of a "fourth round" between India and Pakistan, by using India's naval supremacy in the Indian Ocean to sever China's vital oil imports. Then there are scenarios of U.S.-PRC conflict over Taiwan that escalated into U.S. naval blockade of

China. None of these contingencies is a high probability, yet military institutions everywhere devote attention to remote but potentially dire scenarios.

In any of these contingencies the ability of PLA-N warships to escort vessels carrying oil from Middle Eastern ports to China might be part of an effort to prevent hostile powers from interfering with delivery of China's oil supply. Development of robust over-land transportation systems between Yunnan and the Bay of Bengal, and between western Xinjiang and Gwadar could substantially strengthen the PLA's ability to sustain intense military operations in the eastern and western Indian Oceans. As a neutral power in a possible U.S.-Iran confrontation, China would enjoy the right under international law to continue trading with both belligerents. But historically neutral powers have often found protection by military force essential to upholding those legal rights. Were China's leaders to conclude PLA-N escort of China's oil commerce across the Indian Ocean necessary, the newly created transport lines via Myanmar and Pakistan could become quite useful. In terms of possible Sino-Indian conflict, the PLA-Navy is substantially superior to the Indian Navy in terms of overall tonnage and ship numbers, but the latter enjoys overwhelming geographical advantages when operating in the Indian Ocean. If the PLA-N could obtain bases on the Indian Ocean littoral (perhaps at Gwadar and Kyaukpyu), and link those forward bases to China by robust road and rail lines, India's geographic advantages would be substantially diminished to the PLA-N's advantage.

SECURITY DISPUTES, NUCLEAR DOCTRINES, AND PROLIFERATION TRENDS

To begin with, proliferation issues in South Asia must be understood in context of vertical and horizontal proliferation. Vertical proliferation takes place as nuclear states modernize their nuclear arsenals with more reliable delivery systems and warheads. Countries including the United States, China, India, and Pakistan, are in the process of modernizing their arsenals through actions such as proposals for "a reliable replacement warhead" (as in the case of the United States). In the context of South Asia, nuclear modernization is mainly a function of prevailing threat perceptions arising from security dilemmas. Modernization of arsenals includes the development and testing of longer-range missiles-such as the tests of the Agni-III by India, and the Shaheen-II by Pakistan in the first half of 2007. Horizontal proliferation is the spread of nuclear weapons technology from nuclear states to other entities, including aspiring nuclear weapon states, as well as non-state actors such as terrorist groups. Horizontal proliferation generally involves a significant role for WMD supply networks that may or may not have a connection to official entities in a nuclear state. In the South Asian context, this variant of proliferation is especially pertinent, given the history of the A.Q. Khan network and its assistance to states such as North Korea and Iran. In addition, horizontal proliferation includes second-tier proliferation, where developing countries trade and barter nuclear technology with each other. While vertical and horizontal proliferation are variants of the proliferation dynamic, it is entirely possible that a nuclear state (such as Pakistan) could make use of non-state networks in the pursuit of nuclear modernization. From the subcontinental perspective, one main question arises-given the lack of a comprehensive resolution of the disputes between India and Pakistan and India and China, how do nuclear doctrines in South Asia impact trends in the acquisition of nuclear and missile technology? The answer to this question links threat perceptions and nuclear doctrines with recent proliferation-related developments and requires a brief discussion of existing nuclear postures of India and Pakistan.

Subcontinental Rivalry

So what are the characteristics of the sub-continental rivalry that make nuclear proliferation in South Asia such a crucial security issue? Threat perceptions based on long-standing security disputes shape nuclear doctrines and proliferation dynamics. The intensity of disputes brings in security dilemmas that ensure continued dependence on nuclear weapons in South

Asia. South Asia is one of the most populated regions of the world, with India and Pakistan alone accounting for about 1.35 billion people. Both countries have been bitter rivals since partition of the subcontinent in 1947 that led to the creation of independent Pakistan and independence for India. The two countries have fought two wars over Kashmir (1947, 1965), one over East Pakistan/Bangladesh (1971), one limited war (Kargil, 1999) and the ongoing insurgency in Kashmir (since 1989). The 2001-2002 crisis further highlighted the dangers of terrorist violence provoking a conventional conflict that could lead to a nuclear crisis. Kashmir, which lies at the heart of the dispute, is more than a simple territorial problem. The province has a Muslim majority, and for India it is a symbol of its secular credentials as well as a repudiation of the partition, which was based on religion. For Pakistan, Kashmir is crucial because it is seen as an unfinished agenda of partition, which was supposed to provide a homeland for the subcontinent's Muslim community. Thus, Kashmir is an integral part of both countries' perceived self-identities. Since the 2001-2002 crisis, Islamabad and New Delhi have conducted several rounds of peace talks aimed at bringing a lasting settlement to the Kashmir issue. This peace process has involved several confidence-building measures such as strengthening of transport links between the two countries. The two sides also signed a crucial agreement on reducing the risk of nuclear accidents in February 2007. Nevertheless, the key dispute, Kashmir, is nowhere near resolution. This implies that both New Delhi and Islamabad are more inclined toward strengthening existing military capabilities, both conventional and non-conventional, to prevent an unfavourably scenario in a future standoff.

Apart from notions of sovereignty and nationhood, Kashmir is also of considerable strategic importance. Rivers originating in the Kashmir region provide crucial water supplies for food producing areas in the heartland. Furthermore, the Siachen glacier is also a region of military significance. The glacier, to the north of Kashmir, commands a strategic overlook of the small border between Pakistan and China and can potentially be used as a point of attack on India from northwest Kashmir.

The glacier became a battle ground between the two armies in April 1984 and despite repeated talks, there has been no movement toward demilitarization. The complex rivalry between India and Pakistan involves territorial disputes based on notions of national identity as well as terrorist violence. Another integral element of the subcontinental security dyad is the role of China.

The China Factor

The role of China in South Asian security issues as well as in future conflict scenarios is crucial when considering two realities-(a) the historical animosity between India and China, and (b) the long standing 'all-weather' political and military alliance between Pakistan and China. Indian analysts often cite transfer of nuclear and missile technology from Beijing to Islamabad as evidence of an encircled threat to India. Through nuclear and missile technology transfers to Pakistan, Beijing restricts India to the South Asian strategic framework, and this constrains New Delhi's stated desire to seek a more global presence.

From the Chinese political establishment's perspective, the concern is over India's defence expansion, its desire and movement toward a stronger regional and global role, and its increasing strategic connections with Washington.

Thus, any examination of the South Asian proliferation framework takes into account the Sino-Indian rivalry and dispute, the lowest point of which was the 1962 border war. In recent years, Indian and Chinese leaders and special representatives have met for regular talks on the border dispute issue; the most recent session (the 10th such round), took place in April 2007.

In early rounds of these talks, China granted de facto recognition of Sikkim as a province of India, while India accepted Tibet as part of China. However, serious differences remain, and strategically important areas such as the state of Arunachal Pradesh have been claimed by China, while India has claimed Aksai Chin and certain parts of Kashmir handed over by Pakistan to China.

Despite periodic meetings, little progress has been made on these issues, and from time to time, controversial statements by each side threaten to derail talks. Whether a hardening of positions or a negotiating strategy, it demonstrates that the potential for friction is ever-present.

Furthermore, there is also some dispute over an earlier agreement between the two sides to not insist on territorial exchanges of areas with settled populations, reflected in Beijing's recent demands that India cede Arunachal Pradesh, especially the Tawang tract. Therefore, in the absence of a permanent settlement, both India and China have adopted a hedging strategy to guard against any future strategic disadvantages.

A hedging strategy involves bolstering military-related capabilities in an ambiguous way that is not directly threatening to the adversary.

At the same time, cooperative ties are encouraged without necessarily making any major concessions. In part, such an approach is chosen due to uncertainty over the adversary's future intentions and capabilities and as a way to safeguard against a downturn in future ties or in the regional or global strategic environment. Therefore, modernization of nuclear arsenals in South Asia has to be considered in this context.

Similarly, in the case of India and Pakistan, despite sustained peace talks and CBMs, the two sides continue a hedging strategy to guard against future uncertainty, such as another crisis situation like Operation Parakram in 2001-2002. This is done by developing more reliable nuclear delivery systems (especially longer range ballistic missiles), perfecting and increasing fissile material stock, and acquiring conventional weaponry in line with contemporary war-fighting doctrines.

Thus, in South Asia, underlying security disputes, based on territorial rivalry and terrorist violence, combined with a need to expand the nation's global and regional position encourages future uncertainties that shape the actors' nuclear policy decision-making. As mentioned earlier, apart from the Indo-Pakistan rivalry, strategic uncertainty, and suspicion in

New Delhi is also generated by Pakistan's close military links with China. With China in the picture as a rival of India and a strategic ally of Pakistan, even if Delhi and Islamabad move towards a peaceful resolution of the Kashmir dispute, Beijing is likely to be the biggest factor in Indian threat calculations.

At the same time, the present threat perceptions between India and China are not the same as between India and Pakistan, which are more immediate and based on a 'hot' territorial dispute and state-sponsored terrorism.

Nevertheless, analysts in New Delhi have long pointed to Chinese military modernization as a coercive threat to India. This modernization includes missile development, such as the current deployment of the DF-21 and DF-3 missiles in Qinghai and Yunnan provinces.

Furthermore, there is some suspicion among Indian analysts that though Beijing's stated policy is that of minimum deterrence, the stationing of missiles such as DF-3 and DF-21 reflects a posture of nuclear coercion, and under some conditions, does not preclude a first strike against its neighbours. It is also possible that since 1998, Beijing may have deployed nuclear weapons on the Tibetan plateau in response to a perceived Indian conventional military advantage and the May 1998 nuclear tests.

Thus, despite growing trade between the two sides, there is some degree of unease in India over China's long-term intentions, more so in light of predictions of increased competition between the two countries for global energy resources. The concern in New Delhi is that if bilateral relations take a negative turn at some point in the future, China's current military modernization will give Beijing a significant advantage.

The Sino-Indian security dilemma is also a function of China's desire to establish close relationships with other countries in the Indian Ocean region (most notably Myanmar), a policy that is seen as a potential threat by India and termed as "strategic containment." For India and China, the security dilemma also arises from threat perceptions based on consequences of future nationalistic tendencies. Both sides fear that a rise in nationalism in the other could lead to more hostile attitudes.

China's concerns over future expansions of the U.S. nuclear arsenal, missile defence and space dominance plans also lessen the possibility of any immediate restraint with respect to Beijing's nuclear plans. Therefore a chain reaction exists in South Asia where New Delhi, at the very least, wants to maintain its current relative capabilities vis-à-vis Beijing, if not actually improve them. The interconnected security dilemmas in the Asia-Pacific region shape defence policies and impact stability.

6

India's Changing Nuclear Strategy, Programme and Disarmament in ASEAN

THE EVOLUTION OF INDIA'S NUCLEAR POLICY

On May 27 th, 1998, the government of the then- prime minister Atal Behari Vajpayee issued a statement to the 12 th Lok Sabha titled the "Evolution of India's Nuclear Policy". This statement came about two weeks after India had successfully completed a total of 5 nuclear tests at the Pokhran range on May 11 th and May 13 th. The monstrousness of these events is reflected most notably in clause 14 of the statement: "India is a nuclear weapon state. This is a reality that cannot be denied." However, in the same clause it is also established that India shall refrain from using "these weapons to commit aggression or to mount threats against any country" and in clause 24 (the final one) it is stated that although "India stands at a defining moment of [her] history" the "rationale for the Government's decision is based on the same policy tenets that have guided the country for five decades".

Thus it is authorise that Vajpayee's government attempted to convince both the Indian and the international public that the nuclear tests would not alter the basics of India's foreign policy while at the same time admitting that indeed a watershed event had occurred.

The question now is whether this argumentation can be seen as reasonable or not. Basically, there are two problems: 1) Can the nuclear tests be seen as being concordant with India's foreign and nuclear policies until then? Were they even a somewhat logical product of these policies? 2) Once the tests had been carried out, would it be possible or even expedient for any future Indian government to keep following traditional policy fundamentals? Understandably, these problems have been addressed by different scholars in deviant ways, depending on their respective backgrounds.

The Indian physicist T. Jayamaran argues that the nuclear tests "signalled the initiation of a sudden and dramatic policy turn on nuclear issues by India's Bharatiya Janata Party-led government" as "the new policy abandoned India's earlier position in favour of using atomic energy only for peaceful purposes and it opened the door for the nuclear weapons option". Consequently, he criticises the government for having conducted the tests without an underlying vision of future policies. Instead, according to him, the government tried to portray the tests as mainly a heroic scientific achievement.

The Vice-Chancellor of the University of Jammu, Prof. Amitabh Mattoo, claims in his key note address presented at the inauguration ceremony of the Think Tank on Defence and Foreign Policy of the University of Kerala's V.K. Krishna Menon Study Centre for International Relations in Trivandrum on April 12 th, 2008, that the nuclear tests of 1998 marked the "beginning of [...] a new phase of realism in India's foreign policy".

The tests made India's small strategic elite realise that a fundamental shift had occurred globally from moral, idealistic foreign policies towards *realpolitik,* a development which had started with the end of the Cold War in the beginning of the 1990s. Thus, while Jayaraman focuses more on official government policies Mattoo concentrates on what was going on behind the scenes where, according to him, indeed a new strategic thinking had begun. The new realism among India's strategic elite has also been noted by Ashley J. Tellis, today a Senior Associate at the Carnegie Endowment for International Peace, who cites two articles from *The Hindu* and *The Indian Express* in which the authors hail the nuclear tests for ending both ambiguity and hypocrisy in India's foreign and nuclear policies. Tellis himself however emphasises the difference between nuclear testing and achieving a true nuclear capability.

According to him, India remained at a crossroad after the tests; and in trying to determine whether nuclear capability, i.e. a sophisticated nuclear weapons program, should be pursued or not India would probably move "in a direction quite different from that which most previous nuclear weapon states have taken".

In Tellis' opinion India's further nuclearization process would rather be slow, gradual and distinctive "thanks to a number of factors—including India's traditional and highly publicized commitment to disarmament; its continuing economic and developmental constraints; its susceptibility to pressures emanating both from existing nuclear weapon states and from the global non- proliferation regime in general; its singular view of nuclear weapons as "pure deterrents" rather than as war-fighting instruments; its unique civil military system, which has few parallels in the Third World; and, finally, the fact that its adversaries' coercive capabilities, while significant, can be countered by a minimal, albeit perhaps not a token, deterrent".

As distinguished as these accounts are they nevertheless have in common that indeed they view the nuclear tests of 1998 as a watershed event with far- reaching consequences.

Can we therefore dismiss Vajpayee's statement to the Lok Sabha as pure politics? Although it seems conceivable that the then- government of India had no clear vision or no sound conception about the consequences of the nuclear tests and how to deal with them it nevertheless cannot be denied that those responsible realised that the world had changed for India.

An example for a new approach is the India- US nuclear deal which will be discussed later. What remains to be examined at this point is whether the nuclear tests are a result of a continuous foreign and nuclear policy or mark an abrupt break.

EXPRESSION OF INDIAN STRATEGIC CULTURE

The exclusion of the armed forces from the nuclear programme decision-making process has been made clear by George Perkovich in his study. The absence of the armed forces from the decision-making loop on the nuclear issue resulted in one army chief, General K. Sundarji, depicting the frustration of the service chiefs through a novel titled *The Blind Men of Hindustan*. On the other hand, various other actors such as the political parties, the Indian Parliament, the bureaucracy and even public opinion, have had little or no impact on decisions relating to the nuclear programme. The real debate on nuclear weapons has been carried on by followers of Mahatma Gandhi who stressed the principles of nonviolence and morality in India's actions. While this paper has argued that Gandhi himself was not against violence when it came to pursuing India's interests, the truth is that some segments of the Indian population came to adhere rigidly to such a concept, as a result of misreading the subtle nature of the thoughts and actions of Gandhi and Nehru. Nevertheless, in the 1970s the seemingly contradictory approaches were merged through a clever synthesis, resulting in a now widely accepted formula. Known as the Subrahmanyam formula, it reinforced the broad strategic culture under which the nuclear programme is located. It stipulated that India would acquire nuclear weapons in order to pressure the nuclear 'haves' to disarm, and to protect itself against nuclear blackmail. Thus, by combining idealism with self-interest, the thunder of the no-bomb lobby – which had a negligible impact, if at all, on the programme – was taken away.

But while in the previous years the armed services had very little to do with nuclear weapons, this now seems to be changing. Further, Indian strategic culture should not be perceived to be static. With the development of an Indian triad, it is undergoing a slow but substantive change, and this is taking place in the balance between the political and operational aspects of deterrence. The once overwhelming political understanding of nuclear weapons manifested through the total absence of the armed forces from the nuclear arena is slowly giving way to a more operational conception of nuclear weapons. The development of various delivery systems – including long range missiles and weapons platform systems like nuclear submarines – is pushing the erstwhile practice of deterrence, which remained restricted to broad declarations on doctrine and the development of limited capabilities, towards more pressing operational questions about the quantity and quality of weapons and the infrastructure surrounding them.

The journey India has taken from the writing of the letter in 1944 by Bhabha to the Tata Foundation, to the nuclear tests of 1998, has been a long and arduous one.

As this paper has tried to show, realist security considerations played the most important role in propelling India towards nuclear weapons. But this realist thinking has been Indian in nature. The motivations for such thinking and behaviour are influenced by what India thinks about herself. Thus, one notices how history, religion and geography have all interacted and produced a distinctively Indian approach to nuclear weapons.

While all the nuclear states of the world have travelled more or less the same path towards developing nuclear weapons, the rationales and the way they went about doing it differed. Strategic culture helps explain these different pathways and styles. In India's case a distinctive style, that of *moralpolitik*, epitomises the Indian way of approaching the nuclear issue. This *moralpolitik* has been brought about by India's history, geography, religious and strategic thinking. It is important to recognize that this culture is not transhistorical, either in the sense that it can be traced back to some 'authentic' pre-colonial tradition or that it is timeless, immutable and unchanging. It is a strategic culture influenced by events, experiences past and present and modified as and when thought necessary. As the world awakens to the growing importance of India, an understanding of Indian strategic culture as discerned from her nuclear policy will certainly help make sense of the way India sees the world.

EMERGENCE OF THE NUCLEAR PROGRAMME

Usually analysts proffer four arguments about proliferation. These are: (i) security concerns, (ii) prestige, (iii) technological imperatives, and (iv) domestic politics. Let us go through each briefly. The security or the realist argument posits that security concerns directly related to a state's physical security and survival ultimately drive a state to acquire nuclear weapons. Thus, a state operating under an anarchic international system and facing serious security pressures might go for the nuclear option. The second position informs us that nuclear weapons are a symbol of prestige. States acquire great power status or international recognition by developing a nuclear arsenal. The third view proposes that a state's decision to go for nuclear weapons is an inevitable outcome of the technological momentum created by nuclear research and development programmes. The final argument is that intra-bureaucratic politics as well as politicians' drive to score domestic political points may lead a state down the nuclear path. In other words, bureaucrats acting on the basis of their own individual policy preferences or bureaucracies carrying out their specific institutional interests may propel a country towards nuclear weapons.

India went for nuclear weapons has followers of all schools vying with each other to explain India's actions. For George Perkovich, domestic factors and prestige issues play the most important role in India's actions. He points out that India's quest for nuclear weapons capabilities began before a Chinese threat emerged and was driven not by military or national security experts but rather by bureaucrats like Homi Bhabha. It was also a reflection of India's moral norms and post colonial identity manifested through Nehru's recognition that India could gain international power, standing and a measure of security if she went for nuclear weapons. Others like C. Raja Mohan and Bhumitra Chakma argue that it was mainly security concerns that led to India's decision to acquire nuclear weapons. Chakma convincingly writes that given India's pressing economic problems it is very difficult to imagine that she would invest such huge resources in a nuclear programme merely to satisfy the need for recognition and prestige. Similarly, India's decision to persist with the nuclear programme was not strongly influenced by technological imperatives or domestic pressures. If such were the case, then India would not have abstained from going nuclear in the 1960s and Indira Gandhi and other prime ministers would have chosen to carry out the tests when their domestic popularity was plummeting. While prestige, technology and domestic factors might have played some role, it was the emergence of China as a nuclear weapon state and later on, the development of the Pakistani nuclear bomb, which led India to acquire a nuclear arsenal. Raja Mohan argues in a similar vein. He mentions the same reasons as Chakma, but adds that in the 1990s the demise of the Soviet Union and the removal of a security back-up, the emergence of the US as the sole superpower, China's rise and international pressure to adhere to the NPT and CTBT" all aggravated India's security concerns and pushed New Delhi inexorably towards the nuclear option. Sumit Ganguly also places emphasis on the realist rationales while conceding that prestige and technological imperatives also had roles to play.

While the role played by prestige, technological and bureaucratic factors in India's nuclear programme must be acknowledged, the arguments made by Chakma, Raja Mohan and Ganguly – regarding the importance of realism in deciphering India's nuclear posture – appear to be the most convincing. At the same time, this 'realism' is strictly an Indian understanding of realism, and a study of Indian strategic culture is necessary to unearth the peculiar ways in which Indians have viewed security. Some argue that realism and culturalist explanations of international events are two distinct approaches. They then consider whether the culturalist explanations might yield superior insight. Stuart Poore, for his part, sees strategic culture protagonists as posing a direct challenge to the hegemony of realist thinking. However, there are, and can be, no unencultured realists. As argued above, India's approach to nuclear weapons – including the means of their development, the rationale for them, and India's stance on global efforts to stem proliferation – reflects a distinctive Indian way of thinking and acting. The use of *moralpolitik* is a good example of such behaviour.

NONPROLIFERATION AUTHORITIES AND INDIA

India's advance to nuclear non-proliferation regimes before the 1998 tests was generally one of opposition. In spite of her vociferous support to global disarmament ever since her independence, she has refused to sign the NPT and the Comprehensive Test Ban Treaty (CTBT). She acceded to the International Atomic Energy Agency (IAEA) in the mid-1950s with substantial reservations, but never allowed international inspections of her most critical facilities. The recent signing of the historic nuclear deal between the US and India, which Indians perceive to be a major accomplishment, also ran into controversy in India over its alleged 'loss of sovereignty' implications. Even though the treaty allows for none of India's uranium-enrichment or plutonium-reprocessing plants or her planned plutonium producing fast-breed reactors to be included in the civilian list, the agreement met with hostility from many groups: the coalition partners of the present government as well as the opposition parties; influential scientists and bureaucrats within India's nuclear establishment; and some respected commentators. Like the Indian quest for the bomb, the Indian approach to non-proliferation has been mired in double talk, is contradictory in nature (at least to Westerners), and can be downright confusing. But if one sifts through the evidence, and delves deeply and critically into Indian policies with regard to proliferation and disarmament issues, then one notices a thread connecting the policies and also how they helped provide a momentum for India's bomb.

How to strike a balance between the dream of having the bomb and the underlying stark realities of the dearth of resources and popular revulsion against the bomb was a challenge Nehru faced. The answer was the application of *moralpolitik*. This time *moralpolitik* was to be applied in the following way: India was to become a vociferous champion of disarmament and of a nuclear weapons-free world, skilfully using Mahatma Gandhi's image as an apostle of non-violence and his messages about the reprehensible nature of nuclear weapons. At the same time, she would use this campaign of disarmament as a shield behind which to build up her own arsenal of nuclear weapons. From the Baruch Plan of the US in 1946, to the NPT of the 1990s, India consistently harped on the theme that strategic arms reductions, while of universal concern, are the exclusive responsibility of the big powers (countries having nuclear weapons), to be furthered primarily by cuts in their weapons inventories, which aim India would support enthusiastically. The Indian negotiating strategy was premised on a brilliant stand. India stated that any regime seeking to control the spread of nuclear technologies had to be applied equally to all states. India's position was that the issue of 'horizontal' proliferation could not be given precedence over that of 'vertical' proliferation. In other words, nuclear weapons powers could not be allowed to continue their arms build-up (vertical proliferation), while non-nuclear countries found themselves facing a range of restrictions as they attempted to develop nuclear technology in their national interest. Thus in 1965, the Indian representative asserted at the UN Disarmament Commission:

Unless the nuclear powers and would-be nuclear Powers [*sic*] undertake from now on not to produce any nuclear weapons or vehicles for weapons delivery, and, in addition, agree to reduce their existing stockpile of nuclear weapons, there is no way of doing away with the proliferation that has already taken place or of preventing further proliferation [...]. We must therefore, stop proliferation urgently. But this was only one part of the Indian argument. The Indian negotiating strategy also brought the issue of national sovereignty to the forefront. The position adopted by the countries possessing nuclear weapons (the US, the Soviet Union, the United Kingdom, France and China) during the negotiations on the issue of proliferation was, according to India, an attempt to place restrictions on the behaviour of non-nuclear weapons states, in effect, informing them of what they could and could not do to further their own national goals and objectives. In an era when the majority of the members of the United Nations were leaving behind their colonial status and emerging as independent countries or had just attained their independence, such a proposal seemed to be signalling a return to their past and was not acceptable. It had the odious connotation of colonialism. India skilfully played on such emotions and made every effort to highlight these points whenever discussions on non-proliferation came up. More recently, after the 1998 explosions, Jaswant Singh, who served as Foreign Minister, and also briefly held the position of the Defence Minister, under the Vajpayee administration, clarified why India opted for the bomb, citing the 'unequal' provisions of the CTBT and the 'discriminatory' policies of official nuclear weapons states. Singh reiterated that India's nuclear policy remained committed to a basic tenet: that the country's national security in a world of nuclear proliferation lies either in global disarmament or in exercise of the principle of equal and legitimate security for all. The title of the article was "Against Nuclear Apartheid", and those three words summed up India's position with regard to proliferation norms.

The Indian negotiating position described above should be read in conjunction with the Indian strategy of striving and ultimately acquiring the nuclear bomb. It did bring useful results for India. Itty Abraham points out that such a 'principled' position helped India to: (a) strengthen her claim to leadership of the non-aligned movement and the developing world; (b) divide the nuclear powers (the erstwhile Soviet Union, hearing the accusation of neo-colonialism, out of ideological necessity had to identify with the 'progressive' Indian position in order to distinguish itself from the 'imperialist' capitalist states) and thus weaken the argument that selective nuclear restraint was for universal good; and (c) proclaim itself as a norm producing country (through her emphasis on different principles like nonalignment, and leader of the silent majority), and thereby allow her to assert a claim to membership in the elite group of states that set the rules and established norms for the international system. But these real or perceived benefits pale in contrast to what Bharat Karnad identifies as the real success stemming from India's position on proliferation issues. Karnad claims Indian thinking was based on the view that if one takes history into consideration then one would realise that the principal powers, even if they agreed to eliminate their large and sophisticated nuclear weapons stockpiles, would insist on a long drawn out process. This would give India the time and the rationale for a nuclear build-up of her own, were that ever needed, without the country attracting any negative fallout in the interim.

The Indian nuclear tests of 1998 put an end to the need for India to stick to the postures she had been following while developing her capabilities. Nowhere is this shift more pronounced than in Indian views with regard to issues like nuclear weapon-free zones, transfer of technology and surprisingly, the dismantling of the Anti-Ballistic Missile (ABM) Treaty by the administration of US President George W. Bush. India's opposition to a nuclear weapons-free zone in South Asia has already been noted. Now, with her objective of being a nuclear weapons state achieved, India has herself suggested such a zone for South Asia, signalling her own responsible role as a nuclear weapons power. She can now extend security guarantees to non-nuclear weapons states in South Asia and thus call for a nuclear weapons free zone. Similarly, India in the past emphasised that non-proliferation measures should never be allowed to prevent the transfer of nuclear technology to any country. With her own nuclearisation process now complete, India has started underscoring the importance of such restrictions lest such arms fall in the hands of countries which might harm her interests. The pragmatic nature of India's policies towards proliferation was however best demonstrated through her support for the dismantling of the ABM Treaty. India sensed concrete benefits if it supported counter-proliferation, i.e. having the military capabilities to deal with an environment in which there is proliferation of weapons of mass destruction. These benefits were: finally being able to join the nuclear rule-making club, solving the problems of proliferation in her neighbourhood, and preventing undesirable elements that do not abide by traditional rules of nuclear deterrence from acquiring nuclear weapons. Global disarmament was the masthead of Indian nuclear diplomacy throughout the Cold War period and well into the 1990s. India's fervent endorsement of this principle, however, has diminished greatly. India has evolved new ways of thinking and acting on nuclear proliferation related issues. Still, the ingrained ideas of disarmament and its relationship with India's acquisition of nuclear weapons find resonance in Indian policy documents and public postures. Commenting on the make-up of the Indian Draft Nuclear Doctrine announced in 1999, Deepa Ollapally notes the presence of an open commitment to pursuing disarmament in an otherwise generally hard-hitting nuclear doctrine. She quotes a member of India's Nuclear Advisory Board who is at pains to point out that global disarmament is the primary issue and that the rest of the doctrine is conditioned by the persistent absence of any serious progress on such disarmament, especially among the permanent members of the United Nations Security Council.

INDIA'S PARTICIPATION IN NUCLEAR COMMERCE

A key development in recent years has been the U.S.-India nuclear cooperation agreement, which was first unveiled in July 2005. This agreement and the subsequent endorsement of India's case by the Nuclear Suppliers Group (NSG) will enable India to engage in international nuclear trade. In return, New Delhi has agreed to allow safeguards on a select number of nuclear facilities that will be classified as "civilian" in purpose. The remaining "military" facilities will remain off-limits to international inspectors. The agreement process required a number of steps, including passage of the Hyde Act by the U.S. Congress to authorize the United States government to negotiate a bilateral nuclear agreement with India (December 2006); adoption of a bilateral 123 agreement between India and the United States under the U.S. Atomic Energy Act; approval of a safeguards agreement between India and the International Atomic Energy Agency (IAEA) (August 2008); and an NSG waiver to its rules allowing Indian participation in nuclear trade (September 2008).

In October 2008, the bilateral '123' nuclear cooperation agreement was approved by the U.S. Congress and signed into law by President George W. Bush. In March 2009, the IAEA formally approved the Additional Protocol (AP) to the Indian safeguards agreement, which differs in several ways from previous APs concluded between the Agency and other states. India signed the safeguards agreement with the IAEA in February 2009, and subsequently the agreement was certified by the U.S. government in February 2010. The first two nuclear power plants, units at the Rajasthan Atomic Power Station (RAPS), have been formally placed under the safeguards agreement. In October 2009, India announced a plan to put 14 out of its 22 nuclear reactors under IAEA safeguards by 2014. In late July 2010, India and the United States signed a bilateral agreement on reprocessing spent fuel, in accordance with the '123' agreement between the two countries. The adoption of appropriate legislation dealing with liability in case of a nuclear accident represented a significant challenge. In August 2010, after contentious debate, the Indian Parliament approved the Civil Liability for Nuclear Damage Bill. The bill imposes liability not only on nuclear facility operators, but also on the suppliers of nuclear equipment and materials in the event of an accident. This clause has greatly concerned U.S. firms, which might find it difficult to obtain insurance coverage for such scenarios, making them less competitive than government-supported suppliers from other countries.

Following the NSG waiver, India signed nuclear cooperation agreements involving the supply of nuclear reactors and uranium, with France (October 2008), Russia (December 2008), Namibia (August 2009), and Argentina (October 2009). India also plans to sign an agreement with Kazakhstan, under which the Central Asian state will provide uranium to India and in return India may build several medium-sized 200 to 300MW nuclear reactors for Kazakhstan. Discussions on nuclear cooperation have also taken place with South Korea and Turkey. The Indian Nuclear Fuel Complex (NFC) received the first batch of 60 tons of uranium from Areva in March 2009, under a December 2008 agreement between the French company and the NPCIL to supply India with 300 tons of uranium. Additionally, the Russian company TVEL supplied a first batch of 30 tons of natural uranium fuel pellets to the NFC in April 2009.

According to Indian officials, New Delhi could import up to 40 nuclear reactors in the next decade. The U.S.-India Business Council stated that India might spend up to $175 billion to expand its nuclear sector in the next 25 years. According to October 2008 reports, in the next five years, India will construct 21 nuclear power facilities, including six French reactors (1,600MW each), four Russian reactors (1,000MW each), and four American reactors (1,500MW each).

In pursuit of these goals, agreements have already been struck with nuclear suppliers. In February 2009, the Nuclear Power Corporation of India Limited (NPCIL) and Areva concluded an agreement for the supply of two European Pressurized Reactors (EPR) of 1650MW each. In March 2010, New Delhi and Moscow signed nuclear deals under which Russia will construct 12 nuclear plants in India. In October 2009, New Delhi identified two locations, in the states of Gujarat and Andhra Pradesh that would host reactors constructed by GE Hitachi and Westinghouse. However, given the constraints on any agreement imposed by the civil nuclear liability law, it is unclear whether U.S. companies will conclude any reactor supply deals in the near future.

NUCLEAR PROLIFERATION POLICIES DURING THE COLD WAR

In the South Asian context, a conflictual bipolar security complex, India and Pakistan's transformational process of emerging as opaque nuclear powers was an example of different motivations, aspirations and ambitions for obtaining nuclear status. While the dominance of *realpolitik* trends over states' nuclear decision-making process is not an entirely surprising phenomena, the evolution of India's approach to the nuclear option is interesting from philosophical and strategic viewpoints. The genesis of the Indian nuclear policy from a categorical opposition to nuclear weapons in the Nehru era to Pokhran I, India's first so-called Peaceful Nuclear Explosion (PNE) in 1974, signified a discontinuity in New Delhi's post-1947 strategic thinking. What caused this discontinuity? What factor(s) led the country of Mohandas Gandhi, who once labelled nuclear weapons as 'diabolic', to obtaining potential nuclear power status under Indira Gandhi? Do the same factors suffice in explaining Pakistan's motives for developing its own nuclear capabilities in the mid-1980s? While some political scientists emphasised national security considerations in locating the roots of India and Pakistan proliferation policy, others have used an alternative theoretical approach with a greater level of structural balance between domestic, military security and symbolic motives. The latter multi-causal approach, summarised by Scott D. Sagan, is particularly useful in providing an inclusive analysis of nuclear proliferation causes. In this context and through the application of Sagan's explanatory models, the essay attempts to analyse the layers in India and Pakistan's 'nuclear thinking' leading to the development of military nuclear technology. The alternative multi-causal explanation constitutes a practically efficient theoretical framework for the comprehensive understanding of states' hybrid logic for nuclear proliferation.

Opposing the neorealist mono-causal security-oriented analysis (i.e. "the security model"), Sagan's approach considers the domestic and norms aspects as effective factors in triggering military nuclear proliferation, thus offering two additional explanations: "the domestic politics model" and "the norms model." According to Sagan, security model states (either weak or strong) perceive nuclear weapons as an enormously powerful means of deterrence to secure their national security in an anarchic international system, if their regional or trans-regional rival(s) acquire nuclear capability. Strong resourceful states develop their own bomb, while weak states, incapable of proliferation, are obliged to join a balancing alliance with a nuclear power to maintain their security and sovereignty with the promise of nuclear retaliation. In contrast, the domestic politics model reflects the influence of three main domestic actors on governments' nuclear proliferation policies: first, states' nuclear energy establishments (consisting of scientific institutions and civil companies); second, the military elites (especially in the Air Force branch) as domestic bureaucratic actors; and third, politicians who tend to profit from the nuclear weapons discourse for political parties or individual standing regarding pro-proliferation public opinion. Therefore, these pro-proliferation actors gain additional influence if nuclear weapons are a positive symbol in states' domestic debates – thus the states proliferate in accordance with the influence of one or more of the aforementioned actors. Finally, in the norms model, states' nuclear policies are pro-proliferation due to 'nuclear symbolism' and the 'nuclear myth': states observe military organisation and advanced weaponry as essential elements in their image as modern and sovereign states. The 'nuclear myth', or symbolic implications of nuclear proliferation (e.g. technological advancement, military might, projection of grandeur, etc), are perceived as a means of forming states' modern identity and enhancing their international prestige. While there seems to be an analytical overlap and theoretical interference between the domestic and symbolic models, Sagan's three models offer an efficient toolbox for examining the deciding factors in India and Pakistan's nuclear policies.

The security-model analysis of Indian nuclear policy prior to Pokhran I can be conducted by analysing India's threat perception at the regional and trans-regional levels. The trans-regional level analysis confirms the gravity of Sino-centrism in India's trans-regional threat perception sphere, and the validity of Sagan's security-model explanation. The dynamics of post-1962 Sino-Indian bilateral relations is the fundamental factor in India's horizontal proliferation policy in the security model. While the Sino-Indian protracted conflict began in 1953 over territorial claims, the 1962 Sino-Indian war and its disastrous consequences for the non-aligned India moved the Chinese threat factor from the periphery of New Delhi's threat perception circle to its centre, triggering incremental yet significant changes in Indian defence policy and military strategy. The subsequent Indian military reorientation towards re-equipment and operational reinforcement (e.g. the creation of ten mountain divisions designed for warfare in the Himalayas and increasing the Army's manpower ceiling to 825,000) confirms the demise of Nehru's *moralpolitik*-type policies regarding China. However, the fundamental shift in India's nuclear weapons position occurred when Beijing shocked New Delhi with the detonation of its first nuclear device in October 1964. New Delhi's subsequent reaction to China's nuclear capability demonstrated a paradigm shift in India's previously Nehruvian anti-proliferation policy towards what then Prime Minister Lal Bahadur Shastri reluctantly phrased as India considering "nuclear explosion for peaceful purposes". Compatible with the security-model's two policy scenarios, India's inability to develop its own nuclear weapons forced New Delhi to secure nuclear deterrence by joining a balancing alliance with a nuclear power. Accordingly, when India's request to the United States, the Soviet Union and the United Kingdom for nuclear guarantee was refused, India's only option for deterring a nuclear China and maintaining its national security was to obtain horizontal proliferation on its own, leading to the 1974 PNE.

Similarly, the regional-level analysis indicates the significance of nuclear weapons in India's quest for regional hegemony and security in the South Asian region, although against the much less significant threat of Pakistan. A quick glance at pro-Indian political scientists' analysis of the motivation of India's quest for regional security through nuclear weapons reveals New Delhi's mindset regarding Pakistani conventional threat as well as India's strategic policy manoeuvre to achieve several objectives at once. In the bipolar South Asian security complex, Pakistan was (and is) India's major regional security and strategic concern. In spite of its conventional inferiority to India, Pakistan attacked its greater and more militarily powerful neighbour in 1948, 1965 and 1971. While India's decisive military victory in the 1971 war, and the subsequent disintegration of Pakistan through the independence of Bangladesh, considerably weakened Pakistan, it managed to retain most of its military infrastructures. The series of Indo-Pakistani military conflicts convinced Indian strategists that Pakistan could use the period of Indian domestic political instability to launch other military attacks on India. In the light of alarming Sino-Pakistani cordial relations, and the presumption of Pakistani will to attack India, India's nuclear proliferation became instrumental in maintaining Indian regional security as well as establishing Indian regional hegemony through deterring Pakistan from future attacks. As Saira Khan formulates, the most efficient war-avoidance strategy for India in such conflictual regional settings was 'deterrence by possession of nuclear weapons.'

Similar to the Indian behavioural pattern for proliferation, but in contrast to India's multi-layered threat perception, the application of the security-model framework on Pakistan's nuclear policy produces a mono-causal explanation: Pakistan's nuclear proliferation was a linear reactionary policy to India's 1974 nuclear detonation. In addition to Indo-Pakistani territorial, ideological and ethnic elements of conflict that have formed the essentials of the South Asian security complex since 1947, the 1971 war and dismemberment of Pakistan reinforced Indo-centrism in Pakistan's threat perception. The war crippled Pakistan's economy and displayed the perceived unreliability of Pakistan's allies (i.e. the United States and China) in the time of crisis. Realising its conventional military inferiority to India, in 1972 President Zulfiquar Ali Bhutto initiated a nuclear policy in pursuit of nuclear weapons. Islamabad's nuclear program, however, gained a critical boost by India's 1974 PNE. Closely resembling the pattern of India's reaction to the 1964 Chinese nuclear test, Pakistan's nuclear policy was decisively directed towards inevitable nuclear proliferation after India's 1974 PNE. Against India's combined conventional military superiority and nuclear weapons capability, Pakistan had to obtain its own nuclear weapons as soon as possible to provide deterrence against the gravest threat to its national security.

In this context, with Islamabad's failure to obtain security guarantees from the nuclear powers against a nuclear India, Pakistan had no other option other than to embark on its own nuclear proliferation program.

Applying the domestic-model of analysis on the Indian case clearly exhibits the decisive influence of two of the three domestic actors outlined by the model on India's nuclear decision for horizontal proliferation: nuclear energy establishments (consisting of pro-proliferation scientists and defence laboratories) and politicians eager to enhance their respective parties or/and individual standing in public opinion. Due to the pattern of the civil-military relationship in India where the former utterly dominates the latter, military elites as bureaucratic domestic actors had practically no influence over New Delhi's process of nuclear decision-making. After the Chinese 1964 nuclear test, Homi Bhabba, the head of India's Atomic Energy Commission (AEC), tenaciously lobbied for the allocation of required resources for developing nuclear weapons. Eventually, the AEC leadership's lobbying for proliferation along with pro-nuclear Congress party pressure on the government forced the reluctant Shastri to order the initiation of a classified project to develop technical ability to design and detonate a PNE within a certain timeframe. In spite of Bhabba's successor, Vikram Sarabhai's fierce opposition to any form of nuclear proliferation, the AEC developed an alliance with defence laboratories for lobbying the new Prime Minister Indira Gandhi. In a meaningful coincidence, the dynamics of Indian domestic politics in the early 1970s were defined in terms of economic recession, large-scale riots in various regions and the internal conflict in the ruling Congress party, thus an all-time low domestic support for Gandhi's government. In such dire circumstances, with the Prime Minister acknowledging that a theatrical nuclear explosion could have been a decisive 'political ace' for increasing her standing in public opinion, Gandhi's approval of 1974 PNE is hardly surprising. In a later interview, in spite of her initial denial, Gandhi admitted that the PNE "would have been useful for election". As the result, immediately after the detonation, public support for Gandhi's government and the ruling Congress party increased by one-third, both being "restored to the nation's confidence." Considering the pre-PNE Indian domestic politics dynamics, the influence of AEC, the Prime Minister and the ruling party on nuclear proliferation is evident.

CHANGING TACK ON CHEMICAL WEAPONS

These new considerations of national security are also evident from India's dilly-dallying with the Chemical Weapons Convention (CWC) earlier this year. After signing the treaty and ratifying it, in the face of uncertainty about the ratification of the CWC by Russia, China, Pakistan, and especially the USA, India suddenly threatened to withdraw from the treaty. To justify this shift, a senior official of the external affairs ministry said "The main problem here is that in the absence of the above countries [that is, the USA, Russia, China and Pakistan] not ratifying it, the CWC is neither universal nor equitable nor non-discriminatory because, as was the case with NPT and CTBT, certain countries will be keeping chemical weapons, while denying the same to others." Thus the CWC which, prior to this switch, India had praised as a model non-discriminatory treaty, and as a "useful model for our future efforts in the field of global disarmament," suddenly became a discriminatory treaty. But, once it became apparent that the U.S. would ratify the CWC after all, India executed another shift and welcomed the "non-discriminatory" CWC. Subsequently, India has revealed that it possessed chemical weapons and is in the process of destroying them in accordance with the CWC. This proved that India lied on several previous occasions when it declared that it did not possess chemical weapons, and in direct violation of the August 1992 joint declaration with Pakistan on the complete prohibition of chemical weapons."

Along with three nuclear weapons states, namely the USA, Russia, and China, India did not sign the land mines treaty in Ottawa in December 1997.

Domestic Trends and Global Disarmament

These recent shifts in India's attitudes towards global disarmament, and its increasingly strident criticisms of any step-by-step measures towards nuclear disarmament, can only be understood by analysing the domestic debate. Ever since the early sixties, hawkish sections of the Indian policy-making community have argued in the domestic media in favour of building a nuclear arsenal. The 1974 nuclear test is, in part, a display of their influence. Subsequently, they have not been able to alter the status quo in any significant way.

All this may change. The last few governments in India have been relatively weak and unstable, all formed by coalitions of various parties with different agendas. With the rise in strength of the Hindu fundamentalist Bharatiya Janata Party (BJP), whose election manifestos have consistently endorsed overtly exercising India's nuclear option no party in power has been spared being attacked on its nuclear policy. The BJP has consistently opposed any restraints on the Indian nuclear and missile programs.

The BJP's policy is not new, but with no political party strong enough to oppose it, global disarmament initiatives take a back seat to preservation of the nuclear option. In this new political climate, the hawks have begun to dominate the nuclear debate. Citing the pressure imposed by the nuclear weapon states, and particularly the USA, on several of the non-nuclear weapon states and the threshold states to achieve this extension, the hawks managed to increase nationalistic feelings among the elite.

The hawks also used the extension to argue that nuclear weapons are here to stay and hence India should go about building its own nuclear arsenal. The effectiveness of this line of argument can be seen subsequently in the domestic CTBT debate. Sections of the Indian population who were otherwise opposed to India going overtly nuclear came to accept that the CTBT, originally championed by India, was a "Western" treaty, and a continuation of the discriminatory nuclear regime set up by the nuclear weapon states.

For the hawks, the rationale for the linkage between a time-bound nuclear disarmament process and the Fissban or the CTBT is two-fold. First, this linkage is needed to be used to gain credibility among the majority of people in India, who support India's official position that India should keep its options open only as long as the other states are not willing to give up their arsenals. Indeed, there is substantial support for global nuclear disarmament among the Indian public. A recent poll conducted by the Kroc Institute and the Fourth Freedom Forum, in conjunction with the Marketing and Research Group (MARG), New Delhi, found that 83% of those polled supported an international agreement for the elimination of all nuclear weapons. The second rationale is that it buys time so that the internal debates can be fought out and some consensus for further nuclear weapons development reached. This extra time is also essential for other reasons. With the increasing norm against nuclear weapons, as codified by agreements like the CTBT, or the decision at the World Court against nuclear weapons, the hawks sense this as their last opportunity to propel India into the ranks of the nuclear weapon states.

The economic liberalization program has also contributed in an indirect way to their campaign. Hand in hand with the 5-10% increases in the Indian economy has been the rise of Indian elite who, like the elite elsewhere, is greatly interested in making their country "powerful." And, conveniently for them, the best example of a country that has recently entered the ranks of the world's rich and mighty is China — which in 1962 had a border war with India and defeated it. Completely ignoring the various economic and social factors that go into making China the power it is, the elite focus on its nuclear arsenal, and in it see their short cut to greatness.

ORIGIN OF INDIA'S NUCLEAR WEAPON PROGRAMME

India's indigenous efforts in nuclear science and technology were established remarkably early. The first step was taken by Dr. Homi Jehangir Bhabha in March 1944 when he submitted a proposal to the Sir Dorab Tata Trust (established in honor of Bhabha's own uncle, Sir Dorab Tata) to found a nuclear research institute, over three years before independence and a year before the first nuclear weapon test. This led to the creation of the Tata Institute of Fundamental Research (TIFR) on 19 December 1945 with Bhabha as its first Director. The new government of India passed the Atomic Energy Act, on 15 April 1948, leading to the establishment of the Indian Atomic Energy Commission (IAEC) not quite one year after independence. At that time Prime Minister Pandit Jawaharlal Nehru declared: We must develop this atomic energy quite apart from war - indeed I think we must develop it for the purpose of using it for peaceful purposes.... Of course, if we are compelled as a nation to use it for other purposes, possibly no pious sentiments of any of us will stop the nation from using it that way."

This note of ambivalence in Nehru's speech foreshadowed his policies on nuclear research for the next decade. Nehru took a prominent role in international politics, founding the Non-Aligned Movement, and advocating nuclear disarmament. However, he refused to foreclose India's nuclear option while other nations maintained nuclear arsenals and supported programs designed to bolster India's weapons potential. In 1954 the Indian nuclear program began to move in a direction that would eventually lead to establishment of nuclear weapons capability. On 3 January 1954 the IAEC decided to set up a new facility - the Atomic Energy Establishment, Trombay (AEET), later to become the "Indian Los Alamos". On 3 August 1954 the Department of Atomic Energy (DAE) was created with Dr. Bhabha as Secretary. This department answered directly to the Prime Minister and has continued to do so down to the present day.

The program grew swiftly. The atomic energy budget increased 12-fold from 1954 to 1956. By 1958 the DAE consumed one third of India's research budget. By 1959 AEET employed over one thousand scientists and engineers. In 1955 construction began on India's first reactor, the 1 MW Apsara research reactor, with British assistance. And in September 1955, after more than a year of negotiation, Canada agreed to supply India with a powerful research reactor - the 40 MW Canada-India Reactor (CIR). Under the Eisenhower Administration's "Atoms for Peace" program the US agreed to supply 21 tons of heavy water for this reactor in Februrary 1956, and the reactor was dubbed the Canada-India Reactor, U.S. or CIRUS (now commonly written as Cirus).

The acquisition of Cirus was a watershed event in nuclear proliferation. Although the sale was made with the understanding that the reactor would only be used for peaceful purposes (the heavy water contract at least made this explicit), it occurred before any international policies were in place to regulate such technology transfers and no provision for inspections were made. And in fact India was careful to ensure that no effective regulation would accompany the reactor. India refusing to accept fuel from Canada for the reactor and set up a program to manufacture the natural uranium fuel for Cirus indigeneously so as to keep complete control of the plutonium produced there. This program, led by metallurgist Brahm Prakash, succeeded in developing the techniques for producing the precisely manufactured, high purity material demanded by the reactor.

The reactor was a design ideal for producing weapons-grade plutonium, and was also extraordinarily large for research purposes, being capable of manufacturing enough plutonium for one to two bombs a year. The acquisition of Cirus was specifically intended by India to provide herself with a weapons option and this reactor produced the plutonium used in India's first nuclear test in 1974; provided the design prototype for India's more powerful Dhruva plutonium production "research" reactor; and is directly responsible for producing nearly half of the weapons grade plutonium currently believed to be in India's stockpile. The sale further set a precedent for similar technology transfers which greatly assisted Israel in obtaining its own plutonium production reactor from France shortly thereafter. The Atomic Energy Establishment, Trombay was formally inaugurated by PM Nehru on 20 January 1957. It acquired its present name — Bhabha Atomic Research Centre (BARC) — on 12 January 1967 when PM Indira Gandhi renamed it in memory of Dr. Bhabha who died in an airplane crash on 24 January 1966.

Apsara, fueled by enriched uranium from the UK, went critical on 4 August 1957, becoming the first operating reactor in Asia outside of the Soviet Union (though only days ahead of Japan's first reactor). Cirus achieved criticality at BARC on 10 July 1960. As a nation India has always placed a premium on self-sufficiency. It is, in fact, the most self-sufficient large economy in the world and does not import any nuclear fuel. [The traditionally closed nature of economy though accounts for the import/export based Chinese economy far outstripping its growth from the late seventies to the early nineties.] Due to its vast domestic resources of thorium (a potential fuel for breeder reactors) but limited supplies of uranium, from the start of its nuclear program India has always placed strong emphasis on the development of breeder reactor fuel cycles. Breeder reactors require highly concentrated fissionable material for reactor fuel: either highly enriched uranium or plutonium. This provided a peaceful rationale for developing a plutonium separation capability, but the principal impetus for the India's first fuel reprocessing plant was to obtain a nuclear option.

In July 1958 PM Nehru authorized project Phoenix to build a plant with a capacity of 20 tonnes of fuel a year - sized to match the production capacity of Cirus. The plant was based on the U.S. developed Purex process and an American firm, Vitro International prepared the plans for it. Construction of the plutonium plant began at Trombay on 27 March 1961 and was commissioned in mid-1964.

India's civilian nuclear program was also established during this period. Discussions with American firms to construct India's first nuclear power plants at Tarapur were held in 1960-61. An interesting incident sheds light on Nehru's amd Bhabha's thinking at that time. In 1960 Kenneth Nichols, a former U.S. Army engineer who played significant roles in the Manhattan

Project, represented Westinghouse in discussions on power plant construction. In a meeting with Nehru and Bhabha, Nichols relates that Nehru turned to Bhabha and asked:

"Can you develop an atomic bomb?" Bhabha assured him that he could and in reply to Nehru's next question about time, he estimated that he would need about a year to do it.... He concluded by saying to Bhabha "Well, don't do it until I tell you to."

INDIA'S NUCLEAR WEAPONS PROGRAMME

The end of World War II marked a revolution in world affairs - the recasting of nations and relations between nations, and the emergence of a new technology which fundamentally changed the role of warfare. Within the span of two years and two months, from 1945 to 1947, three critical events occurred whose reverberations have brought the threat of nuclear war in South Asia seemingly daily to the front pages of newspapers everywhere. The three events were - in chronological order - the establishment of the United Nations on 26 June 1945; the dramatic demonstration of the destruction of which even crude nuclear weapons are capable in August 1945; and the calamitous partition of British India into the modern states of India and Pakistan at midnight on 14-15 August 1947.

It is clear to everyone that the legacy of partition is a key driving force behind the nuclear standoff that now exists between India and Pakistan. Partition split apart a region that had been united for millenia amid communal massacres on a scale never before seen, leaving in its wake the unresolved issue of contested Kashmir - a Muslim-majority region held by Hindu-majority India. The skirmishing that has continued now for over fifty years, punctuated by outbreaks of full-scale war (in 1947, 1965, and 1971), have given both nations ample motivation to develop potent weapons to gain advantage over — or restore balance with — the other. Another motivation for India's acquisition of nuclear weapons, less often considered in the West, is the potential threat and regional challenge presented by the nuclear-armed state of China, which faces India along much of its northern border. Disputes covering 80,000 square kilometers of this border region exist:

- China currently occupies the Aksai Chin plateau adjacent to Ladakh in Kashmir;
- India occupies the North-East Frontier Agency claimed by China.

These territorial disputes, a legacy of British rule, erupted into the Sino-Indian War on 20 October 1962, when China launched a massive attack on India to which India was powerless to respond. India had relied for years on a warm relationship with the Soviet Union as a counterweight to China, but with the USSR facing down the United States at the same moment in the Cuban Missile Crisis, India was shocked to find the Politburo suddenly switching to support China in an effort to bolster its own position. PM Nehru was forced to appeal to the U.S. for help. U.S. naval air forces arrived off the coast, but before the USAF could deploy to India, China halted its attack on 21 November and partially withdrew. China continues to hold the Aksai Chin region captured in the initial advance. The legacy of this incident was the discovery that the Soviet Union was an unreliable ally, and the deep resolve not to be at a similar disadvantage with respect to China in the future.

Finally, an even less well known factor is a deep-seated drive to achieve international influence commensurate with India's size, and its importance throughout history as one of the world's principle civilizations. At the founding of the United Nations in 1945 the composition of the UN Security Council, the world's most influential and powerful international body, was fixed and has never changed from that time. By an accident of history India was not an independent state at that moment, and its only hope for representation at the conference was the Churchill administration, then in its closing days, which vehemently opposed India's national aspirations. As a result China - with a similar geographic size, population, and state of economic development - was given a seat on Security Council, but India was not. Nuclear weapons did not exist at the time the Security Council composition was debated, but over time the five Council members all acquired nuclear, then thermonuclear, arms. With the signing of the Nuclear Non-Proliferation treaty in 1970, and the replacement on the Council of the non-nuclear Taipei Chinese government with the nuclear armed government in Beijing shortly thereafter, the de facto principle that Security Council permanent members and the "nuclear club" were one and the same was firmly established.

The crucial importance of the desire for recognition of India as a world power in driving forward the nuclear weapons program, even overshadowing considerations of military necessity and deterrence is underscored by remarks by former weapons program leader Raj Ramanna: "There was never a discussion among us over whether we shouldn't make the bomb. How to do it was more important. For us it was a matter of prestige that would justify our ancient past. The question of deterrence came much later. Also, as Indian scientists we were keen to show our Western counterparts, who thought little of us those days, that we too could do it."

Thus it should be no surprise that India, now tied for third place among the world's largest economies (with Germany), and soon to become the most populous nation on Earth, has concluded that to be given its due in world affairs, it must become a member of the nuclear club as well.

What is notable however is how the world's largest democracy developed such capabilities. The decisions were made by a handful of people, with virtually no input or oversight by the public or the legislature. India's nuclear weapons program from its outset has answered only to the Prime Minister's office, and only the Prime Minister and a select few of his or her appointees have ever had any say in its development and acquisition.

ASIA AND THE PACIFIC REGION

In Asia and the Pacific region, interest has been expanding in a broad range of nuclear technologies. The reliance on nuclear power as a source of electricity is already substantial, with well established programmes in China (including Taiwan, China),

Japan, the Republic of Korea, India and Pakistan — and when compared to any region in the world, Asia holds the strongest current growth market for nuclear power. In addition, more than 50 research reactors and accelerators are operating in 15 Asian countries. Nuclear applications are also playing a strong role in development. Nuclear and isotopic techniques are being used, inter alia: to diagnose and treat cancer patients; to study and improve child nutrition; to produce higher yielding, disease resistant crops; to manage drinking water supplies; to eradicate disease-bearing pests; to increase industrial productivity; and to help address many other development issues.

Effective and credible national and regional approaches to security are therefore essential — not only for nuclear power plants, but also for research reactors, accelerators, and the ubiquitous array of radioactive sources that support these nuclear applications. To optimize the effectiveness of these efforts, it will be important for efforts to be prioritized by focusing on those facilities where the risk is greatest — and to maintain a balance between security needs and the many peaceful applications of nuclear technology.

For example, the recent increase in the denial of shipments of radioactive material, while driven by perceived security issues, can be a matter of significant humanitarian concern — particularly when such shipments involve radionuclides intended for use in medical applications. While we should be strongly focused on ensuring the security of nuclear and other radioactive materials globally, we should equally seek solutions that will ensure the continued delivery of the benefits that these materials and related applications provide.

For nuclear installations such as nuclear power plants and fuel cycle facilities, it is also important to understand how safety and security aspects come together in the identification and protection of vulnerabilities. The IAEA has increasingly been asked to provide guidance on how to reconcile the need for transparency, in matters of nuclear and radiation safety, with the need for confidentiality, from a security perspective. Effective risk management requires striking a balance that protects the security of sensitive information while ensuring that safety concerns are addressed in a transparent manner, and that lessons learned, relating to both safety and security, are shared for the benefit of the entire nuclear community.

Focus of Future Efforts

Looking to the future, it is clear that the imperatives that first led to the development of the IAEA´s nuclear security plan have not diminished. We are now beginning a major review of our nuclear security activities. The main elements of a revised plan of activities are already emerging. One aspect of the new plan is to complete the international infrastructure of legal instruments, as well as relevant recommendations and guidelines.

One such legal instrument is the *Convention on Physical Protection of Nuclear Material (CPPNM)*. For a number of years, work has been progressing on a draft amendment to the CPPNM that would expand its scope and strengthen existing provisions. In July, at the request of the Government of Austria and 24 co-sponsoring States, I circulated proposed amendments to the *CPPNM* to all States Parties. The aim of these amendments, as proposed, is to extend the scope of the Convention to cover nuclear material used for peaceful purposes not only in international transport and storage, but also in domestic transport, storage and use, as well as the protection of nuclear material and facilities used for peaceful purposes from sabotage. While consultations are ongoing to resolve a few outstanding issues, it is my hope that we can convene a diplomatic conference early next year to amend the *Convention* and expand its scope.

A second aspect of the new plan will be to accelerate a shift in emphasis from evaluation to action. While we will continue to deliver advisory and needs assessment services, the work of the past three years have given us a much better understanding of Member State needs, and we will be working with States to give more emphasis to security upgrades and technical assistance.

A third point of focus will be to enhance the sustainability and self-reliance of nuclear security programmes in Member States. This will include helping States establish the needed regulatory frameworks, assisting in the implementation of international guidelines, and addressing continued training needs. For example, major security enhancements are expected as we assist States in implementing the revised Code of Conduct on source safety and security. More than 60 States have already begun working towards implementation of the Code. The Agency is also developing Integrated Nuclear Security Support Plans with individual Member States, as frameworks for helping to address their nuclear security needs over the longer term.

NUCLEAR WEAPONS AND NON-PROLIFERATION TREATY

The Treaty on the Non-Proliferation of Nuclear Weapons, commonly known as the Non-Proliferation Treaty or NPT, is a landmark international treaty whose objective is to prevent the spread of nuclear weapons and weapons technology, to promote cooperation in the peaceful uses of nuclear energy and to further the goal of achieving nuclear disarmament and general and complete disarmament. Opened for signature in 1968, the Treaty entered into force in 1970. On 11 May 1995, the Treaty was extended indefinitely. A total of 190 parties have joined the Treaty, including the five nuclear-weapon States: the United States, Russia, the United Kingdom, France, and China (also the five permanent members of the United Nations Security Council). More countries have ratified the NPT than any other arms limitation and disarmament agreement, a testament to the Treaty's significance. Four non-parties to the treaty are known or believed to possess nuclear weapons: India, Pakistan and North Korea have openly tested and declared that they possess nuclear weapons, while Israel has had a policy of opacity regarding its own nuclear weapons program. North Korea acceded to the treaty in 1985, but never came into compliance, and announced its withdrawal in 2003.

The NPT consists of a preamble and eleven articles. Although the concept of "pillars" is not expressed anywhere in the NPT, the treaty is nevertheless sometimes interpreted as a *three-pillar* system, with an implicit balance among them:

1. *non-proliferation*,
2. *disarmament*, and
3. *the right to peacefully use nuclear technology*.

The NPT is often seen to be based on a central bargain: "the NPT non-nuclear-weapon states agree never to acquire nuclear weapons and the NPT nuclear-weapon states in exchange agree to share the benefits of peaceful nuclear technology and to pursue nuclear disarmament aimed at the ultimate elimination of their nuclear arsenals". The treaty is reviewed every five years in meetings called Review Conferences of the Parties to the Treaty of Non-Proliferation of Nuclear Weapons. Even though the treaty was originally conceived with a limited duration of 25 years, the signing parties decided, by consensus, to extend the treaty indefinitely and without conditions during the Review Conference in New York City on May 11, 1995.

At the time the NPT was proposed, there were predictions of 25-30 nuclear weapon states within 20 years. Instead, over forty years later, only four states are not parties to the NPT, and they are the only additional states believed to possess nuclear weapons. Several additional measures have been adopted to strengthen the NPT and the broader nuclear nonproliferation regime and make it difficult for states to acquire the capability to produce nuclear weapons, including the export controls of the Nuclear Suppliers Group and the enhanced verification measures of the IAEA Additional Protocol. However, critics argue that the NPT cannot stop the proliferation of nuclear weapons or the motivation to acquire them. They express disappointment with the limited progress on nuclear disarmament, where the five authorized nuclear weapons states still have 22,000 warheads in their combined stockpile and have shown a reluctance to disarm further. Several high-ranking officials within the United Nations have said that they can do little to stop states using nuclear reactors to produce nuclear weapons.

Treaty "pillars"

The NPT is commonly described as having three main "pillars": non-proliferation, disarmament, and peaceful use. This "pillars" concept has been questioned by some who believe that the NPT is, as its name suggests, principally about nonproliferation, and who worry that "three pillars" language misleadingly implies that the three elements have equivalent importance.

First Pillar: Non-proliferation

Five states are recognized by the Non-Proliferation Treaty as nuclear weapon states (NWS): China (signed 1992), France (1992), the Soviet Union (1968; obligations and rights now assumed by the Russian Federation), the United Kingdom (1968), and the United States (1968) (The United States, UK, and the Soviet Union were the only states openly possessing such weapons among the original ratifiers of the treaty, which entered into force in 1970). These five nations are also the five permanent members of the United Nations Security Council. These five NWS agree not to transfer "nuclear weapons or other nuclear explosive devices" and "not in any way to assist, encourage, or induce" a non-nuclear weapon state (NNWS) to acquire nuclear weapons (Article I). NNWS parties to the NPT agree not to "receive," "manufacture" or "acquire" nuclear weapons or to "seek or receive any assistance in the manufacture of nuclear weapons" (Article II). NNWS parties also agree to accept safeguards by the International Atomic Energy Agency (IAEA) to verify that they are not diverting nuclear energy from peaceful uses to nuclear weapons or other nuclear explosive devices (Article III).

The five NWS parties have made undertakings not to use their nuclear weapons against a non-NWS party except in response to a nuclear attack, or a conventional attack in alliance with a Nuclear Weapons State. However, these undertakings have not been incorporated formally into the treaty, and the exact details have varied over time. The U.S. also had nuclear warheads targeted at North Korea, a non-NWS, from 1959 until 1991. The previous United Kingdom Secretary of State for Defence, Geoff Hoon, has also explicitly invoked the possibility of the use of the country's nuclear weapons in response to a non-conventional attack by "rogue states". In January 2006, President Jacques Chirac of France indicated that an incident of state-sponsored terrorism on France could trigger a small-scale nuclear retaliation aimed at destroying the "rogue state's" power centres.

Second Pillar: Disarmament

Article VI of the NPT represents the only binding commitment in a multilateral treaty to the goal of disarmament by the nuclear-weapon States. The NPT's preamble contains language affirming the desire of treaty signatories to ease international tension and strengthen international trust so as to create someday the conditions for a halt to the production of nuclear weapons, and treaty on general and complete disarmament that liquidates, in particular, nuclear weapons and their delivery vehicles from national arsenals.

The wording of the NPT's Article VI arguably imposes only a vague obligation on all NPT signatories to move in the general direction of nuclear and total disarmament, saying, "Each of the Parties to the Treaty undertakes to pursue negotiations in good faith on effective measures relating to cessation of the nuclear arms race at an early date and to nuclear disarmament, and on a treaty on general and complete disarmament." Under this interpretation, Article VI does not strictly require all signatories to actually conclude a disarmament treaty. Rather, it only requires them "to negotiate in good faith."

On the other hand, some governments, especially non-nuclear-weapon states belonging to the Non-Aligned Movement, have interpreted Article VI's language as being anything but vague. In their view, Article VI constitutes a formal and specific obligation on the NPT-recognized nuclear-weapon states to disarm themselves of nuclear weapons, and argue that these states have failed to meet their obligation. The International Court of Justice (ICJ), in its advisory opinion on the Legality of the Threat or Use of Nuclear Weapons, issued 8 July 1996, unanimously interprets the text of Article VI as implying that

"There exists an obligation to pursue in good faith and bring to a conclusion negotiations leading to nuclear disarmament in all its aspects under strict and effective international control." The ICJ opinion notes that this obligation involves all NPT parties (not just the nuclear weapon states) and does not suggest a specific time frame for nuclear disarmament. Critics of the NPT-recognized nuclear-weapon states sometimes argue that what they view as the failure of the NPT-recognized nuclear weapon states to disarm themselves of nuclear weapons, especially in the post–Cold War era, has angered some non-nuclear-weapon NPT signatories of the NPT. Such failure, these critics add, provides justification for the non-nuclear-weapon signatories to quit the NPT and develop their own nuclear arsenals.

Other observers have suggested that the linkage between proliferation and disarmament may also work the other way, i.e., that the failure to resolve proliferation threats in Iran and North Korea, for instance, will cripple the prospects for disarmament. No current nuclear weapons state, the argument goes, would seriously consider eliminating its last nuclear weapons without high confidence that other countries would not acquire them. Some observers have even suggested that the very progress of disarmament by the superpowers—which has led to the elimination of thousands of weapons and delivery systems —could eventually make the possession of nuclear weapons more attractive by increasing the perceived strategic value of a small arsenal. As one U.S. official and NPT expert warned in 2007, "logic suggests that as the number of nuclear weapons decreases, the 'marginal utility' of a nuclear weapon as an instrument of military power increases. At the extreme, which it is precisely disarmament's hope to create, the strategic utility of even one or two nuclear weapons would be huge."

Third Pillar: Peaceful use of Nuclear Energy

The third pillar allows for and agrees upon the transfer of nuclear technology and materials to NPT signatory countries for the development of civilian nuclear energy programs in those countries, as long as they can demonstrate that their nuclear programs are not being used for the development of nuclear weapons.

Since very few of the states with nuclear energy programs are willing to abandon the use of nuclear energy, the third pillar of the NPT under Article IV provides other states with the possibility to do the same, but under conditions intended to make it difficult to develop nuclear weapons.

The treaty recognizes the inalienable right of sovereign states to use nuclear energy for peaceful purposes, but restricts this right for NPT parties to be exercised "in conformity with Articles I and II" (the basic nonproliferation obligations that constitute the "first pillar" of the Treaty). As the commercially popular light water reactor nuclear power station uses enriched uranium fuel, it follows that states must be able either to enrich uranium or purchase it on an international market. Mohamed ElBaradei, then Director General of the International Atomic Energy Agency, has called the spread of enrichment and reprocessing capabilities the "Achilles' heel" of the nuclear nonproliferation regime.

As of 2007 13 states have an enrichment capability. Because the availability of fissile material has long been considered the principal obstacle to, and "pacing element" for, a country's nuclear weapons development effort, it was declared a major emphasis of U.S. policy in 2004 to prevent the further spread of uranium enrichment and plutonium reprocessing (a.k.a. "ENR") technology.

Countries that have signed the treaty as Non-Nuclear Weapons States and maintained that status have an unbroken record of not building nuclear weapons. However, Iraq was cited by the IAEA with punitive sanctions enacted against it by the UN Security Council for violating its NPT safeguards obligations; North Korea never came into compliance with its NPT safeguards agreement and was cited repeatedly for these violations, and later withdrew from the NPT and tested multiple nuclear devices; Iran was found in non-compliance with its

NPT safeguards obligations in an unusual non-consensus decision because it "failed in a number of instances over an extended period of time" to report aspects of its enrichment program; and Libya pursued a clandestine nuclear weapons program before abandoning it in December 2003. In 1991 Romania reported previously undeclared nuclear activities by the former regime and the IAEA reported this non-compliance to the Security Council for information only. In some regions, the fact that all neighbours are verifiably free of nuclear weapons reduces any pressure individual states might feel to build those weapons themselves, even if neighbours are known to have peaceful nuclear energy programs that might otherwise be suspicious. In this, the treaty works as designed.

BASIC EFFECTS OF NUCLEAR WEAPONS

Nuclear explosions produce both immediate and delayed destructive effects. Blast, thermal radiation, and prompt ionizing radiation cause significant destruction within seconds or minutes of a nuclear detonation. The delayed effects, such as radioactive fallout and other possible environmental effects, inflict damage over an extended period ranging from hours to years. Each of these effects are calculated from the point of detonation.

Ground Zero

The term "ground zero" refers to the point on the earth's surface immediately below (or above) the point of detonation. For a burst over (or under) water, the corresponding point is generally called "surface zero". The term "surface zero" or "surface ground zero" is also commonly used for ground surface and underground explosions. In some publications, ground (or surface) zero is called the "hypocenter" of the explosion.

Blast Effects

Most damage comes from the explosive blast. The shock wave of air radiates outward, producing sudden changes in air pressure that can crush objects, and high winds that can knock objects down. In general, large buildings are destroyed by the change in air pressure, while people and objects such as trees and utility poles are destroyed by the wind. The magnitude of the blast effect is related to the height of the burst above ground level.

For any given distance from the centre of the explosion, there is an optimum burst height that will produce the greatest change in air pressure, called overpressure, and the greater the distance the greater the optimum burst height. As a result, a burst on the surface produces the greatest overpressure at very close ranges, but less overpressure than an air burst at somewhat longer ranges.

When a nuclear weapon is detonated on or near Earth's surface, the blast digs out a large crater. Some of the material that used in be in the crater is deposited on the rim of the crater; the rest is carried up into the air and returns to Earth as radioactive fallout. An explosion that is farther above the Earth's surface than the radius of the fireball does not dig a crater and produces negligible immediate fallout. For the most part, a nuclear blast kills people by indirect means rather than by direct pressure.

Thermal Radiation Effects

Approximately 35 percent of the energy from a nuclear explosion is an intense burst of thermal radiation, i.e., heat. The effects are similar to the effect of a two-second flash from an enormous sunlamp. Since the thermal radiation travels at roughly the speed of light, the flash of light and heat precedes the blast wave by several seconds, just as lightning is seen before thunder is heard.

The visible light will produce "flashblindness" in people who are looking in the direction of the explosion. Flashblindness can last for several minutes, after which recovery is total. If the flash is focused through the lens of the eye, a permanent retinal burn will result. At Hiroshima and Nagasaki, there were many cases of flashblindness, but only one case of retinal burn, among the survivors. On the other hand, anyone flashblinded while driving a car could easily cause permanent injury to himself and to others.

Skin burns result from higher intensities of light, and therefore take place closer to the point of explosion. First-degree, second-degree and third-degree burns can occur at distances of five miles away from the blast or more.

Third-degree burns over 24 percent of the body, or second-degree burns over 30 percent of the body, will result in serious shock, and will probably prove fatal unless prompt, specialized medical care is available. The entire United States has facilities to treat 1,000 or 2,000 severe burn cases. A single nuclear weapon could produce more than 10,000.

The thermal radiation from a nuclear explosion can directly ignite kindling materials. In general, ignitable materials outside the house, such as leaves or newspapers, are not surrounded by enough combustible material to generate a self-sustaining fire. Fires more likely to spread are those caused by thermal radiation passing through windows to ignite beds and overstuffed furniture inside houses. Another possible source of fires, which might be more damaging in urban areas, is indirect. Blast damage to Stores, water heaters, furnaces, electrical circuits or gas lines would ignite fires where fuel is plentiful.

INDIA AND THE CTBT

The US stepped up its efforts to strike a deal with India beginning last June when Warren Christopher met with I.K.Gujral in the Far East and carried it through the UN General Assembly vote in September. Even after the vote, Bill Clinton hinted that negotiations were not over when he remarked cryptically that "we will work to find a way to address India's concerns."

In this regard, it is probably not a coincidence that in the thick of the CTBT negotiations between June - August 1996, the US suddenly shifted its position on Kashmir to a decidedly more "pro-India" stance and engineered some curious manoeuvres in the UN to reflect this. Many experts believe that the US had previously struck a similar "deal" with India in 1995 that kept India from lobbying world opinion against the NPT - which is far more naked in its aims and iniquities than the CTBT. India has carefully cultivated a policy of "nuclear ambiguity" over the past twenty years - a policy that would end if India were to comply with the CTBT and give up its nuclear option. India's aspirations are clear, and it is also clear that the objections India has raised are not really against the paradigm of big power domination, but at the fact that the CTBT will permanently freeze India out from fulfilling its aspirations to big power status and exerting such domination itself some day.

What made the situation acute was that while India could simply opt out of the NPT, the entry into force provisions of the CTBT required India's participation and signature as one of the 44 states with nuclear technology and as one of the three "threshold states".

Post-Cold War Geopolitics

The post-cold war period is frequently characterised as a unipolar world. Whereas the world was previously held hostage to the agendae and competing claims to domination of two rival superpowers, the end of the cold war did not end this notion of polarity. What changed was merely that one superpower (and perhaps only temporarily) left the scene, leaving the other with its supremacy unchallenged. The US continues to this day, to impose its political, economic and ideological domination over the world as do the other powers to a lesser extent. But as evidenced in the numerous conflicts that have erupted since the end of the cold war, this new paradigm is yet to find stability and has not ended the disequilibrium brought about at the end of the cold war.

The unipolar world, in its strict sense, enjoyed unchallenged supremacy only for a very brief period of time that extended roughly between the U.S. invasion of Panama in December 1989 to the end of the Gulf War in January 1991. What has been witnessed since the Gulf War, (and which has sharpened since then), is an increasing opposition to US hegemony worldwide. This is evidenced in the sharp opposition that Canada, Mexico or the EU have shown to its embargoes against

Cuba and Iran. These and numerous other such instances ranging from Bosnia to Zaire have demonstrated that the interests of France or even Britain are no longer synchronous with that of the US. Even sharper differences though, are emerging between the US and the likes of Russia, China and a number of other regional and extra-regional powers who are seriously dissatisfied with the direction of the unipolar world.

India figures very seriously within this list of regional powers and has long nursed ambitions to become an extra-regional power. India went through a massive wave of militarisation during the 1980's, placing emphasis not just on its traditionally large army, but on new naval bases, sophisticated submarines, a new Southern Air Command, and the development of short and medium-range missile systems capable of carrying nuclear warheads. India has already deployed its short-range (200 km) Prithvi missile with conventional loads and is reportedly finalising the development of a medium-range Agni missile that has a reach of 1,500 km.

But the most important ingredient of this, and key to the ambitions of India's ruling establishment, are India's neo-liberal economic policies that seem designed to ensure that India's business houses gets the access to capital, technology and infrastructure that they need to emerge with the economic clout that can support - and in turn benefit from the rise of India as a extra-regional power.

It was abundantly clear to the world at large that India's self-righteous position in Geneva did not emerge from a principled opposition to big- power politics - but rather from the simple fact that the CTBT draft threatened to interfere with the ambitions of India's ruling circles. Perhaps this helps to explain why India failed to rally almost any international support for its position in Geneva or New York.

At the same time, India's ruling circles have a long history of compromising and collaborating with the big powers in order to gain acceptance and join their ranks and indeed, India continues to negotiate for an amicable settlement with the US. One likely scenario that can unfold over the next three years is that India reaches agreement with the US and accedes to the CTBT in exchange for some technology favours similar to the agreement with China.

But regardless of whether the current text ever comes into force or not, the controversy it stirred internationally helped to expose some of its cleverly hidden subterfuge. Many well-intentioned advocates still support the CTBT as an incremental, though flawed step towards a "nuclear-free world". But if anything, the sheer brazenness and duplicity with which the NPT and CTBT were passed (for the price of a few tongue-in-cheek "commitments" to disarmament) can have only further emboldened the nuclear states and reinforced their belief that their global eminence exists by virtue of their ability to threaten everyone with nuclear annihilation. And in spite of Bill Clinton's assurances to the contrary, the world cannot possibly be a "safer place" if most of its peoples continue to live under the menace his "smart-nukes".

Ultimately, the CTBT itself is a reflection of the extremely unequal and undemocratic nature of international relations today - a situation that is even enshrined for example, in the membership of the Security Council. What the CTBT controversy that erupted last summer demonstrates is that fundamental changes to this situation will not arrive through the chance interventions of those who cry foul only when they feel they have been cheated of their fair share of the spoils.

7

The First Gulf War: Changing the Politics in Asia

OPERATION DESERT STORM AND THE POOL SYSTEM

Recommendations regarding incorporation of journalists into military operations were put into practice during Operations Desert Shield and Desert Storm. However, I believe that these "improvements" tied the media to the military even more. Though the military managed to remove some criticized aspects of the pool system (the media relations were included in the planning phase of operation, and members of the pools were to become the journalists already operating in Saudi Arabia), restrictions justified by security measures were still perceived as a strict censorship by the media.

Journalists had to agree to military guidelines in order to receive their credentials. The most criticized point was the obligation to stay with a military adviser at all times. So as long as the journalists were "guided" by the military escort, every interview with American soldiers and officials was under watch. Every report was then subject to security review. Only short before Operation Desert Storm, the Pentagon decided on access to the operation through the limited press pools. In addition, the pools were not to be disbanded as expected, considering the original principles of the pool system, but the pools were to be the only form of war coverage. Pool reporters were assigned to a particular unit, and what they reported on was determined by the military (DeParle). Among common practice regarding visiting the units was choosing reporters who "do not cause problems". Some words in reports could be replaced by more proper expressions, or the whole report was said to be a "breach of security" and thus not suitable for publishing. The so-called "Annex Foxtrot" represented a strategic document for dealing with the media with an aim to keep reporters from a front line action. And the military managed the media very successfully: no images of frontline combat exist. Military officials regarded the term "censorship" used by the media as overstated, but how would you call the situation when every move and every image and information to be transmitted is controlled by military officials?

The War in the Persian Gulf

When Iraq invaded Kuwait in August 1990, the whole world was shocked. Nobody believed that Saddam Hussein would be so daring to invade an independent state, actually, he was considered to be a mad man. American government and the media were making an effort to nourish this image every which way during the intervention in the Persian Gulf. The improved pool system was to be tested again in a much larger military operation.

Some speculations about the operation in Panama being nothing more than the preparing phase for the Gulf War also emerged (*Panama Deception*). What differed substantially was the background of these operations. While information about Operation Just Cause was withheld to the last moment, the beginning of Operation Desert Storm was awaited with restlessness. Moreover, the military intervention in Panama was labeled as very swift, surprising action; on the other hand, the involvement in the Persian Gulf had two phases, Operation Desert Shield (a defensive phase) and Operation Desert Storm (an offensive phase). Another and more important difference was the fact that the international community condemned unanimously the Panama invasion; on the contrary, Operation Desert Storm drew on the United Nations' resolution. Thus this intervention was more or less perceived to be just.

What did that mean for the media? Operations Desert Shield and Desert Storm received an international support from most of the countries, even Arab countries supported United Nations' position. Positive image of the war given by the media was expected. Before the offensive phase of the operation, the media was already prepared to cover the war. Journalists were "ready" to bring new information about what Saddam Hussein later called the "mother of all battles". And with a new technology the audience could hear and see what was actually going on in the Persian Gulf. With the live coverage they got their "slice of the action".

The Representation of the Gulf War

The Gulf War coverage was revolutionary considering the form of reporting. A new phenomenon, 24-hour war reporting by CNN, changed war reporting dramatically. But first the form of war coverage by other television stations should be described. Patriotic tone of the coverage was one part of "drama" television created. Statements such as "our brave sons" or "the clock ticks, the world waits" were given by an anchor once in a while. Most of the images of the war the public could see on the screen were the images of weaponry, tanks, fighters, rocket batteries firing on their targets, images of precise smart bombs hitting the target, and of course images of highly professional soldiers who operated the machinery. But the public could not see any pictures of direct combat. First because the initial phase of Operation Desert Storm was waged in the air, then during the ground war journalists were not allowed to cover front line combat. In the Gulf War the weapons were the heroes of the battle.

Actually, an anchor in the television studio was a face of the war. He distributed news to the public putting information from various sources together. Whether he was involved in a discussion with a war correspondent (Saudi Arabia, Jordan, and Israel) or with a military consultant, they appeared to be just a "club of talking heads" giving their assumptions "what would happen if". Though for example Dan Rather from CBS repeatedly stated that the first information was usually misleading, that "psychological games are under way", as well as the reports had been censored, no efforts of abandoning the official line were made. As a rule, television stations were cooperating with consultants, usually retired military officers, who gave their opinions on tactics and information about American weaponry in action. And again, the military point of view was presented to the public through them ("1991 Gulf War").

When the first pictures of the bombing of Baghdad were to be broadcasted on CBS, they were censored. Voice of a reporter commenting on the horrors of this war was replaced by the anchor's own interpretation. The public could not "see" the real image of war. Provided we accept the fact that the media broadcasted images showing military superiority of the United States without questioning the official line, we have to take into consideration the matter of media manipulation. I believe that regular and frequent briefings were one of the most effective tools for managing the media message. These official briefings were the only means of receiving any information about the course of the war as the journalists had no direct access to the battlefield. Here very positive and optimistic assessments of the war were presented together with clips of smart bombs. It is clear that the military wanted to offer the new image of war. War was depicted as clean, without death and blood, nothing else than technological mastery (*Enemy Image*). Some media experts called this form of presentation a "Nintendo style" (Franklin 42). Without negative emotions the war became a kind of "entertainment" people could not resist. And it could be said that a live coverage by CNN largely contributed to it.

By the live coverage the audience could see and hear "war in reality". Only CNN obtained technology to ensure continuous coverage of the operation. And it was a CNN reporter, Peter Arnett, who was permitted to stay in Baghdad when other reporters had to leave. He was the only journalist that reported on destruction of bombing in Baghdad. For his reports he was repeatedly blamed for biased coverage and called an Iraqi "sympathizer". And his reporting was not positively perceived by the public either.

Not only CNN, but also other television stations covering the war were criticized for being "stuck in the present". They were giving information about the actual conflict, its progress, tactics, and weaponry used, but not scrutinizing the military intervention in broader context. Neither historical and political background, nor American interests, except for liberation of Kuwait, were discussed (Thussu; Noorami; Petras). Little emphasis on casualties was also characteristic for maintaining the positive image of the war; almost no images of dead civilians in Baghdad were broadcasted. Especially alarming was the case of the "Highway of Death". American fighters attacked Iraqi troops withdrawing from Kuwait; more than sixty miles of road remained littered with smashed and crushed cars, buses, tanks, trucks and thousands of dead Iraqi soldiers. It was estimated that civilians (Iraqi and Palestinians) fleeing Kuwait were also among the casualties. The United States was charged with war crimes but this case was never addressed before the world tribunal (Chediac). And how did the media depict this massacre? Tanks were chosen for background emphasizing the retreat of Iraqi troops, civilian casualties were not mentioned at all and the interpretation of this slaughter was left on the military (*Enemy Image*).

Though day-and-night coverage, most of the pictures Americans could see were from the briefing rooms praising American soldiers and weapons. No documentation of direct combat existed, which was criticized not only considering media censorship but also from a historical point of view. This part of history was lost (*Reporting America at War*). It cannot be said that no efforts to abandon the official line of coverage was made regarding "pool" reporters and independent journalists in Baghdad. For instance, the CBS correspondent Bob Simon and his crew in Saudi Arabia left the pool and were then captured by Iraqi troops. Some reporters were also stripped of their credentials for violating military guidelines (such as talking to a soldier without a military escort). Similarly, reporters in

Baghdad were censored as well by Iraqi military and more importantly, by their home stations. John Alpert, the NBC correspondent in Baghdad, gained pictures of collateral damage after intensive bombing, images of casualties and destruction American people did not see on television. After returning to the United States, he brought these pictures to NBC to be broadcasted, and he was dismissed. After offering this reportage to an ABC executive producer, these pictures were to be shown in the evening news the next day. But this did not happen, and the ABC executive producer was, what a surprise, dismissed (*Enemy Image*). This kind of "home" censorship is alarming considering the principle of independence and it clearly shows that political and commercial pressures count in the time of war intervention. For the Gulf War in particular, the censorship could be also explained by avoiding any possible resemblance to the Vietnam War. Blood and destruction are part of any war but an important goal is to suppress all that and create a reasonable image of war. The Vietnam syndrome was finally "kicked", with a substantial media contribution.

Stereotypes in the Gulf War Reporting

After the end of the first Gulf War, many military officials praised the media for their best war reporting ever. This coverage was considered to be in-depth and sufficient even by the public. The form in which the war in the Persian Gulf was presented corresponded with the official governmental policy in this region. And the Gulf War was exactly the type of military involvement that would put the Vietnam behind and American president George H. W. Bush knew this. Before the war started (the offensive phase), neither the public nor power elites were united over this issue, a fear of the Gulf War becoming a quagmire as Vietnam was omnipresent. Therefore, it was repeatedly emphasized that the United States could not be defeated this time. As President Bush expressed before the Gulf War, "Let me assure you, should military action be required, this will not be another Vietnam" (Harlow 68), and above all, with such "precise" weaponry the United States and its allies possessed it could not be. This military intervention was also perceived as an endeavor to renew American identity so much "wounded" in the Vietnam War (American identity meaning national unity, order, prestige for the United States as a world power). And George Bush confirmed that after the War ended, "By God, we've kicked the Vietnam syndrome once and for all!" (Solomon, "Beyond the 'Vietnam'").

The positive image of the Gulf War presented through the media was of great importance and therefore all the guidelines and restrictions were targeted at managing the media message "on no account will we lose". So what kind of information and image did the public receive? As reporters had no other option to cover the war, they had to agree to military guidelines to be accredited. Thus, most of the information broadcasted was obtained from official sources, or in other words, the military and the government. However, military restrictions and the use of official sources are not an excuse for not reporting critical approaches to governmental actions. Patriotism so much emphasized by the government dominated the media coverage of the Gulf War as well. As the journalist Marvin Kalb evaluated this situation, "Patriotism...robbed U.S. reporters of their most important function...the ability to think critically, act in a detached manner, ask questions, remain unemotional, and resist...the strong temptation during war to cheer for the American side and denounce the enemy" (4).

The line between good and evil was clear cut, Americans as "bearers of liberation", Saddam Hussein as "the demon of enslavement". The Gulf War brought an opportunity to retrieve once for all basic principles of American society, no wonder that the media accepted. The Gulf War was presented as "our" war in which patriotic themes were very often emphasized. The audience could see reports about soldiers' families as well as pictures of soldiers reading their "last mail before the war". I believe this patriotic flag-waving was more apparent on the side of home broadcast studios than the "work" of foreign correspondents.

In addition, depiction of George Bush and Saddam Hussein could be also regarded as very stereotypical. The American president was portrayed as a leader of united community striving for democratic and moral values. In his presidential address, after the beginning of Operation Desert Storm, he emphasizes national unity and liberty, and praises American soldiers, "Sons and daughters...they are the Nation's finest...magnificently trained, highly motivated. The troops know why they're there. And listen to what they say...'Let's free these people, so we can go home and be free again'" (Bush, "Address to the Nation"). It seemed to be just a kind of playing on sentiments; his tone of voice could be compared to "a grandfather is telling a fairy tale". This direct access to the public was aimed to maintain public support for the war. I believe that "there wasn't a dry eye in the house". On the other hand, in accordance with "good and evil rhetoric", Saddam Hussein was portrayed as pure evil, the "new Hitler". This human interest story helped to promote a positive assessment of American intervention, all blame was directed to Saddam Hussein, and as a consequence, potential civilian casualties were presented as "inevitable". He had to be stopped by all means, the media not excepting.

It could be said that the reporting of the Gulf War was highly influenced by an ideology that stemmed from American foreign policy redefined after the Cold War period – the liberation of oppressed nation, protection from the aggressor, and restoration of democracy. But the Gulf War was more than that; by this military intervention the United States reinforced its position in the world by putting Vietnam behind. By stressing the message that "it must work this time", American government took all pains to ensure the victory, and media depiction of the war represented one part of this endeavor.

Dominating patriotic tone of war coverage corresponds with war reporting of Panama invasion in 1989. However, the image of war was different. Though images of brave "sons and daughters of America" appeared very often and pictures of casualties and destruction were sanitized, the main emphasis was put on technological superiority of the United States. The military created a new surgical image of war without blood. With a "dramatic envelope" the media gave to the Gulf War,

war became an entertainment. Live coverage offered the public an opportunity to be right in the action. Though no images of front line combat and only a few pictures of collateral damage exist, the war was perceived by the public as thoroughly covered. Restrictions applied by the military helped to reinforce the positive image of war, these restrictions were seen as a stringent censorship by the media, and actually, the military could very successfully suppress any negative or critical message. The Gulf War was often contrasted to the Vietnam War and its coverage without official censorship. I think that the great difference is not only in censoring critical reports by the military, but also by the owners and top representatives of home broadcasting companies. The media cannot fully exercise their watchdog role because it has become part of the great business of politics.

THE WAR IN IRAQ: WAR AS A VISUAL SPECTACLE

The "Preemptive" Strike

The first thing that enters everybody's mind when "the war in Iraq" is mentioned is the word "controversial". The so-called preemptive strike against Iraq considering justifications and legitimacy of the conflict, American interests, governmental propaganda, censorship and particularly the role of the media in this process of information management became subject to debate especially after the official military intervention ended. All studies dealing with this issue arrived at more or less the same conclusions: Bush administration and the Pentagon succeeded in managing the media message in order to gain and maintain public support by techniques of information management, in which the media played a key role, but not the role of a watchdog.

The Iraq War started in a different context regarding its political background compared with previous military involvements discussed in the thesis. Debates over Iraq being a threat to American national security emerged in the aftermath of the September 11 attacks, thus in the atmosphere of fear of subsequent terrorist attacks. After 9/11 the American

Congress approved the Patriot Act redefining security laws and establishing new tools in the war on terrorism (expanded surveillance, improved intelligence, or new investigation capabilities). American foreign policy was also revised into a new form involving information gathering and preemptive military action. According to the new foreign policy, in his presidential address in January 2002 George W. Bush assessed the threat of terrorism in a much broader context naming the North Korea, Iran, and Iraq the "Axis of Evil" (Bush, "State of the Union Address"). And during the subsequent months Bush administration intensified the campaign against Iraq being imminent danger to the United States.

First argument for American intervention was presented by Bush administration in the shape of link between al Qaeda and Saddam Hussein. An assertion that Saddam Hussein participated in the 9/11 terrorist attacks would make this preemptive strike acceptable in the eyes of the public. However, public polls showed that while the War in Afghanistan was perceived as a legitimate action, a substantial number of Americans opposed the Iraq War. This had to be supported by something more convincing. Claims about Iraq possessing weapons of mass destruction appeared to be suitable supplement to justify and gain a Congress approval for American intervention in Iraq. But as it was revealed later, none of these "reasons" for the war were based on truth. In addition, the war in Iraq cannot be seen as a legitimate intervention considering international support, as it did not receive the United Nations approval.

In fact, the United States did not demand a vote on the war with Iraq as the opposition in the international community was apparent. In accordance with a new National Security Strategy, the focus of the United States would be "those terrorist organizations of global reach and *any terrorist or state sponsor of terrorism which attempts to gain or use weapons of mass destruction* [emphasis mine]". As the United States declared themselves a guardian of freedom and campaigner against the spread of communism in the Cold War period, they adopted the same position but with a different enemy – global terrorism. International approval was not needed; the right was on American side, at least from a governmental point of view. However, it was needed to "sell the war" to the domestic as well as international public, and here the assistance of the media appeared to be crucial.

It could be stated that information management was concentrated into two directions: home front and the theater of war. The pool system used in the Gulf War for war coverage and praised by the military but criticized by the media was replaced by the embedding system. Reporters gained access to the battlefield and the military to an effective tool in media relations strategy. The second and I believe more influential aspect during managing the media message was external and internal pressures: political pressures as well as media policy to make a profit. As far as this issue is concerned, the government maintained conditions for successful information management from the start of the anti-Iraq campaign through the whole war in Iraq without substantial media "interference" in the form of authority actions scrutiny.

Journalists Embedded

From the first Gulf War in 1991 ten years passed until another major military involvement began. The fact that no images of the Gulf War battlefield existed and remaining criticism from the media about limited access to the front lines as well as censorship led to another revision of media-military relations throughout subsequent years. Though the embedding system maintained much of the pool system, it was "revolutionary". For the first time since the Vietnam War reporters had gained access to front line soldiers and combat, but conditions were considerably different.

Operation Iraqi Freedom started on March 20, 2003, with more than seven hundred embedded reporters. By embedding the reporter became part of a unit. They were not allocated individually but according to places assigned to news organizations. This tool enabled the military to control the media even more, because for the freelancers it became very complicated to gain accreditation; simultaneously, the news organization became more responsible for reporter's misbehavior. Journalists had to sign a document dealing with military guidelines (what to report or not to report on, security review, military escorts). Another important difference was durability of "being embedded". While the press pools were to function for a limited period of time according to original pool system policy, an embedded journalist was a permanent part of a unit. Of course, journalists could leave the unit, but after abandoning the embedded status, they were banned to continue in war coverage in that area. Becoming a unilateral and then potentially joining another unit was not possible.

Moreover, the reporter was much more integrated into the assigned unit. Embedded reporters had to attend an "Embed Boot Camp" before war, where they were trained in military jargon, tactics in the case of direct fire, biological and chemical attacks, or combat first aid. With the same equipment as soldiers had they were almost unrecognizable. By signing a contract the reporter became part of a command structure and thus dependent on military orders. The key phrase for embedded reporters regarding files approval was the "level above us" (Miller 12).

The last aspect of the embedding process, but with possibly controversial consequences, is the notion of identification with soldiers. Ronald Paul Larson, an embedded reporter, saw this process of socialization and identification as a potential threat to journalistic objectivity. When a reporter participates in war dangers with soldiers for a longer time period, he becomes part of a social structure called a military unit. This process is usually compared to the so-called Stockholm syndrome, according to which reporters integrated into the military identify with it and therefore report from the military point of view. Andrew M. Lindner explains this subject matter by arguing that the military not only influences individual activities, but also forms personal identities. Individualism is suppressed in order to achieve higher values of the community, in this case, the military. He suggests that the process of embedding "encourages journalists to adopt a positive outlook on both the soldiers with whom they live and the military mission as whole". Under such conditions (restrictions, integration into the military, identification, and constant control) it is very problematic to fulfill professional standards of objective reporting, and as it seems, the military proved to be a successful media organizer.

Some alternatives to the embedding system existed; however, when we consider the number of reporters, the embedded journalists dominated the screen. The first option for the news organizations was to station its correspondents into Baghdad. Another alternative represents the most demanding form of war coverage concerning conditions for reporting. Independent reporters called unilaterals or "cowboy" journalists are expected to "cruise" the battlefield without military restrictions, but the experience of independent reporters in Iraq revealed that this was not true. In Iraq, the American military controlled borders and checkpoints as well as military bases causing difficulties for unilaterals to gain any information about the conflict. Geoffrey York commented on this situation, "Unilateral is the Pentagon's bureaucratic term for the distrusted rabble of independent minded journalists in Kuwait...We are outsiders, powerless and marginal, lacking any propaganda value in Washington's media strategy". In addition, the military could not guarantee security to them. Security of journalists during the war in Iraq is connected to another issue. Since the number of reporters being killed during previous military conflicts had increased substantially, security of reporters and especially how the "enemy" perceives them became subject to debate. It was clear that the journalist became a target in war.

How to Sell the War in Iraq

We have already introduced two arguments of Bush administration used for justification of the war in Iraq, the link of Saddam Hussein to events of 9/11 and possession of weapons of mass destruction. Now we would like to deal with the role of the media during the campaign against Iraq. Governmental public affairs strategy focused on constantly making connections between Saddam Hussein and al Qaeda by leading figures of Bush administration (President George W. Bush, Vice President Dick Cheney, or James Woolsey, former director of the CIA). For example, Collin Powell, former Secretary of the State, stated in his speech to the United Nations in February 2003: "Iraqi denials of supporting terrorism take place alongside the other Iraqi denials of weapons of mass destruction. It is all a web of lies" ("Transcript"). In addition, certain kind of sensationalism was used as well. In presidential address about the initiation of offensive strike against Iraq George W. Bush speaks about weapons of mass "murder" ("Bush Announces"). Deepa Kumar sees information strategies of establishing "guilt through suggestion and speculation" as crucial in gaining public support for war. Repetitions of this connection as well as hypothetical scenarios "what would happen if" resulted in relatively high public support of preemptive strike against Iraq. Repeated falsehoods finally became the truth in the eyes of the public. According to public polls conducted in March 2003, 72% of respondents considered the use of military force in Iraq to be the right decision ("Public Attitudes").

And how did the media report on the eventuality of the American military action in Iraq? They simply accepted the governmental line and became part of official "propaganda". However, the media should not be "damned" so easily. There were many factors that resulted in this position of "mouthpiece" of the government. First of all, reporting of official statements represents an inherent part of a journalist's job, particularly regarding the issue of national security. The officials retain certain credibility stemming from their position of authority, so a mediation of official information to the public is nothing to be criticized. However, the media has the obligation to scrutinize such arguments considering their accuracy especially in the time of potential war. And this did not happen. Actually, the media did not react even when it was revealed that justifications used for the war in Iraq were just speculations and falsehoods.

Also, Bush administration was considered to be the least friendly to the media. According to David Dadge, the government denied a check and balance function of the media and viewed them as a special interest group with a role of furthering its commercial interests and profits. By denial of the function of the Fourth Estate, the media was shifted into a new position where their oppositional reactions could be marginalized. Here the main aim of the government appeared to be getting the message to the public without the media representing an obstacle in this effort. As for information provided by Bush administration, off-the-record briefings belonged to main communication strategies. This enabled the officials to be quoted while staying in anonymity. Nevertheless, the level of credibility was low. Thus repeatedly emphasizing certain points (al Qaeda, weapons of mass destruction, national security, or terrorism), off-the-record briefings and the assigned role of a mouthpiece created conditions under which the watchdog role appeared to be difficult to perform. This position was also reinforced by other pressures.

Again, "old good patriotism" played an essential role in the period before and during the war in Iraq. Dan Rather, former anchor for the *CBS Evening News*, expressed it in this way: "George Bush is the president, he makes the decisions, and, you know, as just one American, wherever he wants me to line up, just tell me where" ("Context of September"). "Flag waving" was typical for the period after the 9/11 attacks and George Bush fully took advantage of it in a buildup of the Iraq War. Opposition against this military intervention was much higher than in the case of the War in Afghanistan (supported by 94% of the public), but whether there was substantial opposition or not, it was perceived as unpatriotic by the government and more importantly, by the majority of Americans. George Bush's rhetoric "either you are with us, or you are with the terrorists" not only referred to other democratic states, but also to the public and of course, the media. This anti-terrorist rhetoric was nourished in the period before the war in Iraq. Therefore, oppositional opinions were usually marginalized or ignored in the media. Questioning of critics' patriotism by the officials became another tool for suppressing oppositional voices. This strong message from the government and the public affected the form of war coverage. The parade of pro-war guests and military experts as in the Gulf War in 1991, together with marginalization of the opposition, shaped the image of the whole conflict. According to the study conducted by a watchdog organization, the Fairness and Accuracy Reporting (FAIR), 76% of all sources used by the mainstream news broadcasters were either current or former officials and only 2% of all sources were opponents or expressed skepticism (*ABC World News Tonight*, *CBS Evening News*, *NBC Nightly News* and the *PBS NewsHour* with Jim Lehrer) ("In Iraq Crisis").

Additionally, journalists who did not correspond to this line were usually disciplined. Peter Arnett, an NBC correspondent in Baghdad during the war, was dismissed for his interview for Iraqi television stating "the first war plan has failed for Iraqi resistance" (Rutenberg). On the home front, Phil Donahue's show was cancelled for presenting antiwar guests criticizing Bush administration. The message was clear: censor yourself or you will be punished.

Moreover, commercial interests belonged to more decisive factors. This media policy was much more emphasized in the campaign against Iraq in comparison with the Gulf War spectacle in 1991. If critical voices are given the space to be broadcasted, it could have an impact on the audience. Thus, when the majority of the public supported the war in Iraq, this represented a threat of outflow of the viewers. As an example FOX News Channel could be stated, the most popular cable channel during the war in Iraq. Not only did they openly criticize opposition to the war, and thus reflected the mood of the public, but their policy was focused on a shift to more popular and entertaining image of news. The strategy aimed at maximizing profits. And the same policy was more or less adopted by all television networks. Furthermore, some critics argue that the FOX channel became one of the tools for governmental propaganda helping to publicly legitimize the war in Iraq. According to this argument, rise in politicization of the facts led to more partisan coverage of the conflict. In particular, FOX News Channel is characterized as a conservative network not only passing official line, but also reinforcing it.

It is clear that an atmosphere of war on terrorism, increasing politicization of the facts, and continuous shift in media policy towards entertainment, commerce and profits created such conditions for the media under which the watchdog role was almost impossible to exercise. But this timid and "lax" approach to such an important issue as the national involvement in a military conflict resulted in the loss of credibility not only of the government, but also of the Fourth Estate, the media.

War as a Spectacle

From the very beginning of the Iraq War it was apparent that the image of the war presented by the American media highly contradicted to war coverage in the European and more contrastingly, Arab media. The war in Iraq was covered by more than twenty broadcasting networks. The form of war coverage and language used for reporting showed that the media was not only engaged in the conflict physically, but that the war was waged semantically, on the screen. While American television networks used such titles as "Operation Iraqi Freedom" (FOX News Channel), "Showdown: Iraq" (CNN), or "America at War" (CBS), the Arab media was referring to the conflict as the "Invasion of Iraq". According to them, the whole war was just an imperialistic intervention without legitimate justification. So it was like following two different wars. American television news channels presented the war as a triumph of American power, freedom, and democracy. Neither historical nor political context was presented. Images of professional soldiers and precise machinery corresponded to the fact that most of the western media journalists were embedded within the troops. The story of war was again told by the soldiers, for the first time since the Vietnam War. In Iraq, the reporters gained again a central role of "being in action", however, better technology, 24-hour live coverage and military restrictions shifted the position of the reporter to being more an "explainer" of what was happening in Iraq. Today embedded reporters lack the professional and time distance that journalists had available in the Vietnam War.

Live coverage directly from the battlefield really brought the war into the living rooms. While the first Gulf War was live but without images from the front lines, in the war in Iraq the audience could see any image conceivable: 20,000 hours of video were shot by television cameras. Nevertheless, most of the reporters did see some "action", but they reported usually on what was happening on the sending but not on the receiving side (*Enemy Image*). According to media analysts, social localities could have influenced reporters' ability to offer balanced picture of the war. The embedded journalists tended to present the war from a military point of view with technical and tactical issues using Iraqi sources minimally; on the other hand, correspondents in Baghdad focused more on the consequences of American intervention, damage and casualties. Independent reporters appeared to be most objective in covering the war regarding the sources and issues covered. As the majority of reporters covering the war were embedded within the troops, dominance of this form of reporting was omnipresent.

Particularly interesting is the difference in coverage of war casualties. As in the first Gulf War, civilian casualties were sanitized in order to create an image of bloodless war. Similarly, when reporting on American casualties, broadcasters did not show any picture of dead soldiers, but the audience could see just a number and the American flag in the background. On the contrary, Arab networks focused primarily on depiction of Iraqi casualties. When these pictures appeared, they could not be simply ignored by American media, so they were either reframed without the sound or put in question: "They look to be civilians but they may have been soldiers." The dead became just anonymous bodies (*Enemy Image*). Considering the form of coverage, it is apparent that the same strategies of propaganda were used by both American and Arab media, but in an effort to reinforce different points of view.

This strategy of creating the positive image of war, together with governmental propaganda, further focused on "what would people remember" from the Iraq War. This war spectacle and drama had to be reinforced by memorable moments. And here two controversial events occur: the toppling of Saddam Hussein's statue and "Saving Private Lynch". Destruction of Saddam Hussein's statue represented a perfect symbol of the fall of Iraq regime. What the audience could see when this event was depicted by television cameras was a spontaneous crowd of Iraqi people trying and finally succeeding in destruction of the symbol of hated dictator. Closer examination showed that the whole action was not so "spontaneous". After entering an empty square, American soldiers used loudspeakers to attract journalists and civilians. It is known that psychological units belong to the American army. And the toppling of Saddam Hussein's statue offered a chance that could not be missed. In addition, the people in the crowd were mostly journalists or soldiers, and those Iraqis actually destroying the statue were later claimed to be members of the Iraqi National Congress supported by the United States.

"Saving Private Lynch" drama was another example of information strategy used by the government. This typical human-interest story constituted a confirmation for the public that the American efforts in Iraq were not senseless, that "our boys and girls" were doing the right thing. Jessica Lynch became a national hero overnight. According to the official version, she was shot and captured, and then tortured by Iraqi soldiers. Several days later she was rescued by Special Forces from the hospital where she was kept. Surprisingly, television cameras were present. It was interesting that at the press conference, when the reporter asked about Jessica's capture, the military spokesperson announced her rescue and played the tape already prepared. As it was revealed later, Jessica was not injured during the gunfire and so dramatic rescue was not necessary because Iraqi troops had left the hospital two days before. After the release of this information, the military announced that Jessica suffered from amnesia. Thus it is evident that the

Pentagon scripted and directed the story for television audience. The fact that the whole story was artificially made was not important: America had its national hero. Broadcast networks competed in gaining an exclusive interview with Jessica, the NBC network shot a television film called "Saving Private Lynch", and a book about her bravery was published as well. Though the story was not true, the myth of heroism could not be suppressed, the bravery of American soldiers was finally personified. Not only the government, the Pentagon and the media strived to reinforce the image of real events in accordance with the official policy, but they also "constructed" stories in order to encourage positive perception of the war both nationally and internationally. Information management reached a new dimension of manipulation of the public.

And it is hardly surprising that a substantial part of American public turned to foreign sources of information (mostly British media). Media coverage of the war was not perceived to be objective and unbiased. A growing mistrust to the mainstream media was the result of the media approach to the whole conflict: governmental motives were not questioned, when converse information proved to be true, broadcasting networks did not refer to previous governmental actions, opposition was marginalized, particular images and sources omitted (casualties, collateral damage), images and stories manipulated. The media created a new image of war: war as a spectacle and virtual reality.

The Iraq War and the role of the media before and during this military intervention raised questions about the ability of the media to perform its role as the Fourth Estate. While such doubts were expressed after each major military conflict in which the United States was involved, the "behaviour" of the media and the form of war coverage before and during the war in Iraq appeared to be the greatest media manipulation ever. Justifications for the decision to intervene in Iraq were not subject to media scrutiny even after they were proved to be falsehoods. The media simply accepted everything what the government said or did. And with so much ease the media provided to Bush administration it was undemanding to convince the American public.

Information management used by the government and the Pentagon could be characterized by "propaganda" strategy. Embedded reporters were encouraged to present the image desirable for transmission: clean, technical and tactical actions, bloodless war with professional soldiers. The public could see war from the soldier's point of view. It was an image of video game. In fact, soldiers are now trained on virtual video games, and precisely these images the public has seen from Iraq – fast, professional, and controllable war (*Enemy Image*). By drawing on post-9/11 moods, together with emphasis on patriotism, Bush administration managed to maintain high public support for the war; oppositional voices were regarded as unpatriotic both by the government and the public. Commercial interests played a crucial role in the whole presentation of the war in the media as well. As the media policy has been shifted to commerce and profits, objective journalism and the watchdog role of the media has been marginalized. It cannot be claimed that independent journalism always occupied the primary position in war reporting (in my opinion it never did), but the Iraq War reporting represents the most serious fail of the role of the media as a watchdog. The media lost its credibility and what remained? Do not believe everything you see on the screen, it is just one version of reality.

8

China's Tibet Policy and India: Changing Scenario

CHINESE INVASION AND DOMINANCE

In 1949 the People's Republic of China began invading, occupying, and colonizing Tibet. China entered into Tibet immediately after the communist victory over the Chinese Nationalists, imposed a treaty of "liberation" on the Tibetans, militarily occupied Tibet's territory, and divided that territory into twelve administrative units. It forcibly repressed Tibetan resistance between 1956 and 1959 and annexed Tibet in 1965. Since then it has engaged in massive colonization of all parts of Tibet. For its part, China claims that Tibet has always been a part of China, that a Tibetan person is a type of Chinese person, and that, therefore, all of the above is an internal affair of the Chinese people. The Chinese government has thus sought to overcome the geographical difference with industrial technology, erase and rewrite Tibet's history, destroy Tibet's language, suppress the culture, eradicate the religion (a priority of communist ideology in general), and replace the Tibetan people with Chinese people.

In China itself, communist leader Mao Zedong's policies caused the death of as many as 60 million Chinese people by war, famine, class struggle, and forced labour in thought-reform labour camps. As many as 1.2 million deaths in Tibet resulted from the same policies, as well as lethal agricultural mismanagement, collectivization, class struggle, cultural destruction, and forced sterilization. However, in the case of Tibet, the special long-term imperative of attempting to remove evidence against and provide justification for the Chinese claim of long-term ownership of the land, its resources, and its people gave these policies an additional edge.

The process of the Chinese takeover since 1949 unfolded in several stages. The first phase of invasion by military force, from 1949 to 1951, led to the imposition of a seventeen-point agreement for the liberation of Tibet and the military takeover of Lhasa. Second, the Chinese military rulers pretended to show support for the existing "local" Tibetan government and culture, from 1951 through 1959, but with gradual infiltration of greater numbers of troops and communist cadres into Tibet. A third phase from 1959 involved violent suppression of government and culture, mass arrests, and formation of a vast network of labour camps, with outright annexation of the whole country from 1959 through 1966. Fourth, violent cultural revolution, from 1966 through 1976, destroyed the remaining monasteries and monuments, killed those resisting the destruction of the "four olds," and sought to eradicate all traces of Tibetan Buddhist culture. A fifth phase of temporary liberalization under Hu Yao Bang was quickly reversed by Chinese leader Deng Xiaoping and led to a mass influx of settlers beginning in the early 1980s. Martial law and renewed suppression took place between 1987 and 1993, with intensified population transfer of Chinese settlers. Finally, from 1993, direct orders of the aging Chinese leadership placed Tibet under the control of an aggressive administrator named Chen Kuei Yuan. Chen proclaimed that the Tibetan identity had to be eradicated in order for remaining Tibetans to develop a Chinese identity. Since Tibetan identity was tied up with Tibetan Buddhism, Tibetan Buddhist culture was in itself seditious, or "splittist," as the Chinese call it.

Chen also was able to use China's growing economic power to invest heavily in internal projects in Tibet, bring in millions more colonists, and he extracted unprecedented amounts of timber, herbs, and minerals from the land. He also toughened up the policies of the People's Liberation Army and the Public Security Bureau.

In 1960 the nongovernmental International Commission of Jurists (ICJ) gave a report titled *Tibet and the Chinese People's Republic* to the United Nations. The report was prepared by the ICJ's Legal Inquiry Committee, composed of eleven international lawyers from around the world. This report accused the Chinese of the crime of genocide in Tibet, after nine years of full occupation, six years before the devastation of the cultural revolution began. The Commission was careful to state that the "genocide" was directed against the Tibetans as a religious group, rather than a racial, "ethnical," or national group.

The report's conclusions reflect the uncertainty felt at that time about Tibetans being a distinct race, ethnicity, or nation. The Commission did state that it considered Tibet a de facto independent state at least from 1913 until 1950. However, the Chinese themselves perceive the Tibetans in terms of race, ethnicity, and even nation. In the Chinese constitution, "national minorities" have certain protections on paper, and smaller minorities living in areas where ethnic Chinese constitute the vast majority of the population receive some of these protections.

In the 2000s, many view the Chinese genocide in Tibet as the result of the territorial ambitions of the PRC leadership. It is seen as stemming from their systematic attempt to expand the traditional territory of China by annexing permanently the vast, approximately 900,000-square-mile territory of traditional Tibet. Tibet represents about 30 percent of China's land surface, while the Tibetans represent.004 percent of China's population. Tibetans were not a minority but an absolute majority in their own historical environment. Chinese government efforts can be seen as aiming at securing permanent control of the Tibetans' land. For this reason, some observers see genocide in Tibet as not merely referring to the matter of religion, that is, of destroying Tibetan Buddhism. Chinese policies have involved the extermination of more than 1 million Tibetans, the forced relocation of millions of Tibetan villagers and nomads, the population transfer of millions of Chinese settlers, and systematic assimilation.

RULE OF THE CHINESE COMMUNIST GOVERNMENT

The Chinese government claims for this time period are a matter of some controversy. For instance they claim to have "liberated the Tibetan serfs" but many Tibetans were nomads or owned their own land rent free, and for those who were under obligations, there is controversy about whether their status is similar to the European serf and how onerous the obligations were.

Also the system based on recognition of "reincarnated Lamas" meant that any children from any family (though mostly males) might become recognised as the religious and political leaders of the next generation. This unusual system of government has no analogy in the European system. There are other differences as well. Also starvation was common in China at the time, but was not common in Tibet. There are widely varying accounts of the effect of the takeover on welfare of Tibetans. See Serfdom in Tibet Controversy-Slavery, and Tibetan welfare after the Chinese takeover

In 1949, seeing that the Communists were gaining control of China, the Kashag expelled all Chinese connected with the Chinese government, over the protests of both the Kuomingtang and the Communists. The Chinese Communist government led by Mao Zedong which came to power in October lost little time in asserting a new Chinese presence in Tibet. In October 1950, the People's Liberation Army entered the Tibetan area of Chamdo, defeating sporadic resistance from the Tibetan army. In 1951, Tibetan representatives participated in negotiations in Beijing with the Chinese government. This resulted in a *Seventeen Point Agreement* which formalised China's sovereignty over Tibet.

From the beginning, it was obvious that incorporating Tibet into Communist China would bring two opposite social systems face-to-face. In Tibet, however, the Chinese Communists opted not to place social reform as an immediate priority. To the contrary, from 1951 to 1959, traditional Tibetan society with its lords and manorial estates continued to function unchanged. Despite the presence of twenty thousand PLA troops in Central Tibet, the Dalai Lama's government was permitted to maintain important symbols from its de facto independence period.

The Chinese quickly abolished slavery and serfdom in their traditional forms. They also claim to have reduced taxes, unemployment, and beggary, and to have started work projects. They established secular schools, thereby breaking the educational monopoly of the monasteries, and they constructed running water and electrical systems in Lhasa.

The Tibetan region of Eastern Kham, previously Xikang province, was incorporated in the province of Sichuan. Western Kham was put under the Chamdo Military Committee. In these areas, land reform was implemented. This involved communist agitators designating "landlords" — sometimes arbitrarily chosen — for public humiliation in *thamzing* or "Struggle Sessions," torture, maiming, and even death.

By 1956 there was unrest in eastern Kham and Amdo, where land reform had been implemented in full. These rebellions eventually spread into western Kham and Ü-Tsang.

In 1956-57, armed Tibetan bands ambushed convoys of the Chinese Peoples Liberation Army. The uprising received extensive assistance from the U.S. Central Intelligence Agency (CIA), including military training, support camps in Nepal, and numerous airlifts. Meanwhile in the United States, the American Society for a Free Asia, a CIA-financed front, energetically publicized the cause of Tibetan resistance, with the Dalai Lama's eldest brother, Thubtan Norbu, playing an active role in that organization. The Dalai Lama's second-eldest brother, Gyalo Thondup, established an intelligence operation with the CIA as early as 1951. He later upgraded it into a CIA-trained guerrilla unit whose recruits parachuted back into Tibet.

Many Tibetan commandos and agents whom the CIA dropped into the country were chiefs of aristocratic clans or the sons of chiefs. Ninety percent of them were never heard from again, according to a report from the CIA itself, meaning they were most likely captured and killed. "Many lamas and lay members of the elite and much of the Tibetan army joined the uprising, but in the main the populace did not, assuring its failure," writes Hugh Deane. In their book on Tibet, Ginsburg and Mathos reach a similar conclusion: "As far as can be ascertained, the great bulk of the common people of Lhasa and of the adjoining countryside failed to join in the fighting against the Chinese both when it first began and as it progressed." Eventually the resistance crumbled.

In 1998, the Dalai Lama's organization itself issued a statement admitting that it had received millions of dollars from the CIA during the 1960s to send armed squads of exiles into Tibet to undermine the Maoist revolution. In 1959, China's military crackdown on rebels in Kham and Amdo led to the "Lhasa Uprising." Full-scale resistance spread throughout Tibet. Fearing capture of the Dalai Lama, unarmed Tibetans surrounded his residence, and the Dalai Lama fled to India.

In 1965, the area that had been under the control of the Dalai Lama's government from the 1910s to 1959 (Ü-Tsang and western Kham) was renamed the Tibet Autonomous Region or TAR. Autonomy provided that the head of government would be an ethnic Tibetan; however, actual power in the TAR is held by the First Secretary of the Tibet Autonomous Regional Committee of the Chinese Communist Party, who has never been a Tibetan. The role of ethnic Tibetans in the higher levels of the TAR Communist Party remains very limited.

The destruction of most of Tibet's more than 6,000 monasteries occurred between 1959 and 1961. During the mid-1960s, the monastic estates were broken up and secular education introduced. During the Cultural Revolution, Red Guards inflicted a campaign of organized vandalism against cultural sites in the entire PRC, including Tibet's Buddhist heritage. According to at least one Chinese source, only a handful of the religiously or culturally most important monasteries remained without major damage, and thousands of Buddhist monks and nuns were killed, tortured or imprisoned.

In 1989, the Panchen Lama died of a massive heart attack at the age of 50. The PRC continues to portray its rule over Tibet as an unalloyed improvement, but a handful of foreign governments continue to make protests about aspects of PRC rule in Tibet as groups such as Human Rights Watch report alleged human rights violations. Most governments, however, recognize the PRC's sovereignty over Tibet today, and none have recognized the Government of Tibet in Exile in India.

Riots flared up again in 2008. Many ethnic Hans and Huis were attacked in the riot, their shops vandalized or burned. The Chinese government reacted swiftly, imposing curfews and strictly limiting access to Tibetan areas. The international response was likewise immediate and robust, with some leaders condemning the crackdown and large protests and some in support of China's actions.

Tibetans in Exile

Following the Lhasa uprising and the Dalai Lama's flight from Tibet in 1959, the government of India accepted the Tibetan refugees. India designated land for the refugees in the mountainous region of Dharamsala, India, where the Dalai Lama and the Tibetan government-in-exile are now based. The plight of the Tibetan refugees garnered international attention when the Dalai Lama, spiritual and religious leader of the Tibetan government in exile, won the Nobel Peace Prize in 1989. The Dalai Lama was awarded the Nobel Prize on the basis of his unswerving commitment to peaceful protest against the Chinese occupation of Tibet. He is highly regarded as a result and has since been received by government leaders throughout the world. Among the most recent ceremonies and awards, he was given the Congressional Gold Medal by President Bush in 2007, and in 2006 he was one of only five people to ever receive an honorary Canadian citizenship. The PRC consistently protests each official contact with the exiled Tibetan leader.

The community of Tibetans in exile established in Dharamsala and Karnataka, South India, has expanded since 1959. Tibetans have duplicated Tibetan monasteries in India and these now house tens of thousands of monks. They have also created Tibetan schools and hospitals, and founded the Library of Tibetan Works and Archives — all aimed at continuing Tibetan tradition and culture. Tibetan festivals such as Lama dances, celebration of Losar (the Tibetan New Year), and the Monlam Prayer Festival, continue in exile.

In 2006, Tenzin Gyatso, the 14th Dalai Lama declared that "Tibet wants autonomy, not independence." However, the Chinese distrust him, believing that he has not really given up the quest for Tibetan independence.

Talks between representatives of the Dalai Lama and the Chinese government began again in May, 2008 with little result.

CHINA AND THE PEACEFUL LIBERATION OF TIBET

The People's Republic of China (PRC) was founded on October 1, 1949, and the Central People's Government under the leadership of the Communist Party of China (CPC) became the sole legitimate government of China. This government immediately won extensive recognition from many countries, and won the natural qualification to exercise sovereignty over the whole of the Chinese territory.

From the winter of 1949 to the spring of 1950, the Central People's Government planned the peaceful liberation of Tibet. In the spring and summer of 1950, the Chinese People's Liberation Army (PLA) marched toward Tibet. After having overcome foreign obstructions, put to rout the resistance by Tibetan separatists and beaten the harsh highland environment, the PLA advance troops arrived in Lhasa and various major towns and border areas in 1951. China's five-star red flag fluttered over the Himalayas. China thus succeeded in the peaceful liberation of Tibet, completing the holy task of unifying the mainland. From then on, Tibet no longer operated under the yoke of foreign forces, and returned to the big family of the motherland known for its national unity and fraternity.

The peaceful liberation of Tibet is a joyful historic event for the Tibetans and peoples of other nationalities in China. Xagabba and Van Praag, however, term the move "aggression."

They even create the "theory of Chinese Communist invasion of Tibet" to shock the world.

"Aggression" or "invasion" has strict meaning and cannot be applied indiscriminately. It involves standards concerning military behaviour of various countries in the world as well as many political issues in the international community. The UN resolution on the meaning of invasion, adopted at the 29th UN General Assembly in December 1974, stipulates that invasion refers to a country which violates, with military forces, another country's sovereignty, territorial integrity or political independence, or uses other forms of military forces which do not conform with the UN Constitution as contained in this resolution. The resolution specifies seven types of behaviour: invading, attacking, occupying, annexing, bombing, blockading, stationing troops and other forms of military behaviour. This should be the most authoritative explanation on invasion or aggression.

The above shows the word aggression or invasion contains two fundamental points: First, the invasion or aggression is possible only when the military move takes place between two countries and when one country takes action against another. No action taken on home soil can be termed invasion or aggression; second, the invasion or aggression is possible only when the military move aims at plundering and enslaving the other country, an action which infringes upon territorial integrity and sovereignty of another country.

World history shows many actions constitute invasion, which are aimed at another country's territory and sovereignty and geared to plunder and enslave people of another country. They include the British invasion of India in 1767, the British invasion of China in 1840, the Eight-Power invasion of China in 1900, the Italian invasion of Ethiopia in 1935, the Japanese invasion of China in 1937, the German invasion of Austria, Czechoslovakia and Poland in 1938-39, the German invasion of the Soviet Union in 1941, and the US invasion of Panama in 1989. All these actions constitute one country's encroachment upon another country's territory and sovereignty, and plundering and enslaving of people of another country. Civil armed conflicts taking place within the same country, though varied in forms, do not fall into the category of invasion. They include conflicts between the Central Government and local government, between various regions, between various nationalities, between various religious factions and between various political groups. Tibet is a part of Chinese territory. Conflicts, including armed conflicts, between Tibet and fraternal regions in China or between the Central Government and the local government of Tibet are the internal affairs of China. Examples include the Qing imperial army sent to suppress the Zungar invasions in Tibet in 1718 and 1720. As the Qing imperial court exercised jurisdiction over Tibet, no one in the world called the two military moves "aggression" or "invasion."

In the early days of the People's Republic of China, PLA advance troops were sent into Tibet to drive imperialist forces out of the region for consolidated national defense and the defense of China's own territory. This constituted the Chinese government's exercise of jurisdiction over Tibet. It was a domestic, instead of an international behaviour, hence legal from beginning to end. Xagabba and Van Praag say nothing of the British military invasion of Tibet in 1888 and 1904. However, they forcibly termed the PLA move in Tibet "aggression." They did so with a view to fundamentally refuting the legality, reasonability and justice of China's peaceful liberation of Tibet. Facts slap them in the face.

In the summer and autumn of 1949, when the liberation war gained much ground in China and was approaching China's Tibetan areas, Britain, the United States and some other countries plotted actively for "Tibetan independence."

In April 1949, US Secretary of State Dean Acheson sent a cable to the American Embassy in India: Washington wishes to see Tibet's military resistance capability secretly beefed up. In July, the Tibet Office of the Commission for Mongolian and Tibetan Affairs under the Kuomintang Government was expelled from Tibet by the Gaxag government. In August, Xagabba managed to have Lowell Thomas, a commentator with the Columbia Radio Station of the United States, enter Tibet together with his son. The Gaxag government attempted to stir up an opinion for "Tibetan independence" by relying on the American radio station. During their stay in Lhasa, they held secret talks with the Prince Regent Dagzha and Hugh Richardson, and met with high Tibetan officials, urging the Tibetan side to organize trained guerrillas to stem the PLA advance troops. In September, the Gaxag government decided to expand its army by 10,000 and reinforce Qamdo and Nagqu. Lowell Thomas and his son called Tibet as "country" and appealed to the US government to offer military aid to Tibet and send diplomatic missions to Lhasa. Upon their return to the United States, they called for the United States to shoulder responsibility for the defense of Tibet.

Reginald Fox, a British spy, plotted construction of the Qamdo Radio Station for Tibet. In July 1949, Robert Ford had it built in Qamdo, and started collecting information concerning the Communist Party of China and the PLA's liberation war. Information thus collected from Xikang and Qinghai was supplied to Lowell Thomas, his son and the Gaxag government. Hugh Richardson and Reginald Fox were responsible for re-sending the information to Britain. At the instigation of Hugh Richardson and some others, the "foreign affairs bureau" of the Gaxag government sent a cable to Chairman Mao Zedong in November 1949: "Please do not send troops to cross the border into Tibet." At the suggestion of Hugh Richardson, Prince Regent Dagzha ordered the Gaxag government to draft a "Tibetan independence declaration" which was revised and turned into English by Hugh Richardson. The English version was brought to the United Nations by Xagabba and Gyalo Toinzhub to seek UN support. Through repeated discussions, Hugh Richardson, Lowell Thomas and his son, and Prince Regent Dagzha sent a "goodwill mission" composed of Tibetan officials to the United States, Britain, India and Nepal in early 1950, seeking their aid and support for "Tibetan independence."

On January 17, Reginald Fox sent a letter to the headquarters of the Tibetan army, making suggestions for its resistance against the PLA advance troops: "It should be extremely difficult for the Communist Party to send troops into Tibet. In order to slow down the advance of the Communist army, various official routes, highways and bridges should be damaged thoroughly. Mines should be planted at various strategically important positions, places where the Communist troops may be ambushed, major rivers with no bridges and mountain entries. Some Communist spies are highly likely to be sent into Tibet to confuse border residents by creating rumors and saying something which will make them change their mind. They will also collect and send information concerning deployment of Tibetan troops to the Communist Party.

"In order to check the possible spread of Communism among residents who are loyal to the 14th Dalai Lama, and in order to stabilize various parts of Tibet, they should be told immediately to prepare for a retreat of at least 20 miles. This is a point of extreme importance. The troops should be deployed in places where the Communist army can hardly cut their escape route and besiege them. Decisions concerning defense matters should be made immediately."

On January 19, the commander-in-chief of the Tibetan army sent a reply to Reginald Fox, expressing sincere thanks for his good suggestion, which he said would "lie embedded in the mind for ever."

Thereafter, the Tibetan army operated basically in accordance with the suggestion made by Reginald Fox. The above facts show how much efforts the British and American forces had made for the control of the Gaxag government. They also show the necessity and urgency for the People's Republic of China to exercise jurisdiction over Tibet.

Patriotic Tibetans, however, ardently demanded and supported the PLA advance troops?entry into Tibet.

On October 1, 1949, the 10th Panchen Erdeni sent a cable to Chairman Mao Zedong and Commander-in-Chief Zhu De: "Northwest China has been liberated and the Central People's Government has been formed. All people who are full of sap feel encouraged. There is hope for the people to lead a happy life and for the country to rejuvenate. Tibet is expected to be liberated at an early date." (Selected Materials on the History of Tibet, p.376)

INDIA SHOULD REVISIT ITS TIBET POLICY

The Indian government's response to the protests in Tibet has been to merely state its "distress" about the situation and reaffirm its position that Tibet is an "internal" affair of China. New Delhi had assured Beijing that its position on the Tibet issue is "clear and consistent" and that this "would not change in the future." The Indian position is based on its traditional opposition to separatist movements and to foreign intervention in support of such movements. Also, given the present dynamics of India-China relations with greater synergy as the goal, New Delhi does not favour supporting the Tibetan cause. However, protests by Tibetans have implications for India as the Tibet issue is entangled with the India-China border dispute.

The Tibet issue is rooted in the histories of the three countries – India, China and Tibet. Tibet has existed throughout history as a distinct civilization with rich culture, language, religion, polity and identity. Through the centuries India and Tibet have maintained strong religious and trade ties, and have shared a peaceful border. But the advent of British power in the Indian sub-continent altered the nature of this relationship.

The British Raj's policy towards Tibet was shaped by the Great Game and the need to prevent Russia from posing a threat to India. It was against this backdrop that the Raj called for the tripartite Simla conference in October 1913, which was attended by representatives from British India (Henry McMahon), Republican China (Chen Yifan) and Tibet (Lonchen Shatra). The goal was to settle the boundary between British India and Tibet on the one hand and between Tibet and China on the other. The result was the Simla Agreement of 1914, which the Chinese representative initialled but only under British pressure. The Agreement divided Tibet into Inner and

Outer Tibet. China was given sovereignty over Inner Tibet but only suzerain control over Outer Tibet. And the boundary between India and Tibet was demarcated, with the Raj retaining trading and extra-territorial rights in Outer Tibet.

Independent India inherited this arrangement, which boiled down to sustaining Tibet as a buffer zone with de facto independent status under Chinese suzerainty. In the post-1949 period, when the People's Republic of China came into being, India urged China to let Tibet continue as an autonomous region in line with its historical status, religious, cultural and political identity. However, the entry of 20,000 PLA troops in 1950-51 into Tibet ended its independent status and eventually brought to the fore the India-China border issue.

During his 1954 visit to China, Jawaharlal Nehru had raised the issue of inaccurate border alignment as depicted in some Chinese maps. Premier Zhou Enlai responded that these maps were reproductions of old Kuomintang maps and that his government has had no time to revise them. However, Nehru's December 14, 1958 letter, in which he had once again raised the issue of Chinese maps depicting the border alignment inaccurately, elicited a different response from Zhou. The Chinese Premier wrote back on January 23, 1959 stating that the Sino-Indian border was never delimited and that China has never recognised the McMahon Line.

After the 1962 India-China war, China began to claim some 90,000 square kilometres of Indian territory in the eastern sector and 38,000 square kilometres in the Aksai Chin area. These claims flow directly from China's control over Tibet and its felt need to consolidate its rule over this rebellious territory.

Between 1947 and 1954, India's position on Tibet was based on recognising it as an independent nation. Tibet represented itself as an independent country at the Asian Relations Conference held in New Delhi in March-April 1947. But India subsequently gave up this position on April 29, 1954, when it signed an agreement with China on trade and intercourse between India and Tibet. Under the terms of the agreement, India gave up all extra-territorial rights and privileges that it had inherited from the British Raj and recognised Tibet as part of China. This, in effect, was a unilateral concession without the Indian government gaining anything in return.

In subsequent decades, New Delhi has repeatedly reiterated that Tibet is a part of China, in spite of the latter's encroachment into and extravagant claims over Indian territory, the border war it imposed on India in 1962, and the unresolved border dispute at the centre of which lies Tibet. In effect, such reiteration has meant the dilution of a bargaining card in the border negotiations. In 2003, the Vajpayee government went further than any other government before by stating that the "Tibetan Autonomous Region of China is part of the territory of China." This has two critical implications for Indian security. First, it excluded Inner Tibet (present day Sichuan, Yunnan and Qinghai provinces) from the geographical notion of Tibet, thus recognising Inner Tibet as Chinese land. Second, it provided China a greater opening to advance its claims on Arunachal Pradesh. For, Outer Tibet or the Tibetan Autonomous Region (TAR), according to the Chinese definition, includes Arunachal Pradesh, which it refers to as its 'southern state'.

India has consistently failed to understand nuances in Chinese diplomatic practice and negotiating tactics. China is tackling the Tibet problem at two levels. One, it is involving the Dalai Lama's representatives in fruitless talks, while also disparaging him as a 'splittist' who aims to disintegrate China. Two, it is arm-twisting India by repeatedly claiming that Arunachal Pradesh is part of China. Here, it is worth noting that at the sixth round of talks with Tibetan representatives Chinese negotiators had conveyed that the Dalai Lama should accept Arunachal Pradesh as part of China, which the Dalai Lama has refused to accept. China is not seriously considering a resolution to the Tibet issue or the border dispute with India. It is simply buying time till the Dalai Lama passes away, after which, it hopes, the Tibetan movement would fizzle out. This would also further weaken India's bargaining position on the border negotiations while at the same time gaining for itself greater manoeuvrability.

The presence of the Dalai Lama in India along with 120,000 Tibetan refugees spread across 35 settlements is leverage for India. But India has so far steadfastly avoided using the Tibetan card. Given the intricate linkage between the Tibet issue and the border dispute, India needs to revise its policy on Tibet. Its present policy of appeasement and unilateral concessions has not stopped China from claiming Indian territory. Chinese maps continue to show Arunachal Pradesh as part of China, and Jammu and Kashmir as falling outside India. Some Chinese maps still do not represent Beijing's revised position on Sikkim.

The latest unrest among Tibetans provides an opportunity for India to revisit and revise its Tibet policy. First, India should make it clear to the Chinese government that developments in Tibet are a concern for India and that it cannot remain unaffected by developments there. Second, on the border issue, instead of merely restating that all of Arunachal Pradesh is an integral part of its territory, India should make it very clear that these are non-negotiable. Third, upholding its democratic principles as well as its cultural affinity with the Tibetans, India should impress upon the Chinese that while it does not support political activity by Tibetans in its soil, it also cannot suppress peaceful demonstrations by them. Fourth, India should move away from its 'over-cautious' and diffident policy on Tibet and adopt a more independent stand that takes into account its national interests.

9

Climate Change, Disasters and Security in Asia

Climate change and disasters are fast emerging as the most defining challenges of the 21st century. The Fourth Assessment Report (AR4) of the Intergovernmental Panel on Climate Change (IPCC); IPCC AR4 has provided compelling evidence that climate change is advancing rapidly as a global risk with impacts far beyond just the environment. Recent projections and analytical studies indicate that the increasing global temperatures, arctic and glacial melt down, sea level rise and other climate change induced environmental degradation will give rise to extreme weather events and overstretch many societies' adaptive capacities within the coming decades thus increasing societal vulnerabilities.

Concomitantly a global review of the statistics of disasters by the Centre for Research on the Epidemiology of Diseases (CRED) indicates that natural disasters are increasing in terms of frequency, complexity, scope and destructive capacity. Hitherto disasters were linked to climate change through short term natural variability manifesting in extreme weather events such as cyclones, storms, floods, droughts, heat waves, windstorms and other natural hazards with potential for catastrophic loss of human lives, damages to infrastructure and environment. However, with the climate change manifesting at an unprecedented rate with increased variability and frequency of extreme events, long term implications and possibility of abrupt change, fuelled largely through anthropogenic cause, these two processes have the potential to coalesce generating destructive forces which could cause mega disasters unless urgent, radical and resolute mitigation actions are not implemented.

For India, tackling the challenge of climate change and increase in disaster risks posits particular significance, presently poised as she in becoming a major global power. Valuable time and resources would be consumed in handling the increasing risks, which would impinge on geo-strategic imperatives, unless appropriate mitigation measures and mechanisms are not put in place now, and policies redefined to address the challenge.

The subsequent arguments analyze the impact of climate change on the risk of natural hazards in India and implications for security and propose preparedness strategies and emergent policy imperatives.

THE CIRCUMSTANCE- CHANGING CLIMATE

IPCC AR4 has categorically established that climate change is advancing rapidly with global warming as a prime causative factor. The warming of the climate system has been termed "unequivocal" by global scientific consensus as evident from observations of increases in global average air and ocean temperatures, widespread melting of snow and ice and rising global average sea level (IPCC, 2007a). This has been unprecedented in the last 1300 years and most of the warming has been convincingly attributed to human influence.

According to the latest evaluations, the average temperature at the surface of the earth has increased by 0.74 (0.56-0.92) °C during the twentieth century. The temperature increase, though widespread, is greater at higher northern latitudes. Land regions have warmed faster than the oceans. Such a rise in global temperature is very large by historical standards, making the 1990s the warmest decade of the past millennium. Eleven of the last twelve years (1995-2006) rank among the twelve warmest years since 1850. Because of warming, the global extent of snow cover has receded by some 10% since 1960s and the annual average Arctic sea ice extent has shrunk by 2.7 % per decade since 1978. Mountain glaciers and snow cover on average have declined in both hemispheres. The global average sea level has risen by 0.1 to 0.2 meters in the century consistent with warming. Precipitation has increased in the higher latitudes of the northern hemisphere while it has decreased in subtropical regions. Climatic phenomena such as heavy rains in parts of the northern hemisphere, warm episodes of the El Niño Southern Oscillation (ENSO) over the tropics, and droughts in some regions of Asia and Africa have gained in intensity and frequency (IPCC, 2007b).

According to the future scenario projections by IPCC AR 4 global warming is expected to intensify during the 21st century. Green House Gases concentration in the atmosphere will be 45% above the present level in 2100 under the most favourable set of hypotheses, and 260% above it in the worst case. Without resolute mitigation, a global increase in temperature of 2-7°C relative to pre industrial levels and a rise of 0.1 to 0.9 meters in the sea level can be expected to occur by 2100 (Parry et al, 2007). Only very rapid and radical changes in emissions of greenhouse gases or aerosols, or unforeseeable events such as a major volcanic eruption or meteorite impact would bring about any marked deviation from the forecast outlined in the next 25 years. Gradual emissions reductions over the coming decades, which would most likely be implemented as part of an effective climate protection policy, would not bring about any notable slowdown in the global warming trend until after 2030 (WBGU, 2008). The IPCC projections are supported and substantiated by other climatic models. A ten-year climate prediction model developed by the Hadley Research Centre of the UK Meteorological Office, predicts that the world is warming up faster than at any time in the past 100 years. It shows that global warming will begin in earnest in 2009, at least half of the years 2009 to 2014 will be hotter than 1998, the warmest year on record. The model predicts 2014 to be 0.3°C warmer globally than 2004 and that by 2015 global temperatures will be 0.5°C above the average value for the last 30 years (Doug, 2007). This is a sharp increase, as the average global temperature has risen by only 0.8°C since 1900. Due to the long lead times involved in climatic changes, global warming is expected to continue during the 21st century. Future projections indicate that there is increased confidence that some weather events and extremes will become more frequent, more widespread and/or more intense during the 21st century and impacts due to altered frequencies and intensities of extreme weather, climate and sea level events are very likely to change (IPCC, 2007c). A few examples of possible impacts of climate change due to changes in extreme weather and climate events to the mid-to late 21st century are (Parry et al, 2007):-.

- Warmer and fewer cold days and nights, warmer and more frequent hot days and nights over most land areas - virtually certain (greater than 99% chance)
- Heat waves frequency increases over most areas - very likely (90–99% chance).
- Heavy precipitation events frequency increases over most areas-very likely (90– 99% chance).
- Area affected by drought increases- likely (66–90% chance).
- Intense tropical cyclone activity increases- likely (66–90% chance).
- Increased incidence of extreme high sea level (excludes tsunamis)-likely (66–90% chance).

CLIMATE MODIFY- DISASTERS-SECURITY NEXUS

Climate Change and Disasters

The United Nations defines disaster as '*a serious disruption of the functioning of the community or society, causing widespread human, material, or environmental losses which exceed the ability of the affected community or society to cope using its own resources*' (UNDHA, 1992). Climate has always been linked with disasters, hitherto, through climate variability manifesting in extreme weather events such as cyclones, storms, floods, droughts, heat waves, windstorms etc, with potential for catastrophic loss of human lives, damage to infrastructure and environment. These short term climate fluctuations and extreme weather events have been the most frequently occurring hazards and in combination with social vulnerability have been responsible for the vast majority of disaster losses worldwide. CRED categorizes these disasters resulting from climatic variability and other climatic and meteorological causes as *hydro-meteorological disasters* (floods, landslides, mudflows, avalanches, tidal waves, windstorms, including typhoons, cyclones, hurricanes, storms, winter storms, tropical storms and tornadoes, droughts, extreme temperatures, and complex disasters associated with drought) as distinct from *geological disasters* (earthquakes, volcanic eruptions and tsunamis) (CRED, 2007). The hydro-meteorological disasters resulting from climate variability and other climatic and meteorological causes are also commonly referred as 'climate disasters' in disaster studies.

Climate disasters have always been a recurring theme in human history, and are on a rising trend.

Trends -20th Century. Over the 20th century, climate related disasters were *seven* times as frequent as those including geo physical hazards globally, and accounted for *nine* times as many deaths and caused economic losses that were *three* times higher (UNDP, 2007b).

Trends -21st Century. In the 21st century over the past three decades, climate related natural disasters occurred *five* times as frequently, killed or affected *seventy* times as many people, and caused *twice* as much damage worldwide as did earthquakes and volcanoes. In the past decade, weather-related natural hazards have been the cause of 90% of natural disasters and 60% of related deaths, and have been responsible for 98% of the impacts on disaster-affected populations, the majority in areas of developing countries (IFRC, 2005). Between 2000 and 2004 an average of 326 climate disasters was reported each year. Some 262 million people were affected annually for 2000-2004, more than double the level in the first half of the 1980's (UNDP, 2007a). Climate Disasters Statistical Review 1987-2006. The global review of the statistics of climate disasters by

CRED also indicates that climate disasters are increasing in terms of frequency, complexity, scope and destructive capacity. A comparison of the occurrences of climate disasters from 1987-2006(CRED, 2007) with averages for periods 1987-1998 and 2000-2006.

Disaster Figures for 2007/08. The recent data from CRED for 2007/08 reveals a marked increase in the number of climate disasters, especially floods, compared with the average of the last seven years, with Asia as the hardest hit continent (UN/ISDR, 2008/01). Eight out of the 10 countries with the highest disaster deaths of 2007 were in Asia, with 4,234 killed in Bangladesh by cyclone Sidr in Nov 2007, and more than 3,000 fatalities from severe floods in Bangladesh, India, North Korea and China. The number of people affected by disasters continued to increase and floods remain the main disaster that affects populations in the world. More than 164 million people were affected by floods in 2007 out of the 197 million affected by disasters.

Climate Change and growing Disasters- Is there a Link?

A number of experts link these current trends in extreme weather events with the increase in the global mean temperature.

The CRED report states that there *'there is increasingly conclusive evidence which confirms that global climate change will have an impact on the occurrence and magnitude of extreme events. These impacts are envisaged to increase human vulnerability to natural disasters, thus emphasizing the need for improved measures of preparedness in every part of the world'* (UN/ISDR, 2008/01). CRED report also surmises that the current trends are consistent with the predictions of IPCC AR4, in that Asia, and also West Africa are already suffering from more severe and frequent floods (Sapir, 2008). The future projections by IPCC AR4 also indicates that there is *'increased confidence that some weather events and extremes will become more frequent, more widespread and/or more intense during the 21st century and impacts due to altered frequencies and intensities of extreme weather, climate and sea level events are very likely to change*' (IPCC, 2007c; Parry et al, 2007).

Notwithstanding the predictions of IPCC AR4, supported by CRED through trend analysis of rising climate disasters, a direct attribution to climate change is not possible as every weather event is the product of random forces and systemic factors. However, climate change will steadily increase the exposure of the poor and vulnerable to climate shocks and place increased pressure on coping strategies and adaptive capacities of societies by resource and environment degradation. Current evidence points very clearly that climate change is creating systemic conditions for extreme weather events and will increase the risk of exposure to climate disasters through increasing societal vulnerabilities. Shifts from long term averages could raise the level of background stress, thereby increasing vulnerability to acute environmental stresses. The character and frequency of the acute stresses themselves could change, manifesting as extreme events. Lastly, climate change could exacerbate the scope and intensity of chronic hazards and contributing elements associated with such stresses by increasing vulnerability because of increasing background environment stress (Hultman et al, 2006).

Also, there is evidence now that climate change, with present developmental trends, will not express itself in through slow shifts in average conditions, but will manifest at an unprecedented rate with increased variability, frequency of extreme events, long term implications and possibility of abrupt change, fuelled largely through anthropogenic causes. Under such trajectory these two processes do have the potential to coalesce generating destructive forces which could cause mega disasters unless urgent, radical and resolute mitigation actions are not implemented.

Disaster and Security

Though viewed principally as cataclysmic events that cause mass losses and upheaval in society, major disasters are much more than mere 'disaster events' and could result in severe social, political, economic and environmental consequences, posing many new threats and challenges to national security and stability. Major disasters disrupt a stable social system and the aftermath is a chaotic unstable random system with conditions of inequality, resource scarcity, social grievances, and political tension-conditions ripe for heightening inter-state and intra-state conflicts. Disasters can cause mass disruption of social functioning, impacting individual behaviour, groups and organisations that serve them. Essential utilities and services are crippled by catastrophic damages, physical infrastructure and the built environment is severely damaged, crops are destroyed, leading to food shortages, famines and localised conflicts over resources. Disasters could also destroy main political and social institutions, threatening political stability. The resulting increased competition for scarce resources, exacerbated inequality, changing power relations between individuals, groups and organisations could create conflict. The earthquake in Guatemala in 1976 caused widespread destruction in the rural mid section of the country that eventually brought an abrupt and violent change of leadership from the 21 year old military regime. Similarly the country of Bangladesh was formed after angered victims of the 1970 typhoon instigated civil war in East Pakistan. A major disaster thus has the potential to reshape society and catalyse political change.

To understand how disasters impact security, an analysis is required that goes beyond the disaster period to look at root causes of vulnerability, inequality, grievances, and resource scarcities. As discussed, a disaster is a disruption in the normal pattern of life generating suffering, socio economic breakdown, damage to environment... to such extent that there is need for external assistance. Much literature exists on what causes disasters and it is well accepted now that disasters are not natural phenomena, but 'acts of society' and are caused by vulnerability at different levels, viz, ecological, economic, social, human and political and are rooted in developmental failures (DFID, 2005). While a hazardous event may take place (a natural phenomenon, or a man made), disasters result from developmental failures which increase the vulnerability to the hazard event. Also while disasters may be natural phenomena, but their impacts are not. Their effects are the result of the actions of human beings and are determined by the circumstances of the country, i.e., poverty, social inequalities, lack of resources, among other factors. There is great risk inherent in treating disasters as discrete events detached from people's lives (Blaike, 1994). In the developing countries, this serves as a warning against analyses that separate natural disasters from their political and socio-economic context, from economic growth, and from the vulnerabilities inherent in the process, which affect the impact of major disasters.

Security, on the other hand, in simple terms, is 'lack of conflict', extant or potential. Conflicts do not occur unexpectedly and there many obvious causes of conflicts. But behind the immediate factors that trigger conflicts, analysis reveals deeper causes, such as territorial demands, socioeconomic inequalities, economic interests, the defence of political ideologies, burgeoning nationalism, and the struggles of ethnic minorities, racism and arms proliferation, ie, vulnerable human conditions. The progression of a hazard event to a disaster and the disaster potential in exacerbating/generating threat to security.

WEATHER CHANGE, DISASTERS AND SECURITY: THE INDIA CONTEXT

Climate Change in India

For the Indian subcontinent, the projected changes by IPCC, based on the General Circulation Model (GCM), project warming of 2-4.7 °C, with the most probable level being around 3.3 °C by the year 2100(A1B scenario) (Solomon et al, 2007). Warming is expected to be more marked in the winter half of the year (3.6 °C) than in summer (2.7 °C), and stronger in the north than in the south. Most scenarios project a decrease in precipitation during the inter dry period and an increase for the rest of the year. At the same time, an increase in heavy rain events is probable, particularly in the north of India. The global sea level rise of 0.1 to 0.9 meters is particularly expected to be high in the Indian Ocean, especially on the west coast. Assessments by Indian Scientist using the Hadley Centre Regional Model (HadRM2) climate models show similar outputs and indicate that over the Indian region the temperatures will increase by 3 to 4°C towards the end of the 21st century.

The warming may be about 2.1 to 2.6 ° C in the 2050s and 3.3 to 3.8 ° C in the 2080s (DEFRA/ GoI, 2005a). The different models/experiments generally indicate the increase of temperature to be of the order of 2-5°C across the country. In case of mean annual temperature, the increase is of the order of 3 to 6°C. The warming is projected to be widespread over the country, and relatively more pronounced over northern parts of India. While the rainfall is projected to increase, there would be variations in the spatial pattern, with some pockets showing increase and others experiencing decline in rainfall. Most models project an increase in rainfall between 10 and 40% from the baseline period (1961–90) to the end of 21st century, with the maximum expected increase in rainfall over northwestern and central India. There is very little or no change noted in the monsoon rainfall over a major part of peninsular India (Kumar R. et tal, 2006). The climate change would cause global sea to rise between 0.09 to 0.88 m by 2100 and enhance extreme events like excessive rain, flash flood, droughts, cyclones and forest fires.

The projected climate change will affect India particularly severely. Its consequences include a rise in sea level, threatening areas such as the densely populated Ganges delta, changes in the monsoon rains, the melting of the glaciers in the Hindukush-Karakorum-Himalaya region(crucial for the water supply in the dry seasons), and the foreseeable increase in heavy rain events and intensity of tropical cyclones (Parry et al, 2007). The thousands of glaciers located across the 2,400 km of the Himalayan range are at the epicenter of an emerging crisis.

The impacts will vary from region to region. The effect of possible changes in the intensity of the monsoons will be particularly sensitive, because large parts of India receive the majority of their annual precipitation during the summer monsoon rains, which already vary noticeably in different regions (Lal et al, 2001). The summer monsoon is crucial to the annual precipitation total of the Indian subcontinent. The effect that global warming will have on the Indian monsoon is still unclear, but increased variability in the monsoon rains is probable (Solomon et al, 2007).

Likely crash of Climate Change on Disasters in India

India is among the world's most disaster prone areas. India support 1/6th of the world's population on just 2 % of it landmass. Nearly 59 % of India's land area is prone to earthquakes of moderate to very high intensity, over 40 million hectares (12 % of land), is prone to floods, close to 5700 kms of its 7516 km coast line (about 8%), is cyclone prone and exposed to tsunamis and storm surges, 2% of land is landslide prone, and 68% of India's arable land is affected by droughts. Of the 35 States and Union Territories, as many as 27 are disaster prone (GoI, 2004a). Most disasters in India are water related.

The global disaster trends are alarming, singularly so in India. The figures for 2006 indicates that Asia remains the continent most hit by disasters, with over 44% of all reported disasters (CRED, 2007). At aggregate country level, India ranks third with 21 significant disasters recorded (China recorded 38, followed by US which recorded 31). In terms of victims India ranked third with 7.3 million victims after China-88 million and Philippines-8.6 million. China, US and India also remained the countries reporting the highest damages (China- 13.5 billion US $, US- 5 billion US $ and India -3.3 billion US $) (CRED, 2007). The available data for 2007/08 also has India reporting third highest number of significant disasters, viz, 18 as against 22 reported by US and 20 by China. In terms of victims India ranked the second highest recorded 1103 deaths, mainly due to floods, as against Bangladesh which recorded 5534(Cyclone Sidr and floods) (ISDR/CRED, 2008). A scrutiny of the past records of 100 years too indicates that India figures in the first 10 in the world in terms of fatalities and economic losses in a variety of disasters.

These trends are likely to exacerbate in future with climate change. The projected increase in precipitation and rainfall, the glacial meltdown and rising sea levels will affect India particularly severely, creating conditions for more hazardous events and will lead to increase in incidence of floods, cyclones, and storm surges. Though it is not possible to predict the future frequency or timings of extreme events but there is evidence that the risk of drought, flooding, and cyclone damage is increasing and will continue to do so. Climate change is also likely to threaten India's food security, increase water stress, and increase occurrences of diseases especially malaria.

Lack of availability and access to technological and financial resources coupled with a high dependence on climate sensitive sectors-agriculture, fisheries, forestry-have made India highly vulnerable to climate change. A large and growing population, densely populated and a low-lying coastline, and an economy closely tied to its natural resource base, further intensifies this vulnerability.

Floods. In India 40 million hectares are prone to floods with 8 million hectares being affected every year. The Brahmaputra and the Gangetic basin are the most flood prone areas. The other flood prone areas are the North West region of west flowing rivers such as the Narmada and the Tapti, Central India and the Deccan region with major rivers flowing like Mahanadi, Krishna and Cauvery (GoI, 2002). Flood disasters are the largest cause of economic damages and losses of human lives in India. The population affected by floods in 2005 was 32.03 million and 1504 lives were lost. In addition about 96,713 livestock were killed and 1683 houses damaged. The crop loss was Rs 4,600.7 million (US $ 103), and the damage to public utilities was Rs 3,772.48 million (US $ 85 million) (Kumar S, 2006). In 2006 India recorded the highest economic damages from floods in the world with losses amounting to 3,390 US $, and with over 40 lakh people affected (second to China, over 41 lakh victims for flood).The floods in 2007 have also taken a significant toll with over 1500 deaths, being the second highest with Bangladesh recording the most (ISDR/CRED, 2008).

Climate change will influence stream flow patterns through changes in the precipitation, changes in volume and timing of snow melt from glaciers, and changes in the type of precipitation, snow or rain, in the Himalayan region. An assessment undertaken by Indian Scientists of the Indian Institute for Technology (IIT) Delhi, India as part of the National Communication (NATCOM) on climate change project under the Ministry of Environment and Forests (MoEF), India, using the HadRM2 daily weather data to determine the spatial-temporal availability of in the river systems in India has indicated that that the severity of floods under the projected climate change is likely to intensify (Gosain et al, 2006). The study shows that western India may experience very high river discharges more frequently than it does at present. Apart from changes in snowmelt and precipitation in the Himalaya, changes in the pattern, intensity and frequency of rainfall will have significant impacts on floods. Climatic changes could result in more frequent high-intensity rainfall events.

Cyclones. India has an 8000 km-long coastline with two cyclone seasons, during the southwest and northeast monsoons. Cyclones have been observed to be more frequent in the Bay of Bengal than the Arabian Sea. Consequently the states of West Bengal, Orissa, Andhra Pradesh, and Tamil Nadu along the Bay of Bengal are the most affected as compared to Maharashtra, Kerala, Karnataka, and Gujarat which are along the Arabian Sea. Most of the destructive cyclonic storms usually occur during the transition periods: pre -(April-May) and post-(September-December) monsoon, the latter being the most active period. The coastal districts of Orissa, Andhra Pradesh and Gujarat are most prone to the impacts of cyclone (GoI, 2006). About 1.3 storms form on an average during a year (GoI, 2004b). The east coast of India, which lies in the path of tropical hurricanes from the Gulf of Bengal, is particularly at risk of being damaged by storms and floods. The projections by the National Institute of Oceanography (NIO), under the Council of Scientific and Industrial Research (CSIR), Government of India on the impacts of climate change on sea level, to assess the degree to which mean sea level and the occurrence of extreme events may change, showed an increased occurrence of cyclones in the Bay of Bengal, particularly in the post-monsoon period, along with increased maximum wind speeds associated with cyclones and a greater number of high surges under climate change (DEFRA/GoI, 2005b). In addition, the strength of tropical cyclones, which represent a threat to the eastern coast of India and to Bangladesh, could increase. The risk to these areas will be aggravated by the rising sea level (WBGU, 2006).

Drought. Along with floods India also suffers acute water shortage. Of the net area sown in the country, 68 percent is prone to drought, and of this 33 percent is chronically drought-prone, receiving rainfall of less than 750 mm per annum, while 35 percent receives rainfall between 750-1,125 mm per annum (GoI, 2002). The steady shrinking of the Himalayan Glacier ranges will drastically cut down water availability in downstream plains of Uttar Pradesh and Bihar. India's initial National Communication to the United Nations Framework Convention (UNFCCC) on Climate Change projects that Luni, the west flowing rivers of Kutchh and Saurashtra occupying about one fourth of the area of Gujarat and 60 % of Rajasthan are likely to experience acute physical water scarcity. The river basins of Mahi, Pennar, Sabarmati and Tapi are also likely to experience constant water scarcities and shortages (GoI, 2004b).

Landslides. Landslides can affect large areas of the country every year during monsoons. They can also be caused by earthquakes. The areas that suffer from landslide hazards are located in the hilly tracts of the Himalayas, Northeast India, Nilgiris, Eastern Ghats and Western Ghats. With the melting of the glaciers in the Hindukush-Karakorum-Himalaya region, and the foreseeable increase in heavy rain events and intensity of tropical cyclones (Parry et al, 2007), the incidences of landslides are likely to increase.

The Coastal Zone. The coastal zone, a highly fragile eco system, is an important and critical region for India. It is densely populated and stretches over 800 km with the Arabian

Sea in the West and the Bay of Bengal in the East. The area occupied by the coastal districts is around 379,610 Km^2, with an average population density of 455 persons per Km^2, which is about 5 times the national average of 324 persons per Km^2. Under the present climate conditions it has been observed that a sea level rise (0.4-2.00 mm) along the Gulf of Kutchh and the coast of West Bengal is the highest. Along the Karnataka coast, however there is a relative decrease in sea level (GoI, 2004b). Future climate change in the coastal zones is likely to be manifested through worsening of some of the existing coastal zonal problems.

Some of the main climate related concerns in the context of the Indian coastal zones are erosions, flooding, submergence and deterioration of coastal ecosystems, such as mangroves and salinization. In many case these are caused by, or, exacerbated by, sea level rise and tropical cyclones. The key climate related risks in the coastal zone include tropical cyclones, sea level rises, and changes in the temperature and precipitation. A rise in sea level is likely to have significant implications on the coastal population and agriculture performance of India. A one meter sea level rise is projected to displace approximately 7.1 million people in India and about 5,764 Km^2 of land are will be lost, along with 4200 Km of road (GoI, 2004b). The diverse impact expected as a result of sea level rise include land loss and population displacement, increased flooding of low lying coastal area, loss of yield and employment resulting from inundation and salinization. Damage to coastal infrastructure, aquaculture and coastal tourism, due to erosion of the sandy beaches is also likely. The extent of vulnerability however depends not just on the physical exposure to sea level rise and the population affected but also on the extent of economic activity of the areas and capacity to cope with impacts. Natural ecosystems such as mangroves, grasslands and coral reefs are also likely to be affected by climate change. Sea level rise would submerge mangroves as well as increase the salinity of wetlands. The projected sea level rise of 0.1-0.9 m seems within the ability of the Sunderban mangrove ecosystems which presently face tidal amplitudes up to 5 m. This may be not true for other mangroves such as the Pichavaram and Muthupet where tidal amplitudes are much lower at 0.64 m (Shukla et al, 2003). However increased snow melt in the Western Himalayas could bring large quantities of fresh water into the Gangetic delta. This would have significant consequences on the composition of Sunderban mangroves species, favoring species that have least tolerance to salinity.

Collision of Climate Change on Security

India's is touted to emerge as a leading global player in future. India's economy is growing at a remarkable 5-7 % per annum (the present economic recession could lower this rate), and if this trend is sustained economic projections indicate that by 2035, India would become the world's third largest economy after China and the US (DCDC, 2007). Much would however depend upon how she manages her environmental, political and demographic challenges and importantly the emerging challenge of climate change and the unexpected shocks to the economy-increasing disasters. For countries with developing economies like India, the financial setbacks disasters inflict can be ruinous, in contrast to developed counterparts, as disasters disrupt short term financial and economic management, simultaneously necessitating substantial realignment in spending plans, adjustments in economic targets and shifts in economic policy, and have negative longer term consequences for economic growth, development and poverty reduction. More than 95% of deaths caused by disasters occur in developing countries and the losses in developing countries are 20 times greater (as percent of GDP) than in industrial countries, because of limited coping mechanisms, prevention, mitigation and adaptation capabilities. Economic losses due to disasters in India were estimated to be Rs 28,678 crores for the period 1994-98, and rose to Rs 47,464 crores in 1998-2003. In 2005 alone, disasters in India caused direct losses approaching Rs 87,500 crores (GoI, 2004a). This was more than the Indian Defence Budget for the year, 83,000 crores. For 2006-07 the direct losses approximate 1,12,000 crores, again greater than the defence budget of 1,07,000 crores. Estimates for 2008 are not yet available, but are also anticipated to be well over the Indian Defence Budget. So much of India's anticipated economic growth and emergence as a leading global power would depend upon how India deals with disaster events.

While India is a high growth economy, there is great inequity and a large human development backlog. Around 28.6 % of the population, some 320 million people, live below the poverty line (UNDP, 2007a). Superimposing the incremental risk of climate change on this large development deficit would compromise the ambition of 'inclusive growth' set out in India's Eleventh Five Year Plan.

India is already battling high population and rapidly increasing urbanization. The population of India is forecast to be around 1.4 thousand million by 2020. The urban population is growing faster than the rural population. The coastal megacities of Chennai (2005: population 6.9 million), Calcutta (14.3 million) and Mumbai (18.2 million) lie generally only a few meters above sea level (WBGU, 2008). The high population pressure combined with increasing cyclone intensity and sea-level rise as a result of climate change will put millions of people at risk of being hit by storm and flood disasters.

With rapid development of coastal areas, industrialization and urbanization, more populations are becoming vulnerable to climate-associated calamities and many have no choice but to move to safer places. It is estimated that approximately 142 million people may inhabit coastal India in 2050 and India's total number of flood zone refugees alone could be anywhere between 20 and 60 million, with 30 million as a conservative figure (Myers, 1993).

Nearly 700 million rural people in India directly depend on climate-sensitive sectors (agriculture, forests and fisheries) and natural resources (water, biodiversity, mangroves, coastal zones and grasslands) for their subsistence and livelihood. Under changing climate, food security of the country might come under threat. In addition, the adaptive capacity of dry-land farmers, forest and coastal communities is low. Climate change is likely to impact all the natural ecosystems as well as health and socio-economic systems, as indicated by the Indian Governments' National Communication to UNFCCC on Climate Change.

The linkages between climate change and national security work both indirectly and directly. In India, climate change is expected to have deep impact on food, energy, water, internally displaced persons and migrants, health and economy. It could aggravate numerous existing conflicts. At the same time, it could generate new stresses, tensions and conflicts. Climate change could become a major issue in India's bilateral relations with its neighbours.

The South Asian region is highly vulnerable to the adverse impact of climate change. According to the various studies, discussed later in this report, the pattern of monsoons in South Asia will become erratic. The overall precipitation may increase but there will be considerable regional variations. The Himalayan glaciers may also melt significantly in the next 40 to 50 years. More floods, droughts, desertification and extreme weather events are predicted for the region. The rise in sea level will have serious impact on the coastal regions of Bangladesh and India. Maldives and island regions of India could be submerged to a considerable extent.

Such geophysical changes will lead to soil erosion and increase in vector borne diseases. The variation in temperature and monsoon, the soil erosion due to floods and sea level rise will create food and water scarcity. The adverse impact on human security would bear on national security as well. There could be more hunger, more law and order problems, overcrowding of cities as a result of food and water scarcity. Since many of the countries in South Asia have weak governance structures, inadequate public health systems and low adaptation capacity, there would be greater strain on governments' resources. Climate change could create chronic economic problems including unemployment. Unemployed youth could take to militancy, terrorism and organised crime. It could create fresh conflicts due to environmental reasons and also aggravate the existing conflicts. Environmental distress due to climate change will create pressure on populations to migrate to safer locations in search of livelihood.

India could also face bilateral problems with neighbouring countries due to climate change reasons. For instance, a large number of environmental refugees could come to India from Bangladesh thereby altering the demographic balance in the Indian states. Migrations could also take place from Sri Lanka, Maldives and Nepal. Water sharing issues could arise between India and China, India and Bangladesh, India and Pakistan.

The frequency and intensity of natural disasters including hurricanes, floods and famines could increase. This will put greater strain on the armed forces in disaster management. The border security forces will have to contend with increased migration flows from the neighbouring countries. The armed forces may also be compelled to change their war-fighting doctrines and operations in light of climate change. They may be required to undertake new humanitarian missions as during the Tsunami 2004, connected with disasters management domestically and internationally. A few implications of greater disasters:

The impacts of the growing risk of disasters and the damaging effects on development could increase the pressure for Indian military forces to participate in inreasing humanitarian assistance, disaster relief and evacuation operations. This has already manifest in the major disasters of the past 4-5 years.

With increasing resource scarcity and environmental security concerns, the key natural resources, especially energy and mineral resources of strategic value, will have to be sourced from unstable areas. Maintaining access and containing instability in these areas is likely to increase in importance, alongside wider developmental and stabilisation roles. Military intervention may be required to protect the integrity of sites where resources are located, and to secure investments.

Defence spending may reduce because of the increasing disasters. Governments may increasingly modify the priority that is afforded to defence, in view of the increased imperatives for disaster risk reduction, and other changes in the dynamics of security.

With increasing disasters, the Indian defence forces would be increasingly used in post disaster reconstruction and development activities. The failure to achieve self sustaining development progress following major disasters will pose instability risks, with likely impacts on neighbours and the international system. The scale and intensification of these risks is likely to elicit military responses as national interests would be threatened. The participation of Indian military contingents in Iraq reconstruction activities testifies this.

The probability of such events taking place are not deterministic as quantitative predictions are not possible. The likely climate change impacts are based on models whose predictions are not totally reliable. Moreover, the impact of climate change would unfold gradually over several decades thereby providing time for adaptation. Therefore, while assuming an alarmist view of the impact of climate change on national security for India may not seem correct, it would be unwise to ignore the issue. With considerable uncertainty about climate change, its impact and its link with national security, it would be useful for India to adopt a risk-based approach. A "no regrets" approach would stand India in good stead.

To cope with these challenges, India will have to devise its strategies carefully. On the one hand, it will have to resist the international pressure on it to take binding objections with regard to CO_2 emissions as this will seriously affect the prospects of economic growth. On the other, it will have to undertake suitable adaptive measures to ensure that its economic growth is based on sound principle of energy efficiency resource conservation. As India is being labelled as a significant emitter, it will also have to craft its negotiating position carefully to safeguard its national interests without being isolated.

Strategy Recommendations

Both climate change and increasing disasters will play out in future against the back drop of other global trends and developments. Both climate change and disasters are largely anthropogenic processes, fuelled largely through development. Development processes are currently largely associated with *risk accumulation* and not *risk reduction.* During the next 20-30 years, every aspect of human life will change at an unprecedented rate, throwing up new features, challenges and opportunities. The Global Risk Network, an initiative of the World Economic Forum, in its Global Risk 2007 Report, identified 23 core global risks to international community over the next ten years. A total of 9 of these 23 risks (39 %), pertain to risks related to natural, health and climate related disasters in the environmental and societal domains (WEF, 2007). Consequently, a nations' ability to prevent, mitigate, respond and recover from catastrophic events is increasingly being recognised as a prime driver for national security and strategic growth. Clearly, the forecast places managing these growing risks as a frontrunner imperative for any aspiring global power. The challenge of climate change and increasing disasters will have to be addressed in the back drop of the key drivers of change, viz, economic growth, population rise, resource competition, changing demographics, increasing diseases, mass displacement and environmental impacts.

Given the lack of resources, and access to technology and finances India has limited capacity to develop an adopt strategies to reduce its vulnerability to changes in climate. To manage the climate change-disasters-security nexus, the country needs to have improved scientific understanding, capacity building, networking and broad consultation processes across every section of the society. A few important policy recommendations are enumerated in the succeeding paragraphs.

Integrated Risk Management Framework. The possibility of climate change and natural disaster forces coalescing and generating greater destructive forces imposes imperatives for a comprehensive integrated risk management framework. In India disaster management is being addressed by the National Disaster Management Authority (NDMA) as the apex body for addressing policy issues and for laying guidelines. Climate change is being addressed at various levels, by the Ministry of Environment and Forests, the Ministry of Science and Technology, the Ministry of External Affairs well as by the Prime Minister's Office. There is wide divergence among these entities. There is an urgent need to bring climate change and disaster communities on a common platform, and develop an integrated risks management framework or model for the challenges of climate change and increasing disasters, which are intrinsically linked through societal vulnerability. An integrated approach would mean: -

- Better coordination among the climate change, disasters and development communities,
- Even-handed attention to the reduction of greenhouse gases and of the risks associated with climate change, including through enhanced disaster management.
- Improved conceptual and methodological approaches to understand and respond to local manifestations of disasters while simultaneously addressing underlying the complex global processes.

Adaptation and Mitigation. Both adaptation and mitigation have been key levers in disaster risk reduction and climate change strategies. An integrated risk management framework needs to build on these two vial strategies. However adaptation, in comparison to mitigation has been the neglected stepchild in both disaster risk reduction and global negotiations and debates over climate change, mainly due to the complexity of separating adaptation from other socio economic, environment and development issues. Mitigation (structural, reduction of green house gases etc) with clear visible manifestation of actions has been the easier chosen option. India has many mitigation projects for disasters, viz, earthquake, flood, drought mitigation, etc, but adaptation is largely spoken about only in discussions. This must change. The key levers of adaptation include poverty reduction, progressive change in economic structures, shifting away from primary (agriculture) livelihoods into (secondary and tertiary) knowledge based forms of economic activity that are less vulnerable to direct impacts of risks, changes in land use and cropping patterns etc and enhancing the resilience of people. Adaptation will involve coping with climate change in the context of several factors that influence vulnerability. The Government of India has many polices in place that are directed to enhancing the adaptive capacity. However, implementation of these at the local level has been poor, as manifest in the slow eradication of poverty, inequity etc and low human development index.

From Structural to Non Structural Mitigation. The Ninth Five-year Plan (1997-2001) of India saw the beginning of a gradual shift away from purely structural measures toward other forms of non-structural mitigation. In the Ninth Plan it was observed that in addition to the progress made in implementing structural flood protection measures, flood forecasting and warning systems had played a great role in mitigating the loss of life and enabling the protection of movable property. However, notwithstanding the growing understanding, the response of governments to floods and droughts (as evidenced from the flood and drought response synthesis reports) reveal that investment strategies focus on structures and other physical interventions designed to increase control over water availability and flow. These investments are intended primarily to increase the physical availability of water during dry periods. In the case of floods, most investments are directed toward the construction and maintenance of embankments and other flood control structures. Both floods and droughts, in the practical sense of investment, are seen as external events that can be controlled through the construction of physical structures. Concepts of flood and drought proofing exist and do include the recognition of wide measures related to the vulnerability of livelihoods. Translating such concepts into governmental programs that actually direct significant investment into something other than the construction of water control structures has not, however, occurred on a widespread basis. Lessons from past efforts toward flood control indicate that structural actions often increase long-term vulnerability. There has been a gradual shift from purely structural measures to nonstructural measures for flood mitigation. This is reflected in the Tenth Five-year Plan of the Government of India, although much of the shift still remains on paper.

Future Climate Change-Disaster Scenarios-Impact Assessment. Practical strategies in an integrated framework risk management would require reliable impact assessment of future risk scenarios. Impact assessment of climate change - disaster – security nexus is complex as it includes geophysical, and socio economic aspects. However tools used for these assessments need to be continuously evolved. Climate change research, monitoring and modeling is an emerging area in India and the assessments are in their nascent stage. The preliminary assessments are mostly sectoral in dimension, which do not explicitly look at inter sectoral connection. Identifying and using appropriate tools for integrated assessment with adequate data inputs can lead to improved projections with reduced uncertainties. There is a need to enhance technical and institutional capacity. Though India has a large science and technology institutional base in many areas relevant to climate change, these have to develop a shared vision, integrated approach and networking for synergistic assessment relevant to policy making.

Climate Change/ Disaster Risk Indices (CCDRI). Quantitative indices are an important tool in risk management. International initiatives and research on developing risk indices for disaster and climate sensitivity exist, though in isolation. UNDP has developed a Disaster Risk Index (DRI) with a global level of observation and a national level of resolution allowing comparison between countries with respect to three types of hazards, viz, earthquakes, cyclones and floods (India ranks highest risk prone to floods with China a close second; for cyclones India ranks second with China leading, and for earthquakes India is ranked 10th) (UNDP, 2004). With the confluence of climate change with disasters, development of climate change induced disaster risks indices need to be initiated. Tyndall Centre for Climate Change in UK has commenced an initiative on this and is in the process of developing a methodology for climate change/disaster risk index at the global level. A similar initiative must commence by the Indian national steering committee on climate change.

Climate Change Modeling. India has presently evaluated the outputs of 10 General Circulation Models (GCMs), and only one regional model, viz, HadRM2 with a resolution of 50 X 50 Km. Regional climate modeling has to be strengthened and it is desirable to acquire /develop and set up more Regional Climate Models (RCM) to ascertain their simulation accuracy of the current India climate, and then use the appropriate RCM for more robust projections.

Vulnerability Atlas. A vulnerability map of India has been developed by the Building Material Council and Technology Promotion (BMCTP) showing multi-hazard zones based on earthquakes, wind and cyclones, and floods. This aids in preparedness, quick risk assessment and action as well as being an invaluable tool for proactive planning and has given enough warning regarding possible hazards that might get converted into disasters in the future. The vulnerability atlas needs to be revised in the context of the climate change projections and extreme weather events that India has faced in the last few years and also in the past on intermittent basis.

Climate Change to 'Climate Affairs'-a Multi Disciplinary Approach. Climate change as become a dominant issue, important to governments, corporations, public and humanitarian organisations. Thus there is a need to make climate science usable by the public as well as the policy makers at all levels of social organization. This can be done by fostering a multidisciplinary approach to climate issues for purposes of awareness. 'Climate affairs' and not climate change should be the way to educate how climate knowledge can improve the quality of climate sensitive decisions. Climate affairs encompasses climate science, climate policies, and laws, climate economics, and climate ethics and equity.

New Approach to Vulnerability. There have been changes in the concept of vulnerability recently, and this requires a new approach. India has a unique vulnerability profile and each disaster affects the other. The poor are the most affected as they are unable to break the cycle. Extreme weather events occur more often and are becoming more severe, and vulnerability will increase. Trends in India show that rescue and rehabilitation do not solve problems, prevention and planning are required. Communities must be made more resilient. Strategies and policies must cope with climate change and adaptability and increasing vulnerability. The top-down approach has been left with very minimal impact. A proactive risk reduction bottom-up driven approach is required and the government should work as a facilitator, for which political will is necessary.

Development as a Tool for Reducing Risk. Climate change and disasters interface with diverse social and natural processes and consequently with the developmental process. The conventional view has been to consider disasters and climate change as a barrier to development and simultaneously developments as a threat to climate change. However development can be the driving force to overcome challenges and risks of climate change. The Indian national perspectives on sustainable development are consistent with this view, and the India Vision 2020 articulates a vision for India's future and throws up a range on interesting possibilities, critical issues and crucial decision points for government and private bodies for future action. Many actions for adaptation and mitigation need to be integrated with and incremental to ongoing projects to meet our vision and the Millennium Development Goals (MDG). Disaster and climate change are increasingly being considered as a development constraint; hence, mainstreaming them into the development policy is all the more pertinent in the current context.

Logical Approach to the Disaster Management Cycle. Until recently the focus of disaster management was on relief and rehabilitation. This focus has shifted to prevention, mitigation, preparedness, response and recovery. The logical approach to the disaster management cycle should be mitigation as the first priority; rehabilitation and reconstruction must also include mitigation in the disaster risk reduction cycle. In a non-disaster scenario, planning, prevention, mitigation and preparedness are all required to address hazard risks and vulnerability reduction. Only this will be relevant in the context of development and environment sustainability.

Centre-State Relations, Policy Issues. The broader and deeper geopolitical dynamics of centre-state relations continue to influence both official perceptions and policies toward climate change-disaster management. In many, if not most, cases the allocation of responsibility among key agencies within each state and between states and the Central government in India, is both highly politicized and far from clear.

Command and Control. The conventional 'command-and control' management, undertaken by 'specialised' and rigid institutions, dictated and driven by govern-mentality, is full of pitfalls. It seriously lacks the capacity to respond to climate change with wisdom and persistence. There is a clash of paradigms which converts natural resource into a geopolitical resource. The nationalisation of nature and natural resources for reasons of the state leads to exploitation of nature and natural resources. Sustainable development calls for a need to return to pre-colonial geographies that will also mean a return to human and cultural geographies.

International Cooperation. Climate change and disasters know no boundaries, and will spread across geographical divides. We need to broaden and deepen the nature and scope of on-going dialogues to encompass the entire subcontinent. Ironically, climate change offers humanity an opportunity for a quantum leap in sustainable development and in peace making. If international cooperation, as opposed to competition, is strengthened in response to the threat of climate change and increasing disasters, international stability, governance, and development could also benefit. As quoted by UNDP regarding MDG 8: *"Climate change, a global phenomenon, calls for a collective response in the form of global partnerships"* (UNDP, 2007c).

Climate Change: Need for Single Authority. In India, on climate change, different ministries feud over turf. With climate change becoming a hot issue, both internationally as well as nationally, several ministries and agencies are now looking to get a bit of the carbon pie (Sethi, 2008). Ministry of Environment and Forests, the Ministry of Science and Technology, the Ministry of External Affairs, the Planning Commission, as well as the recently appointed office of the Prime Minister's special envoy are all addressing climate change from their perspectives. The integrated climate change and disaster risk management framework proposed above needs to be put under one authority/ ministry.

CURRENT TRENDS IN SECURITY SECTOR EXPENDITURES

Security sector expenditures have been growing very rapidly during the past three years, and growth is projected to continue in the current financial year. Whether in absolute terms (an estimated $1.3 billion in 2004/05 not including most counter-narcotics expenditures) or as a share of GDP (23%), the size of the security sector is daunting. The security sector spending reached a very high share of GDP by 2003/04 and has remained high, albeit with External Budget expenditures on security declining modestly as a share of GDP (while continuing to grow robustly in absolute terms). If maintained, and particularly with an expected shift from the External Budget to the Core Budget, such a high level of security sector expenditures would carry serious fiscal risks and would threaten the sustainability of the security sector.

The main driver of security sector expenditures has been the Afghan National Army (ANA), which after a start-up phase in 2002/03 has been absorbing large amounts of funds on the order of $800 million per year during 2003/04 - 2005/06. Equally striking more recently has been the growth of police expenditures, which are targeted to quintuple in two years to nearly $600 million (budgeted) in 2005/06. Other components, while much smaller in terms of their impact on aggregate security sector spending, have also seen very large increases, notably mine action and (starting from a tiny base) and justice.

Not surprisingly in Afghanistan's difficult post-conflict circumstances, the overall pattern has been one of considerable fluctuations and at times large, order-of-magnitude increases in expenditures on different components, amid continuing rapid growth of overall security spending.

PROSPECT EXPENDITURE DRIVERS AND PROGRAMMED EXPANSION

The rapid growth of security sector expenditures seen in recent years has not yet reached a plateau, and there are a number of drivers which can be expected to generate further increases in coming years. The investment component of security sector spending (construction and equipment) may decline after another couple of years, but other drivers can be expected to further increase recurrent expenditures.

Continuing investments and equipment purchases: The large one-time investments in setting up ANA base facilities and in equipping the ANA are expected to taper off over the next several years. However, substantial investments in the ANP have been programmed for 2005/06 and can be expected to continue for a time. It has been reported that the US is expected to commit some $700-800 million for the ANP in the coming two years, much of which would be used for infrastructure development and equipment purchases.

Moreover, the costs associated with maintaining the ANA and ANP "capital stock", as well as similar investments in the counter-narcotics field, are not precisely known but can be expected to be substantial. This underlines the importance of instituting a multi-year planning and budgeting cycle and of fully costing equipment acquisitions and other capital investments. It also should be kept in mind that forecasts made by security-related ministries of investment expenditures over several years are likely to understate the requirements in outer years, as plans and investment programs have not yet been formulated. Moreover, since virtually all security investment costs are currently borne by the External Budget and external financing for the security sector can be expected to decline by at least as much as these investments fall (if not more), there is no net benefit to the Afghan budget from this expected future trend.

Continuing programmed expansion of security forces: Target force levels were set based on various considerations (including the expected need to accommodate existing combatants in the new order), without the benefit of a carefully thought out or agreed threat assessment. Continuing expansion of employment in the security sector will be required to reach these target force levels, most notably in the case of the ANA (targeted level 70,000, as compared with around 26,000 combat troops at present), but there will also be additional recruitment into the police. The annual fiscal impact of increasing the ANA by another 40,000 or so to reach the 70,000 target would be more than $100 million for salaries alone. The total salary bill for the ANA at full strength can be estimated at just under $200 million annually. All in all, if expansion continues, ANA salaries will be a major driver of security sector expenditures (and indeed of total budgetary expenditures) in coming years. Although not as dramatic as in the case of the ANA, other security forces also are programmed to expand, including the ANP. Moreover, there has been a proposal to double the number of border guards from the targeted level of 12,000 to 24,000.

High salary scales, being applied to an increasing proportion of security sector staff: Salary and wage levels in the recent past have varied considerably among the different security institutions. In the ANA they range from a low of US$70 to a maximum of US$850 per month. In contrast, MoI staff (including police) have received between US$30 and US$122 per month. A new pay and grading structure has been proposed for the ANP that will bring their pay structure on par with (and in some grades above) that of the ANA. The new Counter-narcotics Ministry also appears to be getting higher salaries and/or top-ups.

The NDS similarly hopes to at least reach parity with ANA. What is more, setting new pay scales has implications for longer-term pension liabilities, although this issue was not addressed when the new ANA and ANP salary structures were set. Clearly, security sector personnel require a living wage. At the same time, a wage rate that is driven by individual Ministry requests and funded by donors through the External Budget, without a Government-wide agreement on an overall wage structure that reflects Afghanistan's fiscal realities, runs a serious risk of not being sustainable should donor support be reduced before adequate local revenue comes on stream.

It is not clear whether and to what extent there will be further wage increases in the security sector, although civil servants in the Government management bodies (i.e. parent ministries) will be included in any general civil service salary increases. Even if further increases in salary scales, particularly for the ANA and ANP, are avoided, these have been set at relatively high total compensation levels in relation to local conditions and the rest of government employees. In addition to the expansion of the ANA referred to above, the progressive shift of most of the police force from its previous relatively low salary structure to the new ANP pay levels will generate substantial increased salary costs. Even if there are no further salary increases during the coming several years, rising wage costs are already built in due to the shift from a low pay structure to a much higher one. A progressively larger proportion of total security sector employees will be earning higher salaries - along the lines of ANA and ANP - and this is likely to exert upward pressure on civil service salaries more generally.

Corresponding growth of non-salary expenditures in the security sector: Security forces need a range of complementary non-salary inputs in order to function effectively and remain at full readiness. Examples include fuel for mobility, uniforms, food, ammunition, etc. And there are also very substantial maintenance costs for military and other security forces' equipment. In the case of the ANA, the non-salary recurrent costs of an ANA of 70,000 have been very roughly and conservatively estimated at around $120 million per year. Combined with salary costs this would be a major fiscal burden in view of Afghanistan's low domestic revenues (only $269 million in 2004/05 and originally budgeted at $333 million in 2005/06).

Counter-narcotics expenditures: While uncertain in magnitude and possibly fluctuating widely, spending on counter-narcotics programs, including both law enforcement and alternative livelihoods, can be expected to be high. Information is incomplete, and there is a risk of double-counting of alternative livelihoods spending with rural development programs. Moreover, the longer-term fiscal and expenditure management implications of the new institutional arrangements for counter-narcotics (oversight and coordination by MCN) are not yet clear. Pay structures are not yet fully clear but appear to be high at least in some parts of the counter-narcotics apparatus, with direct payments of salaries/top-ups by donors playing a prominent role. Spending on counter-narcotics (both ordinary and development budgets) may increase considerably, and there is a concern that the costs of counter-narcotics may spiral out of control, or at least overtake spending on the ANA and ANP. It is very difficult to capture all information regarding counter narcotics funding because (i) many expenditures are not budgeted (and much is provided "in kind") and (ii) little information is available more than one year ahead (largely because the program is evolving fast, and is supported by donors who make only annual commitments). Nevertheless, it seems likely that spending on counter-narcotics activities in coming years will be in the $500-1,000 million range annually.

These various drivers of security sector expenditures and very rough estimates of their likely future impact (on an annual basis) are outline. Taking into account the substantial double-counting that most likely exists between counter-narcotics spending and other categories inside and outside the security budget, it nevertheless seems likely that the overall costs of Afghanistan's security sector will be in the range of US$ 900-1,000 million per year over the medium term, if not more.

In conclusion, it is frequently the case in international experience that when, often as part of a security sector reform initiative, salaries and wages increase in the security sector and modern equipment is procured, staffing levels in the security services decline. Afghanistan is in quite a different position. Due to its problematic historical legacy and the urgent need to build up security forces, the country faces the prospect for at least some years to come of simultaneously rising average salaries, staffing levels, non-salary expenditures, and equipment/maintenance costs. This, combined with the fragmented character of decisions on key security parameters, will place enormous fiscal pressures on Afghanistan's budget. Counter-narcotics spending is highly uncertain but is likely to further augment total security expenditures, with associated issues for fiscal sustainability.

Moreover, within total security sector spending, important shifts between the External and Core budgets can be expected, with major fiscal implications which could be unsustainable if not well-managed. Currently very large amounts of recurrent expenditures in the security sector - on wages and purchases of good and services - are paid directly by donors through the External Budget. Available data do not allow much precision, but it would appear that very roughly on the order of 60% of security sector spending in the External Budget consists of recurrent expenditures.

In this regard, there are already pressures from key donors for the Core Budget to pay progressively more of the security sector wage bill over time. If this shift occurs rapidly, it will put enormous pressure on the Government's domestic revenues. Similar pressures are likely for non-wage recurrent expenditures, and already the cost of food for ANA troops has been shifted from the External to the Core Budget. Just adding up the recurrent drivers listed above and excluding counter-narcotics, the total well exceeds current and forecast domestic revenues.

NEAR PERFORMANCE DIMENSION IN THE SECURITY SECTOR

It is difficult if not impossible to measure outcomes in much of the security sector, the importance of security as an enabling factor in development becomes very clear in its absence. Moreover, it is also difficult to identify performance indicators that do not inadvertently generate inappropriate incentives for security agencies. Nevertheless, and notwithstanding data limitations, as in the case of other public services it is necessary to monitor performance as best possible and in the process generate useful information for feedback and decision making. Appropriate performance indicators inevitably will vary across sectors, and as important as the information itself is ensuring that it feeds into subsequent decisions including through the budget process. While detailed consideration of performance indicators and monitoring in the security sector would get into technical aspects beyond the scope of this volume, some initial ideas for different sectors are put forward below, for illustrative purposes and further consideration. The Government, in defining its MDGs, has established targets, indicators, and baselines for the security sector (mainly for Defence), and moving toward a performance-based budgeting system for the security sector will keep efforts focused on outcomes.

In the container of *defence,* PFM specialists generally consider that indicators of preparedness (although they are more akin to output indicators than to outcome indicators) are the most appropriate performance indicator in peacetime. Another set of indicators which may be useful are the number, types, and results of training exercises conducted. It should be noted in this context that the Government has put forward the level of defence expenditures as a ratio to GDP as a (negative) performance indicator for its MDG target of enhancing security. While other things equal, a lower level of defence expenditure allows a greater proportion of Government budgetary resources to be spent on other development priorities, the relationship between the level of defence expenditure and actual security is complex and unlikely to be linear in either the positive or the negative direction.

Intended for *the police,* and for the *internal security* system more generally, the ultimate outcome of local security and rule of law is very difficult to measure but can be roughly proxied by some indicators. Official crime statistics are a partial and not very accurate (negative) indicator of security and rule of law, since they are affected by various factors such as the extent to which crimes are reported and recorded. Hence these are hard to use in monitoring performance over time or especially across countries. Household surveys generating information on the number and types of crime encountered by households can provide a useful check on the validity of official statistics, and they can also shed light on people's perceptions of the local security situation and their degree of trust in police. The effectiveness of the police and prosecutorial services can be measured by the percentage of different categories of cases resulting in convictions, based on which type of evidence (confessions, physical evidence etc.). The availability of female police officers and separate detention facilities for women are also indicative of mitigating the risks women face during detention.

In adding, the performance of the *justice system* can be measured by various indicators like numbers of cases handled, timeliness of processing court cases, and households' perceptions of the justice system and their indications of willingness (or otherwise) to use formal justice channels when seeking redress. The existence of Family Courts and Juvenile Courts and their functioning is also indicative of how sensitively and even-handedly the justice system deals with women and children. Furthermore, Afghanistan has signed a number of international conventions related to gender, including the Convention on the Political Rights of Women and on Elimination of all forms of Discrimination Against Women, which like the other international conventions ratified will require legislative and administrative measures to give legal backing to the nation's commitment to fair treatment and advancement of its women. In the container of *mine action,* outcomes of mine clearance activities (land and areas free of landmines - with clear linkage to ultimate development benefits) can be specified and measured reasonably well, and compared with the costs of mine clearance. On the other hand, the performance and effectiveness of mine awareness-raising activities are difficult to measure. For *counter-narcotics,* the outcome indicator at the national level can be specified relatively clearly: progressive and sustained reduction over time and eventual elimination of the opium economy on a sustainable basis (i.e. pressures to resume cultivation are manageable), accompanied by a corresponding reduction in trade in opiates (the latter may occur with a lag due to remaining inventories). However, measuring the performance of various actors and activities involved in counter-narcotics activities is not easy, and linking such performance to progress toward achieving this strategic objective is even more difficult. Given the variety of activities encompassed under the counter-narcotics rubric - ranging from eradication and interdiction to judiciary and penal development, demand reduction, and rural development programs - performance indicators for the different components will need to be appropriate to their varying characteristics.

More generally, in all parts of the security sector *basic indicators of inputs* can be useful in measuring performance. Examples include number and ratio of staff on the job (confirmed by spot-inspections), percentage of staff in security services properly equipped, proportion of staff who have received designated training, percentage of budget resources spent (covering both Core and External Budget to the extent possible), etc. A related option is *expenditure tracking surveys,* which are rarely used in the security sector as compared with social sectors, but which are feasible and provide information on actual flows of funds to, for example, police stations.

Unit costs, although not an outcome indicator, nevertheless can be useful performance indicators of the efficiency with which inputs for service delivery are being provided. All this leads to a rather formidable agenda for generating and effectively utilizing monitoring information. While there will be a need to focus attention and resources on this aspect, developing performance indicators and monitoring progress can start with small steps and make progress incrementally over time. One promising option is to generate and regularly monitor basic financial information on security sector expenditures in the Core Budget, and encourage donor partners to provide similar information on as consistent a basis as possible for External Budget expenditures in the security sector. This will provide useful information on expenditure of funds (a critical input) that can be monitored. To illustrate how straightforward monitoring of basic financial data can provide meaningful insights and feedback for resource allocation and other budgetary decision-making, compares estimated actual expenditures with budget targets for various categories of security sector expenditures in 2003/04 and 2004/05. Key points that emerge from these simple comparisons include the following:

There are sizable deviations between budgeted and estimated actual spending for most categories of security expenditures and also major fluctuations over time, suggesting that there is still a way to go before the budget targets become reasonably good predictors of actual expenditures. Within the security sector, External Budget expenditures are substantially higher in relation to budget targets than are Core Budget expenditures. Defence expenditures tended to perform better in relation to budget targets than other parts of the security sector, especially in 2004/05.

Finally, comparing the security sector with the budget as a whole, it is clear that the security sector achieves considerably higher expenditures in relation to budget targets than does the overall budget.

Another important area for basic input monitoring is employment levels. Staffing data, which have suffered from inconsistencies, need to be improved and regularly monitored throughout the security sector, including staff in security services paid through the External Budget. Such data can be augmented with indicators of numbers or proportions of staff on duty and available to carry out their duties.

Building on monitoring of basic data on inputs, simple indicators of output/performance could be compiled and used in monitoring. It is more important to collect and effectively utilize simple information than to devise highly sophisticated data and monitoring systems which are difficult to implement and become a burden on scarce Government capacity.

Finally, the institutions concerned need to take on the role of monitoring and evaluation and treat it as a serious part of their work. Most important they need to make meaningful use of performance indicators in decision making.

Intensification funds Execution

The budget can be a useful policy tool only if it is properly executed. The Government has made significant progress in developing institutions and systems to raise fiduciary standards, including implementation of the AFMIS in the Treasury, establishment of the Central Procurement Facility, and promulgation of procurement, public finance and expenditure management, and audit laws. However, because most of the expenditures in the security sector are in the External Budget, these systems are bypassed. Ongoing reforms to strengthen accountability mechanisms will develop institutions and systems that give civil servants the incentives and tools to use public resources effectively, but this will take some time. Many of these reforms will also reduce corruption, which may be considerable in certain parts of the security sector.

Currently, execution of the ordinary budget proceeds largely in accordance with the usual process of meeting day-to-day recurrent costs for both the security services and associated civilian staff. Based on the approved annual budget, quarterly advances are provided to security sector entities, against which recurrent costs (O&M) and food allowances are paid. In nearly all cases, execution of the development budget is via donor funded projects in the External Budget. .The only notable exception is DDR.

The ANA payment system has been a parallel budget execution system, although OMC-A is strengthening the budget department of MoD, and future salaries are expected to be paid through the new payroll system. The US Army/OMC-A maintain full expenditure authority over US Government funding.

Salaries for AMF were provided through the national budget, but the AMF has now been phased out through DDR. Food allowances for the ANA had been provided in-kind directly by the US Army but are now paid through the Core Budget. Investment expenditures are procured directly by the US Army.

Core Budget funding is accounted for through the Government / Treasury accounting system. In the case of reimbursement through ARTF, expenditures are verified through AFMIS by the ARTF Monitoring Agent. The Auditor General's Office currently conducts an audit of Government accounts, although the audit methodology (sampling frame and extrapolation technique) needs to be upgraded. In reporting all operating expenditures, the standard economic object classification is used, allowing comparative analysis between sectors.

Implementation of the External Development Budget differs substantially from the recurrent or operating budget in that, with the exception of some Core Budget funding for law enforcement (US$16.8 million in 2004/05), mine action (US$3.9 million), and Justice (US$3.1 million), all other development budget spending is drawn from the External Budget. The External Budget is fully projectized, under funding from bilateral donors. As a consequence, donors procure works, supplies, and services directly through their own procurement services. For the External Budget, accounting and auditing procedures are determined by the policies of each bilateral donor. As financial information is internal to bilateral agencies, actual recurrent spending in the External Budget remains unknown. However, given the requirement to move toward an integrated security budget, greater disclosure will be required to enable the longer-term fiscal implications of External Budget spending to be calculated.

Procurement. An external Procurement Advisor (Agent) has been retained by the Government, reporting to the Afghanistan Reconstruction and Development Services (ARDS) and supervised by the Ministers of Planning and Reconstruction. However, in spite of being the procurement agent for over 17 national Ministries, it has not so far handled procurement for any part of the security sector. A new Procurement Law has recently been passed. Hitherto, procurement of supplies, services, and works in the security ministries has not been unified around a single procurement system due to the different sources of finance and the multiplicity of actors. Instead, all core operating budget expenditures appear to follow the various procurement laws established by the budget entities directly. What is more, none of the 110-150 procurement staff from line ministries who have received training in basic and specific procurement rules have come from security-related ministries. With the approval of the new Procurement Law, this situation will need to change. Indeed, OMC-A has embarked on adapting procurement processes for MoD to the new law. Currently, Government security sector funding is limited to payroll and non payroll recurrent costs, so no large procurements have taken place to date.

LOTFA has its own set of procurement procedures and policies, covering both payroll and purchase of supplies such as vehicles and radio sets as well as works contracts for construction of police offices. Procurement is based on open international competitive bidding overseen by the management support unit, which is formally responsible for "procurement of goods, services and works on a transparent and competitive basis."

Procurement of defence items by bilateral agencies is determined by the bilateral procurement policies of the different contracting authorities (US DoD, UK Government, and so on). Clearly, if procurement policies are to be unified within the framework of the national budget, bilateral commitments in support of national security will need to be progressively drawn within the national budget framework. In essence, this would require that defence and non-defence procurement be harmonized to enhance (i) transparency, (ii) cost-efficiency, (iii) and cost-effectiveness. However, given bilateral donors' procedures and interests, this is unlikely to be possible any time soon. In the case of counter-narcotics, large contracts are being tendered, with few market operators able to deliver in such a complicated political and security environment, and contract costs probably reflecting this situation.

In the case of mine clearance, there are some issues related to procurement (i.e. contracting) for this activity. While very specific to de-mining, these issues and the options for addressing them do provide an illustration of how constraints elsewhere in the security sector might be addressed. The general message is that while the specific features may vary, it is extremely important to ensure that sound procurement principles are followed.

Another area of procurement related to the security sector - very important in the current situation in Afghanistan - is procurement by international security forces for various goods and services that they require, ranging from certain security services to water, fuel, other goods, construction, construction materials, etc.

Although difficult to ascertain with any precision, these activities are sizable and comprise a significant source of demand in the Afghan economy. Such contracts in many cases comprise an opportunity for development of the Afghan private sector which should be exploited. As argued with respect to other security-related procurement, these also should follow good-practice principles for procurement, particularly with respect to transparency and competition. However, it appears that such principles often are not followed in contracting for services by international military forces.

Accounting and reporting. As indicated earlier, accounting standards and reporting requirements should be uniform as between the security sector and non-security sectors. Within the Core Budget this condition is basically met, although there is room for further improvement in the case of security as well as other sectors. Major improvements in terms of timeliness, quality, and harmonized information standards for expenditures in the External Budget are needed. It is also very important that information on staffing and payrolls be improved in both Core and External Budgets.

External scrutiny and audit. It is essential that security expenditures be properly audited by a suitable external auditor, and that findings of audit reviews are made available to the Government and public. Core Budget expenditures (including those on security) are audited through regular Government procedures, whose quality needs to be improved. But it is very important that External Budget expenditures have proper external scrutiny and audit, and that findings are shared with the Government. LOTFA's accounts also need to be regularly audited by an external auditor on a timely basis. With the formation of Parliament, review of audit reports by the legislature should become a regular practice.

In sum, security expenditures within the Core Budget are essentially subject to similar control mechanisms, accounting and reporting requirements, and procurement arrangements as in the rest of the Core Budget. The main difference is the absence of a strong internal audit function - a role that in the case of the civilian budget is to a large extent played by the Monitoring Agent of the ARTF. The absence of such a mechanism - albeit extraordinary (and temporary) - in the security sector means a weaker control framework despite the beneficial application of other elements of the budget execution process for the Core Budget.

Security spending in the External Budget occurs outside these Government processes. Although this spending is subject to financial controls exercised by donors, associated disadvantages are potentially very important with respect to the quality and consistency of information flows, and procurement. Another major problem is the wide variety of salary levels, payment channels, and top-up arrangements in the security sector, which risk fragmenting the accountability and loyalties of security sector staff.

Bibliography

Ahmad, Imtiaz: *State and Foreign Policy: India's Role in South Asia*, New Delhi, Vikas, 1993.

Allison, Graham: *Nuclear Terrorism: The Ultimate Preventable Catastrophe*, New York: Times Books, 2004.

Amitabh Sikdar: *India and China : Strategic Energy Management and Security*, Manas, Delhi, 2009.

Ashok K. : *The Royal Nepal Army : Meeting the Maoist Challenge*, Rupa, Delhi, 2005.

Basrur, Rajesh M., and Hasan-Askari Rizvi, *Nuclear Terrorism and South Asia*, Albuquerque, NM: Sandia National Laboratories, February 2003.

Basu, Prahlad K.: *Governance and Public Administration for Poverty Reduction*, Salvador, Brazil, 1997.

Brooks, Constance : *Disaster Preparedness*, Washington, DC, Association for Research Libraries, 1993.

Cheek, Timothy: *Mao Zedong and China's Revolutions: A Brief History with Documents.* Boston: Bedford/St. Martin's, 2002.

Conway, G. 1992. *Sustainable Rural Livelihoods: Practical Concepts for 21st Century.* Sussex: Institute of Development Studies.

Damrosch, L.F.: *Law and Force in the New International Order*, Boulder, Westview Press, 1991.

Debray, Regis. *Revolution in the Revolution*. New York: Grove Press, Inc., 1993.

Dhagamwar, Vasudha : *Law, Power and Justice : Protection of Personal Rights under Islam*, Popular Prakashan, Bombay, 2001.

Digumarti Bhaskara Rao: *Military Conversion : Impact on Science and Technology*, Discovery, Delhi, 2003.

Evelyn Goh, *Meeting the China Challenge: The U.S. in Southeast Asian Regional Security Strategies*, DC: East-West Center, 2005.

Fletcher, Arnold: *Afghanistan, Highway of Conquest*, Ithaca, New York, Cornell University, 1965.

Friedman, G.: *The Future of War of Cyber Crimes*, N.Y., Random House, 1996.

Gao, Mobo: *The Battle for China's Past: Mao and the Cultural Revolution,* London, Pluto Press, 2008.

Habberton, William: *Anglo-Russian Relations Concerning Afghanistan 1837-1907*, Urbana, University of Illinois, 1937.

Hasan-Askari Rizvi, *Nuclear Terrorism and South Asia*, Albuquerque, NM: Sandia National Laboratories, February 2003.

Hoffman, Bruce, *Inside Terrorism in Afghanistan*, New York: Columbia University Press, 1998.

Holsti, K.: *The State, War, and the State of War,* Cambridge, Cambridge Univ. Press, 1996.

Huntington, S.P.: *The China Modernisation Military and the State*, N.Y., Vintage Books, 1964.

Jagannath P. Panda: *China's Path to Power : Party, Military and the Politics of State Transition*, Pentagon, Delhi, 2010.

Keane J.: *Democracy and Civil Liberty in Afghanistan*, London, Verso, 1988.

Kelly, John B.: *Britain and the Persian Gulf 1795-1880*, Oxford, Clarendon Press, 1968.

Marie Lecomte : *Hindu Kingship, Ethnic Revival, and Maoist Rebellion in Nepal*, Oxford University Press, Delhi, 2009.

Moseley, Philip E.: *Russian Diplomacy and the Opening of the Eastern Question*, Cambridge, Harvard University Press, 1934.

Norris, James A.: *The First Afghan War 1838-1842*, Cambridge, University Press, 1967.

Peter Lambron Wilson : *Traditional Modes of Contemplation and Action*, University Press, Tehran, 1977.

Posen, B.R.: *The Sources of Military Doctrine*, Ithaca, 1984, Cornell Univ. Press.

Rosen, P.: *Societies and Military Power: India and its Armies*, Ithaca, Cornell University Press, 1996.

Schroeer, Dietrich, *Science, Technology, and the Nuclear Arms Race*, Ontario: John Wiley & Sons, 1984.

Shaun Narine, *Explaining ASEAN: Regionalism in Southeast Asia*, Boulder, CO: Lynne Rienner Publishers, 2002.

Spector, Leonard S., *Going Nuclear*, Cambridge, MA: Ballinger Publishing Company, 1987.

Walker, Benjamin : *Foundation of Islam : the Making of World Faith*, Rupa & Co., New Delhi, 2001.

Worster, Donald : *Dust Bowl: The Southern Plains in the 1930s*, New York, Oxford University Press, 1979.

Index

□□□